The Story of a

Mrs. Oliphant

Alpha Editions

This edition published in 2024

ISBN : 9789362928399

Design and Setting By
Alpha Editions
www.alphaedis.com
Email - info@alphaedis.com

Contents

CHAPTER I.

JANET SUMMERHAYES did not start in life with the feelings usually attributed to the young governess when beginning what is certainly a very thankless trade, with about as little prospect of continued prosperity as any in the world. Many representations of that sad and resigned young heroine have appeared before the world. We all know the appearance of the slight girl in deep mourning shyly coming into a strange house and a new world, shrinking alike from kindness and neglect; feeling that she is likely to be shut out there from everything that is agreeable, expecting humiliation, and, if not ready to take offence, at least quite aware that nobody is likely to take her feelings into consideration, or think that she is made of young flesh and blood like the others. There are many excuses for this frame of mind, and in many cases the worst prognostics are carried out. But I am very glad to say that this was not at all the idea with which the subject of this story prepared to go forth upon the world.

Her position up to this time had not been like that of the young and gentle governess of romance, an exceptionally sheltered and happy one. She had not been the only daughter of a doting father or mother, whose want of means to provide for her was only discovered upon their sudden death. On the contrary, Janet's experience was entirely that of a dependent. It is true the dependence was more or less a natural one. She was a relation of her patroness, and she had grown up from childhood in Miss Philipson's house, without any consciousness that it was not her home, and with much of the feelings of a child, always subject, always liable to be ordered about and reproved, and little considered, but only in a way common to children. She had been very well educated on the whole, very well cared for, nicely dressed, since that was quite according to the fitness of things, and not allowed in anything to fall behind the neighboring girls of her age in any pleasure or accomplishment. It would have been contrary to Miss Philipson's credit, and it would have impaired her comfort, if Janet had not been on a level with the rest, or if she had not been cheerful and happy in her life. She was always kind to the girl, not being naturally unkind to anyone. She liked to have everything pleasant about her, and she had a conscience besides—both which things were very good for her little cousin. She did not provide for Janet, but that was all—and indeed, having done so much for her, and given her on the whole such a happy life up to her twentieth year, there was no failure of duty in this; and though some of Janet's friends were inclined to blame Miss Philipson, Janet herself was much more just, and neither felt nor expressed any blame.

"Aunt Mary was always good to me," the girl said. "I had no right to that, but she gave it me freely, and we were very happy together, and certainly I had no right to expect any more."

"My dear, I would not for the world impair your gratitude or your affection for your poor aunt," said the vicar's wife; "in many things she deserved it fully, but——"

"There is no 'but,'" said Janet. She was not perhaps quite so much overcome by grief as her friends would have liked to see her. There is a very simple standard in this respect which people like to see followed. They like to see a grief which is overwhelming for the moment, tears without measure, a sorrow which can take no comfort, all the better if it makes the mourner ill, and perhaps confines her to bed for a few days in a shrouded room, without any occupation but that of brooding and weeping over her loss. And then they expect her to cheer up—not too quickly, but with a little visible advance every day, an advance which they can feel to be owing more or less to their own sympathetic kindness and good offices. Janet had to a certain extent followed this unspoken rule. She had cried a great deal, though her health had not at all suffered; but after the funeral she had perhaps too quickly regained her cheerfulness. When the doctor proposed to her, which was a thing that happened very soon after, it had been all she could do not to laugh at the droll idea that anyone should think it possible she would marry a middle-aged country doctor, she—Janet! She did laugh in the safety of her own room where nobody could hear her, recalling his look, and all the peculiarities of his unattractive person and his rough riding dress. He wanted to save her from the life of a governess by binding her to him, and his shabby house, and his busy, dry, joyless existence. How extraordinary, how ludicrous it was that anybody should think it was better to vegetate than to go out into the world and seek your fortune! Janet had lived at Clover all her life, and she liked the little place. The scenes were all so familiar, the people were all friends; but then she never for a moment supposed that she could be bound to such a seclusion. It had always been her expectation that one time or another she was to fling herself forth upon the world.

At the vicarage they were exceedingly tender of the girl who was going forth upon fate like this. Mrs. Bland made a survey of all her clothes, and mended some and condemned others with a pathetic tenderness.

"You must have all your linen in order," she said, "for there is nothing a girl is so apt to forget. I was in rags myself when my first wedding outfit wore out before I ever thought of getting a new set of things. A girl can see when she wants a new frock, but as for her under-things she always leaves that to her mother."

"But you forget, Mrs. Bland, I have never had a mother," said Janet.

"Ah, my poor child! but you were very kindly thought of, Janet, very kindly."

"Do you think I meant any reproach to poor Aunt Mary? Oh, no, no! She liked me to have everything. She liked me to be the best dressed child in the parish. But as I grew up I saw to it myself. She thought it was best for me. But I shall always take the most care of the buttons you have sewed on. Fancy sewing on buttons and seeing after tapes for me!"

"It is the most natural thing in the world," said the vicaress. "I only wish I could always take the charge of you, Janet; but we are old people, and we have little to leave, and it would only be putting off a little what would have to be faced at last."

"Dear Mrs. Bland!" cried Janet, looking at her with something like tears in her eyes: they were real tears—and yet even while they sprang by instinct of nature, the little thing could not help the rising of a revolt against the thought of settling again at Clover after she had once been unseated from her corner. At Clover! when what she was thinking of was the world.

"But you must promise me, my dear," said the old lady, with a tremor in her voice, "that as long as we live you will always look on the vicarage as your home. If this Mrs. Harwood should not turn out all you expect, you must not think it necessary to stay on, you know, and fret yourself to death trying to make it do. You must always remember you have a home to come back to, Janet."

"But the vicar thought Mrs. Harwood was very nice."

"So he did, but in such cases a man's opinion does not go for very much. If a woman looks nice and talks nicely, and has an agreeable smile, it is all the vicar thinks of: and most people are nice to him."

"How could they help it, he is so delightful himself?"

"Well, I tell you, he is no judge; and in the best of places, Janet, there is a great deal to put up with. Every family has its own ways, and you will be a stranger, and it will be hard for you to be left out and to feel yourself always an outsider. There is a young lady, and she will go out to her parties and balls and you will be left behind. I don't mean that you will feel it now, when your spirit is broken, but by and by, when in the course of nature——"

"It would be just the same at Clover," said Janet; "there are neither balls nor parties."

"Ah, but everything there is you are asked to. That makes such a difference: and it will not be the case there. My dear, I am frightened about you, for you are too bold. You don't realize the difference. It will be a great difference," said Mrs. Bland, shaking her head.

Janet could have laughed, but did not. She was very bold. The new life and the strange family had no terrors for her. Novelty was dear, an exhilaration not a terror, to this little girl. Her heart was beating high with expectation while all these prophecies were poured into her ear. But it would not have been in good taste (Janet felt) to exhibit the real state of her feelings, so she answered, demurely, that she hoped she was not too bold.

"But, dear Mrs. Bland, when one has to do it, don't you think one had better try to do it cheerily and think the best? Don't you remember the old song in the play that the vicar likes so much—

"'A merry heart goes all the way
A sad one tires in a mile, a'!'"

"That's true enough," said Mrs. Bland, still shaking her head, "but men don't know half that women have to put up with. Anyhow, Janet, my poor dear, you must always recollect this, that if it should ever become more than you can bear you must just give up the struggle and come back home. This is home so long as he and I are alive, and, if he goes first, whatever poor little cottage I may get to hide my old head in, you'll just be as welcome there; and if I go first there will be all the more occasion, for he will sorely want somebody to look after him."

At the mingled prospect of Janet's need, and her own poor little problematical cottage as the vicar's widow, and the vicar's want of somebody to look after him, Mrs. Bland broke down entirely, and shed salt tears. Indeed, those things were all possible, though only one of the last two sorrows could be. But when an old pair come to the end of life, it is almost certain that one of them must be left one day to survive and miss the other, though, to be sure, it does happen now and then that they are so blessed as to die within a day or two of each other, which is by far the best.

Janet went to her old friend, and kissed her, and was, as Mrs. Bland said, very sweet, comforting the old lady with tender words and letting fall a few tears, as it is easy on any provocation to do at nineteen. And immediately after it was tea-time, and the vicar came in from his study, where he was writing his sermon, and everything became cheerful again. Afterwards Mrs. Bland put all Janet's "things" together, and looked at them with affectionate, complacent eyes, patting each snowy heap.

"Now, Janet," she said, "you have a dozen of each, my dear, and not a button or a tape wanting, and all the trimmings nice and in good order. That will last you for a long time. You must keep an eye upon the trimming, which London washerwomen tear dreadfully. I've put our old-fashioned Buckinghamshire lace, made in my old parish where I was born, upon all the new ones. There is nothing that wears and washes so well. You never have had to think of these things till now; but you must promise me to look them over carefully every Saturday. You know, 'A stitch in time——'"

Janet gave the promise with all necessary earnestness, and the "things" were carried upstairs and carefully packed. It was a sad evening at the vicarage. The old people said all manner of sweet and pretty things to the neophyte, which Janet tried when she could to ward off by a little joke, or one of the merry little speeches which all the Clover people expected from her: but, though this might turn the edge of a piece of serious advice for a moment, the grave tone always came back. A sentence might be begun lightly, but it was sure to end with "remember, Janet——" The old people both kissed her and blessed her when she went upstairs to bed—"The last night," they said to each other with an interchange of sympathetic glances.

"And she takes it so easily. She is not a bit daunted," said Mrs. Bland, shaking her head.

"Perhaps that's all the better," said the vicar; but the old couple were almost alarmed, in spite of themselves, at Janet's calm.

If they had but known! She went upstairs quietly enough with a composed step. But when she got to her own room, which was, happily, at the other end of the house, Janet threw down on her bed the things she was carrying, which were presents from her old friends—a writing-case from one, a work-basket from the other—and danced, actually danced a lively old hornpipe step, which she had learned when she was a child. She did it before the glass, and nodded and smiled at herself as she bobbed up and down. Then stretching out her arms, flung herself in the old easy-chair and, said, "Hurrah! hurrah! hurrah!" softly under her breath "The last night," said Janet to herself. The last of all this dull old life, which she knew in every feature, which never had anything new in it—no excitement, no change: but to do the same things at the same hours every day, and come in to meals and sit down in the same chair, and go to church and go to bed. She was not at all without affection for the people who were so kind to her, but to feel herself upon the edge of the unknown went to Janet's head. It was like laughing gas, or champagne, or any other stimulant to gayety. The idea intoxicated her. As for all the dolorous pictures that had been placed before her, she believed none of them. To go off among people she had never seen, to plunge into the midst of a life she knew nothing about, to become a member of a family whose name alone she knew—it was like beginning a new world to Janet. She would have everything to find about them—their Christian names, their stories, if they had any; perhaps the family story, if there was one—the skeleton in the closet, the romance; whatever there might be. What fun! she said to herself, clapping her hands. Even the new place would be something to begin with—the new home and customs, the new rooms.

It appeared to her altogether in a bright light of expectation—everything nice, everything new. The name of Mrs. Harwood, a widow lady with three children, living in St. John's Wood, will not, perhaps, appear exciting at the first glance. She was Mrs. Novelty, the gatekeeper of the new world, to Janet, and her three children were three romances about to begin, in each of which Janet would come by degrees to be the heroine. The house in St. John's Wood was the theatre, the stage on which she was to make her first appearance. She knew no more of that respectable (or disrespectable) region than she did of Timbuctoo. As for the naughtiness, that was all a sealed book to Janet. Her wildest thoughts were as innocent as a child's. She had absolute ignorance as a guard to her imagination, which is a guard always to be desired, and most so at nineteen. The life she longed to know was the common life of the world. Not even in her dreams had she thought of the transgression of any law. She expected to have her own merits recognized, to have adoration and homage laid at her feet, to find not only Prince Charming in the end, but, no doubt, many others whose sighs and glances would make existence very amusing. She expected that admiration would meet her, that she would be in the midst of a story before she knew. She expected to triumph all along the line. "The world's my oyster, which with this glance I'll open." That was the light in which Janet contemplated the life of a governess in St. John's Wood, which she was to begin next day.

CHAPTER II.

THE household at the vicarage was astir earlier than usual next morning, which was altogether unnecessary, for Jane did not leave Clover till after twelve o'clock; but that was a kind of tribute to the excitement in which everybody had a part. The morning was spent in investigations as to whether anything was wanting in Janet's little travelling work-case, where she kept (by special provision of Mrs. Bland) a reel of black silk and one of white cotton, needles, thimble, and scissors; or in her little writing-case, where (supplied by the vicar) she had two sheets of notepaper, two envelopes, two post-cards, the same of postage stamps, a pen on an ivory-holder, and a small travelling inkbottle. These little articles were quite independent of the handsome work-box and writing-case, severally given her by her kind friends, and were intended solely for the necessities of the journey, though, perhaps, as it was only three hours by railway to London such careful provisions were scarcely necessary.

Janet's box was not locked till ten o'clock, in case some one might recollect something that had been forgotten; but after every precaution had been taken, the last strap fastened, her railway rug and cloak neatly, nay, almost more than neatly, put up, her own hat put on, and her coat buttoned to the throat, not one detail left which had not been attended to, there was still one hour to spare before the train left. They went out into the wintry garden, where everything was bare, and strolled round the walks—the three together, the vicar in his greatcoat, prepared to accompany Janet to the railway, and Mrs. Bland with a large white shawl over her cap. It was a beautiful morning, the sun shining red through the mist, and everything so warmed in color and sentiment by those ruddy rays that it was almost impossible to believe that it was a cold November day.

"I wish now," said the vicar, "that I had insisted, as I always wished, on going up with Janet to town, and seeing her safe in Mrs. Harwood's hands."

"I almost wish you had, dear," said Mrs. Bland.

"But I don't," cried Janet. "Oh, please don't think of such a thing! How am I to learn to manage for myself if you pet me like this, as if I could do nothing? No, dear vicar, I should so much prefer to part with you here, in our own dear Clover, and to keep the—image quite unbroken."

Janet was a little at a loss how to finish her sentence, but felt very successful when she thought of these words.

Mrs. Bland put up her handkerchief to her eyes.

"There's something in that," she said, "to leave us just as I hope you will find us when you come back. And always do remember, Janet, if any difficulty should arise, that here we are, always so happy to have you—only sorry that we can't keep you altogether."

"Always delighted to have you," echoed the vicar, "and sorry above measure——"

"But I hope no difficulty will arise," said Janet, very briskly; "I don't intend there should. I am not quite like a little novice, am I? I have seen a little of the world. I remember watching how the governess at the Grange got on, or rather how she didn't get on, and thinking had I been in her place—! So you see I am not unprepared. And then it will be everything to know I may come back here for my holidays, when I have any."

"We ought to have made a condition about that," said the vicar. "I have been thinking so for some time. We should have put it down in black and white, so many weeks at a certain time, say Christmas or Easter, instead of leaving it to chance as we have done."

"Not Christmas," said Mrs. Bland, "nor Easter either, for that would not be so convenient; but in August, when every child has holidays."

"Only then," said the vicar—"for I thought of that—they might be going abroad, or to the seaside, or somewhere where it would be nice for Janet to go."

"People very seldom take the governess with them when they go abroad," said Mrs. Bland, shaking her head.

"But, dear Mrs. Bland," said Janet, "you always used to say one should not think of holidays till one had done some work. And it will come all right about that. The grand thing is having a place to come to when one is free; a place," she said, with a little moisture springing into a corner of her bright eyes—a little real moisture, which Janet was quite pleased and almost proud to feel, as it carried out every necessity of her position—"which will feel like home."

"In every way, I hope, my dear child," said Mrs. Bland, with a sob, enfolding Janet in her arms and her white shawl, which were both motherly, warm, and ample, like her heart. The vicar put his hand upon her shoulder, and patted it tenderly as she was held against his wife's breast.

When the girl freed herself (and a dreadful thought about her hat darted into her mind as she did so, for it is so easy to crush crape) she gave a little laugh, and cried,

"You must not spoil me too much. I can't go away crying; it would not be lucky. Dear vicar, there is one bud left in the china vase beside your study window. Do get it for me to put in my coat, and that will be the last thing, and a cheerful thing: for it is nearly time for the train, and I must go now."

Janet kept her point, and pinned the rose to her breast, after she had given Mrs. Bland her farewell kiss, and went away, looking back smiling and waving her hand till she was out of sight from the vicarage gate.

"Bless her, she do have a spirit to keep up like that," said the vicarage cook, who stood behind her mistress to see the last of Miss Janet.

"It's all excitement," said Mrs. Bland, drying her eyes. "I know she'll break down dreadfully as soon as she gets into the railway carriage by herself."

"Now, Janet, you are sure you would not wish me to go with you: for there is time enough yet to get a ticket, and send Mrs. Bland a message?" said the vicar, at the carriage door.

"No, no. No, indeed. It is far better to begin at once—to begin when I am not forced to do it," said Janet. "And perhaps next time I travel alone it will be to come home, which will make everything delightful. Good-bye and, oh, thank you, thank you, a thousand times!"

"God bless you, my dear child."

When he had said these last words, the vicar turned right round and walked away, for his eyes were full; and I am glad to say that Janet too saw his back, as for the first time he turned it upon her, through a tear. It was an old back, in a somewhat rusty black coat, and with stooping shoulders, and there was a slight quiver of emotion in it as he turned away. Poor child! poor little thing, setting out upon that world which is so cruel, which makes so small account of soft things and little things like a bit of a girl, carrying them away upon its stream, drifting them into corners, taking all the courage and the happiness out of them. "God bless her! God help her!" the vicar said within himself as he hurried away.

Janet had been deposited in a first-class carriage alone, with all her little properties carefully arranged about her. Henceforward probably she would have to travel by second or even third-class; but Mr. Bland had got her ticket for this last occasion regardless of expense, and had fee'd the guard to take care of her, and done everything for her as if she had been a princess. And I am happy to state that for the first mile or two Janet saw the familiar landscape all dilated and out of drawing through the medium of tears. They were not many, nor were they bitter, but at least they were genuine.

"Poor old vicar," she said to herself; "poor Mrs. Bland; poor Aunt Mary——"

Even at that moment it was not herself she pitied, but those whom she left behind. She added at the end of a minute,

"Poor old doctor," and burst into a laugh: and her heart jumped up again after its momentary sympathetic depression, and the tears dried of themselves. Her heart jumped up with a throb almost of exultation. At last she had fairly escaped—got away from the village and all the enveloping kindness and cares that had been lavished upon her.

Janet was not ungrateful any more than youth in the abstract is ungrateful, but the first sensation of freedom had something intoxicating in it! Setting out to face the world! She had been told all her life that she would have to do it some day; and though that eventuality had always been held before her as a dreadful though inevitable prospect, it had lost all its terrors as contrasted with the monotony of the village life, which she knew by heart, and all the quiet evenings and dull days in which Janet had often felt as if her young activity and energy of mind must burst the very walls of the dainty decorous cottage where it was so happy for her, so fortunate to have found a home. How often had she felt there as if she would like to take hold of the posts as Samson did, and shake it till it toppled down about her ears, not with any ill meaning, but for sheer need of movement, mischief, something to happen. To face the world! She looked it in the face with a smile of triumph and delight, as a sea-boy faces the smiling ocean that is in time to be his grave, as it had been his father's before him.

Janet was not afraid. The world's mine oyster. Her feeling was even more buoyant than that of the young man who goes up to London to seek his fortune, as being more entirely ignorant, visionary, and without foundation. A young man can at least amuse himself for his day, even if he is to be swept off upon the dark waters of ruin to-morrow; but a girl, a little governess, going to a house in St. John's Wood! What amazing folly, what wonderful self-delusion, what a little dauntless, unforeboding, almost heroic heart! the ideal of a governess is very different, but Janet felt no regrets, no alarms. She was going to conquer fate. What she would have liked would have been to have had a longer journey before her, to have travelled the whole day in order to have been able to *savourer* her release, her freedom, the novelty of everything. She would have liked to arrive in her new sphere when it was dark, when she could only have a mysterious glimpse of the life before her, so as to save up a sensation for the next day, which would bring a full discovery of all her surroundings. But as things were she was very well content.

And then Janet began to think what sort of a person Mrs. Harwood would be. Would she be the nice sweet motherly person who sometimes in a novel took the young governess to her heart and made her feel at home at once? Janet almost hoped not, for that would be too easy, too commonplace and unexciting—to go from one kind home to another, and find everything made smooth for her on every side. Or would she be the purse-proud rich woman who would consider the governess as beneath her notice, with a footman who would ask "Any name?" as was done to Tom Pinch in "Chuzzlewit" when he went to look after his sister. Foolish Janet, in the exuberance of her life and untried power, thought it would be "rather fun" to have to do with such a specimen of the employer. She felt with delight that she would be able to hold her own, that no person of the kind should overcome her, and that the fight would be rather exhilarating than otherwise. Or would she perhaps be a fine lady, too fine to be rude, who would take as little notice as possible of the young stranger, ignore her existence, and consider her only as a medium to grind a little knowledge into her children? All of these types Janet had beheld in veracious fiction, which holds the mirror up to nature: which of them should she encounter? She was not afraid of any, but the consciousness that a battle of one kind or other would soon declare itself gave excitement to her mind and light to her eye.

There were several other points in which Janet, I fear, took the vulgar and superficial view. She felt with an instinctive certainty that the men of the house, if there were any, would be on her side, and that the visitors who ought to admire the young lady of the house would probably find the governess more attractive. She had an expectation, almost going the length of a certainty, that she would be fallen in love with by two or more very eligible persons at the least, and that whenever she was visible in the room, and, most of all, if she were conspicuously neglected, the eye of "the gentlemen" would pick her out, and that they would make flattering comparisons between her and the other young ladies in a happier position, and comment upon the feminine spite and jealousy that kept her in the background. This she considered to be one of the recognized certainties of her future existence, and that assurance of being preferred and vindicated gave her a great deal of pleasure. But to do her justice this conviction did not occupy a very great part of her thoughts.

Thus Janet rattled on through all the brightest hours of the day towards her fate.

CHAPTER III.

IT was between three and four in the afternoon when Janet arrived at her destination. She knew London well enough as country young ladies know it—the parks and Belgravia, Piccadilly and the exhibitions; but St. John's Wood was as unknown to her as if it had been a country town in the depths of the shires. She thought it looked like a country town as she drove along the quiet road between garden walls with trees looking over them, and stopped at the door in the wall which was all the entrance.

That it had no carriage entrance was rather a trouble to the young people in the house, but they had been used to it all their lives. The door when it was opened showed a paved line of pathway to the house, covered by a light permanent awning, supported on slight iron pillars, which were covered by strong climbing roses, now almost bare of leaves. The house door was also open, and showed rather a pleasant vista, for the red of the setting sun was in a long window at the back of the house, and lighted up an old-fashioned hall and winding staircase with a warm and comfortable light. Janet had all her wits about her, though her heart was beating loudly in her ears. She noted that it was only a parlor-maid who came to the door, with momentary discouragement—but was slightly relieved when a man came round the corner of the house to take her boxes. These perceptions and variations of feeling occurred in about a minute of time, during which she paid her cabman, and turned to follow the parlor-maid into the house. The garden looked pleasant and sheltered within its walls, and there was still a scent of late mignonette in the air of the November afternoon, though scarcely any mignonette was left at Clover. Janet walked in with her firm little step, not at all bold, but neither was she abashed. She had come now to a very critical moment, and was about to have her first look at fate.

If this was fate, it was not alarming. The room into which she was shown was evidently one which occupied the whole breadth of the house, though it was divided unequally by a large curtained doorway, through which, where the curtains hung open, came the same gleam of red sunset color which had lighted up the hall. But it was twilight in the other end to which Janet was introduced, except for a bright circle of firelight coming from an old-fashioned high grate of glimmering steel and brass, which threw forth the most brilliant reflections, and made all the shadows warm. By its side sat an old lady in a large chair—that is, a lady whom Janet took to be very old, with white hair, a white cap, and a white shawl over her shoulders, a very pleasing piece of light and suggested color, in the pleasant gloom.

"Is it Miss Summerhayes?" said this lady, in a soft voice, holding out her hand. "Gussy! My dear, I am very glad to see you, though I scarcely can see you in this faint light. Don't think me rude for not getting up. The fact is I can't get up, except with difficulty. Gussy! Priscilla, call Miss Gussy and Miss Julia; tell them I want them at once, and give Miss Summerhayes a chair. Come near the fire, you must be cold after your journey. It's grown very cold this afternoon, don't you think?"

"Oh, no," said Janet, whose heart had stopped that unnecessary racket, and dropped down quite comfortably into its usual place of beating. "It is not so cold at all; it looks so warm and cheerful here."

"Do you think so, my dear?" cried the old lady; "indeed, I am very glad to hear you say so, and it is a pretty thing to say. I fancied everything would be dismal to you, your first coming out into the world. Oh, here is Gussy at last. Gussy, this is Miss Summerhayes."

Janet could not well make out the appearance of the figure which came out quickly from within the curtained doorway, and held out a hand to her. The daughter of the house was taller than herself, very slim, clothed in a dress rather too light for the season, and with hair which seemed very light also. She, too, had a soft, long hand which clasped Janet's lightly, and a soft voice, which said, "I am very glad to see you." Altogether, a more genial pleasant welcome could not have been desired.

"Miss Summerhayes thinks it is not at all cold and that we look very warm and cheerful," said Mrs. Harwood, "which is very nice of her, and I hope she will always find us cheerful and comfortable, Gussy. Where is your sister? for after all she must want most to see Ju."

"Don't trouble about Ju all at once, mamma," said Miss Gussy, "there is plenty of time, and we are just going to have tea. Won't you take off your boa, Miss Summerhayes? Mamma's room is always too warm, I think. Have you had a long journey? We could not quite make out how far it was."

"Only since twelve o'clock," said Janet; "it is not so very far."

"Gussy! the poor child can have had no proper lunch. Tell Priscilla to bring some sandwiches with the tea."

"Oh, no, please! I have had sandwiches and everything I could want. I came from the kindest friends, who could never do enough for me," said Janet. She felt, and was pleased with herself for feeling, that at thought of the kind vicar and his wife a little water had come into her eyes.

"Well, that is very pleasant to know of," said Mrs. Harwood. "I always like to hear that people with whom I am connected have kind friends, for those who have very kind friends are generally nice themselves; and it is a great quality to be able to appreciate kindness. I am sorry to hear that you are an—an orphan, Miss Summerhayes."

"Yes," said Janet, "but I must not claim too much sympathy on that account, for I have never known anything different. I have been an orphan all my life."

"Oh," said Mrs. Harwood, slightly checked in the flow of ready feeling. "But you have lost a—a—dear relation; a—a—some one who has filled up the place?"

"I have lost the dear lady whom I lived with always. She was my mother's cousin, but she let me call her my aunt. Nobody could be more good. I shall be grateful to her as long as ever I live," said Janet, with a little emotion.

"My dear, I hope I have not recalled painful recollections; but one always likes to know. It is very pretty what you say about this good lady. Still, it is not the same thing as losing your mother, and I hope you will soon be able to look at things more cheerfully," said Mrs. Harwood, feeling that this was a little out of the regular course, and not knowing what to say.

The tea had been apparently in the course of being carried in to the other end of the room while this conversation was going on, for there was a jingle of china and teaspoons, and a little movement of furniture, and a figure flitting across the opening from time to time. When this point had been reached a faint glow of light suddenly sprang up behind the curtains, and Gussy appeared once more.

"Are you going through your examination, Miss Summerhayes? We all have to do it—but mamma might have let you off for a little. Come into this room and have some tea. It is not so warm here. I'll bring you yours directly, mamma."

"Attend to the traveller first," said the kind old lady, and Janet followed Gussy into the other room, where there was a lamp burning. The end of this room seemed all window, an ample bay, almost to the ground, though tempered by the shade of a veranda outside. The glow in the west had just died away, the definite contrasted domestic light came in. In the shining of this, which was reflected in a large mirror over the mantelpiece, and another opposite to it, Janet saw what Miss Harwood was like. She was very fair, hair scarcely more than flaxen, eyes blue but somewhat pale, soft features not too correct, with a little droop and sway of her tall figure when she moved which was not without grace, and suggested the soft swaying of a tall flower in the air, though matter-of-fact people regarded it sometimes as a sign of weakness. She drew a chair near the tea-table for Janet, and poured out tea for her, and pressed all the good things on the table upon her acceptance—then disappeared for a moment to the other side of the curtain to take her share of these good things to her mother. Janet, with her quick ears, heard the whispered conversation between them which was only half put into words. "Yes, I like her"—"Don't make too much"—"You are a nice one to say so, mamma!" This last phrase was distinct enough, and Janet with a smile acknowledged its truth. She also recognized the perfect justice of the observation, "Don't make too much of her"—which, of course, was what had been said. No; it would be foolish really to make too much of her. She felt like a young lady coming on a visit—not in the least like a little governess without friends, arriving among strangers, to a new life. If this was all which was meant by going out to seek her fortune—going out to meet her fate!

Gussy came back and sat down and began to talk to the new-comer.

"This is where I always sit," she said, "and where our visitors come, unless when they are mamma's great friends. Mamma is not very strong, but it is only right to admit that she is lazy and won't try to get up out of her chair."

At this a voice came from the other side of the curtain, slightly affected by the fact that the mouth was full.

"Don't forget, Gussy, that I hear every word you say."

"Oh! I know that very well, mamma. She has had rheumatism, and she is stout, and she is lazy—oh, not in any other way; neither in talking, nor in working, nor in thinking. She manages everything at home, and she will be quite willing to manage all your affairs if you wish it; but she is lazy about moving. She won't walk——"

"Gussy, how unkind, when you know I *can't!*"

"That is all a delusion, Miss Summerhayes: but we need not discuss it. She has to be wheeled about in her chair, and nothing but a visit from the Queen will make her get out of it. Now we've disposed of mamma, I won't say anything about myself, for you are forming your opinion of me all the while, as I talk. I don't think I am very hard to get on with; but we must tell you, and that is the chief point of all, that the most difficult of the family is Ju."

"And Ju is——?" said Janet.

"Of course your pupil. She is fourteen, and she is as obstinate as a pig. We can do nothing with her, mamma and I—it is not that there is any harm in her. Perhaps if we did not think so much about it things would go better; but we think, and we consult, and we compare notes, and end by worrying ourselves very much—at least mamma worries herself. We hope that some one quite new, whom she is not accustomed to, who is a novelty to her, and whom she must be civil to, will produce quite a different effect."

Janet felt a little thrill run over her at this description.

"I hope you know," she said, somewhat faintly; "I hope Mr. Bland told you—that I have really no experience at all."

"We think that is all the better," said Gussy. "She is up to all the ways of the experienced people. We don't like to say anything against governesses, but they run very much in grooves, like most other people, for that matter. Now you are not professional at all; you have not got into any of their dodges. Oh, don't say anything, mamma; I must use the handiest word. You are just a girl, like any of us: I don't see how she can be nasty with you—at least not at first," said Gussy, reflectively, "and by the time she is familiar enough to begin her tricks we hope you will have got an ascendancy."

Miss Harwood stopped for a moment and listened.

"Hush! don't look as if we had been talking in particular; she is coming."

Janet did not know what to expect. She listened, thinking of the whoop and crash of some young savage; but there was nothing of the kind, and she gave a little start in the most spontaneous manner, and rose up quickly, when Gussy said, in her soft voice:

"My sister Julia—Miss Summerhayes."

CHAPTER IV.

SHE was a tall girl, taller than Janet, but considerably less so than her sister, with a well-knit and active figure, clad in the shapeless garments which are considered appropriate to her age, a great mane of light brown hair falling on her shoulders, and a pair of gray eyes, which were not soft like Gussy's, nor with any tone of blue in them; but with a glimmer of that yellow light which makes gray eyes fierce. Her eyebrows were slightly puckered, giving a keen arch over her eyes, to which this gave (when one was looking for it) a look of repression, a hint of a possible blaze and spring. But otherwise there was no sign in Miss Julia of anything out of the way or alarming. She thrust out a hot hand to Janet, said "How d'ye do?" because she could not help herself, accepted without any thanks her tea from her sister, and retired at once to the background. Gussy gave a significant look to Janet, and elevated her eyebrows; but the new-comer saw nothing remarkable in the drawing back of the half-grown, shy girl who established herself at a table, ingenuously set up an open book, which she had apparently brought in with her, so that she could read while she consumed her cake and bread and butter, and made herself comfortable in a way which Janet envied, but did not feel herself called upon to disapprove. To-morrow, perhaps, when she was the governess in charge—but at present her mind was still free of any responsibility. A certain restraint, however, seemed to fall upon the conversation after the entrance of Julia. The very monologue of Gussy, the little chirp of protest from the other side of the curtain did not seem so free. They asked Janet a few questions about her journey, which had been inconsiderable, which was absolutely so unimportant, and then it was suggested she might like to go upstairs.

It was evident that the Harwoods intended to be very good to their governess, for she found a pretty room, well furnished and warm with firelight, awaiting her—a better room than had been hers at Rose Cottage, or even in the vicarage.

"I hope you will be comfortable, and I hope you will like us," said Miss Harwood, as she left her.

Janet sat down in a comfortable chair by the fire. She felt very comfortable, in a state of pleasant exhilaration, but also with a faint consciousness of having had, so to speak, the ground cut from under her feet. If this was what it was to go out governessing, what was the meaning of all the fables which she had been told from her childhood? From *Jane Eyre*, to the *Family Herald*, they had all been in one tale—there had been compensations of an exciting character, no doubt, always, or almost always—but never a reception like this. She laughed to herself as she sat and watched the firelight dancing in the mirror over the mantelpiece, and in the dressing-glass on the table. Quite as nice as coming on a visit, in short, just the same, though perhaps had she come on a visit she would not have been at once and so fully taken into the family concerns of her hosts. At the same time there was a trifling disappointment in Janet's little soul. She had fully intended to conquer fate, to make a brilliant fight, to come out triumphant and victorious more than words could say. And to find that there was nothing to fight about, that all was to be easy and agreeable, every authority on her side, and circumstances in her favor—took the wind out of her sails, to change the metaphor. It brought a little ridicule into the whole matter. To think that she had been so screwing up her courage, fortifying herself, and that her heart had beat so high, and that she had walked into this new world with such a determined little step, as if she were marching to military music, with her colors flying and her bugle sounding, all to fall into a lap of luxury, to be received with open arms and almost caresses at the last!

In course of time, however, Janet reminded herself that instead of being the last, this after all was only the very first of her new experiences. Mrs. Harwood might turn out to be very different from the amiable and jocular old lady she appeared at first. Gussy, instead of being the nicest of fair-haired girls, might develop the falseness and treachery which some people thought went with that complexion. Other complications might arise. And then there was Ju.

Ah! Ju! Janet felt a little injured, wounded in her pride, when that consideration suddenly came in and thrust itself upon her. She had anticipated a great many evils, but she had never thought that to master an unruly girl taller than herself would be the chief or the first feature of her warfare. It was almost ludicrous to think of Ju, that child, in her short petticoats and flying hair, as a synonym of fate. Janet had been accustomed to be the favorite of the children wherever she went. The little ones had always liked her, gathered about her, petitioned her to tell them stories, to sing them some of her funny songs, to make up games for them. She was famous in Clover and for quite twelve miles round for this quality. "Delightful with children!" that was what was said of her. And in looking forward upon the future she had never taken into account any difficulty in that respect. The difficulties she had expected had been in (perhaps) the exacting and unjust mother, (perhaps) the jealous and spiteful girl, (perhaps) the undue admiration of the male persons about, and their universal feeling that the governess was much better worth looking at and talking to than the ladies of the house.

These are the difficulties chiefly set forth in novels, and, after all, it was from novels that Janet derived her chief conceptions of life. But a struggle with a wayward pupil had not occurred to her as one of her possible trials. After all, to look at it impartially, it was a not unnatural difficulty. She ought to have considered it one of the things most likely to happen, but it was a poor unromantic difficulty with nothing at all spirit-stirring in it. To wrestle in spirit with a naughty girl, to fight for obedience, for nice manners, for lessons learnt! Oh dear, oh dear! These were no doubt things as distinctly belonging to a governess's business as her grammar or her book of marks—but Janet had not taken them into account, and they seemed disappointing and ignoble trifles after the things for which she was prepared.

The dinner was good; the table was nicely served. It was apparent that the Harwoods were not people of yesterday. Their silver was heavy and old, marked not with a crest, but with a solemn "H," as a family perhaps not deeply acquainted with fantastic trophies of heraldry, but extremely conscious of the credit of their name. And everything shone and sparkled with that nicety of good usage which is never more perceptible than in those well-to-do English houses were splendor is never aimed at.

Mrs. Harwood was wheeled in in her chair, and, now that Janet could see her, proved to be a pretty old lady, rather different from her daughters, not, indeed, a similar type at all—a woman with lively dark eyes and warm tones of color in her complexion, and, even in her crippled condition, much more active in her movements than her eldest daughter at least. They had all dressed for dinner, according to that all-prevailing English practice which no other country knows—Gussy, in a pretty blue dress, which lent a little animation to her extreme fairness; Julia, in a white frock; even Mrs. Harwood, in a changed cap and shawl. How strange it was to sit down in the midst of this unaccustomed company, amid all these unknown surroundings, in one's mourning—a little black figure unlike any of them, yet one of the family! It gave Janet once more a thrill of novel sensation that ran all over her. She sat opposite to the mirror which was over the mantelpiece (there were mirrors over all the mantelpieces), and as it was tilted forward a little Janet could see herself, which gave her much amusement and encouragement. She looked very different from all the rest in her black frock. The second time she looked she had a vague perception that certainly she looked no worse than the rest—perhaps, better. At all events, there is no harm in being consoled about your appearance and feeling that you are no worse than the people about you. Janet felt disposed to have an occasional laugh and pleasant little remark now and then between herself and the little girl in black opposite to her in the glass. Somehow she liked the looks of that little thing the best.

And the talk flowed on, all through dinner and afterwards in Mrs. Harwood's room, where they sat after dinner round the twinkling fireplace, all made of shining brass and steel. How it shone and twinkled and reflected every flame, and threw off glimmers of concentrated light! The mother was wheeled back to her usual place. Gussy took up her position by a screen on the other side, and Julia and Miss Summerhayes found their places between. This nomenclature had been adopted at once, to Janet's great amazement. It was as if a partnership had been made which nobody could interfere with. Mrs. Harwood and her elder daughter were distinct personalities, but the other pair were Ju and Miss Summerhayes.

"It ought to be Miss Summerhayes and Ju," said Gussy, "but it does not run so well. One can't end off well with a ridiculous little syllable. This is where I always sit, and you must find a place according to what you like best. We live very quietly, partly because mamma will not get out of that chair."

"Can't, Gussy. Don't let Miss Summerhayes form such a bad opinion of your mother."

"Miss Summerhayes will form her own opinion quickly enough. I only give her a sketch of the circumstances. This is how we are night after night, often the whole winter through. It ought to be very dull, and it must look very dull to you, but, somehow, we are hardened, and don't feel it, except when Dolff is at home. When Dolff is at home, we ought to tell you, Miss Summerhayes, that there are sometimes a few parties—dinner parties, not very interesting, friends of the family; and on those occasions—it is better to say it to Miss Summerhayes just at once, without waiting till the time comes—don't you think, mamma?"

"Miss Summerhayes has so much sense. I am sure she will understand the size of the room and all that sort of thing," said Mrs. Harwood.

"Just so. I was sure you would think it best. It is just this, that when Dolff is at home and there are dinners, sometimes we may be unable to ask you to make one, Miss Summerhayes."

"Oh, is that all!" said Janet. She laughed with almost a little relief, for she had not known what she might be about to be told. "I did not expect even to dine downstairs," she said. "I was told a governess never did. Mrs. Bland told me all I should have to do—to dine at two with my pupil, perhaps to come in to afternoon tea, then to disappear upstairs and be seen no more. The vicar and she are saying to each other at present: 'Now Janet will be feeling very lonely. She will be finding out what a solitary evening is.' Dear people! I wish they could only see me now."

"Yes," said the old lady; "and all you say, my dear, about them, and about your arrival and everything, is very pretty. But your friends were really quite right, for that is usually the case when a—young lady—is in a family in this way. For you know every family has its own ways—and—and a person, a lady who is not acquainted with them may be—well, made uncomfortable, or the others may be obliged to stop speaking with freedom when she is there. It does not matter among us, who are all ladies together—and no secrets to discuss. But occasionally, my dear, when my son is at home, or when circumstances require it—you won't think it means any unkindness?—but we are obliged to recur to ordinary rules—for a few days—for a little while—perhaps only for two or three times. It is just a sort of necessity. We can't help ourselves. I always think it easier to explain everything and set everything on a simple footing at once."

This was a very long speech for Mrs. Harwood to make, and Janet strove to interrupt her a dozen times, to declare that she understood and that no explanations were necessary. But it came to an end at last, and the old lady pushed back her chair a little, and made a slight flourish with her handkerchief, in the satisfaction of having relieved her mind. Gussy immediately took up the *parole* without a pause.

"You said 'Janet,' Miss Summerhayes—what a nice little prepossessing natural name to have! Do you know what we are called, the unfortunate members of this family? Oh, I see, she can scarcely keep from laughing, mamma."

"I! no, indeed; my name is dreadful, like a Scotch housemaid; everybody says so," said Janet, in some trouble, not knowing what was coming next.

"Wait till you know. I am Augusta, which is Minerva Press of the finest water. And that poor child is Julia, and our only brother is Adolphus—conceive such a thing!—born John if ever man was; such an honest countenance, no pretension about it, and Adolphus put on him like a pinchbeck coronet. It is too bad. Mamma denies any responsibility. She says it was all my father's fault."

"I say," said Mrs. Harwood, "that it was the family—don't blame your poor father. The Harwoods were always queer, and it was they who liked those grand names."

"You call them grand! I have to sink to Gussy, and she to Ju, and Dolff, poor boy! did you ever hear a more miserable thing for a name? Dolff! There is nothing in it, neither meaning nor sense. I know he would come home a great deal happier if he were Jack."

"What can the boy's name have to do with his happiness?" cried Mrs. Harwood, testily, pushing back her chair a little more.

"If he were in a more exalted sphere he would be called Dolly," said his sister, sadly. "Dolly! imagine, a man's name!—Now if we had been born in mamma's time we would have been Mary and Elizabeth and John—how much better! Or we might be, had mamma insisted on being in the fashion, Dorothy and Mabel and Harold: not bad, though perhaps a little artificial. But Augusta, Julia, and Adolphus! Can you wonder, Miss Summerhayes, that we are all sometimes on the eve of rebellion, and if mamma was not really so good might be tempted even to assault her, though she declares it was not her fault?"

"Ju," said Mrs. Harwood, "get up and read by the lamp. The firelight, I am always telling you, will destroy your eyes."

Julia was stretched out on the carpet with a book laid out close by the gleaming, dazzling fire. She had her head supported in her hands, and had not moved or shown any sign of life while this conversation was going on. She took not the smallest notice of what her mother said.

"Ju," said Gussy, "do you know that your hair will be ruined in that heat? Nurse is always complaining it is scorched off your head."

"And that is why you have such dreadful headaches. Get up and sit at the table beside Miss Summerhayes.

But Ju neither moved nor spoke.

CHAPTER V.

IT is one of the most curious sensations of modern life to find one's self engulfed in a new family, wrapped round and round by novel circumstances, made, momentarily, to feel as if the centre of the world had somehow changed, and its most important features were now the peculiarities of a single race, or even of a small division of that race. People who hurry through visit after visit, it is probable, do not feel this amusing change in the direction of all things which takes place when an unsophisticated spirit suddenly leaves its own small centre, where the revolution of the planets has been round some well-known local or domestic sun, and plunges into another, where the forces are all the other way, and a circle of completely novel phenomena comes into sight. Janet, who still felt as if she were a young lady visitor come from one star to another to discover a new life, went upstairs that evening wrapped up in Harwoodism penetrated with a new flavor, feeling these new figures of Gussy, Ju, and Dolff, Augusta, Julia and Adolphus, one of whom was as yet entirely in the mists—and the ludicrous family grievance of their names, and their unaccustomed ways of living, and the blaze of firelight, and the comfort, and the sober limits of their life, surrounded apparently by the garden wall, and extending no farther—to turn her round and round, absorbing her own individuality into theirs. It seemed quite impossible to believe, when she reached her own room, and found herself alone, that she had left a totally different world that morning, and indeed, up to half-past three in the afternoon, had never heard of Gussy, or Ju, or Dolff, or known that such persons existed. Janet sat down to think it all over in her comfortable arm-chair by her blazing fire. Surely there never had been such fires. Her own grate was old-fashioned, too, bright brass, which reflected the flames and the glow of red-hot combustion, with which it played with a brilliancy which seemed to redouble the heat: the whole room was full of the leaping light, in the midst of which two white candles burned pale, like quite unnecessary things. Gussy and Ju, and Dolff—Dolff, Gussy, and Ju, their names made a sing-song in her head as the ruddy light darted and dazzled in her eyes. It was not even as if she had begun to speculate on the effect upon herself and her own life which these new surroundings would have. It was simply that she was enveloped in them, swallowed up, feeling it almost impossible to believe that there was still room in the world for Clover and such places, with their old-fashioned interests. When she tried to think of the vicarage, it had become like a faded old photograph to her mind—far away, at least a year, if not an age beyond anything she could recall. The new centre of the world was in St. John's Wood. And all the air was filled with circling reflections and echoes of Gussy, Dolff, and Ju.

This rhyme was the first thing that came into her mind in the morning when she sprang up a little confused, not quite sure where she was. But Janet was now as fresh as the morning, having shaken off her youthful superficial fatigue, and feeling quite ready for a more reasonable view of her new surroundings. The garden upon which she looked out was getting into trim winter order, though the lawn was still liable to renewed showers of falling leaves, and the late mignonette all weedy and straggling along with long shoots of nasturtiums and heads of geraniums, disorderly with decay, were still lingering in the borders. Some tall trees at the end lent a respectable background to the broad but closely-enclosed space with the very visible boundary of its brick walls. It all looked bright in the misty ruddy sunshine of the November morning. The gardener was moving about at his work, a boy after him, trundling a little wheelbarrow, with weeds and rubbish: the most familiar sights and sounds in the hazy morning air. The new world had thus some points of junction with the old, which made it look more real, not so much like a story. Janet felt her heart jump to meet the new day. She was going to be exceedingly comfortable at least, and amused at first, even if it should be a little dull after. But perhaps it would not even be dull. She herself would have something to say to that—and it is impossible to tell at twenty in what unsuspected circumstances "fun" may be lurking. It is one of the inextinguishable elements in life always to be found in one corner or another.

Janet did not make this reflection in so many words, but she was more keenly alive to the fact than is her historian; and with this confidence went down to breakfast, when Gussy met her with all the kind greetings possible. The breakfast-table was quite brilliant to behold, with a silver tea-urn of old-fashioned form, silver tea-pot, coffee-pot, a glitter of silver everywhere: and so well kept! and so heavy and respectable! with such an air of sober, modest, consciously undemonstrative comfort and wealth!

Gussy's dress was still too light for Janet's taste, being an exceedingly pale gray, which was not very becoming to a person with so little color; but she looked as *nice*, and purled forth her soft speeches just as on the night before. One thing she said, however, which was of more importance than all these friendly purlings, gave Janet the first touch of the real in this mild domestic elysium. She put out her long soft hand from behind the urn, and laid it on Janet's arm.

"Before she appears, just one word, Miss Summerhayes. Please strike your blow at once."

"What blow?" asked Janet, amazed.

"To get the upper hand of Ju. You are quite a novelty; she does not know you at all. You might startle her into submitting, if you took advantage of the circumstances. Don't ask anything unreasonable of her, but never give in when you have insisted on anything. Don't let her beat you. She's coming down now; I can't say any more. And there's really no more to say. Never let her win the day."

These words tingling in her ears gave Janet the strangest little shock, like the sudden touch of an electric battery, in the midst of the comfort and quiet. She could scarcely keep from jumping up, starting out of her seat. Her black sleeve, when Gussy took her long fingers from it, seemed to give out sparks. To strike a blow, to win a battle, never to allow herself to be beat. What curious words in this absolutely quiet and ordinary domestic calm?

Ju came in with a nod to Miss Summerhayes, and said nothing at all while she despatched her breakfast. But then Gussy was talking all the time, and there was not much room for anyone else. She was certainly a most self-absorbed young person; but, save her silence and that acute small curve over each eyebrow, caused by a sort of permanent frown, there seemed nothing else to alarm a stranger.

Janet's heart still beat more quickly than before, but she gradually got more calm, and assured herself there could be no real danger. In some families all the molehills are made into mountains, and perhaps that was the case here.

It was with a little excitement, however, that Janet walked into the school-room, which she found communicated with her own room by a short passage, and which occupied a corner of the house with one window to the garden and another in the other wall, from which a view could be obtained into the outer world, meaning in this case the exceedingly quiet suburban road between two lines of garden walls which had reminded Janet of a country town. The young governess of twenty came into this room, which was still in the shadow, though expectant of a gleam of sunshine from the south when the sun should have made a little more progress, with some excitement, of which, however, she was able to conceal the signs. It gave a brightness to her eyes and a little thrill to her upper lip, but that was all. She had not the least idea of what she was going to encounter. The young knight in the story of the Sleeping Beauty was not more ignorant, nor was she at all sure that she knew how to fight, or had the coolness and the courage necessary for an important encounter. With a child of fourteen! she tried to say to herself with a laugh. But, after all, twenty is not so very far elevated over fourteen, and the child was taller and almost more developed than the woman. It was at ten o'clock that lessons were to begin, and at ten minutes to ten Janet opened the school-room door. Mystery and expectation made her heart beat. She stepped in once more, feeling the thrill as of an electric machine; and her breathing was slightly affected, though she would not show it. She had almost feared she would find emptiness, which would have been the most embarrassing of all, for how fight when your opponent does not show? But, fortunately, Julia was already there. This was what Janet found: a table set out in the middle of the room, with books and writing things, all in good order; the piano open at the back, with music upon it. Meanwhile, at the south window, seated at another table, with both her elbows resting upon it as if riveted to the mahogany—Julia, her head supported on her hands, a book lying open before her, in precisely the same attitude in which she had lain on the previous night scorching her head in the heat and blaze of the fire.

Janet stood for a moment looking at her pupil with an internal shiver. Her pupil—to whom she was not at all sure of being able to teach anything—whom in any circumstances she would have felt an alarmed respect for, as a being probably destined to find her out, and expose her little pretences. Julia remained like a statue, immovable, not turning to see who had come in according to weak mortal usage, far too strong in the instincts of rebellion and individuality for any such betrayal of weakness. Miss Summerhayes then moved a little about the room—looked at the music, took up the books on the table, glanced out from the window. Ten o'clock had not yet struck. She finally went and seated herself in the chair placed for her, and waited until the ten tiny strokes, tingling from the clock on the mantelpiece, had been answered by all the church towers in the neighborhood. Then there came an awful moment.

"Julia, it is time for lessons."

Janet heard her own voice falter, but the tremor was not audible to any listener. Julia did not move nor reply.

"I am waiting to begin lessons," Janet repeated more sharply, after a moment.

Dead silence—not by the merest quiver of movement did Julia betray that she had heard.

"It is ten o'clock, and I am waiting to begin lessons. Julia!"

Julia sat like a figure of wood or stone.

Miss Janet Summerhayes rose from her chair, pale, with her eyes shining. Her little temper came to her aid. The fun disappeared. The moment of conflict had come.

CHAPTER VI.

JANET had as pretty a little temper of her own as you could meet anywhere. It flashed up in a moment into her eyes. No one, schoolgirl or otherwise, was likely to get a cheap bargain of this little governess. She rose, and, turning the key in the door as she passed, walked up to the table at which Miss Julia sat with her book. The girl was not aware that her own absolute immovability proved to her antagonist that she was not absorbed in her book but in the battle which had begun. Miss Summerhayes stood opposite to her for a moment looking down upon Julia's bent head. She felt the key of the door in her pocket, which, perhaps, was rather a desperate step so early in the fight; as in doing this she had at once burnt her ships, and committed herself to a policy of absolute no-surrender; but still it inspired her, for she could now neither draw back nor temporize.

"Julia! I have told you three times that it is ten o'clock, and I am waiting to begin lessons."

There was still not a movement, not a sound. Julia sat as if made of stone. Then Janet made the great *coup* she had been contemplating. With a sudden swift movement she took the book from under the reader's bent face, closed it, and carried it away. In a moment Julia was erect, getting to her feet with a bound, her gray eyes dilating into great globes of gold, her spring like that of a tiger. Janet had scarcely time, though her movements were very quick, to get back to the shelter of her arm-chair. But she managed to do so, and to lock up the offending volume in a drawer, with Julia's grip on her shoulder, and a shriek of "How dare you, how dare you!" ringing in her ears.

"Miss Summerhayes! give me back my book. How dare you take my book? Give it me this moment—do you hear me! do you hear me!" cried the girl, passionately, holding Janet's shoulders in a grasp of steel.

"I hear you perfectly well—as you heard me just now. Take your hands from my shoulders. I did not touch you; if we are to fight, let us fight fair."

Julia's hands dropped, and a shade of consternation came over her eyes. Then she stamped her foot violently upon the floor—"Miss Summerhayes, give me back my book?"

"Sit down," said Janet, not uncheerfully, "and we can have it out."

"Give me back my book!"

"Well," said Janet, "now we have both got through that formula, *trois sommations*—though I am afraid not very *respectueuses*. Do you know what that means? I called you three times and you have called me three times. We are equal, so far. Now sit down and let us talk it out."

"Equal!" said Julia, with a shriek, "me and you, Miss Summerhayes! You are only the governess—that's no better than a servant. You may suppose they think different downstairs, because of their way of talking, and because Gussy thinks it's grand to be like that. But they think just the same. And mamma will stand up for me. She pretends she wants me to be mastered, but she doesn't, and you'll find the difference when you go to her with your complaints."

"But I don't mean to go to her with any complaints," said Janet, putting on the best smile she could. "If we are to get on, we must manage it between ourselves; if not, there is a very easy remedy for me. You had better sit down, and discuss the matter, so that we may know what we are about."

"What's your remedy?" cried Julia, breathing hard.

"It will be quite effectual, as far as I am concerned: but I don't like to be beaten, so I shall try some others first. Sit down there."

"I shan't," Miss Julia said.

"Well, stand on your head then," said Janet, "perhaps you may like that better: only let us get all the necessary tricks over, and come to business, for it may as well be decided once for all."

"How dare you talk of tricks! What do you call my tricks?"

"They are quite easy to describe. To pretend to be deaf, dumb, and blind; to pretend to be a wild beast; to shriek and snort and talk loud. I don't know what others you may still have to get through, but you must know as well as I do that all these are tricks, and of no consequence. When they are exhausted, then we can begin to talk."

"Me a wild beast! Me of no consequence! I should like," cried Julia, with her eyes blazing like red-hot flames, and her fingers clasping and unclasping, "just to give it you hot, for once! just to stamp upon you, and tear off your fal-lals and pitch you out of the window!"

Janet nodded her head at each threat, not by way of approbation, but of acquiescence as in an argument she had foreseen.

"I know," she said, "I told you so. It would be a great saving of time if you would consider all that sort of thing as said, and come to the real question."

"What is the real question?" said Julia, staring, with her hands grasping the top of the chair on which she had been requested to sit down—whether because she was checked in her childish rage, or whether because she meant to use it as a weapon, it was difficult to say.

"The real question is, whether we are to be able to get on together or not. It's the only one of any importance. I want to come to that."

"What an awful fool you must be," said Julia, bending over the back of the chair towards Janet with flaming looks of wrath.

"Yes," said Janet. "One of us is so, that is very evident: but why should it strike you at this moment?"

"To think that it isn't settled already, to think I would ever give in to you for a moment. Knuckle under! me! Oh! you think you can come over me with smiling, when you are in as blue a funk—— You, a bit of a governess hired just like the housemaid: and that's exactly what mamma will say."

Janet yawned a little in the girl's furious face, a gentle little yawn which did not at all distort her own countenance.

"My poor child," she said, "if you would only consider that I understand all that, and that we'd so much better come to business! You can't frighten me, and though, of course, you can insult me, that's of equally little use, for I don't care."

"Because you're used to it," cried Julia.

"No—once only before. It was a tramp on the road, an old woman, and I would not give her any money. It is curious to think where you can have learned the same sort of thing—brought up, I suppose, more or less like a lady—but it must be in the blood."

"Do you mean to say I'm not a lady—you—? Oh-h!" for Janet had gently shrugged those little shoulders which still felt the young fury's grip. "I'll go," cried Julia, fiercely, "I'll go this moment and tell mamma."

Janet sat quietly in her chair awaiting the discovery of the locked door, and somewhat alarmed lest there should ensue a physical struggle which would be undignified and unladylike. Then followed a whirlwind of noise, stamping, shrieking, and wild talk.

"Give me the key! Open the door! I want to go to mamma. Mamma! Let me out. Let me out! I want to open the door,"—then a furious kick upon the panel. "Mamma! Gussy! I'm locked in; come, come, and open the door."

"It is a pity that all the servants should know you are in trouble, Julia. Let it remain between you and me," said Janet, laying her hand upon the girl's shoulder.

"Open the door!"

"No, I shall not open the door—nor shall anyone else, if I can help it. Let this remain between you and me."

"Mamma will send and order you to do it. Mamma! mamma! I am locked in. I can't get out. Come and open the door!"

How it was that no one heard these outcries Janet could not imagine: but they were at the top of the house: the kitchen was thoroughly occupied with its own affairs, and Mrs. Harwood, as she found out afterwards, had been wheeled out for her morning airing, so that silence alone replied to Julia's passionate appeals. She rushed to the window and flung it open, but the gardener was not visible in the garden. After half-an-hour of tumult, an enforced silence fell upon the school-room. But Julia was not yet overcome.

"I shall keep you here all your life—you shan't go—not a step. If I am to be shut in, you shall be shut in too. You shall have no lunch; you shall have no tea; you shall have no dinner!" said Julia, *crescendo*, rising to a climax.

"Well," said Janet, "if you think it better to put off our conversation till to-morrow, I make no objection. It will be very uncomfortable—but there are worse things than discomfort in this world. I have done without my dinner before now."

"Yes! often, I shouldn't wonder—when you had nobody to give you a dinner," cried Julia.

Janet looked at the furious girl with a glance of astonishment in her eyes. She laughed a little.

"You silly child," she said.

And then in the midst of the agitation and tumult there occurred a moment of quiet. Julia was at the end of her resources. She was worn out with her own passion, dismayed by being thus left to the tender mercies of the governess, and discouraged beyond description by the indifference and contempt of the stranger whom she had been so certain of subduing—a little thing not so big as herself, a little governess without a friend—a subject creature whom it was safe for everybody to jump upon. Julia's experience contained no stronger picture of the governess than that of the one who ran away next morning after complaining to Mrs. Harwood that she was not accustomed to such young ladies. The others had all coaxed and cringed and endeavored to temporize.

Julia went and sat down panting at the other table, and watched this new kind of human being seated in the middle of the room as if nothing had happened, calmly writing, not a hair turned upon her head, not a bit of frill crumpled about her neck. It was natural to Janet to be neat, and her self-control was wonderful. Besides, of course she knew that she was being looked at, watched with all the keen observation of a vindictive child to see where her weakness lay. That she had supported this struggle so long without moments of weakness it would be vain to say—that she had not felt the stings and resented the blows. Her heart had beat as if it was bursting from her breast. She had felt herself trembling all over with excitement and alarm. But she had managed somehow to keep calm all along, and she was still calm now, keeping in her breath, holding herself with all her might to look indifferent. Julia's observation was keen, but not so keen as to pierce Janet's armour of mail. The girl sat staring at her with eyes that became less and less like orbs of flame, and more like ordinary big gray eyes with a golden glow. And Janet wrote a letter. It was the only thing she could think of to give her the support of an occupation. She wrote a narrative of what had passed, writing "Dear Mrs. Bland" at the top to give herself a countenance, though the last thing in the world she would have done was to send the vicar's wife such a description of her first day in her new situation. She smiled, however, to herself involuntarily as she went on with her story, making it very amusing. And Julia saw her smile, and something like awe came over the exhausted spirit of the little rebel. To go through all that, one tithe of which would have broken the spirit of any other governess, and yet to smile!

After a long interval of silence, and when Janet began to wonder with some alarm how she would meet a long strain of passive resistance had Julia strength of mind to keep it up, a sudden voice once more made itself heard.

"Miss Summerhayes! the first thing I shall do when I get out of this will be to tell mamma."

"That is exactly what I should recommend," said Janet, looking up from her writing; "one's mother should always know everything," and with a little friendly nod she returned to her letter.

Julia could not tell what to think: there was more in it than her puzzled understanding had ever encountered before. After a while she said, with some hesitation, "Miss Summerhayes!" again.

"Yes," said Janet, looking up once more.

"What did you mean about conversation? I hate you! I shall never speak to you three words if I can help it; but what did you mean about putting off the conversation? I want to know——"

"Perhaps it will be better to put it off till to-morrow."

"I want to have it now. Conversation! as if there ever could be any between you and me."

"That is what I have just said. It will be better to put it off," said Janet, without raising her head, turning over the page of her supposed letter.

The next thing she heard was a stamp on the floor, suppressed so that it was scarcely a stamp, and an exclamation,

"I prefer to have it now."

"I cannot talk to anyone so far off," said Janet, and there was another pause.

Presently she could hear the faint rustling of a person about to get up from a chair, which went on for some time, there being an evident and great reluctance to move. Then there was a sudden plunge. Julia alighted opposite her, on the other side of the table.

"I want to know what it is—— I want to know what you want with me."

Janet sat up, raised her head, putting down her pen.

"Honestly, and without any more preliminaries?" she said.

Julia's eyes gave a single dart of fire.

"No one ever said I was a thief. I want to know what you want with me."

"That is what I call honestly," Janet replied, and she put away her writing things for the second encounter, the first having thus been successful beyond her hopes.

CHAPTER VII.

"WELL," said Janet, when she found herself looking into the blurred and flushed countenance of the passionate girl. Julia had given vent, in spite of herself, to some tears, and had dashed them away with her hand or her sleeve, leaving a smear, and her hair was hanging wildly round her face, and there was a general air of dilapidation and ruin, though accompanied by few actual signs of warfare. She ought to have torn her frock from top to bottom to justify the general aspect of affairs, but she had not done so, and the smeared cheek and the ragged hair were the only physical certainties of the conflict past. There was still a pucker over each eye, but it was not an assured and dauntless pucker. The fortunes of war, for once, had not turned the usual way.

"Well—you have been behaving like a fool, but a fool has no meaning. When one can behave like a fool with a meaning I think there must be some sense at the bottom. If I am right, nothing matters that has happened; but if I am wrong——"

Julia stared with faint comprehension and much impatience. She said—

"Don't palaver. What do you want with me?"

Now, Janet had expected to exercise a little feminine philosophy upon the girl when she had got her in hand—a little banter, a little seriousness—to make her ashamed of herself in the first place, and then to make her see. She was taken a little aback. If she could not make her ashamed nor make her see, what was to be done? The question grew a great deal more serious thus than when it concerned only a locked door. She ran over the circumstances rapidly in her mind, and she saw it would not do to answer according as it at first occurred to her, that she (Janet) personally wanted nothing at all with Julia, except as little to do with her as might be.

"What I want is simple," she said, with a smile. "I want to do the work I have been engaged to do, and that is to educate you for as many hours as your mother has fixed for your education. How am I to get that done? for, you may be sure, I mean to do it one way or other. I want to talk it over and discover how it is to be done."

"I don't want it to be done at all"

"Neither do I," said Janet, facing the rebel bravely, and bursting into a laugh. "But if you will reflect," she said, "that does not get us a bit further on, for it must be done. Unless it is done you will grow up like the tramp woman I was telling you of—not at all an interesting person—and I shall break my word. Now, I don't like to break my word. You don't care at present about becoming like a tramp, but you will later on."

"How dare you say——"

"Julia," said the little governess, "I dare to say anything I think proper, or to do anything, so you had better make up your mind to that at once. Such questions are silly. I am not afraid of anyone or anything."

Janet threw back her head, which was smaller—as she was smaller in every part—than that of her tall pupil. There is nothing so fearless in life as a girl who is without fear. It is true that the kind of dauntless courage she possesses is largely made up of ignorance, and also comes a little perhaps from the conventional precautions which defend her, though she does not know it. However, the quality is absolute, and Janet had it. She feared nothing, as she said.

Julia, from under her puckered eyebrows, glared into the clear brown eyes, which had something in them like the sparkle of a Highland stream, and admired the valor which she did not possess: for she was afraid of the coercion which she was always fighting against. She stared, but she said nothing in reply.

"You see," said Janet, "I will do what I've promised: and if I were you I'd say I will too. It's much nicer than to have to say I must——"

Still Julia stared; her lips moved as if she would have spoken, but she uttered no sound.

"Downstairs," said Janet, "they expect us to fight. I am afraid you have been so silly that they think you are a fool, and don't understand anything about what is expected from a gentlewoman. That's not my opinion, as I told you: but as I shall not give in, whatever you do, it would be very silly to go on fighting forever. We can make something better of it: if you will be convinced that I never shall be afraid of you—no, nor of anyone else," Janet repeated, with the color mounting in her cheeks.

Julia continued silent for some time; then, with a sudden burst of harsh sound, asked, "What do you want of me?" and was abruptly silent again, as if a spring had been touched to give forth that voice.

"I want you to speak when you are spoken to," said Janet.

The girl, who evidently expected something of much larger scope, cried "Oh!" but said no more.

"I want you to do as I tell you—for so many hours in the day—from ten to one, is it? That's not very long. You can be a demon after that, if you please, and dance your war-dance."

"What do you mean by—dancing my war-dance?"

"Behaving like a fiend, or a Red Indian, or a tramp in the roads: so long as you are in your senses from ten to one."

Julia stared again, but made no reply.

"But you must remember," said Janet, "that in the place I come from, where there are no Red Indians, there is a point of honor; and whatever one undertakes to do one does. If you see the sense of what I say, and give me your word, it is once and forever; not promise one day and break it the next. That is a sort of thing I don't understand. One promises, and it is for life and death. It does not matter what comes in the way. If you were to be killed for it, it would have to be done."

Julia stared for a few moments more, and then——

"I can see the sense of that," she said.

"To be sure. I knew you would when you gave yourself time to look at it. Well, then, you can see that to call in other people or other considerations is of no use between you and me. At the last we should always have to talk it over between ourselves. If you like, you can make it quite easy and rather pleasant; if you don't, I must think of some other way."

When the hour of luncheon arrived, the respectable household in St. John's Wood was considerably excited as to the fate of the new governess. Perhaps the servants had not been so completely out of hearing as had appeared. Perhaps some stray notes of the fray had been blown out of the open windows or conveyed through the chinks of the woodwork. At all events, there was a prevailing curiosity in the house, which became apparent almost as soon as the governess and her pupil left the shelter of those rooms in which already so many varied scenes in the life and education of Julia Harwood had taken place. Mrs. Harwood's maid met them on the stairs, and gave Janet an inquiring look, to which the governess, you may be sure, made no reply. Half-way down they were again met by the parlor-maid, who, looking somewhat "flustered," announced that Mrs. Harwood was afraid they might not have heard the bell.

"Oh, yes, we can hear the bell perfectly," said Janet.

She went into the dining-room with Julia so close behind her that they formed one shadow. Mrs. Harwood's face was turned anxiously towards the door. Gussy, more astute, had her eyes intent upon the mirror, in which everything was reflected. There was a long breath of relief drawn by both, not, perhaps, audible by any uninterested spectator, but affecting the entire atmosphere to Janet's excited consciousness. She felt as if her triumph must be of more importance than the mere victory over a naughty child, and wondered, with a passing thrill, was there any mystery involved? But in face of the decorous, gentle household, so correct, so punctilious, which had not a fold awry, or a corner neglected in all its careful economy, it was ludicrous to think of any mystery. However, there could be no doubt that her entrance was greeted with extreme pleasure.

"Sit here, my dear Miss Summerhayes," said the mistress of the house. "This is the warm corner; there is no draught at this side. Well, you have got over your first morning's work. And how do you like teaching? It's very tedious, I'm afraid."

"Oh, not where there is intelligence and brains," said Janet, with great composure. "Children who cannot keep up their attention are very trying; but not anyone who is old enough to understand. There has not been much teaching, however, this morning, we have been chiefly talking things over. Two strangers forced together without any mutual knowledge, I thought it best that we should understand each other first."

This statement, which was given with the most natural air in the world, was listened to by all her audience with the most flattering interest, but perfect decorum, the only transgressor of which was the parlor-maid, from whose direction there came one or two faint muffled sounds, whether of painfully suppressed laughter, or of something giving way in the effort of controlling emotion, Janet could not tell. Gussy fixed the culprit with a glittering eye from behind the screen which sheltered her from the blazing fire, and Mrs. Harwood cast a cursory glance behind her. None of these things would have been noticed at all by a stranger who was less prepared than Janet, but she perceived everything in her own suppressed excitement. There was something amusing, however, in the comment made by the strain upon the parlor-maid's stays.

"That is so sensible," said Mrs. Harwood, "it is for want of getting to understand each other that so many relationships go wrong. Ju, push your chair back a little, the sun is in your face."

Julia paid no attention to this command.

"Ju, the sun is in your face, sit nearer this way; your eye-sight will be gone before you are twenty. Child, do you hear me!" Mrs. Harwood cried.

"And her complexion: you will have none at all left, not a tint," said Gussy, "before you come out."

Julia did not betray by a movement that she had heard either speak, but put her head forward into a brilliant ray of sunshine which streamed across the table, so as to get the full glow upon her face. She had not much to boast of in the way of complexion. Whether it was the blaze of sunlight and firelight combined to which she loved to expose herself, or whether it was nature, her face thus brought into prominence was sallow and freckled, only relieved by the golden light in her gray eyes.

"The winter sun cannot do much harm," said Janet, with a friendly impulse. "It makes a pretty picture."

"Ah," said Gussy, shaking her head, "you should have seen that child once; she had such a color. We have nothing to brag of in the way of complexion in our family, but I once thought Ju would redeem us in that respect. Alas!" and Miss Harwood shook her head.

"And did you find her very backward, Miss Summerhayes? and is there any special thing you think she is more fit for than others? I always like young people to have some particular turn. Do you remember, Gussy, how we used to try and try with Dolff to get him to say what he would like to be. But he never would take an attitude of his own. 'Whatever you please, mother,' he used to say."

"That was all his goodness, mamma," said Gussy. "What he wanted was travel and that sort of thing—and he knew you would not like it. We have never travelled much in this family. And then he knew he would not on any great occasion have to work for himself."

"We never can tell that," said the old lady. "Land's gone down, and perhaps the Funds may soon go down. In these dreadful times, you never can know. Ju, take your elbows off the table. You sit like a washer-woman. I never saw such shoulders."

"The Funds are the country," said Gussy, "they can't go down, or England will be ruined. Ju, do you hear what mamma says? Her shoulders are something dreadful. Take your elbows off the table, for goodness' sake!"

Julia took not the slightest notice of these remarks. She sat with both elbows on the tablecloth, eating bread-and-butter at an elevation of many inches over her neglected plate.

"I have heard," said Janet, "that the people who are called smart people do that now. It has become the fashion: so Julia is in advance of us instead of being behind, as you think."

"Ah," said Mrs. Harwood, shaking her head, "bad manners are the fashion, and that is a dreadful thing to say. I remember in my young days—but fortunately we don't know anything about smart people here."

Julia's elbows had disappeared with the rapidity of magic. She would not have it supposed that she meant to be smart or in the fashion whatever anyone might say.

CHAPTER VIII.

JANET found after this experience was over that she had perhaps discounted too quickly the excitement of her position. She had gone too fast, as was the impulse of her nature. Julia Harwood, who had been used to continued "nagging," which never came to anything, a continual and frivolous demand to which obedience was never exacted, had been taken entirely by surprise by the rapid movements of the little governess. Reason, which had never before been applied to her case, had made a considerable impression upon her; but still more the conviction that Miss Summerhayes would "stand no nonsense," the wholesome sense of a force which she could not overcome: and between the two the temporary effect produced had been great. And a certain amount of order had followed in the school-room. When the two were alone, Julia replied when she was spoken to, and did more or less what she was told. There was a frame-work created of lessons and rules which helped the hours along, and to which the girl gave a sort of submission. But apart from this, which occupied the mornings of her new existence, poor Janet found herself immersed, submerged, drowned in a sort of tepid bath of Harwoodism which was an experience quite unlooked-for and unthought-of.

Some families, and those perhaps the most amiable in existence, have this tendency so strong that there is no escape from it; they compare everything, judge everything, estimate everything by the rule of their own case—"in our family we do," or "we don't do," so and so, were words continually on Augusta Harwood's lips. She was a very good, considerate, kind young woman, trying to make everybody comfortable about her, eager to anticipate every want, to see that the stranger was warm enough, cool enough, had just the right amount of sugar in her tea, was not over-tired, did not have damp feet or wear too thin a dress, or get the sun or the firelight in her eyes. Gussy achieved the difficult feat of making a dependent perfectly at her ease, and obliterating almost every trace of that embarrassment which attends the position of a governess. It was not that she fell into one of those sudden enthusiastic friendships which sometimes unites the daughter of the house with the stranger in it, but only that she was constitutionally kind, thoroughly good-hearted and good-natured. It would seem difficult to say any more in her favor than this. And yet, from her gentle, amiable, and good-humored sway there arose one fixed impression: and in her pleasant person there breathed out, embracing all things, one mild, universal atmosphere of the family.

It was as if she knew nothing but Harwoods in the world. Church—even Church!—and State, and laws and governments, and business and books were outside of the oasis in which she dwelt—the universe in general lay beyond, as great London lay beyond the brick walls of the garden in St. John's Wood. London existed for the advantage of that house, and so did the universe in which London is but a point. But they were outside, and of secondary importance. The Harwoods, their habits, their ways, their ancestors, their relationships, and, above all, their characteristics were within, and everything without took a tinge from this prevailing atmosphere.

It might be some time before the spectators found out what it was. It was like the transparent veil of tarlatan which is sometimes stretched between a drawing-room assembly of spectators and an exhibition of *tableaux vivants*, to give distance and softness to the mimic scene; it was like the tint sometimes supposed to be becoming to the complexion, which faintly rose-colored glass gives to the air of a boudoir: it was a medium, an atmosphere, all pervading, something from which there was no escape.

Janet had been prepared, as has been seen, for many of the deprivations of a governess, none of which she was called upon to bear. The letters she received from her old friends at Clover, to whom she had narrated her first experiences, were almost enthusiastic in their congratulations.

"You seem to have been fortunate above anything that could be hoped for," Mrs. Bland wrote. "I never heard of such kind people."

And so they were, Janet assured herself. Never were people so kind; they cared for her comfort as if she had been a favored visitor; they never allowed her to feel herself *de trop*. They accepted her into the bosom of the family with the most open as well as the most considerate kindness. Nevertheless, it was not very long before Janet began to feel the creeping in of something not strong enough to be called miasma, a sort of closeness in the air. She felt the heavens contracting round her, and the horizon closing up. These sensations were more or less physically justified by the fact that there is a great deal of vegetation in St. John's Wood; that the trees grew too close in a hundred gardens, and that though their foliage and greenness were delightful in summer, the fall of the leaf was attended with disagreeables there as in other leafy places; but that was not the heart of the matter.

Janet began to feel herself drawing long breaths of relief when she got outside the garden gate. This was generally in company with Julia, who did not share in the family worship, and whose conversation was very jerky and irregular, leaving the governess free either to lead the dialogue or to refrain from any. And when Janet escaped altogether by herself, as sometimes she did, to go to church, sometimes to the circulating library to get a book, sometimes to the nearest repository of art needlework to match some silk or crewels for Mrs. Harwood, she was still more delighted and relieved.

To escape for an hour from the Harwoods—to become once more conscious of her own individuality, and of the existence of crowds, nay, worlds of people who did not bear that respectable name, became the greatest refreshment to her. She would run out even in the wet if anything was wanted in the most cheerful and, as the family thought, self-denying way.

"But, my dear, it rains. I couldn't possibly let you go out in the rain, to take all the stiffening out of your crape, and, perhaps, catch cold, all because I want that book," Mrs. Harwood would say, divided between her desire for a new novel (which is so doubly acceptable on a wet day) and her concern for Janet.

This was a thing that the gardener could not do, nor even her own maid—could that functionary have been persuaded to wet her feet—for maids and gardeners never know what books you have read, even though they themselves have brought them from the library, and produce the same three volumes again and again, as Mrs. Harwood complained, till you are nearly driven out of your senses.

"If you really think you would like a run," the old lady added, with a sudden sense of the advantage. "I remember when I was your age I never minded the rain—but it will take all the stiffening out of your crape."

"She has no crape on that dress," said Gussy, "which I very much approve of, for what is the good of a thing you have always to be thinking of? We never go in for mourning very much in our family. But, mamma, I do think, what with your books and your crewels, and so forth, you impose very much on Miss Summerhayes."

"Oh, I like it," cried Janet, "it gives me the greatest pleasure. I only wish I could run on errands all day long, if I could be of any use—you are all so good to me."

"That is a grateful little thing, Gussy," said Mrs. Harwood, as Janet, wrapped in a mackintosh, with her skirts drawn up, and a little felt hat upon her head which could not be spoilt, ran lightly along the glistening path to the garden door.

"Yes," said Gussy, sedately, "she is a kind little thing: and I am sure she would do anything to please you, mamma. And such a good influence over Ju. Dolff will not believe his eyes when he comes home and sees her actually doing her lessons like any other girl."

"I hope Miss Summerhayes does not humor her too much," said Mrs. Harwood, with a sigh.

In the meantime, Janet was running along with the rain in her face, and a sense of freedom which made her heart dance. It was not an attractive day to be out, and the long roads in St. John's Wood, between the garden walls, with here and there a little oasis formed by a few shops, were not, perhaps, exhilarating to pedestrians generally. On a wet day there was nothing at all to be seen or met with in these roads any more than had they been the suburbs of a country town. On fine days the children and their nurserymaids made a great deal of variety, and the old ladies going out for their airings in their bath chairs. It is not, perhaps, a very gay kind of traffic which is represented by bath chairs and perambulators. But there were the tradesmen, too, and occasional cabs passing to add to the effect. But when it rained everything was desolate. The garden doors were closely shut: the houses invisible behind among the bare branches of the trees from which the last shabby leaves were tumbling like rags among the droppings of the rain. What it is to be twenty, and to have a heart free of care! Janet ran along the glistening pavement with her skirts held up, delighted, glad to be out, though she breathed almost as much rain as air, glad to have escaped from the all-enveloping Harwoods, and to be herself for a moment. She was only going on an errand for her employer, and her return was anxiously looked for, so that she knew that she must not be long: but every moment was good. She carried her umbrella shut; she would not lose the feeling of the soft rain on her forehead. A conviction that this was against all the traditions of the Harwoods made it doubly agreeable. They were all afraid of catching cold and getting wet, but not Janet. She liked it. It meant a mark of freedom and independence. It meant being herself without a thought of Harwoodism, as she had been in the old days.

Janet skipped into the stationer's shop to which she was bound, and which stood only (alas!) about a quarter-of-a-mile off in one of the oases already described. In St. John's Wood there are a great many stationers' shops. They are doubled with a circulating library, usually a branch of the all-pervading Mudie, and they sell all manner of "fancy" articles, cardboarding of every description. There is a great sale for menu cards, for little mounts and frames, for calendars and almanacs, and every sort of little composition of paper, pictures, and mottoes in pretty colors, in such districts. Pencils in boxes and out of them, with little holders, with silver cases, and unadorned for drawing purposes: writing materials in pretty colored covers: little books such as innocent minds love, with texts for every day, or pretty verses, or scraps of genteel philosophy. It would fill all my space if I were to give a catalogue of half the things in these stationers' shops. In addition to all this and the library, with its rows of novels, a little dilapidated, there was a counter for music in this particular example of the stationers of St. John's Wood, and another one for newspapers both these things forming a portion of the well-established business carried on by the Misses Mimpriss in Laburnum Place.

When Janet skipped in, her face fresh from the rain and cold air, her eyes dancing with freedom and satisfaction, she almost ran against a gentleman who was standing inside turning over the music, and who turned round quickly with a mixture of surprise and curiosity. He was a young man and rather handsome, Janet thought; not very tall but strong and well built, with dark hair and a fine complexion, a little like, perhaps, the male beauties in the hairdressers' shops. She was so much taken by surprise to find a man in that feminine place that she was, perhaps, a little severe in her hasty judgment. He interfered with her satisfaction somehow, though he was perfectly well-bred, and after the one glance of surprised attention—which was quite justifiable surely when a girl came like a bombshell into a little shop, where no such projectile could have been expected on a wet day—returned to his music and took no further notice. The momentary shock, however, made Janet's fresh countenance blaze with its surprise and unexpectedness. She went back into the further part of the shop to look over the novels and choose one which Mrs. Harwood would like, which was no easy task. She had to ask for the help of the disengaged sister, who presided over that shrine of fiction, and had a long consultation with her to see which books Mrs. Harwood had already read. Finally, she chose one with much internal doubt, intensified, she could scarcely tell how, by the presence of the man who stood with his back to her, certainly not interfering in any way with that simple operation. And it happened to make matters worse that the sister whom Janet was consulting was not the sister whose business it was to enter the books. Accordingly, when Janet's Miss Mimpriss said to the other Miss Mimpriss "391,-121 for Mrs. Harwood," the gentleman who was buying music turned half round again, exactly as if he had said, "Oh!" and gave Janet a look, not like the former look, which was merely conventional, but one which was personal to herself, and meant several things. It was a glance full of understanding, as if he knew all about her, and of criticism, and amusement. His eyebrows went up a little, and he seemed to say, "Oh! so that is who you are? It is you, is it?" which made Janet very angry, though for the life of her she could not have told why. She took her three battered volumes in her hands and left the shop, feeling her little expedition to be quite spoiled. She had meant to make an investigation herself among the music and to look over the "fancy" articles. She was only after all a country young lady; and she believed that among the many pretty things which the Miss Mimprisses sold at a cost of from one to two shillings, she could have found something which Mrs. Bland would have set upon the drawing-room mantelpiece in the vicarage, bidding her visitors look what a pretty thing Janet had sent her from London, and was it not kind of the child?

Janet could not linger, however, to make any such purchase under that man's eye. She would not have liked to do it before anybody, and had, indeed, jibed at the fancy articles when she had entered the shop with Miss Harwood; but she felt much aggrieved to be so balked.

"Very like a barber's block," she said to herself; the sort of man whom you might expect to see in that respectable part of St. John's Wood, buying music, which perhaps he was going to take with him to some tea-party, to sing to the ladies.

When she had exhaled her annoyance in this angry criticism, Janet recovered some portion of her pleasure, and walked home, but much more slowly, in order that she might have the enjoyment of every moment of her freedom, and not go in too soon. We are all much displeased when maids and page-boys, and other light-hearted but slow-footed messengers, do this, and keep our letters or our novels from us, forgetting that these functionaries too might, like Janet, have need to feel themselves now and then, and be able to think, as they walk along Acacia Road, that they are John or Mary, and not mere officials executing our will.

That night began just as other evenings had begun after dinner. The family group was very comfortable, warm and safe from all contention of the elements which had settled into a downpour outside, from all inharmonious noises or interruptions within. Mrs. Harwood and Gussy at opposite sides of the fire, Miss Summerhayes seated at a little distance with the book upon the table, the very book which she had got from the library, and which she had volunteered to read aloud while the others worked. Very comfortable, but rather dull, but for the book, which was something, and lent an interest to the monotonous night.

When lo! all at once, in the midst of this monotony and unbroken calm, the stillness was suddenly broken by the tingle of the house bell. Somebody at the door! Late in the evening, nearly nine, an hour at which no stranger step or sound ever disturbed the house. Janet stopped reading involuntarily, and grew pale in her surprise, looking round upon her companions with a sort of appeal.

"Bless us," cried Mrs. Harwood, "who can this be so late at night?"

"It is, perhaps, a telegram," said Gussy. And then she glanced at the clock, and added, "It is not so very late. We have had people come later than this."

Gussy had a little light, not usually there, kindled in her eyes. She let her work drop upon her knees and listened. The sound of the unwilling parlor-maid sallying out in the wet to unlock the door, the sound of a voice and another step, even of a dripping umbrella placed in a stand, and an overcoat being taken off, were listened to by the ladies with much unanimity of interest. Even Janet was glad that something was coming to break the calm routine. When this last stage of suspense was reached, Gussy said,

"It will be Charley Meredith and his songs," and laughed a little, as it were, under her breath.

And then the door opened, and there walked in, with the assured step of one who knew himself welcome, the man of the music and the stationer's shop, the man who had looked round upon Janet as she got her novel, saying, "Oh!" with his eyes.

CHAPTER IX.

JANET drew instinctively a little out of the way of the new-comer. It was not, we fear, with any intention of effacing herself, but to satisfy the spectator's privilege of watching all that happened and understanding every new situation. The change that had come over Gussy's countenance took her by surprise. She had not thought it possible that such an illumination and transformation could take place in so calm a face, and it betrayed Miss Harwood instantly to Janet's quick perceptions. She was a little person whose reflections were very rapid—who saw in a moment a whole succession of possibilities. Her mind flashed from one to another in sudden surprise, conviction, imagination, asking herself was the man worth it? almost in the same flash of intelligence with which she perceived that to Gussy he was the first of men.

Janet saw various other matters in the moment of pushing back her chair. She saw that the stranger, now in the act of approaching Gussy, whose interest in him was so visible, recognized herself, and was surprised, with the slightest, scarcely visible, elevation of his eyebrows, as if asking an explanation. She saw also that Mrs. Harwood made a slight movement of pleasure in the chair which she never quitted, as if in her mind making the same little start of welcome which her daughter actually did. Janet would not perhaps have gone farther than this if her attention had not been called by another movement of a different kind. Julia, who had been lying as usual on the rug with her book between her mother's chair and the fire—a position which she could not be persuaded or forced to resign—suddenly disappeared with a sort of scrambling sound and movement, which came in not unlike a hiss into the very different sentiment with which the welcome of the others was given. Did she actually make some such sound between her closed teeth? At all events, Janet's rapid judgment flew to the conclusion that Julia detested while the others cherished the visitor. Her own keen eyes made an inventory of him and all his visible qualities in a moment. Was he worth it? He was well-looking, nay, very good-looking, she concluded in that instantaneous survey: but a little of the order of the barber's block—good features, very white where whiteness was becoming, very bright in color where color was necessary: good eyes, dark, and with considerable power of expression, which he entirely understood and could manage; the whiskers of respectability carefully kept under, disturbed by no extravagance of moustache or beard; dark hair that curled in a very attractive way in close vigorous rings; not tall. This, in Janet's opinion, was the worst thing about him; for a girl's hero has always six feet of stature at the least. And he was perfectly well dressed in well-fitting evening clothes, which, though so generally objected to in matter of form, are yet, with their large foreground of dazzling linen and background of blackness, almost always becoming to men. All these things Janet remarked in a glance; but as for her first question, was he worth it? she had not yet come to any decision at all.

Gussy made no movement to present the stranger to the governess. She gave him a chair so near herself that Janet was obliged to draw back a little more to get herself out of the way. It was the first time that she had found herself *de trop* in the little circle. She was not, however, at all wounded by this, being very curious and much excited by the little drama which thus seemed to come to light under her eyes. It must have been existing for some time, Janet thought. They must have reached at least the end of the second, if not the third, act, and with quite a flush of interest she settled herself to watch its progress. Was she *de trop?* Would they rather she went away? Was Julia's disappearance a signal for her—a hint that she was not wanted. These ideas passed through Janet's head, but without disturbing her. She wanted above all things to follow this story out.

"I have only just got back to town," said Mr. Meredith. "I have had a longer holiday than usual this year."

"So we suppose, or I made sure we should have seen you," said Gussy, with undisguised pleasure in her face.

"That seems like making a claim of right upon Charley's time," said Mrs. Harwood; "we must not do that, for it is the last thing that young men like."

"I think Gussy understands me best," he said, "so far as that goes. Of course I should have come in any case the first evening I had."

Janet said to herself that they must at least have begun the third act, as they called each other by their Christian names.

"You say in any case?" said Gussy, with an inquiring look.

"Yes; fancy what was the first thing I heard to-day. I went into Mimpriss's on my way to the Temple to get some pencils, and there was some one inquiring for books for Mrs. Harwood: so I knew that you also had reached home."

"Oh, yes, we have been at home a long time!" said Gussy. "Mamma never likes to be long away: and Ju—you know Ju—was going down hill like an express train, getting more and more unmanageable and refractory every day."

"But I am happy to tell you, Charley, that Miss Summerhayes seems likely to work marvels."

This was the only thing that approached an introduction, and Janet did not know whether to take any notice. Mr. Meredith, however, jumped to his feet, and made her a bow.

"It was Miss Summerhayes I saw changing the books," he said.

Gussy made no remark. She was not in the least disturbed by this greeting. Janet had not even the satisfaction of thinking that Miss Harwood did not wish her to seek the visitor's acquaintance. She ignored her altogether, as if she was of absolutely no importance—which was much harder to bear, and a great surprise to the governess, who had hitherto been treated with so much regard.

"Mamma cannot do without her books," she said, calmly. "As for me, I have not heard a note of music since you have been away."

"We must take order about that," he said. "I brought something with me to-night, a new thing by—what's his name—one of the men you like. The soprano part is very nice. We can try it over to-night."

"And how did you leave your Aunt Owen, Charley, and what are they doing down in that part of the country? Dear me, what changes I should find, to be sure, if I were to go down there again. All the Plinlimmons swept away, and my friends at the Grange, and Agatha Lloyd, and——"

"Don't think of it, mamma," said Gussy, humming over the air with the music in her hand, and interrupting herself to run in a few words between the bars. "Think of your own people, and how well we all are—tum— tum—ti-tum—tum—and don't let us distress ourselves about strangers, tu-tu—tu-tu—tum-tum. Yes, I think I shall like this."

"Your friends at the Grange have not been swept away, Mrs. Harwood. They are in perfectly good case, and made the most tender inquiries for you. I came home full of Welsh news for you; but it blows away after a day in chambers. Ask me as many questions as you please, and it will all come back."

"Oh, never mind!" said Gussy, with an impatience quite unusual to her. "Tell us rather what you have been doing yourself. Have you had any sport? Have you met any nice people while you have been away? Have you been singing a great deal, or met anybody whose voice goes with yours?"

"Not one like you," he said, with a glance that made Gussy's color rise. He added, after a moment, "There were some ladies at the Lloyds' who were very good musicians. We had a little practice now and then.

"Young ladies?" asked Gussy.

"Well—yes, some of them were young. One was a capital accompanist, and her sister's voice was something quite remarkable. We managed that duet, don't you know, that we never could master, of Brahm's."

"Oh!" said Gussy. The color went slowly out of her face, leaving her very pale and gray. "You must have enjoyed yourself very much," she said, in a subdued tone.

"Not so much as I do—here," he said, lowering his voice and bending towards her: and Janet, ever watching, saw Gussy's face take fire again and glow with a tender flush. Was the man worth it? He seemed to play upon her like an instrument, blowing her upwards one moment, the next bringing her down to the ground.

All this time not the least notice had been taken of the governess, who went on with her sewing with a little thrill of observation and attention in her which ran to her very finger points. Even these finger points seemed to be roused into seeing and hearing, reading meanings, and judging looks. Janet felt as if she were sitting apart at the rehearsal of a play. In this end of the room where the personages of the drama were sitting everything was light and brightness; but the other was like an unoccupied auditorium, the lights low, and the space vacant, though quite in the depths of the scene there was an open piano with a gleam of white keys showing out of the dimness. Had Gussy left the piano open on purpose? She had been in the habit of scolding Julia for that injurious habit, but Janet now remembered that it had been left open for several nights. And where was Julia? and was it perhaps, understood that she should vanish with her pupil? All these things perplexed and disturbed Janet, who did not know what was meant.

Presently the scene changed, the dim background lighted up, and there were two people between her and the gleaming white keyboard of the piano. The episode grew more exciting than ever, for the two—lovers? surely they must be lovers—were going to sing together. Janet's attention, however, was distracted for a moment or two by the same little stifled sound which she had heard before, and looking up she saw Julia glide from behind the curtains and come back to her place on the rug.

"Julia," cried Mrs. Harwood, "you will end by making me frightened. What do you mean by that elfish way of stealing out and in? Can't you have a little respect for your sister? It is not so often that she sings."

Julia fixed upon her mother her usual dogged look, lifting her head from her book, then, to Janet's supreme surprise, vouchsafed an answer.

"She's so silly," the girl said, with a glance of scorn.

"Do you hear, Miss Summerhayes?" said the old lady. "She is incorrigible. I thought we had come to an end of all that, Ju?"

Julia gave her mother another look, then returned to her book, with again a faint hiss from between her closed teeth.

"She is so much interested in her book," Janet made haste to say. "When one gets into the heart of a story at her age one thinks of nothing else."

"Do you think, Miss Summerhayes, that Ju ought to read so many novels?"

"I thought," said Janet, faltering, "that it was with your permission."

"Oh," cried Mrs. Harwood, "I thought you might have seen by this time how little they care for anything I say."

She looked irritable, cross, disturbed, as Janet thought she had never seen her before, and moved uneasily in her chair. But she had shown no such annoyance when the visitor came in. She had received him with a cheerful welcome, and he had seemed in no doubt on that subject. Indeed, the young man had come in and taken his place among them with the familiarity and complacency of a favored visitor who expected to confer as well as to receive pleasure. That line in Mrs. Harwood's brow had not appeared till Julia, with her dogged look, had stared into her mother's face.

"I wish," cried the old lady, "oh, I wish that Adolphus would come home!" and she wrung her white, plump hands with almost a tragic gesture, which was so strangely unlike her comfortable person, and all that Janet had hitherto known of her, that the little governess had hard ado not to laugh.

"Do you expect Mr. Harwood soon?" she asked.

"They are all very self-willed, Miss Summerhayes. You must have seen that, already. Gussy of course will not be guided by me. She thinks that things are meant which probably are not meant at all—except to pass the time. And Julia, though she is not more than a child, sets herself up in judgment as if she were—do you think I can do anything to stop it?—even if it were desirable to stop it. And why should I, for that matter, even if I could? It would be suitable enough. How am I to tell, Miss Summerhayes, with no one to advise me, and such self-willed children to deal with? Oh, I wish—I wish that Adolphus were here!"

Janet did not know what to make of this sudden burst of confidence. She was afraid to seem to wish to pry into her employer's concerns, yet, with the impulse of youth, which is at once a kind meaning and a movement of vanity, wanted to say something which should be consolatory—to put forth her own little hand as a guide in the circumstances of which she was so entirely ignorant.

"I am sure, dear Mrs. Harwood, no one would do anything which they knew you really disliked—you are so good. Perhaps they don't know that you really dislike—anything that may be going on."

To Janet's surprise, Mrs. Harwood received this enigmatical utterance as if it had thrown real light upon the situation. She put her handkerchief to her eyes.

"I dare say you are right, my dear. I always said you were full of understanding for so young a thing. Perhaps that's what it is, after all. I don't speak out. It would be much more sensible if I were to speak out."

There was a momentary silence, and the sound of the singing came in, the two voices "going" together, rising into a burst of melody in the higher notes which made Janet pause and hold her breath. Mr. Meredith had a beautiful tenor voice, and Gussy's, though not so good, aided the effect with a somewhat tremulous second, twining out and in of the clear and liquid masculine notes. Janet let her work drop and her attempt at consolation together, and sat rapt gazing at the pair. She was too young, too energetic, too ambitious for pure sympathy. She gazed with impatient longing to be in the midst of it.

"Oh! what a weak accompaniment!" she said to herself. "Why don't they ask me to play it for them? She might sing to her heart's content; but *why* doesn't she ask me to play?"

Jane forgot Mrs. Harwood, whom she had been in the act of advising and consoling, and Julia, who was her special care. She could scarcely restrain herself.

"It is too much for Miss Harwood to sing and play both," she said, with a sudden impulse, dropping her work upon the floor, half rising as if to rush to the rescue. Her own movement, however, brought her to herself; for what right had she, a stranger and a hireling, to interfere?

"Miss Summerhayes!" said Mrs. Harwood.

As this was all that was said, Janet detached her eyes from the scene at the piano, and looked at the old lady in the chair. Mrs. Harwood was talking energetically with her eyes and gestures, though she said nothing. She indicated Julia with a glance, then looked towards the door. She put her plump hands together with a little pantomimic prayer. Janet saw and understood, and sighed. She wanted to have a hand in the music; she wanted to watch the story which was going on, which as yet she did not understand. But no. Her duty lay in another direction. It was the first time that she had felt her chains.

"Julia, come, come; it is our time," she said briskly.

Miss Harwood at the piano, who had her back turned, took no notice of the little commotion of the withdrawal; but Mr. Meredith turned round, still singing, and gave Janet a look out of those eyes which she had declared to herself were too black, too bright, too ostentatiously fringed with eyelashes—a look which meant respectful regret, a tinge of remonstrance, a veiled entreaty to stay, a sort of *au revoir* unspoken but eloquent. He could not make more than a slight inclination of his head, as he was singing, but the effect was that of the most deferential bow. Janet was taken altogether by surprise. Had he appreciated her position all in a moment, read her abilities in her eyes, longed to have her at the piano as she longed to be there? or was it a mere impulse of subjugation, the instinct of the conqueror who desired another victim? She was so startled that her heart jumped up suddenly like a bird as she left the room, and made one or two big beats in her ears. And then she laughed to herself apparently without any meaning at all.

CHAPTER X.

"Miss Summerhayes! why did you laugh as we came upstairs?"

"Oh!" said Janet, quite restored from that momentary impression. "I don't know. Because it is curious to come into the middle of a story; it is like beginning a book, as you do sometimes, at the third volume. One wonders what has happened before, as well as what is going to happen now."

"You think that's a story!" cried Julia, with scorn; "because Gussy's a fool, and that man—I can't endure that man."

"You make that too easy for anyone to see. I think you made a sound like what they do in the theatre."

"I hissed him," said Julia, her lowering eyebrows closing down over her eyes. "I always do. He can't bear to be hissed. He is just like an actor: it makes him mad, and that is why I do it, and I always shall. I don't care what anyone says."

"That is a pity," said Janet; "for it will not harm him, but you. You forget that people care very little for the opinion of a girl at your age, especially when it is rudely expressed."

"They don't care much for your opinion," said Julia, furiously.

"No; I did not expect it; and I have no opinion, except that you must learn to be a gentlewoman—if that can be learnt—or else I must go away."

Julia received this, as she usually did Janet's remonstrances, with a look of rage, a flush of shame, and then a sudden self-subdual.

"You want to go away," she said. "You are the only nice one that has ever been here; and you want to go and leave me. I know you do. You'll go before Dolff comes home, and then he'll never know you, and will think—will just think I am a stupid and don't know anything, as they all do!"

"Well, my dear child," said Janet, who understood this broken speech perfectly well, and knew that she was being represented to "Dolff" in the brightest colors, a thing by no means indifferent to her, "they are not very far wrong if they think so; for a girl who hisses—even in the theatre——"

"I did once," cried Julia, "in the theatre! They had a hideous ballet in the pantomime like what one reads of in books—a woman making a show of herself—oh!" The girl's cheeks blazed crimson at the thought. "And I hissed—like this." Here Julia uttered a sound, in comparison with which a whole serpent-house in highest exasperation would have retired defeated, with the whole force of her youthful energy and breath. "Gussy pinched me black and blue to stop me, and I wouldn't. They never would take me to the theatre again."

"I don't wonder," said Janet "So now you hiss the people who come to call."

"Only Charley Meredith," said Julia. "And," she added, subduing her tones, "if he came in the morning I should not mind: but he comes at night without being invited, with his music, as if mamma was obliged to have him whether she liked or not. And he gives himself such airs, as if he knew that Gussy—you think I don't care for Gussy, Miss Summerhayes—but I do. I could kill her when she looks silly like that! A woman! to let a man see that she——oh! I could kill her when she looks at him like that!"

"That is a pleasant way of showing how much you care for her," said Janet. "It is quite natural that at fourteen you should think you know best; but if I hear you hiss again,"—the governess kissed the tips of her fingers—"good-bye, my dear; that's all that there will be to say."

"You say that to beat me down," cried Julia. "You don't really care, not a bit, whether I behave myself or not. I am not sure that you are any better than Charley Meredith. I don't know that there is not just a pair of you. Well, then, do it if you like, there! take him away from Gussy, break everybody's heart, make Dolff think me a stupid for all I've said. I can see in your eyes that's what you'd like to do."

"You have made me out a very pretty programme," said Janet, laughing. "I think I shall begin by looking over your exercises, and giving you double black marks for everything. We need not have come upstairs so early but for that pretty habit of yours; and, for my part, I would rather listen to the music than to a little girl storming. Oh, yes, my dear, I know you are taller than I am, but that makes no difference. Be quiet; we can hear it mounting up now that I've opened the window a little. Ah! bravo! that was well done."

"Do you really care for that squalling?" Julia demanded, with a mixture of wonder and scorn.

Janet was standing by the window which she had opened. The school-room was over the drawing-room, though on the second floor, and in the quiet of the night Mr. Meredith's fine voice came out like the blast of a silver trumpet. The night was mild and very still, and perhaps Janet's youthful bosom was still a little fluttered by that sudden surprise which had made her heart beat. She leaned a little out, listening, with a natural self-pity that she was not there, and realization of the different fate of Gussy, to whom music and love and all the softnesses of life were open, while she was sent away out of sight with a naughty child. Janet had far too much strength to give in or permit anyone to see that she suffered from this, nor, indeed, did she suffer more than the vague and momentary sensation of being at a disadvantage. But she leaned out to listen with a little wistfulness, impatient of the childish vehemence, and as yet but little awakened to the deeper nature of her unmanageable pupil. This pensive mood, however, was soon to be interrupted. In the very midst of the liquid notes ascending from below, there came suddenly, as if it rent the air, a wild and wailing cry—the cry as of a spirit in pain. It seemed to Janet to rise almost from her side, close by. She started back from the window and turned round with a scared and terrified exclamation,

"What is that? What is that?"

For a moment it occurred to her that some terrible accident or hurt must have happened to the girl by her side.

"I—don't know," said Julia, stammering as if she could not get out the words. But she was not terrified as Janet was. The governess did not notice this at first in her own panic. She ran to the door of Julia's room, from which direction the sound seemed to come, and flung it open crying, "Who is there? Who is there?" then shut it again in terror of what she might see.

"Oh, run and fetch some one! oh, go and alarm the house, Julia! there must be something dreadful in there."

"There's nothing," said Julia. "What are you making such a fuss about? It's—a boy outside—they make such hideous noises—it's——"

She stopped, for the same sound was repeated, this time lower and further off, as it seemed—a cry of pain dropping into a low prolonged wail. Janet rushed to the school-room door and out upon the staircase, calling for help, for some one to come. She was wild with alarm. There was no doubt in her mind that some wretched creature, a madman, probably, had got into the rooms.

But all was quiet in the house below, the doors all shut, everybody occupied with their own business, singing going on in the drawing-room, talk in the servants' apartments downstairs—nothing it would seem had been disturbed but Janet alone.

"It's nothing," repeated Julia. "Oh, Miss Summerhayes, come back, please, and don't make a fuss. Mamma is so angry if there's any fuss made. If I go into my room and look all round, and convince you there's nobody, will that do? There's nobody, I know. It's either a boy passing outside, or it's an owl or something that lives under the ivy in the wing. Mamma knows. If you ask her to-morrow she'll tell you; but, oh, for goodness' sake, Miss Summerhayes, don't make a fuss to-night."

"Your mother knows? Do you mean that—it has been heard before?"

"You look as if you thought it was a ghost," said Julia, who, however, was very pale. "We have no ghosts in our house."

"It was like the cry of a mad creature—it was———Julia, if it comes again I can't bear it. It must be some madman who has got in."

"If it's a madman he can't get near us," cried Julia, "for he's in the wing."

Janet came back into the school-room, still trembling with her fright. She dropped into a chair, unable to support herself.

"You know—you know what it is," she said, faintly.

"I know—it's something in the wing. It does no harm. Sometimes it will cry like that—oh, once in a year, perhaps. It can't do any harm. Oh, Miss Summerhayes, do be reasonable when I tell you. What does it matter? I don't know what you mean, to be so taken up with their squalling and shouting, and in such a state when you hear a cry. I don't care either for one or the other," Julia said.

It cannot be said that Janet showed much interest in the "squalling and shouting" of which her pupil was so contemptuous after this. The two changed their *rôles* completely for the rest of the evening, during which Julia, though not without a titter for her companion's weakness, soothed and patronized Miss Summerhayes, and addressed to her many philosophical admonitions, which naturally were much more self-confident even than the exhortations of Janet, in themselves by no means deficient in the certainty of youth.

"What can it matter to us," said Julia, "what a noise is?—unless you happen to like noises which people make, squalling at the top of their voices and call music. A noise can't hurt you; it can't do you any harm. You hear it, and that's all—especially when it's only like a voice. I am not fond of thunder, myself, for a thunderbolt might fall on the house or crush you; but a cry—what does it matter? People are always crying out, or making some nasty noise. You should pay no attention to it. I never pay any attention; it is not worth while. Why, you might spend your life thinking of such things, if you were to be disturbed by every sound you hear."

This discourse did not satisfy Janet or even calm her mind, but she reflected after a while that it was not the part of a governess to put visionary terrors into the mind of her pupil, and so far recovered herself with an effort as to satisfy Julia that it was safe to go to bed and leave Miss Summerhayes. Poor little Janet, when left alone, felt for the first time how terrible it was to be so young, so impressionable, and among strangers. She dared not run downstairs, as a girl at home would, to shake off her terrors by confiding them to some one who could authoritatively calm and reassure her. Mrs. Harwood had been very kind to her governess, but to go down again after she had been dismissed, to meet Gussy's astonished look turning round from the piano, and the mother's suspicious glance which would ask what she wanted, why she came?—was impossible to Janet. She felt to-night, for the first time, what it was to be a governess, although to-night, for almost the first time, she had realized what she had expected when she came out into the world, how amusing it was to watch a story going on. How soon had all interest in the story disappeared from her mind in the face of this terror which froze her very blood! What was it?—was it a spirit or a living creature in pain? Where was it?—in this tranquil house, as Julia seemed to allow? And worst and most dreadful question of all—would it come again? This last thought was the one that kept all her faculties awake. Might it at any moment burst once more out of the quiet? Janet thought that if she had to undergo that moment of horror again she must go mad or die. She was afraid to go to bed—afraid to close her eyes—lest she should be awakened by that cry. The singing went on late downstairs, and Janet listened anxiously to the departing of the visitor, the bolting of the door behind him, the little bustle as Mrs. Harwood was wheeled to her room on the ground floor, and Gussy came upstairs. But she did not come as far as the school-room, which she sometimes did to see if all was well. It was too late to disturb any one—to wake up the sleepers. Janet heard Miss Harwood coming upstairs singing softly over to herself her part in one of the duets. Gussy was happy; no alarm or sense of desolation was in her.

"If I were happy like that I would come upstairs to see how the poor little governess, all alone, was getting on," Janet said to herself, opening her eyes in the dark. But, indeed, she would have done nothing of the kind. She would have been perhaps more indifferent than Gussy was to the governess in causeless trouble, feeling "out of it"—or else in a visionary panic thinking that she had heard a ghost.

The night wore away gradually, and nothing happened. When it was between three and four, Janet, worn out, fell fast asleep. She slept till the breakfast-bell rang, and had to hurry her dressing and hasten downstairs with an apology, wondering at herself and her own foolish terror in the red light of the wintry morning. Gussy was very ready, it was evident, to be questioned about last night. She began her self by expressing her distress that Janet had been hastened away for "*that* child," and narrated to her with subdued triumph how many "things" Mr. Meredith and she had gone through, and what good practice it was.

"The Harwoods generally are so unmusical," Gussy said; "I never did get any encouragement at home. But fortunately mamma likes Charley, and he may do what he pleases. I do enjoy a musical evening so. Hasn't he a delicious voice?"

"It is a charming voice," said Janet.

"And he is so well trained. To sing with him it is like getting a lesson. He wanted to know whether you were musical, but I said I feared——"

"I used to be thought pretty good for accompaniments," said Janet.

"Oh, really!" but Gussy did not receive this statement with much delight. "Perhaps you'll help me to practise my part," she said, and returned to sound the praises of Charley.

Janet would not introduce the subject of her own terrors, and if she had been ever so intent upon doing so, there was no opportunity, for Charley and his songs and his perfections left no room for any other discourse. And when Mrs. Harwood appeared matters were not much better. The old lady remarked that Janet was pale, and feared that she had not been able to sleep for the singing.

"The fact is that Mr. Meredith has not been in London for a long time, and I could not cut them short, could I, the first night?"

To describe the impatience with which Janet heard all this would not be easy. She said to herself, what was Mr. Meredith to her? What were his songs, his attentions, the grief of his absence, the joy of his return? She listened with a great eagerness to interrupt, to break through this eternal burden of the self-occupied to whom their own little affairs were everything, with her own questions. But when Mrs. Harwood's voice stopped Janet did not find hers. What could she say?

"I heard a dreadful cry last night. What was it? You know what it was!" It seemed to her when she turned this question in her mind that it was a thing impossible to say. "I heard—last night," she began.

"Ah, the singing!" cried both ladies together. "I hope it did not keep you from your sleep, my dear," said Mrs. Harwood. And, "I'm sure you could not hear me, and Charley's voice is always a pleasure," cried Gussy.

Janet's mouth was closed, and she could say no more.

CHAPTER XI.

JANET'S life seemed to herself to change from this day, though no one else seemed aware of any difference, and all its outward expressions went on as before. For a few nights she was afraid to sit alone upstairs, and hurried to bed in the hope of getting to sleep, and thus avoiding any repetition of the cry which had so rung through and through her on the night of Mr. Meredith's first appearance; but, as the days and nights passed in perfect tranquillity, this scare passed away from her mind, and she began to be able to explain to herself that it must have been some boy in the road outside, belated and anxious to make a sensation in that still neighborhood, or perhaps that fancy had exaggerated the fantastic wailings of a love-sick cat into something portentous and terrible. Both these things were possible, but that anything mysterious could exist in this comfortable, modern, respectable house, where everything went as on velvet by carefully kept rule and order, was an idea too ridiculous to be entertained. At night, it is true, Janet had various fallings back from this confidence, and reminded herself with renewed panic that Julia had heard and had not been astonished as she was, but evidently was aware of some explanation which she did not give. These grew fainter and fainter, however, as one week passed after another, and nothing occurred.

There was one thing, however, which Janet only remarked after this period, though she was afterwards assured that it was no secret, but might have been seen from the first day, and that was the appearance of a man-servant in the house where none but women ever waited upon the family. She met him one day going across the hall, a respectable, serious man of middle age, just such a butler as Mrs. Harwood ought to have had. But the ladies had no butler; they had a highly-respectable parlor-maid, just such as, failing the butler, a family in St. John's Wood, entirely *comme il faut*, must have had— tall, staid, good-looking, but not too good-looking, well-dressed, and thirty-five. The man, who had all the air of perfect familiarity with the house, and who was in indoor dress, with noiseless shoes, went across the hall from the servant's quarters towards the side upon which was the wing, an apparently unoccupied part of the dwelling.

After that first meeting, which startled her, Janet saw this man again and again. There was no explanation of him, he was never seen but in these chance encounters, yet he was no secret, nor was his presence in any way concealed. What, after all, had a stranger to do with it? It was nothing to Janet. But her strong sense of spectatorship, and the curiosity of imagination which made her keen to find indications of a story anywhere or everywhere, caused a half-conscious groping on the part of the governess among unexplained incidents. It was some time, however, before she began to associate the mysterious man-servant with the alarming outcry which had almost, she thought, deprived her of her wits, ringing as it did into the silence of the night. After a few weeks had passed, she asked herself if, indeed, she ever had heard it at all—whether it was not a delusion of her senses, the reverberation of some well-known and vulgar sound. Needless to say that Janet had read "Northanger Abbey," and had been taught to smile at the investigations of our dear little Catherine, and their amusing issue: though, to tell the truth, her sympathy in Catherine Morland's thirst for romantic adventure had been more strong than her amusement in the result, which disappointed her a little too.

However, not even a romantic imagination disposed towards discoveries can survive the uneventful progress of weeks in which nothing happens. And Janet meantime had the other story going on before her eyes which she could study at her ease. Mr. Charles Meredith and his visits became now the chief interest of life in the house in St. John's Wood. He dined once or twice, but only in company with another visitor; and on those occasions Janet did not form one of the party. Gussy explained that it would "put out the table."

"If I were to invite gentlemen for you and Ju, it would make quite a party, and mamma does not like parties when Dolff is away. And then Ju is too young to dine when there is company," said Miss Harwood.

"Oh, you must not think of me!" Janet would reply; but when she heard the gentlemen arrive, and the increased sound of voices as the servants went out and in of the dining-room, and the little cheerful commotion, it is undeniable that Janet remembered Mrs. Bland's little sermons about the fate of a governess.

She did not like it. She had never been left out in her life before. Janet was not shy; she had always been used to take a somewhat privileged place in the little society she was acquainted with. She could talk; she was not afraid of anybody who might drift into the little world of Clover; and she loved variety, which is a thing not permitted to governesses. On these occasions supper was brought up to the school-room for Miss Summerhayes and her pupil. It was brought late, and they had to wait and yawn on opposite sides of the table for the cold and tardy meal. On such occasions it was difficult to make herself amusing to Julia, or to find Julia amusing. It was dull. It produced a certain mortification in Janet's mind to find that she cared. She said to herself, with a little bitterness of which she was ashamed, that she had no doubt it was a very dull party, and that the two strangers were not in the least interesting. She recalled to herself her previous conviction, that to be left alone to do what she pleased, to read a novel or write a letter, would be a pleasant relief. No, it was not so; she wanted to be in the dining-room with the rest, hearing what was said, even if she had to remember her own position and take little part. She wanted to see how the drama was going on, and how the hero looked when there was some one to compare him with. That scene would glide in her imagination in front of her novel, with the attraction of a pleasure out of reach. And Julia was a dull companion on these occasions. She yawned and wondered when they would bring the supper.

"It's disgusting to be kept so long waiting, and all the things like stones when they do come," Julia would say; "I shall complain to mamma. If all the others are so busy, Vicars might bring it up, once in a way."

"Who is Vicars?" said Janet.

"Oh, he is the man; he never goes into the dining-room except when Dolff is here—but he might bring up our supper if all the rest are so busy. As if there was any reason to make such a fuss! Two men to dinner! You would think there were twenty, all fine ladies and gentlemen, to see how Gussy goes on."

"They are probably great friends, and more important than twenty ladies and gentlemen," said Janet, with her most correct governess air.

"Oh, you know well enough! It is Charley Meredith, and they will caterwaul afterwards till it makes me quite ill to hear them. And Gussy will look so silly. Oh, why does a woman look so silly when there is nonsense like that going on?"

"It is generally the man who is supposed to look silly," said Janet. Involuntarily she thought of poor Dr. Harding and his proposal; and the hard-hearted young woman laughed in spite of herself.

"What are you laughing at? You are remembering something. Tell me, tell me, Miss Summerhayes! I suppose," said Julia, with deep discrimination, "that the man looks silly when it is he who wants it most. Now, here it is Gussy who wants it most."

"Julia, you have no right to discuss your sister."

"Oh, but you can't stop me doing it!" said Julia, with composure; "you can stop me when—when I'm silly myself. I was a great fool, I know. I thought once I could drive you away—no, I didn't want to drive you away. I wanted to get the upper hand; but you've got the upper hand of me, and I don't mind now. However, that's quite different. This is a free country, and I can say what I please of Gussy. I say that it's she——"

"As it is a free country, you can't compel me to listen," said Janet; "but there is one thing in which it is not a free country, and that is that you are not permitted to be ill-bred. It is not allowed to be vulgar."

"Oh!" cried Julia, coloring to her eyes, but affecting to laugh, "as if there were not hundreds and thousands?"

Janet shrugged her little shoulders in a manner which her pupil, rebellious, but admiring, thought irresistible.

"Out in the streets, perhaps: so are there applewomen, and people who sell matches. But in good time here comes the tray, and something for you to do."

Janet, however, was not far from being of Julia's opinion. Miss Harwood, who had been so calm, who had explained that the quiet family life so unbroken, the long evenings of needlework and talk, might appear dull to Janet, but were never dull to her mother and herself, now went through these evenings as in a dream. Meredith came twice, sometimes three times, in a week, after dinner, as he had done on his first appearance. He had privileges which were extended to no one else, and it was never known on which evening he would appear. He even took pains, Janet thought, to have no rule, to appear suddenly when he was not looked for. But to this spectator, whose attention was fixed upon Gussy, as on the heroine of the drama, it was very easily apparent that there was no evening on which he was not expected. She worked, she talked, she made her little disquisitions as usual, but there was a certain fixed attitude of her head, a little almost imperceptible pause now and then in the movements of her hands, which showed that she was listening for the summons at the door, the step outside. In the quietness of the semi-rural suburban road the step of the rare passenger was sometimes heard even outside the garden wall. Sometimes Mrs. Harwood would say,

"I wonder if that is Charley Meredith?" to which Gussy would reply, with beautiful composure,

"Oh, no; he is always engaged on Thursdays!" or, "This is never one of his free nights."

But it was not lost either upon Janet or Julia that her hands were for a moment still, that her downcast eyes were fixed not on her work, and her entire frame rigid with intent listening. The attitude relaxed in a moment when the welcome sound of the bell pealed into the silence, a little faint sigh of ease and happiness came from the bottom of her heart, her head regained its easy poise. Whether the mother also saw these indications of supreme suspense and then of delightful relief, even Janet, whom no circumstance escaped, could not tell. Perhaps, like Gussy, she thought that the visitor was of more account than the other bystanders believed him to be.

A little of the same enchantment hung over Gussy through all the ordinary affairs of life. There was a liquid softness in her eyes that had not been there before; her want of color, which was her great deficiency, seemed to be half compensated be the faintest rose-flush of feeling and sensibility which had come to her, no one could tell how. Was it a sign of better health, greater vigor, than her tranquil temperament usually enjoyed? Her mother said so, rejoicing over the fact that Gussy was "so well."

"She has quite a color," the visitors said. "What a good thing you went to Malvern this year; it has quite set Augusta up."

But the governess and her pupil knew it was not Malvern. The piano in the larger drawing-room was always open now, the lights were always prepared, and Gussy practiced her songs in the morning with a devotion for which Janet, a little moved by the *esprit de corps*, and unwilling that a woman should betray herself, blushed sometimes when the unwearying watchfulness of Julia, to whom no such awakening had come, pointed out the performance going on below.

"She's practising again," Julia would say, in the midst of a lesson.

"She knows how necessary it is," cried quick-witted Janet. "I wish you were half as sensible."

But these little snubs, which were frequent, did not turn aside Julia's keen perceptions or break the unspoken sympathy of spectatorship that was between the two.

Julia, however, made no further demonstration of her dislike to the visitor, and Mrs. Harwood's satisfaction with the "good influence" which Miss Summerhayes had acquired over the rebellious girl went on increasing.

"She looks no more than a girl herself—and so she is, quite young, and never was out before—but her power over that unmanageable child is something wonderful. You know, my dear, what poor Ju was."

"Oh, yes, I know what Ju was!" replied, with fervor, the friend to whom Mrs. Harwood confided her satisfaction. With too much fervor, perhaps; for when the person we blame is our own child, we desire no warmth of conviction, but rather a good-natured deprecation, as who should say, "I never remarked it," or a warmer assertion, "She was always very nice to me." But the mother's confidant was not enlightened in this case. She acknowledged her perfect consciousness of the demerits of Ju.

This checked Mrs. Harwood in full flow.

"She had always a great many defects of manner, but she was right in her heart, poor child, and as soon as you could get to that—— Well! Miss Summerhayes has just that knack. She divined my poor Julia's warm heart, and to see her now you never would believe there had ever been any trouble. She was always more sensible than most girls, but self-willed and too frank. Now, I think you would say there are few girls with better manners, and all that little thing's doing, who really sometimes looks far more a child than Ju herself."

"Dear me," said the visitor; "but I am glad, with my houseful of sons, that I have not got such a fascinating personage. What is so good for the girls might be dangerous for the boys. When do you expect Dolff to come back?"

"Not before Christmas," said Mrs. Harwood; but she did not take the good-natured insinuation; she was too full of her present subject. "He will be so delighted with the improvement in his sister. Dolff is very fond of his sister; he is so domestic. Sometimes it is a little difficult to get him back from Oxford. They enjoy themselves so much in their college with all their friends about them. But, when he does come home, he is so good in taking Julia about and giving her treats. Julia was always his favorite, even when she was most hard to deal with. He will be quite delighted now."

"And Miss Summerhayes will go away, I suppose, for her holidays?" said the far-seeing friend.

Mrs. Harwood looked across the room at Gussy, with a half-alarmed, half-inquiring glance. But Gussy, who was once so quick to perceive all possible imbroglios—Gussy shook her head. She had been thinking with satisfaction that Miss Summerhayes would amuse Dolff, that her own pursuits need not be interrupted for the sake of her brother. She shook her head in answer to her mother's unspoken question.

"Oh, no; she never thought of wanting a holiday so soon," Gussy said.

And so, unmoved by any warning, the Harwood family rushed on their fate.

CHAPTER XII.

THESE musical evenings became now the central events in the life of the house in St. John's Wood. When they did not occur, and the evening passed in its former quiet fashion, with the mother knitting in her chair, and Gussy and Janet on the other side at their work, and Julia on the rug with her book, it was to all of them as if life were arrested, and that day did not count. Everything went on as usual, but nothing was of any consequence. That this should be the case to the heroine of the drama who had the first *rôle* to play, and whose future might perhaps be entirely shaped and colored by what took place on these occasions, was natural enough; but it may be thought strange that an entire household should hang, as it were, on the comings and goings of a presumed lover, whose actions could affect materially only one individual, and to whom one at least of the lookers-on was indifferent and one hostile. But the hostility quickened the interest, and the indifference did not take away from it. The course of a wooing is always an excitement to a household of women. It is "as good as a play." After it is concluded, in that moment of absorption when two engaged people follow each other about, and parade their special privileges and rights, it becomes odious, we are ready to allow; and the only desire in the minds of all reasonable persons is to get the marriage hurried on and the turtle-doves disposed of. But when all is still in the mists of uncertainty, when it cannot be asserted that the entire fabric of the drama may not melt away again, and new complications take place, then it is that the spectators gather round, and every woman keeps a watch under her eyelids upon the progress of the affair. This is especially the case when there is little doubt about the sentiments of one of the parties, and more so still when that one is the woman. The story will then acquire a sometimes painful interest, and the women who watch will feel something of humiliation, something perhaps of resentment, against the girl who has given her affections without sufficient warrant, or the man who is dull enough not to perceive, or wicked enough to disregard, the gift thus bestowed upon him.

Thus the party of women in Mrs. Harwood's drawing-room were diversely moved, but all to the same end. The mother herself felt nothing but anxiety about her child. She was not an enthusiast for Charley Meredith, though she liked him well enough. His blue-black hair, his fine moustache, his bloom of roses or wax, his seductive eyes, and fine voice were not much to the old lady. And she thought him too fond of music and society, not sufficiently anxious to establish his practice and make his name known at the Bar, which was to be his means of living. As she sat and knitted, and listened, and looked on, her mind was full of calculations, often gone over, as to how much the two could scrape together between them to begin housekeeping upon, and whether it would do? Mrs. Harwood naturally knew to a penny what her daughter's fortune would be, although she was not without anxieties lying deep in her soul, even upon that point, which nobody guessed. And as she was well acquainted with his Aunt Owen and his other relatives in Wales, and knew how the family had been "left" at his father's death, she had a tolerably good guess as to what young Meredith was worth in the way of money, and wished it had been more. Still, if, when this period of courtship was over, he would more or less give up music, and devote himself to work, what with Gussy's little fortune, and the remnants of what he had from his father, they might do. It was not a very brilliant conclusion, but yet it might do. When she had come to the end of one such long course of calculations and thoughts, Mrs. Harwood would nod her head and say, "That is very pretty; what is it? Who is it by?"—questions of which in a general way no one took any notice; and then she would begin with her calculations again.

Janet naturally approached the question from an entirely different side. She said to herself that there was not the least doubt about Miss Harwood's sentiments, but she herself was generally treated as if she were a cabbage on these musical evenings. There was no notice taken of her. Though they were so kind in all other ways, and though even Gussy never wavered in her friendliness on other occasions, on these she ignored Janet altogether. Mr. Meredith made her a bow when he shook hands with Mrs. Harwood, and, if he were not absolutely in the middle of a song, he would make a rush to open the door for her when Julia and she retired with their candles. But that was all, and Gussy went on all the time with her accompaniment (which she played so badly!), and took no notice, except to call him back sometimes, the governess thought, with a little sharpness. But that was all.

Was it all? In the depths of her heart Janet felt that it was not. Mr. Meredith's eyes were fine, with almost too much eyelash for a man; they were undeniably like those bold orbs which shine from waxen faces in a barber's shop: but they had a way of opening very wide and expressing a great deal of sentiment, which is not given to those representations of manhood, though at first Janet was wicked enough to think that if the waxen busts could look sentimental they would do it in a similar way. When Janet, however, found that these great eyes were made for herself—when she discovered that Mr. Charles Meredith was asking pardon of her for his scant greeting, and throwing a good deal of respectful admiration into the momentary but intense gaze which was from time to time directed upon her—and when, finally, she found herself almost by this same medium taken into his confidence, made to sympathize with him when, having settled down for a comfortable chat, and secured a place near herself where he could conduct these telegraphic communications easily, he was carried off without compunction by Gussy to the piano—Janet's opinion undeniably changed a little.

There is nothing more flattering than to be made the confidant, to be put behind the scenes, to have the *dessous des cartes* revealed to you; and the piquancy of the revelation, which was never put into words, which was half her own quick perception, which could not have been made to any one whose understanding was less vivid, charmed her imagination, which was still mischievous and curious like that of a child. Sometimes, when Gussy led him away triumphant, he would give a rueful glance, and it was hard ado for Janet to restrain her impulse to laugh. Gussy swept him away in her train as if he had been her own property, as if his visit had no other object than that piano, always open in the background, which afforded such an easy mode of separation from the others, and the suggestive delightful semi-privacy in which the two voices mingled as the two hearts were learning to mingle. That was Gussy's view of the question, but it did not long continue to be Janet's. When poor Gussy made, as now and then she did, a false note, when she went wrong in those somewhat elaborate accompaniments which Janet knew she herself could play so much better, a momentary gleam from Mr. Meredith's eyes, the pointed shrug of his shoulders or elevation of his brows, gave Janet once more that inclination to laugh which it was so difficult to restrain.

It did not at all occur to the girl behind backs that she was an accomplice in a piece of domestic treachery. It was ludicrous to see the unconscious performer, full of complacency in her accomplishment, producing those false notes; it was at once horrifying and laughable to hear the strange discords with which the piano came in. Janet, who could have done it so much better herself, felt a little shiver steal over her at the first jarring thrill, and what so natural as that he, who was evidently a good musician, should discover it, too, and seek her sympathy. As these communications grew more frequent, it is true that Janet did feel a little shame now and then steal over her. Poor Miss Harwood! She would not like it, the governess felt sure, if she surprised one of these glances; and thus, in the complacence of knowing better, in the secret superiority of divining the sentiments of Gussy's lover even better than Gussy did, the girl felt it almost impossible not to burst into a little laugh again.

Were these two floating on—as Gussy thought in her confident tenderness and glamour of love, as Mrs. Harwood thought in her anxious calculations and adding up of this and that to see whether it would do, as Julia, in her eager dislike and scorn and childish inexperience, was certain of—towards a happy *dénouement* and a life of harmony together? This was what Janet did not know. She sat and wondered, going on with her needlework. Janet, who was not at all without experience, and who had seen that people in most things consider their own advantage and pleasure first, as the protectress of her own childhood had done in adopting her, did not jump to the conclusion that Meredith had not the intentions which the others attributed to him. But she had a doubt which none of the others had. She sat and wondered, working on, anxious to be a little nearer, and hear what they were saying, longing to be asked to take that accompaniment, to be in the middle of what was going on. The uncertainty lent the scene, which in any case would have been as good as a play, a still more vivid interest. Her heart beat with the sensation of knowing so much more than the others, with wondering from day to day what would be the next event, and how it would end. Strangely enough, she did not enter at all into Gussy's feelings, or conceive any sympathy for her. Like Julia, like the very young in general, Janet was angry with Miss Harwood for being "silly," for letting the visitor see his advantage. She could not forgive the woman who made the advances, who was deceived and fancied herself beloved, and flung herself at the head, or at the feet, of a tardy lover. She was more impatient with Gussy for the glamour in her eyes, than with Meredith for having none, for shrugging his shoulders at the false notes.

It came about, however, one evening, in the most natural manner in the world, that Janet, trembling with impatience behind backs, and longing to be in the midst of it, achieved at last the active share she desired in what was going on. She never could tell whether it was accident or whether Meredith had chosen on purpose a duet of which the accompaniment was extremely difficult, such as Miss Harwood was quite incapable of.

After a few trials and failures, the practising came to a sudden end, and a little controversy evidently went on over the piano. He proposed something which she did not consent to willingly. By-and-bye Gussy's voice, a little raised in vexation, reached the other end of the room.

"I have no reason to suppose she can play at all," she said.

Then there was a murmur from Meredith and the name of Julia.

"Oh, yes! enough to teach Ju; but Ju has no ear and no taste, and never will do anything."

Again the lover made a representation, inaudible, in Gussy's ear.

"Well, if you like we can ask her; but it's always introducing a third, and spoiling——"

Janet's ears were so quickened by this time that she heard, or thought she heard, him say, stooping close to Gussy's ear,

"Who can feel that like me? But she's only—seems to know her place."

Heavens! how the heart jumped up in Janet's breast! She was sure she heard him say, "seems to know her place." Her place! and he who had made her his confidant, made her the judge, making fun of Gussy to her, as he now set her down so contemptuously to Gussy! The blood boiled in Janet's veins, a flood of thoughts and resolutions rushed through her mind. She would not play for them! They might break down, and Miss Harwood might jar him to death with her discords, for anything Janet cared. Her place! behind their backs, without notice, without a word! Oh, yes, she would keep it, she would understand what it was, she would do nothing for them! And then the pendulum swung the other way. Yes, she would play for them. She would show Gussy what a bungler she was. She would let them both see that it was quite simple, nothing to make any fuss about, to herself no more than the easiest exercise! She would play, but never betray again that she was conscious of Mr. Meredith's existence, never seem to see his looks, treat him as if he were the cabbage——

All this ran through her thoughts in the moment, while Miss Harwood turned slowly round on her music stool, and he advanced a step, turning towards Janet a look of entreaty, and at the same time of private intelligence, such as all her resolution not to look could not prevent her from seeing. Gussy had never treated Janet with unkindness, never shown any want of consideration, save in ignoring her on these occasions; but at present her voice sounded careless, disrespectful, almost insulting.

"Miss Summerhayes!" she called out, carelessly.

Janet, with still that tumult in her breast, did not lift her eyes or move in her seat.

"Miss Summerhayes!" cried Gussy again.

"My dear," said Mrs. Harwood, "my daughter is calling you. I think you did not hear."

"Oh!" said Janet, and looked up as if she had heard for the first time; indeed, the force of her indignation gave her something of the feeling of one awakened from a dream.

"Will you come here, please?" said Miss Harwood.

Never before had there been between them the tone of command and obedience. Janet reflected to herself bitterly that she was supposed to know her place, and rose, but with a reluctance that anybody could see.

This reluctance softened Gussy. She thought the other girl felt all the inappropriateness of being made the third between two——

"Please come and look at this accompaniment. I have never seen it before, and it seems difficult. Will you try it for us? You said you could play."

"Yes, I can play." Janet went slowly towards the piano. He might make eyes as he chose, she would not see them. She looked at the music while Gussy rose and left the place for her. Easy? why, it was child's play! "I will play it if you wish me to do so;" her fingers were crisp with impatience to get at the keys.

"Oh, do, do, Miss Summerhayes! we are waiting for you. A new accompaniment and a new song at once are too much for anyone. Is that the proper height for you? is the light as you like it? Ah!" he said, with a deep breath, "that is something like; now, Gussy!"

He took her hand to draw her to his side, and over Gussy's colorless face there sprang anew that light as if it came through rose-leaves, through some ethereal medium, a light ineffable, which neither sunlight nor lamplight ever gave.

Poor Gussy! this was the look which made her sister's childish countenance lower, which was "silly," which moved Janet to mingled ridicule, wrath, and shame. These young critics had no mercy. But as she stood by her lover's side and sang, all unkindly thoughts and every little irritation went out of Gussy's soul. She was the only one of them whose mind was in true harmony with the music; the others were better performers. She forgot that she had been displeased to have Janet called in. She touched the girl's shoulder tenderly, gratefully with her hand; her heart went out in the song, though she was not so very certain about the notes.

It was not at all with these beautiful emotions that Janet plunged into the mazes of the notes. She played with rage, with fury, beating down the man who had wounded her, helping out the tremulous soprano; and Meredith, roused to the conflict, sang against her, till he, too, excelled himself. It was like a musical duel, carried out to the last note with an intention which the two chief performers only were aware of; and Janet was ringing out the last symphony with her cheeks burning and her heart beating, when suddenly she sprang up from the piano and covered her face and her ears with her hands.

"Oh, there it is!" she cried, "there it is again!"

"There is—what?" said Miss Harwood. She had been standing a step apart, contemplating with mixed feelings the performance from which she herself had dropped. She came forward and laid her hand on Janet's shoulder. "What is the matter, Miss Summerhayes? Have you done too much? are you ill? What is it?"

"The voice, the voice!" said Janet, still with her hands on her ears.

"The voice! I heard the wind in the chimney, if that is what you mean."

"And I heard nothing at all, except Miss Summerhayes' brilliant performance," said Mr. Meredith.

"Miss Summerhayes is not so complimentary to you. She evidently was not thinking of your brilliant performance. Why, you are quite upset," said Gussy with the faintest tone of contempt.

"What is it? What did she hear?" cried Mrs. Harwood, sharply, from her chair.

CHAPTER XIII.

THIS little incident could not be said to have much effect upon Janet's relations with the family in which she was living, but yet it was not without some influence on the new order of things. She had an interview next morning with Mrs. Harwood, who complimented her very much on the beneficial influence she was exercising over Julia.

"I begin to hope that, after all, she will become a reasonable creature, and like other people," said the mother. "I need not tell you that she has been a great trouble to me, and nobody we have had has ever got such command of her before. She is growing very fond of you, Miss Summerhayes, and I hope nothing will occur to disturb this good understanding," she continued, with a little significance in her tone. Then, after a pause, she resumed, as with an afterthought, "Oh! there is just one thing I wanted to speak to you about. I am afraid, my dear, from what happened last night, that you are a little fanciful, easily-frightened, terrified, they tell me," she said, with a little laugh, "for ghosts, and that sort of nonsense."

"No—oh, no! indeed, indeed I never was."

"Then, my dear," said Mrs. Harwood, laying her hand, not unkindly, on Janet's arm, "don't begin now. They told me you heard something that frightened you. Be quite sure that there's always a perfectly natural explanation of anything you may hear. There is nothing whatever in this house to be frightened about. Make yourself quite sure on that point, and we shall always get on perfectly well, I am convinced. Now run away, you and her. I won't keep you longer. I am sure it is time for your walk."

"But, Mrs. Harwood——" said Janet, with some timidity.

"No," said the old lady, "I won't keep you any longer. You must not lose the sunshiny part of the day."

Janet lingered a moment longer, but her courage failed her. How could she insist upon a thing which nobody paid any attention to but herself? Perhaps, indeed, nobody but herself heard it at all. It might be something which was addressed to herself alone; some mysterious warning; something which could not find any other utterance. The little governess, however, was so sensible and so perfectly modern in her views that, though such a flattering and thrilling idea did occur to her, she did not entertain the notion. Why should she have a ghostly voice all to herself? What could there be that she required to be warned about in such a way? Janet knew very little of her family, but they were not distinguished enough to possess a ghost. She did not believe that it was a ghost at all; it was something in trouble, something that had been caught in a trap, or perhaps the cry of some one who was mad, which was a very terrible suggestion. To see a ghost would be exciting indeed, though even the youthful imagination of the nineteenth century has overcome these kind of terrors—and there would be a distinction in the vision of something supernatural which would more than make up for the strain upon the nerves; but to encounter a madman about the house or garden would be very different, a horror which would have no compensating superiority. How could she ask, however, of that calm old lady in her chair whether she was quite sure there was no dangerous madman about? Such a suggestion might bring on something terrible; it might produce a fit, or something; it might kill Mrs. Harwood. Janet made up her mind it was better to forbear, to wait a little longer, to see what might happen. And she had not been insensible to the significance of Mrs. Harwood's tone when she hoped that nothing would occur to disturb their good understanding. Janet was very quick-witted, and the tone was not lost upon her. It brought before her very distinctly the fact that Mrs. Harwood, if she pleased, could send her away, and that it would not be pleasant to be sent away. To go of her own accord might be supportable, though she did not by any means desire it: but to be sent away would not do at all. She knew what all the gossips at Clover would say. They would say they knew from the beginning that Janet Summerhayes never would do in a situation; that she had been too much spoiled ever to get on in a place where she had to consider other people and not herself, and that they were quite convinced she would soon turn up to be a burden on the good Blands, who were foolishly kind to her. Rather any self-denial, Janet said to herself, than encounter this? So she restrained her alarms, kept a careful eye upon all the dark corners when she went up or downstairs, always carried a light with her wherever she went, and determined to say nothing, whatever might happen, so long as she could bear it. In this way she kept herself calm, although she could not divest herself of an alarmed expectation and sense that at any moment she might be startled into overpowering terror again.

Another consequence, however, followed, which she did not become aware of at once, yet which was of more practical importance—and that was that her presence in the drawing-room in the long evenings was not so much a matter of course as it had been. The little dinner-parties, at which the guests consisted only of Mr. Charles Meredith and one other man, or sometimes of Mr. Charles Meredith (as she discovered) alone, took place more frequently, and it was occasionally discovered by Miss Harwood or her mother that Julia ought to prepare her lessons better in the evening, which meant, of course, the exclusion of Miss Summerhayes too. When Janet saw that this had become a system she was, of course, disturbed by it; but she was so reasonable that she did not take offence, as some young women might do. She concluded, on the whole, after the first prick of annoyance, that it was quite a natural thing, and one that she had no right to complain of. Miss Harwood liked to have her suitor (if he was her suitor) to herself. She did not want a third person coming in between them, especially a third person who, in one particular at least, surpassed herself. Janet acknowledged that it was quite natural. In such circumstances she too, she felt, would invent reasons why the other girl should not come downstairs, why she should not be allowed to interfere. It was a pity, and she did not like it. It was dull with Julia in the school-room, and not to be able to note how the play was going was a disappointment. But she behaved herself like a little heroine, and did not complain. It certainly did not occur to her, at this period of her history, that to be prevented from improving her acquaintance with Charles Meredith was a grievance of which, even to herself, she could complain.

It happened to her, however, during this period, when again she had volunteered to match crewels for Mrs. Harwood, on a day when nobody else was going out, to meet Meredith exactly as she had done when she saw him first. She had run into the little shop on her mission—the St. John's Wood shop, with all its little merchandises, like a superior village repository: and there, once more, exactly in the same spot, looking over the music, was the now well-known figure, correct yet easy in his morning suit, with his black hair and dark eyes and waxen bloom. The old ladies in the shop thought Mr. Meredith a model of manly beauty, and even Janet could not refrain from an involuntary glance of satisfaction. She was half-ashamed this time of having thought that he was like a barber's block. And his eyes lighted up with such evident pleasure at the sight of her that it would have been impossible for a little girl long abstracted from any look of admiration not to be pleased.

"Come and help me to choose a new song for to-night," he said, after a warm greeting. "I have not seen you for a fortnight, Miss Summerhayes. I hope we shall meet to-night."

"Not if you are coming to dinner," said Janet, demurely; "we do not come down to dinner when there is company, Julia and I."

"Oh, that is the explanation?" said Meredith, and, with a widening of his eyes and elevation of his eyebrows, he added, "Then I shall not come to dinner to-night."

Janet said nothing, for what had she to say? She had no part in these arrangements of her superiors. She gave a glance at the song he held in his hand.

"It would be better to practise those you have than to bring anything new."

"Ah, if you could persuade her of that! and if we singers could be left free to think of the song without hammering at the accompaniment! How well you play, Miss Summerhayes."

"I can do nothing else," said Janet; "I was taught only for that."

"Yes," said Meredith, "that is the right way—to do one thing well, and stick to it; but, unfortunately, everybody is not of that opinion. Most ladies think that they can do anything—or, at least, try."

"No more than most men," said Janet, quickly.

"Oh, don't you think so? I think you'll allow we've a different way of setting to work. We do what we can, what we have studied; but you ladies try a little of everything without having studied at all. Miss Harwood has a nice little voice, but no science even in that, and she knows no more of the piano than of the steam-engine. Don't contradict me, Miss Summerhayes, for I am sure I must know best. I have suffered from it too much."

"You have no appearance of suffering at all," said Janet.

"Ah, that's all my power of dissembling," he said.

Janet had got her crewels by this time, and she had a vague consciousness that it would be well not to continue this conversation, so she said, "Good-morning!" and was about to pass him on her way home when he put out his hand to detain her.

"Miss Summerhayes, don't run away. I am going in the same direction. We are prevented from making friends in the evening, but I should not like to let an opportunity slip."

"Who keeps us from making friends, Mr. Meredith? You are making a great mistake."

"Am I? If you think you know Gussy Harwood, it is you that are quite mistaken, Miss Summerhayes. How quickly you walk; I can scarcely keep up with you." He laughed, and took a stride or two which made Janet's attempt to hurry away ridiculous. "There is no harm in walking along the same pavement, even with a person you disapprove of."

"I don't disapprove of—any one," said Janet.

"Oh, that is more than I bargained for. You must promise to play for me to-night."

"But you said you were not coming to-night," said Janet.

"So I did," he answered, laughing; "but never mind—not to dinner, certainly. You must promise me to play, and not to stop short all at once, as you did the other night, whatever you may hear."

"Oh, did you hear it too?" Janet cried, clasping her hands.

"I don't think I heard anything. There are queer sounds sometimes about that Harwood house—and old Vicars is queer; don't you think so? Never mind, Miss Summerhayes, you and I have nothing to do with that."

"I don't understand what you mean," said Janet. "I have nothing at all to do with it; but you, who are a great friend of the family, and have known them so long, you ought not to talk like that."

"What am I saying?" said Meredith; "that you and I have nothing to do with the secrets of the family, if they have any. Isn't that quite true?"

"We are not at all in the same position," said Janet, indignantly. "I am a stranger and the governess. You are their—dear friend."

Mr. Meredith laughed low, with vanity and self-complacence.

"Am I a 'dear friend'?—you flatter me very much, Miss Summerhayes—of Julia, for instance, who says the prettiest things about me. I see you've been working in my favor, for she's no longer so uncivil as she used to be."

"Oh, Mr. Meredith, she means no harm; she's only so—so———"

"Sincere," he said; "so she is, and I am half sorry you have taught her to mend her ways: for she is less amusing when she behaves like other people. The brother, too—but you've not yet made acquaintance with the charming Dolff—I know what will happen to that young man before he has been two days in the house."

"What?" cried Janet.

She felt more than ever that the conversation was undesirable; but she was full of curiosity, and her companion had ways and modes of securing the feminine attention. He made great play with those eyes of his, which expressed so much more than his words. Even now he answered her question with them in a way which made Janet blush before he had said a word.

"What will happen to him? Oh, I know; but I will not forestall the pleasure of the discovery. I suppose it's always more or less a pleasure to a young lady when she finds—— Oh, I am not going to say any more. You need not blush, Miss Summerhayes."

"I am not blushing," cried Janet, angrily, feeling her countenance blaze.

"Oh, no, I see; it is only the effect of walking so quickly, which brings the most agreeable color to the cheek. About Mr. Dolff, we shall see what we shall see. But keep your head, whatever you do, Miss Summerhayes, and we shall have some fun. It will be as good as a play."

"You are as good as a play," cried Janet, indignant, eager to give him a prick in return.

"Who, I?" He gave her a momentary stare, then laughed. "We," he said; "I don't pretend not to understand. I daresay we give you a good deal of amusement as you sit and make your remarks. I saw the very first night what a keen pair of eyes had come into the scene. But do not be too sure of anything. People who look on don't always see the whole of the game."

"I think I see a great deal of the game; and I don't like it at all," Janet cried.

"You don't like me at all, Miss Summerhayes. After that home-thrust I have nothing for it but to make my bow and take my leave."

CHAPTER XIV.

MISS HARWOOD came into the drawing-room in the afternoon, at five o'clock, when the little party were all assembled, with an open note in her hand.

"Fancy, mamma, how annoying," she said, "Charley cannot come to dinner. Some engagement, business, has turned up; and he says, since you kindly allow him to dispense with ceremony——"

"Oh, I should think so," cried Mrs. Harwood. "Let him keep any business engagement, for goodness' sake. He has not too many of them, I fear."

"He has more than you think," said Gussy. "His time is far more taken up than you suppose."

"Well," said Mrs. Harwood, "he might have let us know sooner, and then I should not have ordered those partridges. Game is thrown away upon women. You all like a chicken just as well."

"I'll tell cook," said Gussy, "to put them aside for to-morrow; but I don't suppose he knew till the last moment."

Janet had been going on with her work very demurely, taking no notice, feeling somewhat guilty, yet recognizing with a throb of elation that she was not the unimportant person they all thought her. Janet was of opinion that it was best to have no secrets, for secrets have an infallible certainty of being found out. So she lifted her voice at this point and said,

"I saw Mr. Meredith in Mimpriss's when I was there for the crewels. He was choosing some music."

"Did he tell you he was not coming?" Gussy asked, somewhat breathlessly.

"He held up a song," said Janet, and said, "This is for to-night."

Which was quite true. To keep back a little is very different, she said to herself, from telling a fib. And now any gossip might tell them she had been seen with Mr. Meredith, and no harm could come.

"Ah! you see it must have been quite sudden, mamma. Did you notice, Miss Summerhayes, what the song was?"

"I saw Tosti's name at the bottom of the page, but I did not look at it more closely," said Janet. "He held it up to me while I was getting my crewels, and said something about your voice."

"He should not speak of my voice or of me at all in a shop," said Gussy, with a bright look and an air of flattered grievance. To think that he could not refrain from speaking of her, even in a shop, to anybody whom he might meet, was sweet to poor Gussy, as it was also sweet to blame him, and resent his foolish, lover-like weakness. "Well," she said, "I suppose it will be for to-morrow night. I will tell cook about the partridges, mamma."

There could be no doubt that Janet felt a little guilty as she dressed for dinner—guilty and curious, too. He had said he should not dine, but he had meant to come all the same. Would he come, after all? and on what pretence? How would he make it seem consistent with his business engagement? What would he do? It was a curious question, and she could not help feeling that her *rôle* and that of Gussy were reversed, and that it was she who would listen for the step and the ringing of the bell, though solely out of curiosity to know what would happen. Janet made herself a little more smart than usual; she could scarcely have told why. She relaxed a little the profound gloom of her mourning. There was a little additional light in her eyes. She was curious, very curious, to know whether he would do it, and how he would do it. Her instinct was mischievous—perhaps a little malicious—a sort of drawing-room wickedness, mere fun, not anything else. It would be interesting to see with what ingenuousness he would account for his unlooked-for appearance, how gravely he would recount the manner in which he got rid of his business engagement. Janet felt that she would have difficulty in keeping her countenance while he ran through his excuses. And she realized to herself Gussy's serious attention, her congratulations to him on having been able to get away, and Mrs. Harwood's remark that she hoped he would never neglect any business engagement which was of importance. Janet held her breath in anticipation, to keep down the laugh which she knew would try to come. And he would look at her with audacious eyes, lifting his eyebrows, claiming her as a fellow conspirator. There could be no doubt that it would be "fun." All of them so serious, taking the matter in the gravest way, while she would receive that glance aside, that reminder that they were in a plot together. Yet it was no plot. Janet could truly say that she had nothing, nothing to do with it. If he was so impudent as to cheat his friends, it was no fault of hers: and no doubt it was very wrong of him. But it was a piquant break upon the monotony, and Janet could not deny even to herself that the fun was uppermost, and that she expected to be much amused.

It all happened exactly as she had foreseen. Gussy took her place opposite her mother with the most absolute tranquillity. Her usual little strain of expectation, which was always there, even on the evenings when he was not expected, when it was only possible that he might come, had altogether fallen to-night. She looked at her work with eyes which had no other meaning, never held her breath at a passing sound, nor paused to listen; became, indeed, again the mild Gussy, undisturbed by emotion, with whom Janet had first made acquaintance. The sight of this relapse into quietude gave Janet a great compunction; more even than had Miss Harwood shown acute disappointment; and she felt in herself, as she had foreseen, all the signs of the suspense and expectation from which the other had escaped. In the stillness of the night she heard, or thought she heard, steps coming from a long distance: she caught her breath at every passing sound. When a cinder fell from the hearth, she gave a little jump, as if it were some one coming. Her ears were keener than they had ever been in her life. The sense of fun gave way in Janet's mind to a sense of guilt as she thus listened and watched in spite of herself. And yet she had done nothing wrong; the fault, she said to herself, if there was one, was not at all her fault. But Janet felt like a little conspirator, sitting there among them, knowing the surprise that was coming and that they were about to be deceived.

When nine o'clock struck, however, which it did very audibly, in the long pauses of conversation, Janet said to herself, half with relief and half with disappointment, that now he would not come. Gussy had closed the piano before dinner; there was no glimmer from the white keyboard. The evening was going to pass over quite tranquilly, like one of the quiet evenings before Mr. Charles Meredith appeared.

Just as she had concluded upon this, with, to do her justice, quite as much relief as disappointment, the sudden sound of the bell came tingling through the quiet, making Janet jump, who was off her guard. Gussy, who expected nothing, scarcely stirred.

"Who can that be so late?" said Mrs. Harwood: "it can't be Charley Meredith to-night."

"It must be a parcel or something," said Gussy, "or perhaps a telegram from Dolff to say when he is coming. He is fond of telegrams—It is some one coming in," she said, after a pause, raising her head.

"Perhaps it's Dolff himself," said Julia, getting up with one spring from the rug. She rushed to the door, while they all watched. Julia opened it, looked out, and closed it again with indignation. "After all, it's Charley Meredith again," said the young lady, "and now, I suppose, we shall have to go to bed."

Gussy rose up, her quietness all gone. She said, "Ah!" in an indescribable tone, as if coming from the bottom of her heart.

"Ju, how rude you are, shutting the door in his face!" said Mrs. Harwood. "You seem to wish to make the very worst impression, as if you were a savage. Well, Charley! this *is* a surprise. We made sure we should not see you to-night."

"I hope it's not disagreeable," said Meredith, coming in briskly with his roll of music, as usual. He managed, even in that first moment, to give a side glance at Janet, which she somehow caught trembling under her eyelids. Oh, it might be fun! but it was horrid, too. She felt herself a conspirator, a deceiver, all that was most dreadful, and did not dare to raise her eyes. But nothing could be more assured and easy than his explanation. "I found I could shake off my man sooner than I expected. Talks about business, don't you know, Mrs. Harwood—you ought to know—mean endless maundering on one side, and half-a-dozen words on the other. If your advice is worth anything, it can always be said in half-a-dozen words."

"I would never hurry a client, Charley," said Mrs. Harwood, shaking her head; "in all I've had to do with the law I've always seen that; and my brother, who, you know, was a Q.C., always said so. Never hurry a client; let them get it all out."

"Oh, I think he got it all out, and we parted the best of friends. He's only in town for a few days, and he wanted to go to the theatre; so I took him to the 'Gayety,' and gave him my blessing. And here I am, not much later than usual. I beg your pardon, Miss Summerhayes, I did not see you. How do you do to-night?"

What a look he gave her as, pretending to see her for the first time, he made a step in her direction. Gussy afterwards took him much to task for slighting the governess.

"Just because she is the governess one ought to be more than usually attentive not to hurt her feelings," said Gussy.

But, then, she did not see that look, which so tempted Janet to laughter, yet overwhelmed her with a sense of guilt. His eyebrows went up almost into his hair as he looked at Janet. He gave her the slightest nod of understanding. "You see!" he seemed to say. Janet felt herself drawn into his circle, made his comrade, his confidant. And it *was* funny; but, oh, so horrid, too!

"Clients come, more or less," he said. "I am not quite so briefless as I was. I think I may say I am getting on, and my devotion to my work is boundless. I know how much depends upon it."

He gave Gussy a look as he said this, which caused two blushes instead of one, for the color came crimson to Janet's face as she stooped over her work, as well as in a soft rose to Gussy's colorless cheeks.

"Ah! it's more music, I fear, than law," said Mrs. Harwood, again shaking her head.

"Well, both are best," said the young man, looking at Gussy again. "Music gets me on in one way, law in the other. I have to consider what is needed all round."

"You can always make out a good case for yourself, Charley."

"I hope so, Mrs. Harwood; and for my clients, too."

Gussy was silenced by these allusions, which were so very plain. Her eyes seemed to swim in a soft and liquid brightness. Her face had the rose-tint which makes up for all deficiencies in character and color. This evening, which had begun in resigned dulness, was it to end more brightly than any other? She was silent in the flood of silent happiness that filled her heart. And Janet sat by, the little conspirator, who was behind the scenes and knew the difference! Oh, how wicked, how angry, how helpless she felt! It was not fun at all, but treachery, a falsehood that made her ashamed to the very bottom of her heart; unless this, indeed, was the truth, and Janet the little dupe whom he was making a fool of, which would be better than the other, yet even more exasperating. She kept her eyes fixed upon her work, and her needle flew, and her cheeks burned. Never, never, never, thought Janet, would she speak to Mr. Meredith again.

There was at least half-an-hour spent in conversation, and then the visitor unrolled his new song.

"I wish you would try this," he said; "our concert is coming on, and we must settle what we are going to do."

"Gussy is to sing in the quartets," said Mrs. Harwood.

"In more than quartets. She is to perform a duet with me."

"Oh, is that what you are thinking of? Isn't it a little conspicuous? These things are all very well in a drawing-room—but on a public platform!"

"Mother—it is to amuse the poor."

"Oh, yes. I know what you mean with your amusements for the poor. You amuse yourselves very much first of all, and then you call it an act of charity. I am not a great person for amusing the poor. It would not amuse me at all to go out in a cold night and listen to your concert, and I don't think a woman of my age in the back slums would like it a bit better. We would both prefer our fireside and our work."

"But suppose the poor creature had no fire, Mrs. Harwood?"

"Then give her some firing, which would be far more sensible. She wants coals, and you give her a song. Of course you will do it your own way. Singing to them is the fad of your generation. Coals and groceries have always been mine."

"But about this duet," said Meredith, with an indulgent smile.

"As for it being conspicuous," said Gussy, "that is nonsense, mamma: for people sing according as their voices suit, and not for any other reason. And Charley and I are such old friends. We surely may sing together."

"Or do anything else together," he said.

"Oh! have it your own way," said Mrs. Harwood. "It is quite useless for me to interfere."

"You mean a much more gracious permission, dear Mrs. Harwood, than you say. Ah! here is Miss Summerhayes to play for us, if she will be so good. And I think you will be so good, for nobody could play so well without liking to do it. No, I can't have you bothered with that, Gussy. You must give your whole attention to the song. Come! Why, the piano is shut up, and there are no lights."

"You forget," said Gussy, "we did not expect you to-night."

"And you never have any music except when I am here! That is a pity, though it's a great compliment. May I light the candles? Now, come—it is to be a lesson to-night. Miss Summerhayes will play, and I shall coach, and correct, and do all sorts of dreadful things, as if I were Cantalino. You shall have everything over again that Cantalino inflicts upon me."

In this way, with every kind of seduction, Gussy was got to the piano, and received her lesson, which was half a gratification and half the reverse, for Miss Harwood did not quite like to be put in the place of a learner before Janet, while it made her happy to be "coached," and trained, and interrupted, praised, and encouraged by her lover. Was he her lover? Janet seated with her back to them, with a new and difficult accompaniment to occupy her fingers, could not resolve this question to herself; sometimes men are not at all loyal and yet are in love. They discuss their beloved one, or even their *fiancée*, with the first comer. They ask other men's opinion of her. They talk of their own execution, when they are to be "turned off," and similar vulgarities, and yet are lovers in the curious contradiction of nature. Was this all? Was his criticism of Gussy only his unmeaning banter? and his joke played upon her to-night, did it mean nothing?

Janet sat at the piano, and thumped and pondered, with her cheeks blazing crimson and her hands flying from one end of the instrument to another. She was a very good accompanist. She might not, perhaps, have any instinct of self-sacrifice in life, but she had learnt that it was of the first importance in art. She played for the singer, not for herself, supporting her in her weak notes, giving place to her strong ones, making her own performance the background of the other. And, as Janet felt much ashamed of herself and of the part which she had been made to play in this night's performance, she was more self-sacrificing, more bent upon making herself secondary and the singer first than ever. When the singing was over, even Mrs. Harwood applauded.

"You should always have Miss Summerhayes to play your accompaniments, Gussy. She does it beautifully. She brings out your voice as I never heard it before. I begin to think that no one can sing and play too. You brought out her voice quite beautifully, Miss Summerhayes."

"A word of applause for the coach, too," said Meredith, with a laugh.

Gussy, pleased with her little success, stood, with an uneasy glance at Janet, not knowing what to say. She was more disposed to applaud the coach than the little governess. She stood hesitating between them, now and then giving Janet a doubtful look. She was far too much assured in her own superior place to be jealous of Janet. Jealous of Janet! She would as soon have thought of being jealous of a cat. But still it annoyed her slightly that Janet should have such a share even in this little drawing-room triumph.

CHAPTER XV.

JANET was not at all satisfied with herself after this performance. She understood, if nobody else did, the attitude of Gussy towards her; the half-defiance, half-sympathy, and entire doubtfulness with which the young lady of the house began to regard her. All the events the evening, taken together, had given Miss Harwood a sensation of doubt. She was not clever enough to put one thing to another, and divine that there was a connection between the meeting with Meredith and the sudden engagement which prevented him from coming to dinner, and his unexpected appearance at night; but she had a vague feeling of doubt, which originated in the instinct of her emotions rather than in any exercise of reflection. She blamed neither of them, unless, indeed, a faint sensation of displeasure, too little to deserve that name, towards Janet could be called blame. She thought that the governess wished to be of the party, to thrust her services upon them, to share the amusement without consideration that something more than amusement was beneath. Her mind did not go any further than this, but it gave her a slight soreness towards the other girl, who did not understand— a soreness modified by a kind of uneasy gratitude to Janet for having really served her after all. Whatever her motive was, Janet in her compunction for her behavior altogether (though, after all, there was nothing for which she could blame herself, the fault lay entirely with the other, or almost entirely), was, after this, very anxious to put herself at the service of Gussy. She put aside occupations of her own to play these accompaniments again and again. She it was who urged upon Miss Harwood the unceasing practice which was necessary to bring her song to perfection.

"It is so different when you are standing up before a crowd of people, and it all seems to float away from you; so different from singing at home."

"Then you have done it yourself?" said Gussy, surprised.

"Oh, only at our little concerts at Clover, where I knew everybody: and I only played, which is not nearly so bad; but I have seen people who, for a minute, forgot everything, and looked as if they would run away."

"I don't think I shall want to run away," said Miss Harwood, with dignity.

"Oh, no, I didn't suppose so; but you will feel so much more comfortable if you know your song well. Shall we go over it once again?"

"It is very kind of Miss Summerhayes," said Mrs. Harwood, feeling a want of warmth in her daughter's reception of this generous offer. "It is very nice of her," the old lady added, "for it can't matter a bit to her. It is not as if she were teaching you, when she might get some credit from it. It is entirely good feeling."

"I am sure I am—much obliged to Miss Summerhayes," said Gussy. And she was aware that what her mother said was quite true. She was not an impulsive person in general, but a sudden movement of remorse for her own ingratitude and appreciation of the other's unselfishness seized her all at once. "I don't see," she said, "why we should go on calling her Miss Summerhayes when she has been three months in the house, and always so nice. I am sure she would prefer it, mamma, if you at least were to call her Janet; and it is a pretty name, too; not like our solemnities in the Harwood family."

Janet was taken very much by surprise. She was not quite sure that she was so much gratified as she expected to be, and it took her a certain effort to get up the little burst of pleasure and gratitude which was becoming. It is a sad thing to be expected to be grateful for a favor which does not appear to yourself in that light. Janet had always been called Janet by everybody all her life, so that she rather preferred at present to be Miss Summerhayes. However, she succeeded in assuming the air of delighted surprise which was necessary in the circumstances, and when Mrs. Harwood kissed her, and said, with her motherly smile, "I shall like so much to call you Janet, my dear," the genuine kindness touched her heart.

"I hope I shall never do anything to vex this dear old lady," she said to herself.

The silent prayer was not realized, but still it may be put on record as a real moment of feeling in Janet's very contradictory little being. She was very uncertain what Gussy could mean in thus opening to her the gates of intimacy, and receiving her, as it were, on a new footing. What did she mean by it? But Miss Harwood herself could not have told. She meant a momentary compunction, a half-apology, and to compensate the girl a little for the involuntary doubt she had of her. If there was anything more in it, Gussy herself was unconscious of further motive. It was something in the nature of a penance, no doubt; for Miss Harwood loved the governess a trifle less as Janet, in the intimacy of the closest intercourse, than she had done as a stranger and Miss Summerhayes.

Thus a vague mist of feeling rose between the two which did not in any way interfere with their present relations, and was, in fact, founded upon almost nothing, yet was full of undeveloped elements in which mischief might lie; while all around this nebulous region of uncertain sentiment shone the easy light of the household, untroubled by any mist, a sober, steady glow, not excessive, of good-humor and kindness, chiefly proceeding from the mild moon or household lamp of Mrs. Harwood, which reflected many different colored rays, reducing them, by the action of a steady, pleasant, good disposition, taking all things soberly and kindly, to a light which was warm without extravagance, and bright without dazzling. How happy were all her friends in Clover to hear that Janet had thus "fallen on her feet!"

The vicar called at the house in St. John's Wood about this time, and carried back the most delightful report with him. The impression he himself produced was the best possible, for he was a handsome old gentleman, and perfect type of a country vicar, well got up and well-to-do. Mrs. Harwood was anxious that he should come back to dinner, and would have liked to pay him a great deal of attention, and Janet rose in everybody's opinion, from that of the head of the house down to Priscilla, the parlor-maid, and Owen, the gardener, to whom Mr. Bland gave a shilling for calling a cab for him.

The vicar assured Mrs. Harwood that he and his wife felt towards little Janet as if she were a child of their own. And when he went back to Clover he assured an anxious party assembled at afternoon tea that he had seldom been more favorably impressed than by the charming family with whom Janet had found a home.

"A delightful, refined house, an admirable mother, and a charming young lady, quite the sort of friend I should have chosen for Janet, I scarcely saw her pupil, but I have no doubt, judging by all that I did see, that she was a sweet child, and worthy of the rest. No complications such as so often beset a young girl's path; indeed, I should say that if we had chosen from one end of the country to the other we could scarcely have selected anything so desirable as Providence has procured for her—by chance, as we say. It is a lesson to me of trustfulness and dependence upon a higher guidance."

The ladies were all deeply edified with this speech, feeling that what the vicar said, especially about Providence, was beautiful: and when they heard that Janet was called by her Christian name, there was a universal chorus of satisfaction. Dr. Harding, who had come in as he passed on his afternoon round, said "Humph!" behind their backs, shaking his head; but then he, as we are all aware, had reasons for thinking very ill of Janet's foolish determination to measure her little strength against the world.

The concert took place shortly after the vicar's visit, and Janet and her pupil, in the charge of a neighbor, Mrs. Hunter, from next door—as Mrs. Harwood was unable to take care of them herself—were present, happy spectators of Gussy's success: for the duet was quite the success of the evening, everybody said. And the pair appeared on the platform together, with a little halo of romance about them, a pair of lovers, as the audience believed, though nothing was as yet announced, or positively known.

"Of course, we shall soon hear that it is all settled," the friends of the family said to each other. "He is never out of the house, and singing together night after night; there is only one way in which that sort of thing can end."

Some thought that Gussy Harwood, who would have a very tolerable fortune, should have secured something better than a briefless barrister. But others added that Charley Meredith had very good connections, and knew a number of solicitors, and was a pushing sort of man, one of those who always get on. And they looked very well together, quite a model couple; she so fair, almost too fair, but very well dressed to-night in a dark dress, which threw up her fairness and neutralized her want of color; and he, on the contrary, with so much color, such dark hair and mustaches, and such a fine bloom. The natural attraction of opposition could not have been more pleasantly set forth. Janet sat in her place among the audience, and looked at them with eyes a little—just a little—envious, yet pleased to shine in the reflected glory. The dark dress which was so successful was her doing. She had wanted Gussy to look her best, with a certain *esprit de corps* and desire for the credit of the house: and it was she who, with much ado, had persuaded both mother and daughter that the pale dresses in which Miss Harwood delighted would be out of place. Also it was she who had trained her in her song. It would not have been half so good but for Janet's painstaking, and her determination to have it fully practised.

Janet sat all impatient not to be on the platform along with them, longing for an occasion to show herself, half-believing to the very last that there would arise a commotion among the performers, and that some one would walk down the room to where she sat to ask if she would kindly come and accompany Mr. Meredith and Miss Harwood in their duet. She kept on expecting this until the very moment when they stood up, and the pianist who had accompanied everybody struck the first notes. Oh! said Janet to herself, impatient, what a mistake they were making! The pianist was a nobody, and did not know their voices, and could not half bring them out. If only she had been there! But she had to sit quiet and listen, which is very hard when you know that you could do it much better.

Janet was not thinking of Mr. Meredith any more than if he had been a cabbage, but she did want to share the triumph, she who had really brought it about, and she wanted to do what she could do so well instead of the inferior performer who did not do it half so well. But this is a trouble which accomplished persons must put up with continually, and after the first mortification was over Janet sat it out bravely, and even led the applause with a most energetic pair of hands, at the points where it ought to come in, and was most wanted to stimulate failing courage or cover a weak point. In this she behaved with the utmost generosity and desire that, notwithstanding their neglect of herself, the performance should succeed; and she listened to all the remarks with eager attention, especially those about the one way in which things of this kind must end. Was this the way in which Gussy's romance was certain to end? Janet felt that she herself would not be nearly so much interested, not to say excited by it, if the conclusion was as certain as people thought. But she perceived clearly that if it did not end so it would be wrong, and Mr. Meredith much to blame. The drama altogether was breathless in its interest to this little spectator, because she felt that there was no certainty in it—that probably Mr. Charles Meredith was (so to speak, in the language of the stage) a villain, and Gussy, perhaps, a victim. Who could tell? It appeared, however, that Janet herself was the only person who had any doubt on the subject, and, an inexperienced little guesser as she was, how was she to know?

"Do you think Gussy and Charley are in love with each other?" said Julia suddenly, on their way home.

"Julia! one doesn't talk of such things till—till they are publicly known."

"For I don't," said Julia. "Gussy, yes, she is too silly. I could kill her when she looks at him so; but, Charley, no—and he's the most important of the two, isn't he, Miss Summerhayes?"

"I don't know why he should be the most important; they are both equally important," said Janet, in her *rôle* of governess; "besides, it is not our business to discuss any such matter."

"Oh! that is all bosh," said Julia. "Of course, I must discuss it when it's my own sister. I'll tell you what I think. He has not made up his mind; he thinks he'll do it, and then something makes him think that he'll not do it. He knows that whenever he likes to put out his hand Gussy will——"

"Julia, I can't let you talk so."

"Whether I talk or not, I know it all the same," said Julia. "I hate Charley Meredith, with his red cheeks. I can't think what she sees in him; but, though I could kill her for being so silly, I don't want our Gussy to be disappointed. I should like him to propose and her to refuse him; but, oh! I'm afraid there is not the least chance of that. Do you think a girl should accept the very first offer, Miss Summerhayes?"

"I don't think at all on the subject," said Janet.

She paused, and gave a little laugh, not a sigh, which would have been more appropriate, to the memory of Dr. Harding, who had procured her that gratification.

"Oh, nonsense!" cried Julia; "why do you laugh? You were thinking of someone, Miss Summerhayes. Look! there's a light in the room over the porch. Don't you see?" The girl gripped her instructress by the arm. "Look, look, Miss Summerhayes; don't you see?"

"Don't be so excited," said Janet. "I see perfectly well: but I don't know why you should excite yourself."

"Oh, wait a bit!" said Julia; "wait a bit, and you'll be excited too. You don't know what it means yet. Janet—I'm going to call you Janet now—I'm so glad. Why, Dolff must have come home—that means Dolff!"

And Julia suddenly flung off from Janet's side, and fled along the road like an arrow from the bow.

CHAPTER XVI.

JANET had no very strong curiosity about Dolff. What she had heard of him had not been calculated to rouse her interest, and still less the photographs about the house in which Dolff appeared in every phase of boyhood and early manhood: for he was still very young, only two and-twenty, and consequently a mere boy to Janet, who was closely approaching her twentieth birthday. She had no interest in young boys. Manhood, in Janet's estimation, did not begin till twenty-five at earliest, and before that period the male youth, who could not in any way be taken seriously, was always more or less objectionable, she lingered a little in the hall, and then she said to herself that it would be better to go upstairs at once, and not disturb the family reunion. Sounds of a loudish voice, bass and rough, an altogether new tone in this feminine house, and of a laugh still louder, came from the dining-room, when Julia rushed in. Priscilla, when she came out, had a demure smile upon her face. There was a little air of excitement about the house, a portmanteau still standing in a corner of the hall, greatcoats and railway-rugs, and railway-novels thrown about.

"I don't think I shall go in to-night," Janet said to the parlor-maid. "Mrs. Harwood must want to have her son to herself. Will you send me up some little thing by Jane, and I shall not come down again to-night."

"Oh, miss," said Priscilla, "I hope you will go in. Mr. Dolff is a most affable young gentleman, he wouldn't wish to keep anybody away."

"Please do as I say," said Janet, running upstairs.

It may be supposed that the description of Dolff as an affable young gentleman who would not mind the governess's appearance did not mend matters. When she went in with her candle into her room to take off her hat and the large shawl which she had wrapped round her over her evening dress, Janet could not help seeing a piquante little face, which glanced at her carelessly from the dark depths of the glass. Her black dress was a little open at the throat, and amid all the surrounding dark her throat was of a dazzling whiteness, and her eyes shone with the excitement of the evening, and many thoughts that were careering through her mind. Janet did not stop to admire herself, but the glance made her realize more deeply the contrast of her circumstances with those of Gussy, who would come in presently accompanied by Charley Meredith and receive all the applause.

"Though she would never have done it but for me," Janet said to herself.

She had much wanted to see them after they came home, to watch how they looked at each other, and whether they would take any notice of the good effect of her teaching. And, therefore, it was with a little sigh that she sat down at the school-room fire, and contented herself with the solitude which was her legitimate surrounding, and in which she was far more safe from any snubs or disappointments than elsewhere.

She was prepared not to like Dolff. Even Mr. Meredith's malicious prophecy of what "would happen" had increased her prejudice against the son of the house. Janet had not that admiration of an Oxford man which is common among young ladies. He was of the least agreeable kind which that refined university produces, she judged by the sound of his voice; and to have him hanging about "paying attention" to the governess, for something to occupy the spare time that would hang heavily on his hands, was an anticipation that made Janet furious. When Julia came up, full of excitement and news of her brother, Janet was so deeply occupied with the book she was reading as to pay scarcely any attention.

"Why didn't you come in," said the girl. "Dolff wanted to see you much more than me. He has heard so much about you. He was so disappointed. He wanted me to go up and bring you down."

"How good that was of Mr. Harwood; but I can't be brought down to be shown like a new cat," said Janet, glancing over the top of her book.

"Oh, Janet, how unkind!" said Julia; "Dolff is not a boy like that. He may not be quite serious, nor work as he ought, but he always was a nice boy. And Gussy came back all in a glow. They had been praising her so. But mamma said you ought to get at least half the credit, and so Charley Meredith thinks too."

"Oh!" said Janet, coldly.

She relapsed into her book, which she declared to herself was far more interesting than all the Harwoods put together. What a thing it is to have a book to retire into when you are a little out of humor with your surroundings—a book full of romantic conditions in which you can compare how you would yourself have behaved with the manner in which the heroine behaved! Janet sat up till midnight reading, till the fire went out, and all was silent in the house. Her candles, too, were nearly exhausted before she perceived and started up in dismay to find one flickering in the socket, and to feel that the room was very chilly and the silence very eerie. It suddenly came into her mind how terrible it would be if at that moment, in the dead of night, the cry should come again which had scared her so twice before. When an idea of this kind gets into one's mind at such an inappropriate moment it is very difficult to shake it off. Janet hurried into her room to prepare for bed, to get rid of the alarming suggestion. Her room was next door to the school-room, and she stole out very quietly, not to disturb the dead silence. But when she came out upon the corridor with her little remnant of candle, she was startled to find that the house was not so dead asleep as she believed it to be. A light was visible downstairs in the hall, and a stealthy sound as of some one moving about.

Janet looked over the bannisters with her heart beating, instantly asking herself what she should do if it turned out to be burglars robbing the house. It was, however, something quite different. It was the respectable man-servant whom she had already seen at long intervals, whose presence nobody explained, and whom Julia, the only one of the family who had ever referred to him, called Vicars. He was going across the hall towards the part of the house which was called the wing, carrying a large tray. The candle which was on the tray shed its light upon sundry articles of food and a bottle or two of wine, which he was carrying very carefully, steadying as much as he could the little jar and tinkle of the dishes. Janet looked down in great consternation at this unexpected scene. He went straight across the hall to a door which Janet had been told was done away with—the door that led to some rooms which were never used—but which opened to Vicars at a touch, closing again upon him and his trayful of food and his twinkling candle.

Janet watched him disappear with a chill of horror. What did it mean? Was he a thief who kept his spoils there? Was he some secret enemy hanging about the house pillaging it in the dead of night? And what, oh, what ought she to do? Should she rush into Mrs. Harwood's room and rouse her, or, at least, her maid? Should she communicate at once the fact that there was a thief in the house? The thing that Janet did eventually was to retire hastily into her room and lock the door. While the bit of candle lasted she made a hurried investigation, feeling it quite possible that some accomplice might be lurking under her own bed or behind her dresses in the wardrobe. And then she jumped hastily into bed, and covered herself over, so that at least, whatever dreadful thing might happen, she should not see.

But nothing happened, dreadful or otherwise, and Janet awoke in the morning in her usual spirits, not remembering at first that anything had ailed her on the previous night. She only came by degrees to recollect the last incident at the end of the others which occurred to her one by one as she opened her eyes upon the foggy, wintry December morning. First of all, the concert, Gussy's singing, and the applause, which she felt was due to herself half as much at least as to the singer, and then the return home, Dolff's arrival, her own withdrawal upstairs, and then——

She sat suddenly bolt upright in her bed, with something of the shock of the previous night, and made up her mind that she would tell Mrs. Harwood, that it was her duty to prevent the house from being robbed; and, in the force of this idea, jumped out of bed and got through her morning preparations hastily, that no time might be lost. But before Janet saw Mrs. Harwood the impression once more had been effaced. She forgot in the morning aspect of the house that anything could happen in it that was not commonplace and ordinary. Gussy, who was the housekeeper, and must know everything, had her keys in their little basket on the table before her, and Janet felt that to suggest any trickery in the house would be to offend that perfectly competent domestic ruler; and after all, what had the governess to do with it? So once more she held her peace.

The breakfast-table was, as usual, surrounded by the three active members of the household—Miss Harwood, Julia, and the governess. The new-comer did not appear.

"My brother is always late, especially at first when he comes home," said Gussy. "I don't suppose they get up very early at Oxford; but he behaves as if they did, as if he had to take a long rest when he gets beyond the reach of lectures. Young men are all lazy in the morning. They sit up half the night and waste their health. They never can stand the fatigue that women do."

"Dolff is always at his football and things—he is very strong; he is as strong as all of us put together," said Julia.

"Oh, yes, in that way," said Gussy. "I hope you liked the concert, Janet. It went off very well, don't you think, on the whole?"

"Your duet went off very well. You sang delightfully. I was so pleased, so happy."

A little flush came over Gussy's face.

"It is very nice of you to say so. I saw you looking at me, and it kept me up, for you looked as if you were pleased. It was once suggested to ask you to come and play, but I thought it would only make a fuss, and that you would not like it. A fuss is what I cannot bear."

"Oh! I should not have minded," said Janet; "but," she added, generously, "it did not matter; it went very well as it was."

It was once suggested! Janet retired with her pupil to their lessons with this little revelation in her mind. It continued in hers that sense of being in the confidence of Mr. Charles Meredith, and knowing more about him than Gussy did, to whom he was paying his court in all the forms, which was half-agreeable and half-humiliating to the governess. She would have no more of it, she said to herself. He ought to ask Gussy to marry him, and be done with it. He ought not to give those side glances, those unspoken avowals, to any one. It had been "fun" that first time to think that he had upset all the arrangements, and disregarded everybody's convenience, and deceived his friends with smiling assurance for the sake of Janet. It was wrong, but it was amusing, and at twenty a mischievous pleasure in a trick of this sort is not out of date. But Janet felt now that it must not go on. She made up her mind not to go down to the drawing-room in the evening, or, at least, not to be beguiled to the piano, nor to take any part. If the accompaniment was spoiled, if Gussy did not do justice to her voice, if the duets were unsuccessful, what was that to Janet, any more than Vicars with his laden tray going across the hall! She had thought that one of the amusing things in the life of a governess, as she had pictured it to herself, would be this very spectatorship, the glimpses behind the scenes which she could not help having, seeing more of the game than the players did. But now it appeared that there were great inconveniences in the *rôle*, and Janet made up her mind that she would play it no more.

Her first sight of Dolff was in this wise. When she came in with Julia from their morning walk, blooming with health and fresh air, she found the Harwood family in the hall. Mrs. Harwood, in her chair, looking on with maternal smiles; Gussy on her knees before the opened portmanteau, which had been left there on the previous night; and a young man with his hat on, perched on the back of his head, seated upon the edge of a table, swinging his legs, and directing the process of unpacking. He was evidently in the happy position of one who was monarch of all he surveyed. He had come home to his kingdom: his vassals were ministering to him in various ways. Priscilla, the parlor-maid, was gathering up an armful of books to carry them away. Mrs. Harwood had got some gloves in her hand, which had evidently been given to her to mend. Dolff, with his hat on his head, and the suspicion of a cigar in the air, gave his orders lightly from his throne.

But when the closing of the hall door, done somewhat loudly by Julia, aroused his attention, and he looked up to see a young lady unknown, with a bloom unknown to the house of Harwood on her cheeks, coming in, Dolff started from that presiding seat, or, rather, slid from it, with a movement of consternation, and his hand stole up to his hat, removing it with evident embarrassment and confusion. It is to be supposed that he had no idea at first that this was the governess of whom he had heard much, but only officially under that name. His hat disappeared as if by magic, and he himself would have disappeared too, had that been possible in his abashed and troubled state. He looked at his mother helplessly, falling half behind her for protection. Janet, it may be believed, was not abashed at all.

"Oh, this is Miss Summerhayes," said Mrs. Harwood. She thought, perhaps, that her son required no introduction in his own house.

"And that's Dolff," said Julia, who was more conscious of the claims of the governess.

The young man himself stood and grinned feebly, an image of confusion and shamefacedness. Janet gave him a bow, a bow which was half a curtsey, with a sweep of grandeur in humility, excessive politeness intended to accentuate the informality of the presentation—and, having said her good-morning to Mrs. Harwood, hurried upstairs. That was all so far as she was concerned, but it was far from being all for the unfortunate Dolff.

"Mother," he said, "why didn't you tell me she was a swell like that?"

"You silly boy! She is no swell at all; but a nice little girl with, now that I think of it, a well-bred air."

"Excessively formal—for her situation in the world," said Gussy.

"Well—I never thought of it before—she has very nice manners; but she has been used to a good deal of attention, and perhaps——"

"You always spoil everybody, mamma. Janet is very nice, but she does not quite know her own place."

"That's not the sort of person a fellow expects to see when he's told there's a new governess," said Dolff. "You might have said something not to let me in for it like this. She'll think me a regular know-nothing, an ignorant cad; everything that's stupid."

Gussy looked up from the unpacking of the portmanteau, now nearly finished, with widely-opened eyes.

"What can it possibly matter what Miss Summerhayes thinks of you?" she said.

"Oh," said Dolff, "I don't see that! Why, she's a—— You mayn't mind, but I do. Let a fellow in for looking as stupid as an owl, and as if he didn't know what's what, and then ask him what does it matter! It does matter to me. I say, Ju, why didn't you tell me she was that sort? I never felt more small in my life."

"I don't think there is any occasion for it, Dolff," said Mrs. Harwood. "Janet's a very sensible girl; she knows exactly what to expect. She is not one of those that are always taking offence. Besides, I don't see that any harm has been done. You took off your hat at once. You're very careless keeping it on and thinking no manners are necessary for your own people, Dolff, that I must say; but so far as concerns Miss Summerhayes——"

"Oh, of course she thinks me a cad, and that's all about it," said the young man; "and you don't care. But, as it happens, I do. What is the good of having people belonging to you, if they can't keep you straight in a business like that? Oh, put the confounded things where you like," said the young man, waving the books away which Priscilla held in her arms waiting for directions; "on the floor, or anywhere; I don't mind anything about your tidiness, but I do mind being shown off as a dashed cad."

He took up his hat, and looked at it, as if that was the cause of offence, then flung it on his head, and stalked out, careless of the calls that followed him.

"Where are you going, Dolff?" his mother said, with a sudden shade of anxiety on her face.

"Mind that you are not late for lunch," said Gussy.

Julia put her arm through his, and accompanied him to the garden door.

"Don't be long; oh, don't be long," said Julia. "Come out for a walk in the afternoon, Dolff, with her and me."

"I don't suppose she'll ever speak to me," said Dolff, shaking his sister off: and he paused to take his pipe from his pocket, and light it before he went forth, while all the ladies looked on through the open hall door. That he should go out with a round hat and a pipe in his mouth was a trial of Gussy's patience, such as was very difficult to endure; and the knowledge that Dolff, when he disappeared in this way, might not, perhaps, come back till midnight wrung the heart of his mother. The first day, too! He was not very much to look at, nor remarkable in any way, but he was of great importance to them.

"It is a mere pretext to get away to follow his own devices," said Gussy, as she rose, red and angry, from her knees.

"Oh, Gussy, the first morning!" said Mrs. Harwood. "I wish some one had told him; he is so particular about being well-bred, poor boy."

"Oh, I have no patience with him," said Gussy, "it is merely a pretence to get away."

CHAPTER XVII.

THE fears of the household, however, were not justified. Dolff dutifully came home to lunch.

Janet, who, instead of being offended and dwelling upon his rudeness, had not thought of him at all, save with a certain passing satisfaction such as moves a woman involuntarily when she perceives that her own appearance has had the effect which it ought to produce—continued to be agreeably impressed during luncheon with the evident awe and admiration which she elicited from the son of the house. He was very quiet, not saying much, civil to his sisters, evidently disposed to please. His appearance did not impress Janet. He was colorless, like the rest of his family, with whiskers and a budding mustache, which, being very light, scarcely showed upon his face: and his form was wanting in those fine proportions which a girl's imagination requires in a hero—the length of limb and commanding height. Dolff was not short, but he was thick, which neutralized his real stature. It is impossible to describe how civil he was—to everybody, to Priscilla when she handed him the potatoes; even to Ju—whom he called Julia. He inquired how she was getting on with her—history. Evidently he did not know what study he ought to inquire into, but selected that as most dignified. This continued during the whole day; for Dolff, to the evident amazement of his family, came in again at five o'clock and drank tea and ate bread-and-butter in large quantities.

"I did not think you ever took tea, Dolff," said his mother, amazed.

"Oh, I think it's very good for a fellow," said Dolff; "better than—other drinks——"

"So do I, my dear," cried his mother, fervently, and was about to make further remarks, even perhaps to improve the occasion, had Gussy not interposed with an imploring glance.

In the evening he suggested a game of backgammon with his mother; the power of virtue could no further go. The ladies kept a close but carefully-concealed watch upon him, expecting the moment when he would break loose, when he would exclaim that he must go out and get a little air, which generally meant that Dolff disappeared for the evening and was seen no more. But he endured like a man these hours of severe domesticity. He looked on while the ladies worked; he stood in front of the fire and told them stories of Oxford, condescending so far to their inferiority as to explain phrases and even to apologize for slang, as well as to throw in several passing biographies of "men" from other colleges with whom he had formed alliances. I could not assert authoritatively that Mrs. Harwood, or even Julia, enjoyed these stories, but they all expressed the utmost interest, plied him with questions, and did everything that could be done to prolong the autobiographical narrative. Occasionally a glance would pass between Mrs. Harwood and her elder daughter—a glance of wonder and satisfaction. Dolff had turned over a new leaf! Dolff had passed without apparent difficulty a long, unbroken evening at home.

The next day Dolff continued in the same good dispositions. He even arranged his books in the little room that was called his study, and retired there for an hour or two to work, as he said. The ladies scarcely ventured to express their delight.

"There is no doubt that Dolff must have turned over a new leaf," said Mrs. Harwood.

"It looks like it," said Gussy, "but we must not build much on the first night."

The second night, however, was even better than the first. Dolff made an offer to Julia to help her with her—history, which made that young lady open her eyes with consternation.

"I'll come and give you a lecture, if you like—if Miss Summerhayes will let me," he said. "I'm an awful dab at history. That's my subject, don't you know. I've given up classics, and I'm going in for history—does a fellow far more good in the world. I'll give you a course of lectures if Miss Summerhayes has no objection."

"Oh, no," cried Janet, demurely, bending her head over her work to hide the laugh which she could scarcely restrain: for it would have been difficult to imagine anything more unlike an academical lecturer than Dolff as he stood, with his legs very wide apart, against the glowing background of the fire. "It would be to my own advantage as well as Julia's," she added, "if Mrs. Harwood would not think it too much——"

"Too much for—me?" asked Dolff. "Oh! mother would be delighted to think I was doing something. I'll come up to-morrow and see what you're about."

"Well, Dolff, I am sure it is very good of you," said Mrs. Harwood; "but I daresay what you learn at the University, where you have the first men to teach you, would perhaps be rather too much for a little girl."

"Oh! if that is all! I think you might trust me, mother, to break it down into nice little scraps," cried Dolff.

"It would only waste Ju's time and keep her back from her—music and other things," said Gussy, suspicious, though she did not well know why.

"Oh, Gussy!—when you know you have always said I never should do anything in music," cried Julia, who saw prospects of fun and congenial idleness in Dolff's proposal.

Janet had suppressed her laugh, and was very grave over her needlework. It was not for her to interfere.

"We'll think it over," said Mrs. Harwood; "you don't always think the same in the morning as in the evening, my dear boy. No doubt it would be for Julia's advantage, for I don't think, any more than Gussy, that she will ever do much at her music. I should like to see into it myself first, and whether it wouldn't interfere with your time, and if you remain in the same mind, and so forth. We'll think it over, Dolff."

"I never knew that the mother considered herself clever about history before," said Dolff, with a laugh. "And what's all this about music? I've grown a great dab at music, too. You've had the piano open these two nights. Who plays? or sings, is it? Oh! I suppose it's you, Gussy. Come along and let us hear."

"I seldom sing alone," said Gussy, with a blush.

"Well, come and sing with me. I'm your man. I've grown quite a dab at it this term. Anything to make the time pass. I thought it was something new when I saw the piano standing open."

"It is nothing at all new, Dolff. Gussy has always had a very pretty voice. She is shy about it by herself, so she generally sings in duets or concerted pieces. But she has a very pretty voice, hasn't she, Janet?"

"Are you musical, Miss Summerhayes?"

"She has a very sweet voice," said Janet. "It came out beautifully the other night."

"Are you musical, Miss Summerhayes?"

Janet paused, believing that some one would answer for her. Then she said.

"I play a little occasionally."

"You could rattle over a little accompaniment?" said Dolff. "Oh, it's not difficult—I could almost do it myself, only one can't play and sing too."

Again Janet hesitated. She cast a glance round the silent company to know what she was expected to do. But Mrs. Harwood gave no sign, and Gussy was abstracted, listening for the step which did not come—and which was so much more important than all the brothers in the world.

"Oh, yes, I think I could rattle over a little accompaniment," said Janet.

"Then come along," cried Dolff, delighted. "I'll fetch some of my songs in a moment. They are not Gussy's sort, and she would not care to play for me, but the mother will like it, won't you, mother? There's a chorus with most of them," said Dolff, pausing half-way to the door. "Perhaps Ju and you could tune up in the chorus? it's not difficult, and it adds to the effect."

"I think, perhaps, I might tune up in the chorus, if it's not very difficult."

"Oh, that's famous," cried Dolff, rushing out of the room.

Janet turned an ingenuous glance to her patronesses.

"Am I doing what you wish?" she said. "Perhaps you will tell me, dear Mrs. Harwood, what it is best to do."

"It will be horrible Christy Minstrels and things," said Gussy; "if any one should come, it would be rather dreadful to have the piano taken up in that way."

"At the same time," cried Mrs. Harwood, "it would be strange if my Dolff could not sing what he pleased in his own mother's house."

"Oh, if you take it in that way," said Gussy.

She gave a furtive glance at the clock. It was getting late; the probabilities were that no one would come to-night. And yet sometimes he came quite late, sometimes he was detained by—business. It was strange that he never should have appeared since that evening of triumph, when they had shared the plaudits of their friends, and had been drawn so close to each other, associated so completely in the common regard. Gussy had felt that something more definite must come into her relations with Charles Meredith after that, and she was restless and *distraite*, unhappy yet subduing her unhappiness, above all things anxious not to betray herself, or to let even her mother suspect what was in her mind. A woman must never betray what she expects, in so far at least as this goes. She went into the other end of the room, voluntarily withdrawing to a distance where she could not hear any step outside, with a fantastic hope that when she was thus out of the way it might come: and moved about, displacing some small pieces of furniture, rustling among the music on the piano, which was chiefly *his* music with his name upon it, in order to give him a chance of arriving unheard. Poor little device of the strained nerves and sick heart! No one suspected what was in Gussy's mind except the last person whom she could have desired to know it—Janet, who followed her movements with a half-contempt, half-sympathy. Janet herself was fancy free; though she was immensely interested in Charles Meredith and his present movements, it was solely with the interest which is felt in a story, to see what would happen next; and she had all a girl's indignation against the woman who thus let herself go and depended upon a man's decision for her happiness. At Janet's age a girl resents and scorns such a renunciation of the woman's rights: yet follows the sufferer with an inalienable pity and wonder, too.

Dolff came back excited with a sheaf of songs.

"Now, Miss Summerhayes, if you will be so good," he said. He threw off the pile of music that was on the piano. "Oh, that's all classic stuff," he said, "I can see with half an eye—and as dull as ditch-water—"C. Meredith"—it seems all to belong to C. Meredith. I hope you'll find mine a little more lively, Miss Summerhayes. It's Meredith and Gussy that carry on all that, ain't it?" he said, with a wink and whisper. "Oh, you needn't be afraid—I know."

Janet sat down at the piano without making any reply, and Julia stood by as audience. Dolff placed himself at one side, facing towards the further room in which his mother was sitting. He had turned her chair round a little, that she might see the performance, which, indeed, was supposed to gain in effect from the looks and gestures of the performer. And then there ensued the most curious exhibition of native fatuity, vanity, and simplicity that could be imagined. Janet (perhaps even more important than any other spectator) had the privilege of seeing his face, too, and all the grimaces he made, as he stood facing an imaginary audience. The ladies listened to him in a silence which was almost awful.

Janet, whose hands were busy now, was in no way responsible for Dolff: and the one who could see everything that was ridiculous in the exhibition without being humiliated by it was the one who was best off. But for Mrs. Harwood, listening with a gasp to her son's performance, seeing his contortions of face, his gestures, his complacency, the moment was terrible. And even Julia, though she was not much more than a child, and disposed to receive all her brother did as admirable, gazed at him open-mouthed with horror in her face. Gussy had given him but one look, and then had strayed out into the hall. She was not capable of judging. Her mind was too much distracted with other thoughts. She went into the hall with a pretence of something to do there, and even into the dining-room on the other side, where all was dark, yet where she penetrated, to carry back a vase with flowers, groping her way. It was so near the garden, the hall door, the outer road. Nobody could pass or come to the gate without being audible. Poor Gussy pretended even to herself that her sole object was to take back the flowers which had been moved into the drawing-room by mistake, though they belonged to the decoration of the dinner-table. She knocked against the displaced chairs and the corner of the table as she went in in the dark, thus preventing herself from hearing any sound outside; and when those noises were still her heart beat so loudly as to drown all sound—of the less importance, as there was no sound to hear!

"Dolff," said Mrs. Harwood, "that is surely a new style for you. I don't remember ever hearing you sing songs like these before."

"I have been having some lessons," said Dolff; "they are all the rage just now. You never learn anything else in Oxford."

"Oh," said Mrs. Harwood; but she said no more, and Dolff, who did not care very much for her opinion, turned to Janet.

"You don't do yourself justice, Miss Summerhayes," he said. "You played that first-rate. You must have heard Arthur Roberts, or some of them, to do it as well as that."

"No," said Janet, "I never heard of Arthur Roberts. Who is he?" a question which made Dolff laugh—"scream with laughing,"—he said to himself.

"Oh, you *are* original! Who is Arthur Roberts?—that is a good one! Who is Shakespeare? You might just as well ask one question as the other. But you play as if—as if you had been all your life at the Vic. I never heard any one play so well before."

CHAPTER XVIII.

IT was not till some evenings after this that Mr. Charles Meredith made his appearance again.

To tell the truth, he had been a little alarmed by his position in respect to Miss Harwood. The applause they had received at the concert, which somehow enveloped both of them in a sort of unity—a oneness which was embarrassing, and provoked inquiries and looks of intelligence, glances and hints of all sorts—had given him a little shock. It had not affected Gussy in the same way, for Gussy was far more deeply and truly touched than her partner in that success. She had given up her whole being to him with the unreasonable confidence which is sometimes to be seen in an otherwise unimaginative and unemotional woman, never doubting from the first the object of his attentions, feeling that he could have but one reason for his frequent visits, and that the gradual manner in which she herself had been separated and swept up, as it were, into his identity, was the natural result of a strong and certain desire on his part to attract and appropriate her—an unquestionable feeling to which her gradually elicited responses were natural and fitting. It never occurred to Gussy, who was a little narrow, as was natural to her education and circumstances, but very sensible and just, that Meredith's sentiments, which had been so distinctly shown, could be anything but definite and certain. To her there appeared nothing accidental, nothing fortuitous, in the way in which it had all come about. Gradually he had secured the *entrée* and the complete freedom of intercourse which is not very common in English houses. There had been a break during his absence in the country, but this break had been followed by a return to all the old habits, by the resumption of all his claims upon her attention and sympathy, those claims to which she had already responded in all sincerity and good faith. Gussy had no sensation of having gone a step further than she had been led and persuaded to go. She had no doubt whatever that of this intercourse, which he had so sought, so organized, so firmly established, every step was intended. He had set himself, she believed, to win her love, to gain her heart. What other reason could there be? It was all his doing. He it was who had pressed for each new extension of privilege: for what?—for no conceivable reason save one, that he loved her, and desired to make her love him.

Such was Gussy's theory. She had been first flattered, then touched by these assiduities, and finally, there being no reason whatever against it, she had yielded to the gradually growing response in her own bosom. She was not unaware that this might attain to greater potency than the demand which had evoked it, for he was a man, about in the world, and having a great many things to distract him, whereas she was a woman with nothing particular in her mind save this new interest which filled her thoughts night and day. There was no doubt that it might grow more engrossing than his love. She was aware of the danger, and quite reasonable about it; but his had been the first—his had been the foundation of all. She was not ashamed of loving him, nor even of the impatience that now devoured her to have him speak and put the whole on the footing of a known and established certainty. It wanted that, at the point to which the matter had now reached. As soon as they had once understood each other, all would be well. Understood each other! Yes, they did so already; but it was necessary that it should be clear—spoken out—settled. Gussy could not tell what it was that restrained her lover. But she was restless and a little impatient, knowing that, by this time, the certainty ought to be fully comprehended of all, and the result known.

It had not been anything in the nature of jealousy which had made her unwilling to take advantage of Janet's services, but only an indisposition to let any third party come in—to have another associated in the already long-lingering duet which she had every reason to believe was to continue all her life. He had chosen that way of drawing her to him which, in the circumstances of the family, was the most effectual way, the easiest—perhaps the only manner in which he could have secured the attention which was due to her mother and sister first, and which it would otherwise have been so difficult to obtain. And it had become a method dear to her—and she did not like to have any one come in, to disturb the isolation in which their music wrapped them. This was all—no fear of a new face or attraction for him—no feeling of rivalry.

Janet was perhaps incapable of comprehending how very far the young woman, so much less clever, less instructed in the usual course of affairs, perhaps less intelligent than herself, was from thinking of any such danger.

But all this was quite apart from Mr. Charles Meredith and his sentiments, which had not at any time been those believed in by Gussy. He had found it amusing and piquant to make his way into that secluded, but most respectably secluded, house in St. John's Wood. A little curiosity of his own, the secret of a something to be found out even in the heart of that respectability, had for a moment mingled with his other motives; but that had found little encouragement in anything he saw or heard, and had gradually died out, leaving behind a pleasurable privilege—an amusing variety to his other engagements, an ever-ready way of spending an evening in which he had nothing else to do. He had known the Harwoods almost all his life, and this familiarity, to begin with, had made the domestic circle the more easily comprehensible to him: the unmanageable child, Ju, who lost no opportunity of showing how undesirable she thought his presence; the mother, mysteriously incapable of leaving her chair, though her children frankly declared their disbelief in her inability; the room so bright and full of comfort with that shadowy background which seemed made for a romance, tickled the fancy of the young man. He had an inclination towards Gussy Harwood—liked her—felt that, if he were ever to come the length of marrying, she would be a very suitable wife for him, and her respectable fortune a very comfortable foundation on which to begin life. And then he was very fond of music—music, that is, represented by new songs and duets in which his own fine tenor might be enhanced by a gentle soprano acknowledged to be very sweet, yet in no way capable of eclipsing the richer tones it accompanied.

All these mingled sentiments had led him to the course of conduct which he had pursued for some time before Janet's appearance, but into which her sudden appearance had imported a little difference. It will be seen that these vague and mingled sentiments were entirely unlike that for which he had credit in the mind of Augusta Harwood—the steady and serious love by which she supposed him to be moved. The foregone conclusion of a happy marriage, a household equally respectable, and still more bright than that in which the preliminaries took place had no existence. It was always on the cards, of course, that Gussy Harwood and he might marry and settle down together. It would not be a very romantic conclusion, still Meredith was aware that he himself was not at all a romantic personage, and it would not in any way be a bad arrangement. But where was the need of going so far as that? He liked to know where he could spend an evening pleasantly when he pleased; he liked to hear the sound of his own voice, and even to feel that the voice of the other performer was not likely to beguile the applauses of their audience away from himself—when they had an audience; he liked to have those excellent dinners from time to time, with the other man who could not help perceiving how entirely the entertainment was for Meredith's gratification. All these things were very pleasant, and Mrs. Harwood was quite able, no doubt, to take care of her own daughter and all the *convenances*, and it was none of his business to watch over Gussy in case his continual visits should be misunderstood.

But the concert had certainly made a little crisis in this easy intercourse—the concert and Janet's appearance on the scene, and the little excitement she had produced, and the additional signs of regard it had been necessary to lavish upon Gussy, to make her feel herself always the first person, notwithstanding any interest that another might call forth. He had felt that a great step had been taken in that concert. To be sure it could not, strictly speaking, be asserted to mean anything at all. A duet between a soprano and a tenor—what more innocent? Their voices suited; what had their persons or their lives to do with it? Charles Meredith knew, however, that though this might be true enough in the case of most tenors and sopranos, it would not be true as between Gussy Harwood and himself. The audience was not an audience drawn from the larger public, which might have known nothing further, but a St. John's Wood audience, which knew everything about him, and that he visited the Harwoods "every day of his life." This was not exactly true, but it was how he heard it stated in the dark, outside the concert-room, by one of the departing hearers. All those present knew them, and knew all about them, and naturally made their remarks: "Of course it will be a match; he is there every day of his life."

What a vulgar definiteness there is in these criticisms! People who pretend to be one's friends, yet speak of one without a gleam of understanding, as if all one's intentions were cut and dry. Meredith felt angry, but he dared not show it, for it was clearly his duty to escort Gussy home, and to tell Mrs. Harwood what a success it had been. But after that he was seized with a panic, and did not come back. He saw that a crisis had come, as well as any one—a crisis which seemed to him very premature, and for which he was unprepared.

I think there is some allowance to be made for young men who in these days hesitate about taking the last step which makes marriage inevitable. We are not now discussing the so-called "smart" people, who live after their kind, and afford no rule for the rest of the world, but young men of occupations, who have, as people say, their own way to make. A small income very often represents a great deal more than it is to an unmarried man, with all the luxury of the clubs behind him: and it represents a great deal less than it is to the man who is going to marry—witness all the foolish statistics periodically placed before the world. It is rather surprising how, when the moment and the impulse comes, all these precautions are so easily thrown to the winds: but there is nobody in modern society so well off as the young man with a small competency, a good club, and a tolerable acquaintance. It is heroic of him to risk all his comforts and immunities, the things he can do, and the things nobody expects him to do, for the sake of a young woman who on her side is much better off at home, if she would only think so. But, fortunately for the race if not for the individual, nature scorns all such judicious reflections, and follows its own impulse at whatsoever expense.

Meredith, however, who was not in love, but only amiably, pleasurably inclined towards Gussy Harwood, felt their full force when he was thus pulled up and brought face to face with inevitable consequences. In his present circumstances he was very well off indeed: he had all that a young man could desire. He knew a number of people, and was civil to them, and derived from this a little benefit of dinner-parties, dances, and invitations from Saturday till Monday, for which he was not expected to do anything except to continue to be civil in return. And he could also entertain at his club a friend or two when he pleased. I do not know whether the dinners at the more modest clubs are as good as those of which we read in novels, at which the very fine gentlemen dispense and enjoy hospitality; but they are almost sure to be better than those which a Mrs. Charles Meredith, in a little villa in the suburbs, or in a little flat high up in the district styled W., could produce with great trouble, a complete *bouleversement* of the small household, and a greengrocer from round the corner to wait. The servants at the club are real servants, the dinners quite genuine, and giving no extra trouble. If Charles Meredith had been in love, it would have been unpardonable in him to have made any such reflection. But then he was not in love. And he was startled, and paused in the face of fate.

He might not perhaps have done so with quite so much perturbation if there had not been at the same time a little point of interest in his mind about the other little girl who had appeared so inopportunely in St. John's Wood. He was not in the least in love with Janet. But she was amusing—a great deal more amusing than Gussy, with all whose opinions and inclinations he was acquainted, and who changed little from any standing-point she had once taken. It amused him to get possession of the governess, to make her play, to watch her looks, and communicate with her telegraphically, nobody being aware of that intercourse. That Janet did not respond, or, at least, did not willingly respond, made it all the more piquant, for even a glance of indignation now and then, a flash of anger, was a reply, and he could read in the involuntary movement of her little shoulders, as she played, a hundred little criticisms and signs of what she was thinking; the thrill of displeasure at a false note made him laugh, and the clang of accompaniment with which she would suddenly drown a failure—all this imported a new element into the evening with which he was delighted. But all these amusements would have to be put a stop to if he married and settled down to domestic felicity and the enjoyment of a sensible companion and a comfortable life at home.

All of which things made Charles Meredith pause; but after a week or so he began to feel that his hesitation, if too prolonged, would in its way produce a decision which he desired as little as the other. And then he remembered that Dolff was at home, which would always make a diversion and stave off explanations. These deliberations have seemed to occupy a long period; yet it was not, after all, a very long period. About ten days after the concert, the door being open to admit of the exit of Dolff, who, in all the glories of evening costume, was stepping forth towards a waiting hansom, ready to convey him to some evening festivity, Charles Meredith slipped in unheard, with his usual little roll of music, but less than his usual confidence and calm. He was met in the hall by Julia, who had come out to superintend her brother's departure, and whose pleasure in Dolff's entertainment and finery was brought to a sudden pause by the apparition of a figure less beloved. She gave vent, having no watch upon her, to that sound which had died from her lips, or rather from her teeth, for so long, but with which she had been wont to welcome Meredith.

"Oh!" or rather "S—s!" said Julia, "so this is you—again——"

"Yes, my dear child, it is I—again," he replied, with a mocking bow and smile.

CHAPTER XIX.

MEREDITH paused at the door inspecting the quiet interior thus thrown open to him—in which he was not looked for, and where, accordingly, his arrival remained unobserved—the doors being all open still for the exit of Dolff. It startled him a little to find in how like its ordinary condition everything was, and how little sign of the absence of a habitual visitor was about the place. There were a hundred signs of Dolff, but even the place near Gussy usually though tacitly reserved for himself was filled up, and Gussy sat at the eternal woman's work which, in some circumstances, is so exasperating to a man, as composed as if he had never crossed her horizon. They were all at it, Mrs. Harwood with her crewels, Janet with something else. He wondered, half-angrily, if they would go on forever with their heads bowed over that infernal sewing whatever might happen, even that quick little thing, that creature born under more variable skies, the governess. She, however, was the first to find him out. A consciousness of some new element in the warm atmosphere, something that had not been there a minute before, moved Janet. She looked up and uttered a faint exclamation.

Ah! he had thought there was no difference, but there had been a difference. Gussy had been sitting like a statue, quite still, but not the faintest thrill of movement in her. She did not expect him, or anyone, she was not thinking of him, or anyone, quite self-contained, self-absorbed. He was almost ashamed to think how he had been thinking of her, complacently realizing her suspense, and disappointment, and wonder at his non-appearance. The extreme composure of her aspect gave Meredith a shock which would have done much to redress the balance between them. She did not even raise her head at Janet's exclamation. It was Mrs. Harwood who did that, crying out, "God bless me! Charley!" with a pleasure of which there could be no doubt. And a sort of shock passed over Gussy, electric, spasmodic, he could not tell what it was, something that moved her from the crown of light hair on her head to the tip of the shoe which was visible under her gown. It all passed in a minute, nay, in a second, as so many a crisis does. He could see it go over her; had not his eyes been opened by a sense of guilt, and by various other convictions, he might have known nothing of it; but he did, and suddenly became aware that he had something more to deal with than a girl's momentary annoyance at the absence of the man whom she was beginning to care for. At the end of that moment, when he had come forward to shake hands with Mrs. Harwood, Gussy rose, and gave him her hand with perfect composure. On her side she was quite sure that she had betrayed nothing, not even the mere surprise which would have been so natural.

"You have been a great stranger, Charley," said Mrs. Harwood.

"Yes, indeed," he said, "no one can know that so well as I. I have been driven to the end of my patience. I kept hoping that one of you would take a little interest, and ask what I was about."

He kept his eyes on Gussy, but Gussy never moved or gave sign of consciousness.

"My dear boy," said Mrs. Harwood, "women never like to interfere—to ask what a young man is about. You are so much more your own masters than we are. We know very well that if you want to come you will come, and if you don't——"

"How unjust you are with your general principles! Here is one poor miserable exception, then, to the rule—who has tried to come, and thought he could manage it evening after evening. Well, it is all in the way of business. You have always been afraid I was idle. What will you say when I tell you that I have been in chambers—sometimes till eight and nine o'clock every night?"

"I shall hope it means a lot of new clients, Charley," the old lady said.

"Well, I think it does."

He did not wink at Janet—oh, no! that would have been vulgarity itself—the sort of communication which takes place between the footman in a play and the chamber-maid who is in his confidence. Mr. Charles Meredith's manners were irreproachable, and vulgarity in that kind of way impossible to him. But he did catch Janet's attention with a corner of his eye, as it were, which expressed something a little different from the open look which was bent on Mrs. Harwood—or, rather, on Gussy, at whom he glanced as he spoke. And then he entered into certain details. Mrs. Harwood, though she was disabled and incapable of getting out of her chair, was an excellent woman of business, and she entered into the particulars of his narrative with great interest. She said at the end, with a satisfied nod of her head,

"Well, Charley, I hope we may now feel that you are beginning to catch the rising tide."

"I hope so, too," said the young man. And then it seemed to dawn upon him that these agreeable auguries might lead him too far. "A little time will tell," he said, "whether it's a real beginning or only a flash in the pan. I am afraid to calculate upon anything too soon. In three months or so, if all goes on well——"

Janet asked herself, with a keenness of inquiry which took her by surprise, what, oh, what did he mean by three months? Was that said for Gussy? Was it said for anyone else? Did he, by any possibility, think that *she* cared—that it pleased her to know that he was deceiving Mrs. Harwood and her daughter? She felt very angry at the whole matter, which she thought she saw through so completely, but which, after all, she did not in the least see through. Janet thought that for some reason or other this young man was "amusing himself," according to the ordinary jargon, with Miss Harwood's too-little concealed devotion, that he secretly made fun of the woman who loved him, and was preparing, when the time came, a disenchantment for her and revelation of his own sentiments, which would probably break Gussy's heart. It can scarcely be said that Janet felt those sentiments of moral indignation which such a deliberate treachery ought to have called forth. She was still so far in the kitten stage that it half amused her to see Mr. Meredith "taking in" Miss Harwood. It amused her to think that probably he had been having some wild party of his young men friends (a party of young men always seems wild, riotous, full of inconceivable frolic and enjoyment to a girl's fancy) in his chambers, on some of those evenings which he so demurely represented to the old lady as full of business. She could not help an inclination to laugh at that. It is the kind of deceit which has always been laughed at from the beginning of time. But she felt angry about the three months. What did he mean by three months? Was it for Gussy to lull her suspicions? Was it for—anyone else? Janet felt as if she were being made a party to some unkind scheme which had not merely fun for its purpose. Why should he look at her in that comic way when he said anything particularly grave? Janet turned round her little shoulder to Mr. Meredith, and became more and more engrossed in her needlework. But yet it was strange that whatever she did he succeeded in catching her eye.

"Some one has been singing," he said, presently, with a little start of surprise. "I brought something with me I thought Gussy would like—but you have been singing without me?"

He turned round upon her suddenly at this point. Gussy had been very quiet; she had said scarcely anything. She had allowed him to go through all those explanations with her mother. At first she had closed her heart, as she thought, against them; but it is not so easy to close a heart when it is suddenly melted by a touch of thaw after a frost. Gussy had been frozen up hard as December—or even February—could do it. But what is frost when there comes that indescribable, that subtle, invisible breath which in a moment undoes what it has taken nights and days of black frost to do?

What a good thing it is to think that the frost which works underhand and throws its ribs across the streams, and its icicles from the roofs by degrees, takes days to make ice that will "bear," and that the sweeter influence can bring all that bondage to ruin in an hour or two! Gussy's heart had frozen up, putting on an additional layer of ice every day; but in a moment it was all gone, sliding away in blocks, in shapeless masses, upon the irresistible flood. The flood, of course, is all the stronger from that mass of melted stuff that sweeps into it, giving an impetus to every swollen current. Gussy made an effort to feel as if this melting and softening had not been, as if she were as she had been an hour before; but what attempt could be more ineffectual? Frost may counterfeit a thaw on the surface when the sun shines; but what thaw can counterfeit frost. It was not among the things that are possible.

"I have not been singing," she said, softly, her eyes wandering, in spite of her, to the little roll in his hand. "You forget we have had something else to amuse us all these evenings. It is Dolff who has been singing."

"And a very nice voice he has got, now that it has been trained a little, poor boy," said his mother, "though I am not very sure that I like his taste in songs."

"And Miss Summerhayes plays for him," said Meredith, turning round upon Janet with a laugh. He faced her this time, looking at her frankly, not trying to catch any corner of her eye. His look had a gleam of merriment and saucy satisfaction which make Janet glow with anger. "Didn't I tell you so?" he seemed to say with his raised eyebrows. He laughed out with a genial roar of amusement. "I knew Miss Summerhayes would play for him," he cried.

How did he know anything of the kind? How dared he laugh in that meaning way? How dared he look at Janet as if he had found her out; as if she, too, had a scheme like himself? Janet gave him a look in return which might have turned a more sensitive man to stone, and she said, with great dignity, wrapping herself up in the humility of her governess-state as in a mantle:

"I am here to play for anyone who wishes for my services, Mr. Meredith, as I think you ought to know."

"Good heavens," cried Mrs. Harwood, "my dear child! I hope you don't take it in that serious way. If it is so disagreeable to you, my dear, you shall never be asked to humor poor Dolff again."

"Oh, Mrs. Harwood, that is not what I meant! I am very glad to do it for anyone, but I don't like to hear people talk—to hear people laugh——"

"The little thing is in a temper," said Meredith, aside to Gussy, "have I said anything so very dreadful? Come and try whether they have thumped the piano all to pieces, and then we can talk."

"I don't know that you have said anything dreadful. And we can talk very well here," said Gussy, in the same undertone.

"She is like a little turkey-cock," said Meredith. "What has been going on? To think that something should always turn up, a farce or a tragedy, when one is out of the way for a few days."

Gussy asked herself, with a catching of the breath, if it were a farce or a tragedy? How true that was! No, it would not be a tragedy now—now that he had come back.

"Nothing has been going on—except some silly songs," she said.

It did not occur to her that her own songs were silly, or that there might be two meanings to the word, but Meredith was more ready in his comprehension.

"Ah, some silly songs!" he said.

Upon which Gussy, feeling more and more the soft welling-up from under the crackling frost, of the warmer waters, felt a compunction.

"Poor Dolff," she said, "is not altogether exalted in his tastes, you know. And he has taken a music-hall craze. I suppose it is from the music-hall they come, all those wonderful performances. But he likes them, it appears, as well—as well——"

"As we like ours," said Meredith.

"Well, ours——" she colored a little as she said the word; but why should she not say it, seeing he had thus given her the cue? "Ours are better worth liking. At the same time," said Gussy, returning to her old self, "we are all so silly in this family that we can't do anything without doing a great deal too much of it. We can't, I fear, take anything moderately. We do it with all our heart."

"That is why you do it so well," said Meredith.

His voice had a slight quaver in it, which might have been taken in more senses than one. It might have meant emotion, and again it might have meant a suppressed laugh, for to imagine that Dolff sang his music-hall songs exceptionally well because he sang them with all his heart was a little trying to the gravity. But now that he had set up a conversation *sotto voce*, and now that Gussy had been brought back to talking of what was habitually done "in the family," Mr. Meredith felt that he had got back upon the old ground.

As for Janet, she packed up her sewing things in her little basket, and begged Mrs. Harwood's permission to retire.

"I have a little headache," she said.

Good Mrs. Harwood was much concerned and very sorry, but agreed that quiet and going to bed early was the best thing for a headache. And when the lovers—were they the lovers?—went to the other room, Janet rose and stole away. She was not gone so soon but that she heard Meredith burst into a laugh over Dolff's songs, which were all scattered about. He sang a snatch of one of them mockingly as she was going out, and caught her with a wave of his hand, an elevation of his eyebrows, and a slight nod of his head. He would not let her escape, he who had so easily made up his own difficulties, but must discharge that arrow at her, hold that whip of mockery over her. Janet closed the door upon herself with a studied quiet, which was even more demonstrative of her state of mind than had she shut it with a violent slam, as Julia would have done; but it was more hard to suppress the pants of her laboring, angry breath.

CHAPTER XX.

JANET sent out before her into the hall a bursting sigh, a hot wave of impatient fiery breath, which seemed to raise a little mist before her eyes as she emerged into the silence and found herself alone, leaving mockery and music, and sentiment true or false, behind. What did he mean, what did he want, that visitor whose non-appearance had held the household in suspense, whose coming had introduced so many elements of disturbance? It cannot be said that Janet herself had been uninfluenced by his absence. It had been a fact of which she could not get rid, always present with her as with Gussy, though in a different way. Certainly he had taken away much of the salt of life with him—the interest, the drama. And now that he had come back the salt had not lost its savor; it was almost too keen: it affected sharply not only the chief personage in the piece, but the audience. He was now more than actor—he was audience also; and that look of intelligence which had conveyed so many confidences on his own part now expressed the most daring suggestions as to hers. Janet burst out of the room with a sense that her period of peace was over. His looks would put motives to the most trifling actions. What had he to do with her? How dared he to suggest that this booby, this music-hall hero, this cherished only son, could in any way affect the life of Janet? "Miss Summerhayes plays his accompaniments." The tone was light enough, the laugh as light; but it stung Janet to the very depths of her heart.

Something cold and fresh blowing in her face made her turn to the door, which had been left inadvertently open, filling the house with the chill of December. Outside it was a beautiful night—the moon shining full, the stars sparkling with that keen glitter which is given by frost, the shadows of the leafless trees standing as if engraved upon the whiteness, not a breath stirring. Moonlight is always an attraction to a girl, and the outer air the best calmer of feverish thoughts. She caught a shawl from the stand, and wrapping it round her, went softly out. Everything was very still. Talk of the silence of the hills! The hills have sounds innumerable that can never be silenced—movements of birds, of insects, of living creatures of all kinds; rustlings among the heather; tinklings of water; the air itself, occupying vast fields of space, has a breath—which means silence, but is not. But, if you like, the silence, in St. John's Wood! That is something worth speaking of. There was not a sound. At long intervals, when anybody moved in the world outside, you could hear the distant footstep walk out of the unknown, advance step by step as if it had been that of a messenger of doom, diverge, pass away again, grow fainter and fainter till it went out in the stillness like the withdrawal of a light. That mystic, unseen passage occurred from time to time, but faintly at a distance. Sometimes there came into the absolute stillness a distant jar of wheels, increasing and diminishing in the same manner, going out in space.

When Janet stole out, in her little thin evening shoes that made no sound, the house stood surrounded by that intense quiet and moonlight like a house in a dream. Like its own enclosure of humble human garden soil, that mystic atmosphere isolated and surrounded it from everything else in the world. It was almost an awe to steal round the white path, and cross the branching shadows that lay over it in all the complication of their elaborate anatomy, and watch the dark and solid dwelling standing in the midst, surrounded by all that reverence of nature, with a touch of yellow light here and there in its windows, and such foolish evanescent fret and jar of feelings and thoughts within! Janet's own little step, which was scarcely so much as the stir of a bird, struck, she felt, a half-guilty little broken note into the profound calm. The chill of the air cooled her little head. She was so small, so insignificant an atom in that silent world, troubled about matters so infinitesimally little, so unworthy to be breathed in the all-listening ear of night.

She had made the round of the garden, which was a long piece of ground, more than half of it grass, and of a very woodland aspect for anything so near London, and was about passing the side of the house on her way back, when Janet's attention was suddenly roused in a very extraordinary way. The house was square, of the commonest comfortable form, but on the western side there had been built on to it, at some previous period, a wing, which projected in front, making a gable, and slightly outpassing the *corps du logis*. This wing, however, was not, so far as Janet knew, ever used at all. If used, it was as a lodging or workshop, whatever his employment might be, for the mysterious Vicars, who yet was not mysterious at all—the man-servant of whom more had been seen since Dolff's return home, and who, Janet had vaguely understood, lived in some corner of the house, carrying on his own avocations, whatever they were, but at hand when he was wanted for any special service—a privilege given by the kindness of Mrs. Harwood to an old servant, but also a convenience to herself. It was after Janet had seen this personage carrying through an open door, which had all the appearance at other times of being hermetically closed, a tray covered with dainties, that Mrs. Harwood herself had explained the position of Vicars to the governess, thus settling the question.

Nothing could possibly be more uninhabited, more shut-up and empty, than the wing. It had two long windows on the upper floor, facing the garden, which were so grown over with ivy that it was clearly apparent no light could enter, or human uses be served by them. The ivy was carefully trained, and perhaps a little thinner than usual at this time of the year. As Janet came opposite the windows, something—she could not tell what—made her look up. The moonlight was streaming full upon them, showing white crevices and reflections in the half-covered window-panes which never showed by day. She stopped short, struck by an alarm and horror which seemed to freeze the blood in her veins. At the nearest window, in an opening made by the curvature of a great ivy branch half denuded of leaves, there appeared to her the face of an old man with white hair and a long, white beard—a white image so like the moonlight that, after the first dreadful realization of what she saw as a face, Janet, in her terror, tried to persuade herself that it was only some effect of the white light shining upon the panes, which were covered by dust and the droppings of the heavy foliage. If she had hurried away then, flying indoors, as was her first impulse, no doubt she would have been able to persuade herself that this was the case. But she was, on the other hand, too much frightened, too much excited, to fly. She stood still, scarcely able to draw her breath.

A pale, very pale face, with a long, white beard—patriarchal, like the beard of a prophet—white hair, deep-sunken, aged eyes, looking up towards the moon. A sort of frenzy of terror caught hold upon Janet, so that she could not move. Who was it? Who was it? Vague recollections flew across her mind of things she had read—of an old, blind, mad king whom she remembered in her history—of—she knew not what. The thoughts thronged over her mind like clouds o'er the sky, and she could take no count of them. For there could be no king, no martyr, no prison, no madhouse here. Who was it? Who was it? In a house in St. John's Wood, the most respectable, the most perfectly well-known and well-established, in the midst of the quiet, within the tranquil garden, surrounded by all the decorums of society. Who—oh, who could it be?

She stood transfixed, not thinking that she herself in the midst of that white light, a little dark figure, all surrounded and isolated by the brightness, was more clearly distinguishable than anything about her, and, indeed, could scarcely fail to catch the eye of any one that might be looking. Janet did not think of this, her whole mind being occupied with her extraordinary discovery. She was afraid of being seen. She never realized the possibility—until suddenly, all in a moment as she stood and gazed, her whole bewildered being lost in wonder and amaze, she discovered, with a second shock even more potent than the first, that the face in the window had changed its direction and turned towards herself. Whether it was that Janet was too terrified to have the strength to fly, or whether that she was not so terrified as she thought, and more eager, more curious than she was frightened, it is certain that, though she shrank back a step upon herself, she did not run away, but stood there gazing with her heart in her mouth, and the sensation tingling through and through her that not only did she see this extraordinary being, a real person, whoever he was, but that he saw her. The head, with its white hair, turned slowly from contemplating the sky to contemplating her. He began to make signs to her, beckoning, bending forward, till the crown of white hair was pressed against the pane, and seemed to sparkle and reflect, as if those patriarchal locks had been spun glass, the hard white blaze of the moon. Janet felt as if she could neither move nor breathe. It was real—it was not a dream—it was a man shut up there, who saw her, made signs, called for her help—an old man—a man in trouble. Her head seemed to go round, though her feet were planted on the path as if they had grown to it, or frozen there. What was she to do? What could she do?

At this moment there came from within, from the room whence there stole a ray or two of yellow lamp-light out into the whiteness of the moon, the sound of music—a few notes—tremulous notes—with which she was very familiar; and then rising together the two voices, also so familiar, every tone of which she could have anticipated. The sound made a diversion in her thoughts. She turned her head for a minute that way with a thrill of sensation, wondering if they could but see what she saw—if they only knew! It was so strange to realize, as she did, with a sudden flash of consciousness, the tranquil room, the mother in her chair with her mild face full of gratification and reflected pleasure turned towards the pair at the piano in perfect composure and ease—the two singers busy with their music, with themselves, thinking of nothing else. She took her eyes from the window in her startled realization of all this, and turned her head for a moment in the direction of those unconscious people, who did not know—
— In that moment, while her eyes were averted, the air was suddenly rent, torn asunder, cleft by the same wild, unnatural, and awful cry which Janet had twice heard before. Her feet, which had seemed growing to the path, were loosened with a spring, and Janet too uttered a scream which she could not restrain. Where was it? Though she was wild with terror, she had yet sense enough left to see that the figure at the window had altered its position, and that it was from thence that the sound came. But her strength was equal to no more. She fled, forgetting all precautions, her feet flying over the hard path to the open door. She was dimly aware that the music had wavered, half stopped, and then gone on again, Gussy's voice coming out loudly upon the night. After that Janet knew no more. She burst into the house, and stood panting in the hall, recovering her breath, not knowing what to do.

What was she to do? She stood leaning against the wall inside, safe from pursuit. And it was not till some time later that it occurred to her that, instead of being safe from pursuit, she was within the very walls of the house which inclosed the mystery, and that the prisoner, the maniac, whoever he was, the pale old man with the white hair, was an inmate of the same dwelling, and therefore she was within his reach far more easily than she had been outside. But this in her panic she did not think of. For the moment she felt securely sheltered, and stood gasping, recovering her breath, asking herself what she should do. They were singing in the drawing-room, singing as if all was right, as if nothing could ever be wrong. Had they not heard it? Did they not care? They had not seen as she had, but how could they remain unconscious after that cry? Should she walk in and tell them—tell them? What should she tell them? That there was some one shut up in the wing—an old man with white hair, with his pallid face pressed against the window between the branches of the ivy? How could she go and tell them this? "Mrs. Harwood, there is a man—an old man—at the window—in the wing——" Was that what she should say? Some door might have been open and some madman got in. But then it was not the first time she had heard that cry. He must have been there for some time— he must have been there before she herself came. Perhaps—perhaps—how could she tell?—perhaps Mrs. Harwood already knew—perhaps—— Janet panted and gasped, but after a time got back her breath. But still she stood there thinking, wondering over her problem. What was she to do? Was it, perhaps, her part to do nothing—to ignore this sight she had seen—to try to forget it? Was it none of her business to interfere? Was it her duty to tell at once her appalling discovery? What was she to do?

In the meantime she had not closed the door, which still stood open, letting in the cold air of the night; and presently, while she still stood trembling, steps approached from the servants' quarters. It was Vicars who made his appearance, and Janet almost had a new shock of terror as the man to whom she had never spoken before came up and looked at her severely with suspicious eyes. He asked, in a tone as severe as his look,

"Was it you, miss, as left the hall door open, to give everybody their death?"

"I—I found it open," Janet said, faltering.

"If a person finds a door open of a cold night it's their part, if they've any sense, to shut it," said Vicars. He never removed his look from her, fixing her with the eyes of a judge. "May I ask, miss, if it's your custom to go ranging about the grounds at this hour of the night?"

"Oh, no," said Janet, "it was only an accident. I never did it before."

"I am only a servant," said Vicars, "but if I was the master I wouldn't hold with folks going round and round of my house in the middle of the night looking things up."

"I have not been looking anything up," said Janet, indignantly. She stood by while he closed the door; but when he turned to go away, made a step after him timidly. "Oh!" she said, "if you would only let me speak to you for a moment. Mr. Vicars, you said you were a servant——"

"Did you take me for the master, miss?" he said, with a low laugh.

"Oh!" said Janet, "if you would but tell me. Who is the old gentleman at the window with the white hair? And why does he cry so? I will never, never say a word if you will but tell me. I am so frightened, I don't know what to do."

"There is no gentleman at the window—and he don't cry," said Vicars, fixing her once more with keen eyes.

"But I saw him—and I've heard him, oh! three times. Mr. Vicars, tell me, for goodness' sake, does Mrs. Harwood know?"

"You'd best go and tell her, and see what she'll say. You'll not stop another night in this house if you bother the missus with what you hear and see. You may take my word for it, Miss Peep and Pry."

"You are very impertinent," said Janet, indignantly, "and I do not care in the least whether I stop here another night or not. Does Mrs. Harwood know?"

"I'd advise you, miss, not to offer her no information," said Vicars, "about things as happen in her own house;" and with this he turned his back on Janet, and went deliberately away.

Should she go and tell Mrs. Harwood what she had seen? She turned towards the drawing-room door, which was so close at hand; but she paused again before she had opened it. Had Vicars remained there she would certainly have done it; but as he was gone, and as there was nobody to see, Janet hesitated, pondered—and, finally, though with a beating heart, and every nerve in her body thrilling, went away in the other direction, and very softly and slowly, hesitating at every second step, retired upstairs.

CHAPTER XXI.

EVERY family has a skeleton in some closet. So says the proverb; but is it true? We are all of us aware of many cases in which it is not true. To half of the world perhaps it is a foolish fiction. They have troubles, but they are above-board, straightforward troubles upon which their neighbors can offer sympathy. Thackeray speaks of the wife or the husband in their intimate domesticity going back secretly, each unknown to the other, perhaps upon a youthful past which contained another image than that of the legitimate partner of their days, but that is a gentle sort of a skeleton, its bones all covered in soft rounded outlines of imagination. The real skeleton is very different: it haunts the house in the form perhaps of a ruined son, a debased and degraded brother, still more dreadful a woman disgraced. Or it is an incipient madness—a dreadful disease of which the miserable people never know at what moment it may blaze forth? It is always in the minds of those to whom it belongs. In the midst of laughter, in the happiest moment, it gives a tug at their hearts, as if it held them in a chain, and the smile fades, and the sweetest tints grow gray.

But how could there be anything like this in the house in St. John's Wood? The Harwoods were people not given to excitement of any kind. They were too orderly in mind, too calm and well-balanced, for any emotion. Their daily round of life was comfort itself, unbroken by any pangs of anxiety. No, Mrs. Harwood was a little anxious lest Dolff should stay out too late, and showed it in a natural, motherly way. Her brow got a little pucker in it when he did not return at the time he was expected; and Gussy had a way of going upstairs to the staircase window, from which she could see, over the garden wall, the road outside, to look out for him. This was visible enough to those who had eyes to see. But a mystery in the house, a secret inhabitant, a prisoner—— It was incredible; it was a thing that could not be.

Janet lay awake for a great part of the night tossing and trembling in her bed. She had locked her door, and she kept her light burning, frightened, she knew not for what, for the old man with the pale face, who might appear at any moment, and congeal the blood in her veins. Janet, of course, argued with herself in every way, that if there was any old man in the wing he was evidently shut up there and guarded and very unlikely to be seen outside; that there was no reason to suppose that he would know where her room was and come to her; that perhaps it was no old man at all, or a mere visitor to Vicars, or a hallucination, or—she knew not what. But all these reflections were not enough to calm the beating of her heart. She heard

Dolff come in from his ball and was comforted by the sound of voices, which gave a feeling of security: but these sounds died away again after a few minutes, and the silence and the darkness settled down. It seemed to Janet that the night had endured for ages before she got to sleep. Perhaps, however, it was not so very late, after all, for she was quite unused to watching.

It was, however, late when she sprang up in the morning, finding that she had overslept herself and too busy in her hurry to think of anything for the first half-hour. Then all that she had seen suddenly flashed over her mind again, and she uttered an involuntary cry. She leaned back in the chair and closed her eyes, and saw again in her mind's eye the apparition of the previous night. Janet started up again and gave a wild look round her, wondering whether she should not pack up at once and go away. If she had been one of the happy girls who have a mother to go to!—but all the possibilities rushed through her mind in a moment. The explanations she would have to give, the mild suspicion at the vicarage, the milder remonstrances, "But, my dear!—when you were so happy; a face at the window! There might be a dozen ways of explaining it; and what had she to do with it, when all was said?

"Janet, what's the matter? Janet, let me in. Why, you have your door locked! Janet, Janet, are you ill? You're late for breakfast and everybody's down. Ja—anet!"

This was Julia beating a tattoo upon the door.

"There is nothing the matter," said Janet, faltering; "I have overslept myself. I shall be down directly. Go away, Julia, please."

"I sha'n't go away. I'll wait here for you. I suppose Dolff woke you up coming home in the middle of the night. Make haste, make haste, Janet, or Gussy will say something nasty about people who are so easily put out."

"Julia, please go away. I am coming; I—have got a headache."

It was not often that Janet had recourse to a headache, which is always the most ready of excuses. But Julia, though she had been subdued by her governess, was not yet a model of subordination. Janet could hear her seat herself noisily on the other side of the door to wait. She could hear her foot drumming impatiently upon the floor, and then Ju, by way of amusing herself, began to give forth discordantly one of Dolff's not very lovely songs. It was quite true that Julia was never likely to do much in music. Her voice was something like that of a crow. She chanted Dolff's song with a very perverted reminiscence of the air, but a perfect memory for the words, which were not admirable. Janet was called back by this performance to the recollection of her duties. It was not possible now to pack up and hurry off.

And then she became conscious of a great many threads that held her, as well as this sentinel with her song keeping watch over her door.

They went down together, though Julia did not fail to impress upon the governess a due sense of the fact that she herself had been ready nearly an hour ago.

"You should always get up the moment you're called, or you are done for," said Julia; "one says just five minutes more, and when one wakes one finds it's an hour. I've learned all that about the kings, which is rubbish. What do I want with all those old kings? I shall just forget them the moment I've said them. I learned it not because I approved of it, but merely to please you."

"Thank you, my dear, that was a very kind motive," said Janet, recalling herself to her duties, "but if there is one thing that you ought to know it is the history of your own country. Everybody will tell you that."

"Well!" said Julia, "if it's all about one putting out another, till you don't know which is which, or who's king and who's not, I don't call that the history of anybody's country. So long as it's just to say off the Henrys and the Edwards I don't mind; but to learn whose sons they all were, and what right they had, and why they fought each other about it, I do it to please you, Janet, but I don't care tuppence."

Janet also did not care tuppence either, nor a fraction of tuppence; but she knew, and feebly tried to do her duty.

"You can't understand how they succeed, or which is right and which is wrong, unless you know about their families," she said. "It is all very complicated in the Wars of the Roses, but it is plain sailing for a long time after that."

"It ought always to be plain sailing," said Julia. "The Prince of Wales comes after the Queen, and Prince George of York after him—any one can understand that. If it went quite straight—father and son, or mother and son when there's a queen—I shouldn't mind; but they just inverted things to make history difficult, with no other reason. If they had only let Richard the Second alone, he would have had a son after a while—Richard the Third, perhaps—and we could have skipped all that nasty bit. But those old people had no consideration. Of course, it stands to nature that the son should always come after the father."

"This is most edifying," said Gussy, for by this time they had arrived at the breakfast-table. "You are late, young ladies, but if you come in discussing historical questions it is clear you must have been making a good use of your time. Good-morning, Janet; I hear you were disturbed—by Dolff or something last night."

"No!" said Janet, faltering a little, "I heard Mr. Harwood come in, but I was not disturbed. It is pleasant to hear voices and people stirring when one can't sleep."

"You left us in a great hurry last night," said Gussy. "I am afraid something put you out. You must not think you are neglected if, when a visitor happens to come—— I am sure there was no such intention. We always like, in this family, to see everybody comfortable, but sometimes, you know, there are circumstances——"

"Indeed, indeed, I was not put out by anything," said Janet. She had really forgotten all about Meredith and the small commotions of the drawing-room. "I had—a headache," she added, by an afterthought.

"I don't wonder, after thumping out all those accompaniments for Dolff. We must not let you be victimized so much. And you ran out to have a turn in the garden. It is very tempting on a moonlight night, but there is nothing that gives cold so easily. You must really take care. You look," said Gussy, raising her eyes full upon Janet, "rather pale, and shivering as if you had caught cold."

What was this in Gussy's eyes? something more than their usual placidity—an inquiry, an examination, almost a menace—they seemed to ask where the other had been, what she had been doing, what she had seen. Janet felt herself shiver under the look.

"I am sure you have caught cold; you ought to stay in and take care of yourself to-day. I am sure my mother would wish you to nurse yourself up. Ju, you must see there is a good fire in the school-room, and if Janet would keep to one room, without exposing herself to any draughts to-day, she will probably be quite well to-morrow. That's what I always do when I feel a cold coming on."

"But I don't think I have any cold——"

"Oh, yes, I can see it in your eyes; they are beginning to run. You must take care of yourself, my dear. And you really must promise to give up this habit of running out into the garden on a cold night."

"Indeed," said Janet, "I never did it before. The door was open, and the moon was shining so brightly——"

"Oh, the door was open! I wonder, now, who could be so silly as to leave the door open in December? I must ask about that."

"It was me, I suppose," said Julia. "I was standing there when Charley Meredith came. And I wasn't at all glad to see him. So I turned round in disgust, and forgot all about the door."

"You are very impertinent to say so!"

"Oh, I've just as good a right to my own opinion as you have, Gussy; as much as you like him, so much I don't; and I should never open the door at all to him if I had my will. He's not nice at all, or true. He has always mocked at me and made eyes, and I can't bear him," said Julia, through her teeth.

"Ju! I thought you had learned a little sense. I thought Miss Summerhayes had taught you how to behave, though your own family never could."

"Oh, I am quite sick and tired of my own family," cried Julia. "Mamma does whatever you please, Gussy. And you're so silly, I could shake you sometimes. And Dolff—Dolff——"

"What of Dolff? It must be delightful for a stranger to hear what we think of each other."

"What do you mean by calling her Miss Summerhayes and a stranger, when you know it was settled she was to be like one of ourselves—and by far the best of us?" cried Julia, with flushed cheeks and blazing eyes.

"Miss Summerhayes," said Gussy, turning again upon Janet, with a wave of her hand towards the indignant Julia, "I think your pupil is not doing you much credit to-day."

Janet had more command of herself in the family squabble than she had in the previous question.

"Julia has forgotten herself," she said. "She will be very sorry for it by-and-bye. I hope you will forgive her. She cannot quite get over her quick temper all at once."

"I hope she won't wear out our patience altogether before she does so," Gussy said, with significant calm.

"Janet! she means she'll persuade my mother to send me to school. Mamma would never do it of her own will. But if Gussy goes on nagging and nagging—— But I'll not go. I'll run away. I am too old to be packed off like a child. I'll——"

"It would do you a great deal of good, Julia, to go to school," said Janet, sedately.

"I have always said so," said Gussy, "and it's very good of you, Janet, to back me up. I have a temper, perhaps, too, and I say what I don't mean when I'm angry. But please don't think that I have ever changed about you. I liked you from the first, and I shall always like you. That little vixen makes one say things—but I know that we owe a great deal to you."

"Oh, no," cried Janet, with a compunction in her heart.

She was not sure that she could return the kind words and declare that she would never change. She felt as if involuntarily she was a traitor to Gussy— in a complot against her—or at least in the confidence of the plotter. And she was glad to retire into the shelter of her supposed cold and withdraw for the day to the school-room, carrying the excited Julia with her, to whom Miss Summerhayes set forth her offences against good taste and decorum with an incisiveness and distinctness which soon reduced that young lady to the depths of self-contempt.

CHAPTER XXII.

THE day had been rainy, some time after these occurrences, and the governess and her pupil were taking their needful exercise in the garden—up one side and down the other under the bare trees. They trudged along, making a sharp noise upon the wet gravel with their heels, occasionally very fast when they thought of it in the true spirit of a constitutional, occasionally lingering when they got into a discussion, and their tongues went faster than their feet.

Things had fallen into comparative tranquillity, and Janet, though far from at ease in more respects than one, was drawn on from day to day with the force of the current, and had no idea, whatever mysteries there might lie under the surface or troubles might be to come, of packing up in a hurry and rushing away. She wanted to see what was going to happen—very curious, a little disturbed, with more things going on in her little mind than were known to any philosophy. Julia was the greatest talker when the two were alone, and Janet carried on her thoughts and the thread of many a reflection through the girl's chatter at her ease—for Julia answered her own questions in a great many cases, or forgot that she asked any, and a very small response on the part of Janet sufficed to keep her satisfied.

What had happened, however, on this particular afternoon was that Dolff had seen from a window, and had sallied forth to join them. Dolff had a very comfortable little study to which he retired for certain hours in the day "to work"—as everybody said. Perhaps in her heart Mrs. Harwood had not very much more confidence than other people in Dolff's work. But she liked to say she had—to deceive, perhaps, a family friend now and then, or, what was more likely, herself.

Dolff, however, smoking a cigarette over his work—which in this case was an old French novel—saw the two figures in the garden, and threw aside his book with as much alacrity as if it had been Aristotle. He did not much care even for a French novel: literature of any kind was not his forte. And it was the afternoon, in which no man, nor woman either, has any call to work. It is going against the very rules of Providence to work between four and five o'clock, and you cannot disregard these laws with impunity. Nothing that is done between these hours is ever good. If it is reading, it runs out of your memory as fast as you put it in; if it is writing, it is so bad that next morning you tear the paper across and throw it into the fire. Dolff was deeply sensible of this penalty of untimely labor. He threw his book aside, picked up his cap, and went downstairs. A walk in the garden before tea, which was a refreshment his mother liked him to share, was exactly what was needed to keep him up to the mark.

It is difficult to say how these things happen; but after Dolff joined the pair, Julia separated herself with an instinct which need not be defined. She found that two was company and three was none. She was a little impatient at the sight of her brother when he first appeared, but afterwards accepted the situation, and began to find that she had a great many things to distract her attention. She wanted to speak to the gardener. She wanted to see whether the snowdrops were appearing which grew in the grass under the trees. She wished to look how the primulas were coming on in the little conservatory. It was well, on the whole, that Dolff had appeared to leave her free, for she could not have allowed Janet to walk alone, and yet she had all these things to do.

Dolff was not very great at conversation, as the reader may imagine; and it was very seldom that he had found a chance of talking to Janet alone, or so nearly alone as they were now. He began with the weather, as was natural. It had been very cold. That night he went to the ball he thought he should have been frozen walking home, coming out of the hot rooms after dancing all night. It was a beautiful moonlight night, indeed, as Miss Summerhayes remarked—but dreadfully cold.

"I hope it was a nice ball?" said Janet.

"Oh, yes; it was a nice enough ball, but I did not know very many people. I wish you had been there, Miss Summerhayes; but perhaps you don't care for that sort of thing?"

"Indeed I do," said Janet. "I am very fond of dancing. At least, I used to be when I was in the way of it."

"I hope you are not out of the way of it now. We must have a dance at Christmas. I am sure you dance to perfection, Miss Summerhayes."

"Oh, no," said Janet, with a laugh. "I don't do anything to perfection, but I confess I am fond of dancing."

"And of music, too," said the grateful Dolff. "I know you are—good music, not my sort. And yet you are so very kind as to play for me."

"Oh, please don't speak so. I am very glad to play—for anyone. Everybody is very kind to me. I am here to be of any use I can."

"I hope, Miss Summerhayes," said Dolff, growing very red, "that you don't think I would presume to ask you—on that ground."

"I don't mean anything disagreeable," said Janet. "I am sure you don't ask me because I am the governess. But if your mother makes me like one of the family in other things, I must be so in this too."

"How strange it is!" cried Dolff; and then he added, growing redder, "Don't be angry with me, Miss Summerhayes. To think that being one of our family should be anything to you!"

"Why not?" said Janet. "It is always a great thing for a governess to have such a kind home."

"A governess!" he said. "It hurts me to hear you call yourself a governess. Don't, oh, don't, please!"

"Why not?" she said again, and laughed. "It does not hurt me at all. I have no objection to being a governess. You need not be so careful of my feelings. I am quite contented to be what I am."

"That is because you are——" Dolff murmured something in his young moustache, and grew redder than ever.

Janet was not sure that it was not 'an angel'; and she was very much amused—not displeased either. There is no harm in being well thought of. She liked it on the whole.

"It is because I had—nothing else to look for," she said; "and I am not a discontented person. One can always get a little fun out of everything. It was rather fun coming out like this upon the world, not knowing what sort of place one might find oneself in. It is the nearest to beginning a brand-new life of anything I know."

"Well, about fun I can't tell," said Dolff, a little abashed. "I—I hope you think there is a little more in us than that."

"There is a great deal more," said Janet, "oh, a great deal more. You have all been so good. I mean before I came that it was fun imagining what my new family would be like, and how I should get on, and what sort of a pupil I should have, and all that."

"I daresay," said Dolff, "you never thought there would be a cub of a brother to bother you with his vulgar songs—oh, I know they're vulgar—at least, I know now. A set of men, you know, is different. We bellow them out at each other's rooms, and make an awful row in the chorus, and think them jolly."

"And so they are, I suppose," said Janet, with a smile.

"I assure you," said Dolff, "I don't think so now. I have been getting more and more ashamed of them, Miss Summerhayes. I've gone on singing them just for the pleasure of your playing. But I'll not do it any more."

"I cannot see why you should give up what is a pleasure to you," said Janet. "If you think I dislike playing for you, it is not so at all."

"That's because you're so good and charitable; they're not fit for you to touch. I can see that now. In a roomful of men that are thinking of nothing but noise and diversion, such things are all very well; but for your hands to touch, no, no—I see it all now."

There was in Dolff's voice a tone of touching regret. He felt the sacrifice he was making, yet he was ready to lay it at the feet of his lady. Between amusement and a certain pleasure in his devotion Janet's countenance shone.

"I can't allow you," she said, "to make such a sacrifice. You must have something to amuse you in the evenings; and your mother likes to hear you sing. Never mind if they are a little—well! some of them are quite nice—they are not all vulgar. I will show you the ones I like best."

"Will you be so very, very kind to me, Miss Summerhayes? It is out of the goodness of your heart, I know. Yes, my mother likes it, and she has good reason. I used always to be going out of nights getting into bad company. I can tell *you*, Miss Janet, though I could not tell anyone else. Poor mother was anxious about me, of course. But now I have no wish to go out at night. The Strand may be in Timbuctoo for anything I care. I never want to spend an evening away from home. So long as you will go on playing them—the best of them, don't you know—you will make both mother and me happy."

"Well," said Janet, "it is very easily done: and there are some others that I think would suit your voice. We might go over them together."

Dolff turned quickly round as if he would have seized her hand, but overawed by the imposing vision of Janet, who met his eager look with a slight elevation of her head and withdrawal from his side, drew back again a little shyly. But he was beaming with happiness and gratitude.

"If you will do that for me, Miss Summerhayes," he said, "I can't tell you how happy you will make me." He paused a moment, and then gave vent to a laugh. "Gussy and Meredith may think they're very grand," he said; "they look down upon me as if I was a clown at the circus; but just you stand by me, Miss Summerhayes," he said, with a little break in his voice; "by Jove, we'll put them on their mettle!"

Dolff was so delighted with the future joys which he saw before him that he smote his manly thigh in exultation. His face was crimsoned with pleasure and satisfaction, shining behind the faint shadows thrown upon it by his colorless hair and light mustache. He was happy and he was proud, doubly repaid for the genuine humility which had prompted his sacrifice. Janet had made him feel his coarseness and imperfection. It was with all the greater exultation that he felt himself mounting up with her into a higher place.

"You must remember, Mr. Harwood," said Janet, "that Mr. Meredith has a beautiful voice. There are not many people that have a voice like that."

"Do you really think so?" said Dolff, somewhat crestfallen. "He thinks a deal of it himself, I know."

"A man cannot have a voice like that," said Janet, "without knowing it. I will do my very best for you, but no one can give you a voice like that. And your sister sings very well, too. I think I could help her a little—but she doesn't think so, which is a pity. But you cannot do as well as that, Mr. Harwood—oh, no, whatever we may do."

"I don't mind," said Dolff, magnanimously, "so long as you back me up, Miss Summerhayes. If you're pleased, that's all I care for. I know you don't like Meredith, I've seen it in your eyes. We'll have concerts of our own, and my mother will like it, for one, better than twenty Merediths. And Gussy can't hold a candle to you—not in any way. Do you think I am so stupid that I can't be trusted to see that?"

Janet's mind was a little excited by this conversation. An uninterrupted course of adulation is not a disagreeable thing altogether: even if we do not have a very high opinion to begin with of the genius of the person who expresses it, our idea of his judgment will probably improve when we see how he appreciates our merits. Janet was no doubt more or less influenced by this natural sentiment; but she was also a little shaken by his confidence in respect to Meredith.

I know you don't like him—was it true? She felt herself pulled up short by that unhesitating expression. I know you don't like Meredith. It gave her heart a quicker beat: it was like the drawing up of a curtain upon a scene—a scene very much confused and covered with clouds, but not what her companion in ignorance of her and of all things had made sure it was. The curtain divided, opened for a moment, and then the folds fell back again, leaving her not much the wiser. No, not much the wiser; but not at least as Dolff supposed. After all he was a lout, though he admired her so much, which was a sign of good taste; but to take it for granted that he understood her was a little too much. Also, it was quite time to change the subject. He might rush upon her at any moment with other words that it might not be easy to answer. Decidedly the subject must be changed. She turned round upon him quite suddenly, though not without a little conscious artifice.

"Mr. Harwood," she said, "I want you to tell me one thing."

"A hundred things, Miss Summerhayes; as many as you like."

"Well, it is just this. Do you put full confidence in Mr. Vicars?" she said, looking him full in the face.

"Mr. Vicars," cried Dolff, with the most comical expression of astonishment and dismay. He had thought, poor fellow, that he was "getting on very well" with Miss Summerhayes; he had felt himself able to speak to her as he never had been able to speak before. Yes, and she had understood him, agreed to what he had scarcely ventured to ask, and, though she had not flattered him (which was so much greater a compliment he had said to himself somewhat ruefully), had at least seemed willing to help him—to stand by him. Decidedly he had been getting on; but what in the world could she mean by this sudden *volte-face*. "Mr. Vicars!" he repeated, with amaze; then slowly dawning into understanding. "Old Vicars?" he said; "the old butler?" then Dolff paused to laugh. "You startled me so, I could not think what you meant. Do I put confidence in him? Well, I suppose so—that is—I can't tell. I know very little about him; but my mother does, I have always heard. Do you—take any interest in Vicars, Miss Summerhayes?"

"Oh, no," said Janet. "I thought as he was such an old servant you must know him very well."

"So I do," said Dolff, "and yet I don't. I have not been much at home— only for the holidays when I was at school, and now only for vacations. And half the time we were always away at the seaside or somewhere. It is strange how little a fellow is at home when he is young, though of course when one is the only man of the family, and all that, I suppose you think I ought to pay some attention to things at my age."

"Oh, it was only an idle question," Janet said.

"But I should like you to know: everything is in my mother's hands for her life. That is—not everything. I have the most of the money, but not till I'm twenty-five: and she has the house and all the management. Of course I ought to pay more attention; and if I was to marry, or that sort of thing, I should have to settle up, and I don't know that she would have enough left to keep up this house. I have never thought of marrying till—quite lately; and I've always left everything in her hands and never interfered. Do you think I ought to pay more attention, Miss Summerhayes?"

"Oh," cried Janet, after two or three attempts to stop him, "I did not indeed want you to tell me about your family matters. It was only an idle question. I—I don't like the look of the man, and I only asked for curiosity. I never wanted to pry into your family affairs."

Dolff gave her a look which was full of meaning. He drew himself up to his full length, and instinctively pulled at his shirt-collar, and smoothed his mustache.

"Miss Summerhayes," he said, with dignity, "never speak of prying, for that is what you could not do. It is I who wanted you to know."

CHAPTER XXIII.

"WELL," said Gussy, "I cannot say that I see any harm in that. We have not had anything of the kind for a long time. We must see what mamma says. It does turn the house upside down, and give a great deal of trouble. But—you know mamma always likes to do anything to please you, and make you fond of your home, Dolff——"

"I should like to see any fellow that is more fond of his home, or sticks to it more," cried Dolff.

"You have been very good lately," said Gussy, in a hesitating tone, "if only one could be quite sure."

Gussy did not know what to think. Mr. Meredith's laughter and innuendoes had opened her eyes as to the cause of the virtue of Dolff; and she did not like the persistence with which Charley came back to the subject. She had no desire to be talked to about Miss Summerhayes and her influence for a whole evening, even if it was by way of jest. And as regarded the matter itself, though Gussy was quite willing to accept Janet's aid in keeping Dolff from nightly wanderings which were not for his advantage, she did not like to be called upon to acknowledge that aid; still less to consider that it might lead to what she called further complications: the idea of "further complications" was highly disagreeable to her. Janet was very well in her way. She was good for Julia, and fortunately for Dolff too. It was a great advantage to have anyone who would keep those troublesome members of the family in order. But—the idea of further complications alarmed her very much. It was the last thing in the world that was desirable for any one concerned.

"I shall tell my mother I have set my heart on having a dance. How can you expect a man to stick to his home as you wish if he has nothing to amuse him? I will settle all that with my mother myself," said Dolff, somewhat magisterially. He turned round upon her, however, after a moment: "If you don't interfere."

"Why should I interfere, if it makes you happy? To be sure it is a great trouble turning everything upside down."

"One would think you were forty, Gussy!"

"I am not so young as you, at all events," she said.

Gussy was as good as her word, and did not interfere. Even when she was privately consulted by her mother she said nothing against Dolff's wish.

"If it keeps him up to the mark," said Mrs. Harwood. "It is such a pleasure to see him so nice, to see him so improved—none of those wanderings out at night."

"Yes, it is a great improvement," said Gussy. She shook her head, with a sigh, and hoped that it would last.

"It has lasted a month," said Mrs. Harwood, "I see no reason why it should not last forever. How can I refuse him anything when he is so good? Vicars will not like it. It distracts his mind, and he says he never knows what may happen: but I think I can smooth down Vicars, Gussy, if you are sure that you approve."

"Oh, yes, I approve," said Gussy, "anything to keep him steady."

But Gussy herself was still young enough, and she thought of all the opportunities of the dance and the talks aside, the conversations in quiet corners, which were legitimate on such an occasion, with a little stir in her heart. At the piano, even though it was at the other end of the room, it was still under her mother's eyes. She never saw her lover, never talked with him except under her mother's eyes. How could he say anything under such circumstances? Her heart was a little sick that it should all go on forever in the same way, without the least progress. He talked about the songs, or about Janet and her influence on Dolff, laughing at what he said he had foreseen from the first. Gussy did not quite like the discussion of her brother, who, after all, *was* her brother, and not to be dissected as Charley loved to do, and she was not fond of hearing so much about Miss Summerhayes. There was no special interest in Miss Summerhayes that she should be the object of so much conversation between the two. And Gussy could not help thinking with a little pleasure of all the possibilities of the ball, where it was not only possible that two could talk together quite untrammelled, but where it was even a necessity that they should do so. To sit apart in a room unobserved with Charley once at least in the evening would be almost her duty; and then—with nothing to disturb them, no occasion for self-restraint—Gussy thought of this with a thrill through her veins yet with a sigh. She was becoming weary. All this had gone on for so long, and it looked as if it might go on forever without change.

Curiously enough it was the governess alone—as if she had any say in the matter!—who objected to the idea. Of course she did not object in words—but she nearly wrecked the project notwithstanding. She said, very innocently, that she did not think—even though Mrs. Harwood was so good as to ask her—that she could be present. There was a great outcry over this, for it was at luncheon, and the whole family was at table.

"Not come to the dance?" said Dolff. "Oh, but, Miss Summerhayes, that will spoil everything. I have—we've all calculated upon you, haven't we, mother. Tell her she must come."

"My dear," said Mrs. Harwood, "this is quite a new idea. I couldn't have a dance in the house, knowing there was a young person upstairs alone. Oh, no, I couldn't do it. Dolff is quite right—you must come."

Gussy had only said "Oh!" raising her eyelids—but Janet read in that exclamation a suspicion and question. Gussy did not believe that she was sincere, and was curious to know what her motive was. The two had drifted apart strangely, but this suspicion was not native to Miss Harwood's mind. It came from all those talks about Janet, and Dolff's subjection to her, which had afforded an opportunity for so much amusement over the piano. Meredith would say, "Ah! I wonder what she means by that?" till Gussy put the question to herself involuntarily as he would have put it, feeling all the same that sick weariness with the subject which translated itself unjustly, but not unnaturally, into an impatience with Janet which sometimes she could hardly restrain.

"I should like to come," said Janet, "but you forget I am in mourning. It is not six months yet——"

"That is true," said the old lady; but she added: "My dear, I like you the better for thinking of it. But, after all, she was not a near relation—not like your mother. For an aunt, six months' mourning is all that any one thinks of nowadays. And I believe the late poor lady was not even an aunt."

"She was all I ever had, for mother or aunt or guardian."

"Yes, I know—but left you to struggle for yourself, which makes a little difference. And what harm can it do her, poor thing, that you should enjoy yourself a little? You don't get so many opportunities in this quiet house. When Dolff goes away we shall all relapse into our needlework again."

"And Charley Meredith," said Julia.

Thought is quicker than the most rapid utterance. Julia's words came instantaneously, almost before her mother had done speaking, but it had flashed into two different minds before she spoke. And Charley Meredith! Gussy added that reflection to the picture of the future with an increasing sickness and impatience of her heart, seeing the same thing over again stretch before her, not without happiness in it, but with a weariness and incompleteness which would grow day by day. And it gleamed into Janet's thoughts with a certain excitement and suspense, as of a thing of which nobody could prophesy how it would end. The sudden movement in both minds was curiously struck as by a false note by Mrs. Harwood's calm reply:

"And Charley Meredith, perhaps. But that can't affect Janet, except the wrong way: for I confess, myself, I get sick of these two always philandering—I beg your pardon, Gussy, my dear, but I've been young in my day—and other young people looking on, you know: why they must either make fun of you or the water must come into their mouths."

The old lady laughed in the heartless way in which old ladies will laugh. She was only the more tickled when Gussy drew herself up, and, looking straight before her with a blank countenance and the sternest gravity, replied,

"I cannot form the slightest idea what you mean, mamma, or what there is in anything that has been said to call forth such a digression. We were speaking of the dance, I think, and of Janet's mourning, which I agree with you is no reason why she should shut herself up."

"I'm sure I beg your pardon, Gussy," said Mrs. Harwood, wiping her eyes, for she had not been able to stop her laugh, "but I'm glad of your support. No, no, my dear, the mourning has nothing to say to it. You have worn it very faithfully, and you have done your poor aunt full justice. I'm sure, poor lady, she would be the first to say, could she know, that you must now begin to enjoy yourself a little. At least, take what enjoyment you can: for you know the men are generally in the minority, and nobody can ever tell till the last moment whether there will be enough partners or not."

"There shall be enough," said Dolff, with a grand air. "I should be ashamed of myself if I couldn't produce a lot of fellows—only you'll have to put some of them up for the night. Couldn't you clear out that old wing? There must be some rooms that could be used if they were tidied up."

"No," said Mrs. Harwood, with a change of countenance. She, too, became perfectly blank, as Gussy had done, dismissing all expression from her face. "It is quite out of the question to open the wing."

"Why?" said Dolff. "I don't see the difficulty. A couple of housemaids and a few brooms——"

"My boy, I must be the judge on this point," said Mrs. Harwood. "There is nothing to be done with the wing."

"But, mother——"

"I will have no more said on the subject," she answered, peremptorily. "You had better come and wheel me into my room, I have some business to do this morning. And, Janet, I hope it's settled, and that I shall hear no more about your mourning."

"You are very kind, Mrs. Harwood. I am afraid I have no dress——"

"You have a very pretty dress; and let me tell you, my dear—though I daresay you know it—that black is always becoming, and that you look very well in that dress. Now, Dolff——"

"I hope we shan't hear any more on that subject," said Gussy, with an air of decision, as her mother's chair was wheeled away. "I'm very glad to humor Dolff, but I shall soon be very tired of it if there are many more difficulties. Dress is always a nuisance on such occasions. One wears a ball dress once—it is as good as new, but when one takes it out it is old-fashioned, or faded, or something, and it is such a waste of good money to get another to be worn again only on one occasion. You may be very glad you are in black, Janet—and there is Ju, she is not out, and won't be for a couple of years. And yet she can't be sent to bed. How is she to be dressed for this one night? I know mamma will overdo it if she is left to herself. All that and the supper, and the musicians, and everything of that kind is left on my hands. A ball may be very nice at the moment—for those who like it—but the trouble it gives, both before and after! Every spare inch of room must, of course, be got ready for Dolff's friends."

"Do you think, then, that Mrs. Harwood will yield about the wing?" said Janet, very curious.

"As if Vicars would!" cried Julia. "Mamma doesn't matter—it's Vicars that won't have it. I've always wanted to get into the wing, but Vicars stands sentinel as if he were a jailer. I've told him a dozen times I was sure he had got something wrong in there. I can't bear Vicars!" said Julia, hurrying out the words to get as much said as possible before Gussy's imperative tones broke in.

"Ju! you are unbearable. I thought at one time there was an improvement, but there's none. Vicars is a most valuable servant. We have the highest respect for him and his opinion, both mamma and I. At such a time as this he is more good than words can say—and always so careful for the credit of the house. Isn't it time you had begun lessons? I must go and see after the house."

As Janet followed her pupil out of the room she was met in the hall by Dolff, very eager and breathless.

"You're coming, Miss Summerhayes? I must stop you just for a moment to make sure. Don't spoil it altogether by saying you'll not come. I shan't care a brass farthing for it if you're not there. But you *will* come—say you will? You won't disappoint us all and ruin it for me——"

"I can't see what difference it would make," said Janet, "especially if there are too many ladies already."

"But that wouldn't affect *you*. You will always—— Miss Summerhayes, I'll throw it all up if you don't come."

"Don't threaten me, Mr. Harwood; besides, after what your mother so kindly said, I am coming—to look on at least."

"Oh, I like that!" cried Dolff. He seized her hand and squeezed it as she passed him. "But you may say anything you like," he said, rejoicing, "so long as you come."

"Janet," said Julia, when they had reached the school-room, "I think this is getting a very queer house. Gussy cares for nothing but Charley Meredith, and Dolff cares for nothing but you. It is—odd—don't you think?"

"It would be if it were true," said Janet; "but as it is a mere fancy, it is not worth discussing. I hope you are quite ready with your preparation to-day."

"I can't see," said Julia, "any signs in you like the other two: but perhaps it's just your artfulness. One thing, Dolff is much nicer than he was before. As for Gussy——"

"We are not here to discuss either your brother or your sister, Julia, and I will not have it. Where are your books?"

"Janet, you have a dreadfully strong will. Mamma says so. I suppose you never would give in to another person; to do what they wanted, and not what you wanted yourself?"

"It does not look as if I had a very strong will," said Janet, with a laugh, "when you run on defying me, instead of getting out your books."

"That's no answer," said Julia. "If Dolff asked you——"

"Come," said Janet, "this is going too far. I think the Wars of the Roses are much more interesting. You have never yet made out that table showing how Henry the Seventh succeeded; and how it was so wise of him to marry Elizabeth of York. Come, you'll understand it all so much the better when you see how it comes——"

"As if I cared," said Julia, opening her books with a sigh; "they were all cousins, and the one that was strongest took everything, and when the other one got stronger he took it all back. I know exactly how it was; all cousins are like that. The very same thing happened with Mary Morgan, who is my cousin. All the toys used to be mine while I had Dolff, and Fred was away; but as soon as Fred came home, who was the biggest, he seized them all. I know it far better than any book could say."

CHAPTER XXIV.

PERHAPS it was Julia's question; perhaps it was the rapid seizure of her hand which she had not been able to prevent, which opened that self-discussion in Janet's mind. "If Dolff asked you——" "What?" she said to herself, "what would Dolff ask?" She had been half pleased with his homage and her evident power over him in the dearth of other excitements—more than half pleased, pleasantly carried on by it with a laugh at him and his clumsy devotion, which was not unpleasant. She thought better of Dolff, on the whole, that he thought so well of her. It was the best trait she knew of him. Her first idea had been that he was a dolt, that he was a vulgar, music-hall frequenting, loud, and foolish young man. But when she had become aware of his admiration, his subjugation, the reference to herself that was in everything he did, Janet could not help entertaining an improved opinion of Dolff. She laughed at him secretly with an amiable and complacent laugh, conscious that there was a great deal to be said for him. He was appreciative—his doltishness had disappeared— his manners had improved. Janet was quite conscious of liking him a great deal better than she had done at first, and she had no objection to allow him to continue on the same footing as long as he should be at home. She had found the quiet evenings, the warmth and friendliness, and the needlework, pleasant enough when she first came to St. John's Wood, having still all the novelty to amuse and carry her on, and the story of this new family to pick up and understand. But no doubt it soon would have ceased to be exciting had it not been for the entrance of Meredith upon the scene, with all the peradventures to which his appearance gave rise and the manner in which he had drawn her into the romance by those asides and confidences, which never were expressed in words, but which she could not help understanding.

And then Dolff. Janet did not feel, as Mrs. Harwood had indiscreetly said, that the sight of the pair "philandering" had brought the water into her mouth. Meredith, with his confidences and the curious doubt she had of him, was too interesting for that. She did not envy Gussy, nor feel the least desire to be in the same situation. What sentiment she had on the subject was a troubled pity for Gussy; but even that only in the background; her curiosity and interest and doubt in respect to Meredith himself being her chief feelings. And Dolff, for a time, had only been an interruption to the other study. But now it was evident that matters were getting serious, and that it was necessary for Janet to take into consideration whither she was going. The ball was a great event in front of her, which might bring with it serious consequences. Balls are but frivolous things, but yet they are sometimes fraught with events of the deepest importance. Miss Harwood, as we know, with ideas far from frivolous, looked forward to this merry-making as perhaps the most serious moment of her life. Janet had not the same feeling, but she was excited and a little disturbed. If Dolff should ask her—whatever he might have to ask: what would happen?

The reader is aware that Janet at the very outset of her career had been brought face to face with a similar problem, which she had solved very summarily without taking much time for thought. But the circumstances now were a little different. Dolff was young (too young, for he was only twenty-two): there was no disparity in that point of view: and whereas, in the first instance, the only drawback in refusing was the breaking of poor Dr. Harding's heart—a contingency at which Janet was disposed to laugh in the cruelty of her youth—the matter was complicated now by the possibility that she would herself suffer by the necessity of giving up a situation that suited her, where she was comfortable and interested. This probability did not please her at all. To leave St. John's Wood, not to be able to follow the curious romance to its end, not to know how things arranged themselves between Gussy and Meredith, to be cut sheer off from that thread of story which it was so exciting to watch as it twisted itself out day by day—Janet was very unwilling to contemplate such a possibility.

And then there came upon her, as if blown upon the fresh winterly breeze which puffed in at her open window, the half-forgotten talk of Clover—the conversations that used to go on by the fire at Rose Cottage in the afternoon, when half-a-dozen ladies would drop in to tea. How severe they were upon a girl who was so fantastic as not to accept a good offer! How they would prophesy that she would never have such another—how they would ask indignantly what she expected! Janet seemed to hear them all talking together, hoping sarcastically that Mary Brown would never repent her folly.

Dolff would have seemed to these ladies a good match. A young man who was at Oxford, who was going in for the Bar, whose mother was so well off, and all the money his, though not to be inherited till he was twenty-five. What was Janet thinking of? they would say. What did she expect? Had she another string to her bow that she was so careless of this? And how could she tell that she would ever have another offer? She, a governess, with nothing to fall back upon, and no resource but to go from one place to another, so long as she pleased her employers or was wanted. Even Mrs. Bland, though she was so kind, would say the same thing. What did Janet expect?

She did not, as will be seen, fling off this new opening of fortune as she flung off Dr. Harding. To get herself provided for, established in life all at once, she knew now that this was something. And she reflected with a kind of pride on the triumph of concluding such a matter at once while the story of Gussy and Meredith still dragged along, and in showing *him* that while he lingered and amused himself another made up his mind.

These ideas fluttered about, now one of them, now another, alighting upon the surface of her thoughts like snowflakes. The opposite arguments did not come in the same manner, probably because it was the opposite she held by, and they stood around her like fortifications round a citadel. It was the others, the temptations, which fluttered about her, and went and came.

"If Dolff should ask you——" To marry Dolff! "Oh, never," cried Janet to herself; "oh, no, no," with a keen conviction that it was impossible.

And then the temptations began to flutter about like snow. It was a serious thing to throw away for no reason—for no particular reason—a good offer, a good house like this, a good income, and all that is certain in life. And then, again, on the other hand—Janet lingered in the garden when Julia ran indoors, saying she would follow instantly. She knew that Dolff was safely disposed of—that he could not come to trouble her, and a moment of solitude was delightful. She walked very quickly under the trees making the round. To be, or not to be? Oh, no; it was not so deep a question as that. To marry, or not to marry. Janet was well aware throughout that it was a foregone conclusion, and that nothing would really tempt her to marry Dolff: but she let her thoughts flutter about her, and pretended to discuss the question—not, however, with much faith in her own thoughts.

In the second round she extended her promenade a little without thinking, and came accordingly along the side of the wing. She looked up at the window, as was natural, and for the hundredth time asked herself how she could have ever fancied that she saw a face between the arching branches of the ivy. The boughs were so strong, the clusters of glossy leaves so thick, how would any one be seen through? I need scarcely say that these arguments did not shake her conviction in the least; and that she was as sure of having seen that face as of anything in her experience, notwithstanding that she argued so strongly that it was impossible. The ivy was like an old tree in thickness, great twisted hairy branches barring the window, the glistening dark leaves concealing everything, stopping the light. How could a man show through that?—particularly in moonlight, under a glare so dazzling and confusing? The whole side of the house looked completely shut up. The windows behind the ivy branches were encrusted with the dirt of years. There was no trace of habitation, no possibility of anyone being there. And as for the face at the window, what tricks fancy will play! It was very evident it could be nothing but that.

Under the wall was a flower border, in which there were some bare rose-bushes, some bulbs showing green points above the ground for spring flowering, some bushes of wallflowers for the same season, but looking very shabby after repeated frost. There was nothing in this to attract any one's attention: but scattered over them, lying on the drooping leaves of the plants and the damp brown soil, were a quantity of small specks of white which caught Janet's eye. She thought at first it might be the beginning flakes of a snowstorm—for the sky was very gray and lowering. On looking up, however, she saw that the atmosphere was still quite clear, though dull. Looking again, she saw that several of those white specks had lodged on the ivy upon the wall, and went forward to the flower border with some curiosity to examine what they were. There was no air, the afternoon was perfectly still, so it could scarcely be a windfall.

To her great astonishment, Janet found that these were little pieces of paper, covered with a large indistinct writing, but torn into such small pieces that it was scarcely possible to trace a single word. She gathered up a handful of them hastily, looking round to see if any one was about, with a sense of doing something clandestine, though she could not tell why. And, indeed, she had scarcely taken a dozen steps in the opposite direction when she heard other steps coming round the front of the house, and, looking back, saw Vicars, who seemed to be continually prowling about, and who, after a glance at the papers on the border, looked after her with a suspicious start, and finally followed her into the long walk which ran along one side of the garden. Janet instinctively concealed the bits of paper in her hands, and turned upon him before he overtook her.

"Do you want me? Has Mrs. Harwood sent for me?" she said.

"I can't say as she has, miss. Seeing you about, I would just like, if you please, to ask you a question. Have you seen anyone a-picking up pieces of paper about these walks?"

"Seen anyone—picking up pieces of papers? No. I have not seen anyone—there has been no one here but myself."

"Ah!" said Vicars, drawing a long breath, and then again he looked at her keenly. "As for yourself, miss—you've got sharp eyes—maybe you've seen some of them papers blown about the walks."

Janet persuaded herself afterwards that she did not tell a fib by premeditation. She answered, hastily.

"I have seen nothing about the walks but fallen leaves—there is no wind to blow anything about."

"That's true enough," said Vicars: then he added, "It's a bit of an old copybook as someone has been tearing up. Missus can't bear a litter—that's why I asked you. Beg your pardon, miss; I hope it's no offence."

"If you mean to me, I am not in the least offended," said Janet, with her most dignified air, and Vicars, though with another searching look at her, turned away.

She watched him go back and collect carefully all the scraps in the border. Those she had seemed to burn her fingers with the impatience she felt to examine them: but in face of Vicars' suspicious looks she would not turn back and run in as she wished to do. She had to make the whole long round sedately before she could take refuge indoors and in her own room. And by that time the afternoon had begun to grow dusk towards evening. She locked her door, and lighted her candle, with an excitement which made her temples throb, and then sat down at the table and began her task to piece the scraps together. It was by no means an easy task—no child's puzzle was ever so difficult—the bits of paper were very small, and of the most obstinately disjointed character. A few of them, a very few, fitted into each other, and the handwriting was large and sprawling, one word going over several lines: for the paper was ruled in lines, as if it had been, as Vicars said, a copy-book. To support this idea further, Janet found, after going over the scraps which she had been able to piece together, that the same words were repeated over and over, and that on several pieces which seemed to have formed the bottom of the page there were some scrawls that looked like a name. She deciphered, by degrees, "I can't," and "I want," and the word "out," written in all kinds of letters, sometimes small and sometimes large.

The name at the end gave her still more trouble. She made out at last an Adol, Char—and then there came a piece of paper more triangular than ever, containing the following curious hieroglyphic—"esHar—w—" She pondered over this till the candle burned down and the dressing-bell rang. "esHar." What did it mean? She dressed hurriedly, with her mind still full of this problem. It only gleamed upon her what it was as she stood, looking in the glass, putting the last touches to her dress. Sometimes, to look at your own face in the glass is like looking into the face of an intelligent friend, and it sharpens your wits. "esHar—w." She spelt it over and over to herself—"e-s-h-a-r—w." What did it mean?

At last Janet threw up her arms over her head and burst into a laugh, though she was alone—a laugh full of confusion and self-ridicule. Mean! Of course what it meant was as clear as daylight. Adol for Adolphus, or Dolff;

Char for Charles, with the two last letters joined on to the Harwood—Adolphus Charles Harwood. What could be more clear? She might have known that it must be Dolff's big, straggling hand. Janet laughed at herself till she cried, but subdued the sound, lest anyone should hear, and flung her scraps of paper into a box as if she had been playing at a letter game. Of course, that was what it was—an old copy-book of Dolff's inscribed with his name—Adolphus Charles Harwood—after the usage of the school-room. How could she have been such a fool? She thought of Catherine Morland in "Northanger Abbey," and blushed crimson and hid her face in her hands, though she was alone. How ridiculous she had made herself? Only, fortunately, nobody knew—not even Vicars knew.

There was not much music downstairs that night, for the time of the ball was now very near, and everybody was interested in talking it over—the people who were coming, and where "Dolff's men" were to be put up, and all the details. It had given the family a great deal of trouble, as Gussy had prophesied it would, and they liked to find a recompense for these fatigues and anxieties in endless discussions. Janet found an opportunity, while they were all busy with the box of programmes which had just arrived, of looking at the autograph upon Dolff's music. It was, to her surprise, not at all like the sprawling hieroglyphics of the copy-book; but then, to be sure, he must have been a child when he had written the others. The music was all inscribed "A. Harwood" in a neat little concise hand. He saw her looking at it, and came up to her.

"You are looking at those wretched old things of mine, Miss Summerhayes?"

"No; I was only looking at your name on it. You don't use your second name?"

"For a very good reason—I haven't got one. It's a ridiculous name, isn't it? I sign 'D.' always to my friends. But 'A.' is a good enough disguise. A great many fellows are Arthur, or Andrew or Alfred, or something like a man, so I creep among them. You never would suspect a man of being Adolphus, eh?" cried the young man, "if you saw only A. standing for his name?"

"I don't think I should," said Janet; "but I thought you were Adolphus Charles."

She had a little tremor in her voice as she spoke, which was, half alarm at this betrayal of herself, and half-suppressed laughter, though she dared not laugh.

"Oh, no; I have no Charles in my name. I wish I had. Shouldn't I use it if I had the chance! You may laugh, Miss Summerhayes, but if you would only think how much nicer for a man it would be if his friends called him Charley instead of calling him Dolff!"

"What are you talking of, Dolff?"

Both Mrs. Harwood and Gussy had turned round at the sound of the name.

"Not much, mother. Miss Summerhayes thought I had Charles in my name, and I tell her I only wish I had."

"How did Miss Summerhayes know?" said Mrs. Harwood, with a faint, scarcely perceptible change of tone. "I beg your pardon, Janet; but how did you know—about that name?"

"How could she know, mother, when it doesn't exist! It was only a mistake she made."

"How did you know, Janet, we had that name—in the family?"

Mrs. Harwood repeated the question with an insistence which was not like her usual easy-going way.

"I suppose I must have—seen it somewhere," Janet said, her color rising.

She felt guilty; she did not know why. There was no harm in it. She might have said it was out of an old copybook; but somehow she did not—scared by she knew not what.

Mrs. Harwood had been wheeled, to that end of the room to see the programmes, and to examine some new arrangements Gussy had been making for the ball. She dropped out of her hand the pretty pink programme which she had been holding, and called to her son to take her back to her place, with a change of mien which brought a chill over the party. Janet felt more and more guilty, though she did not know what she had done, nor why she could not confess frankly where she had got her information. The others soon recovered the momentary depression, and resumed their talk over the approaching event, but Janet stood at the piano, running over the notes of a waltz softly with one hand, and wondering why she should have produced, without intending it, so great an effect. Presently Mrs. Harwood called her, clapping her hands as she had a way of doing to secure attention. Janet hurried to her side. The old lady had recovered her composure, but she still looked grave.

"My dear," she said, "you will wonder that I was so startled. There was no reason. Of course you could know nothing. That was my husband's name."

"Oh, Mrs. Harwood, I am so sorry. I can't think what made me ask. It was because most people, I suppose, have more names than one: and Charles was the first that came into my head."

It will be seen that Janet told a little fib again, but she said it in a hurry, and did not mean it, or at least this was how she afterwards explained it to herself.

"Then it was only what people call a curious coincidence," said Mrs. Harwood, with a smile.

CHAPTER XXV.

THE night of the ball arrived at last. It was a long time in coming to the impatience of Dolff and Julia: and even to Gussy, who was not impatient, who would rather have held it off a little when the day at last came, and to whom so many things were involved in the hours which would be but amusement to the rest. Nobody suspected what was going on under Gussy's tranquil looks. She was one of those people whom many think to be incapable of feeling at all. She had a force of resolution not to expose herself, not to let anybody know what she endured, which was equal to almost any trial. There are many women who possess this power, but it is most frequently exercised to shield and cover the delinquencies of others. Gussy's reticence was only for herself; but strength of any kind is respectable; and if any one had known the fever that was in her breast, the chance upon which the fortune of her life seemed to turn, and the absolute tranquillity with which, to all appearance, she prepared for the evening's pleasure, no doubt she would have earned the admiration of some and the respect of others.

But our best qualities, as well as our worst, remain for the most part blank to those who surround us, and nobody suspected either the trouble in which Miss Harwood was, or the empire she exercised over her own soul. Janet, perhaps, was the only member of the party who was in the least degree cognizant of it, but even Janet was chiefly aware, with a feeling of provoked sympathy, that Gussy, as she generally did, had dressed herself unbecomingly on an occasion on which the little, quick-witted governess divined she would have wished to look her best. Gussy was not clever in the matter of dress. She arrayed herself in the lightest of tints and materials—she who was herself so colorless, who wanted something solid and distinct "to throw her up."

Janet had done her duty in this respect by the other young woman, who could scarcely now be called her friend, so conscious were both of a mist that had come between them. It was one of Janet's good qualities that she had no jealous feeling, but that unfeigned pleasure in dress which made her so anxious to see everybody else becomingly attired, that she was impatient of failure. She had given many hints and suggestions as to Miss Harwood's dress on this particular occasion, but they had not been attended to. And Gussy had enveloped herself in something that was not quite white nor yet any other color, with the persistency common to persons who are without any real instinct in the matter; and, instead of looking her best, looked more colorless than usual.

Janet could scarcely restrain a cry of impatience when they all met in the drawing-room, which had been cleared for dancing. If Gussy had but worn her own black gown, what a difference it would have made! But Gussy was altogether unconscious of that, as all the others were unconscious of the way in which her heart was beating under her *fade* and foolish dress.

Janet, for her part, had received her programme from Dolff, with his own neat little "A. H." written on a great many lines; but she was too wise to permit the son of the house to make himself and her remarkable. Janet had a great terror of what the opportunities of the evening might lead to, very different from that sentiment which moved Gussy. She managed to escape, if not with some other partner, then alone, anywhere, even going so far as to make a rush upstairs till some of the dances bespoken by Dolff were over. She was determined not to lay herself open to any comments in that respect, or to expose herself to the chances of what Dolff might say in the excitement of the evening. But she had no such terror of Meredith, who, after he had done his duty in various directions was so polite as to ask the governess for a dance. Nor was she alarmed by the eagerness with which he plunged into conversation, leading her away, when half the dance was over, to a quiet corner.

"I am sure you are tired," he said; "you have been dancing all the evening, and so have I. Come and let us talk a little. I never have a chance of half-a-dozen words with you, Miss Summerhayes."

"That cannot matter much," said Janet, "for I don't suppose we have anything very particular to say to each other, Mr. Meredith."

"You must, of course, speak for yourself; but you cannot for me, and I have a hundred things I want to say to you. We have never had a good talk but once, and that was the day I walked with you from the circulating library, when you were quite afraid to be seen with me."

"Not in the least afraid to be seen with any one," said Janet; "but it did not seem suitable somehow. And as we are talking of that, Mr. Meredith, I don't think it's very suitable——"

Here Janet thought better of what she was going to say, and stopped short.

"What does not seem suitable? Tell me, I implore you! How can I regulate my conduct according to your wishes, which is my highest ambition, if you will not tell me what to do?"

"I have nothing to do with your conduct, Mr. Meredith, I don't understand why you should wish to sneer at me——"

"I—sneer! but you know you don't mean that. I sometimes try to secure your sympathy, I allow, when I'm at a particularly hard place. They say that the lookers-on see most of the game, and I soon saw in your eyes, if you'll forgive me, that you——"

"I don't see any game," cried Janet, with indignation, "and if you are playing one you ought to be ashamed of yourself; and, at all events, I will not be in your confidence!"

"Hush!" he said, "don't be so fiery. If you get up and leave me you will make everybody ask why, and we don't want to raise any talk, do we? Look there, Miss Summerhayes—for I must talk of something—look at that man Vicars. What a hang-dog face he has! Like a man that is up to some mischief, don't you think?"

"I don't like Vicars," said Janet, hastily; "he would like to be insolent, if he dared."

"Insolent, the beast! You have only to give Dolff a hint," said Meredith, with a laugh, "and he'll soon put a stop to that. I should like, all the same, to know a little what's Vicars's mission in this house. Oh, I know he's an old servant, and all that. I have my little curiosities, Miss Summerhayes; haven't you? There are some things I should like to know."

"I thought you must know everything," said Janet; "you are such a very old friend."

Now Janet was bursting with desire to communicate to somebody her own wonderings and the things she had seen, or had imagined herself to see. She was held back by many things—by regard for the law which forbids you to talk to strangers of things you have observed in the house in which you live: and also by a principle of honor, which is but feeble in such matters in most bosoms, and by a lingering sense of loyalty towards Gussy, whose property this man was—and by a general prejudice against making mischief. But, on the other hand, she was impelled to speak by her own curiosity and conviction that there was something to find out, and eagerness to communicate her discoveries. And then Meredith was not a stranger; and if there was anything to find out he had a right to know it; and, of course, as Gussy's husband he would know everything. Janet's heart began to beat with excitement. Should she tell him? She wanted so much to do it that she scarcely knew how to keep in the words.

"I am an old friend," said Meredith. "I have known them all my life; therefore I have a kind of right, don't you think, to want to know? And I am one of the very few men who come familiarly about the house, so if there was any way in which that fellow Vicars was taking them in, or playing upon them, I am just the person who ought to be told, for I could take steps to put them on their guard."

It was on this argument, which seemed so unanswerable, and especially applicable if Meredith became, as Janet assured herself was inevitable, the son of the house, that at last she spoke. After all, it did not seem as if she had very much to tell. She confided to him her suspicions that Vicars had somebody shut up in the wing whom no one knew about, and that she herself had seen—she was certain she had seen—a face pressed against the window-panes, visible between the branches of the ivy; and how, just below the same window, there had been the other day that little shower of scraps of paper, which looked as if they had been thrown out.

Meredith listened with the greatest eagerness. He leaned his elbow on his knee, and his head in his hand, looking up into her face, and shielding her thus from observation in her dark corner, so that even Gussy, passing by at a little distance on the arm of her partner, could not make out who the lady was to whom he was talking, though the sight increased almost beyond bearing the agitation in her mind. Meredith's eyes on Janet's face, so near, and the manner in which he surrounded her, shutting off the world, confused her and gave her a vague sort of guilt; but, after all, how could she have helped it? She could not have refused to dance with him. She could not refuse to sit down to talk, to sit out the Lancers which was then being played, and which Gussy was going in dutifully with her partner to dance. Any other girl whom he had asked would have done that, and how could Janet refuse? But there was no doubt that she felt a pang as Gussy, in her pale dress which did not become her, and with a look in her eyes dimly divined by this little interloper, passed into the bright room beyond to perform her duty dance.

Janet went on with her revelations after this episode. She had seen Vicars crossing the hall with a heavy tray covered with dainties very late one night, after everybody was in bed. She had seen the door in the hall, which was said to lead to the wing which was believed to be permanently shut up, open to him——

At these words Meredith started up. They were quite alone in their corner—nobody was about. The dance was going on gayly—the ball-room crowded, a little hedge of men standing round the door.

"Everything is quiet," he said, hastily; "let us go and see."

"Go and see—what?"

He drew her arm within his, with a smile upon her, which dazzled Janet and made her cast down her eyes. She was so startled that she was scarcely aware that he kept her hand in his as he led her along.

"We have five minutes," he said, "and there is nobody here. Let's go and see." It seemed half a schoolboy frolic, half a righteous mission. He hurried her into the hall, which was deserted, enveloping her so in his shadow that Janet felt as if she had no longer any will of her own. "Which is it?" he asked, bending over her so that she felt his breath on her neck.

They spoke in whispers, and crowded together on their clandestine enterprise so that they seemed but one figure. She put out her hand, trembling, and touched the door.

Janet's heart had been beating loudly before. It jumped up now as if it would choke her when she felt the door move slightly under her hand. When Meredith added quickly the pressure of his fingers it swung open. He drew her in, scarcely conscious of what he was doing. "Oh-h!" Janet breathed a low cry of excitement upon his shoulder. Whatever the discovery might be there was now no escape. He silenced her, pressing her against him. They were in a dark, narrow passage, which ended in thick curtains closely drawn, and was lighted by the feeblest spark of light.

"We must follow it on now," he said, in her ear. "Not a word—not a word."

Inside the curtains was a door which opened outward, and admitted to a steep, straight staircase. Everything was dark, muffled, breathless. They groped their way up this, and found before them another closed door at the top, which yielded also to pressure, moving noiselessly. Within this were curtains again, in which they both stumbled, unable at first to open or put them aside. But the circumstances were desperate, and somehow they made their way through. They found themselves then in a room lighted only by the window, which was the very window, covered with ivy, at which Janet had seen that old man's face. But the room was void and dark. They stood for a moment looking round, but, though they could see next to nothing, it was certain there was nobody there.

By this time Meredith's excitement had so grown that he forgot Janet. At least he dropped her arm involuntarily, and leaving her trembling, scarcely able to support herself, made a long step forward to where his keen eye had found out a crevice, through which came a faint ray of light. Once more he held back a curtain and pushed a door; then with a sudden, quick movement, held out his hand to Janet. Her eyes by this time had become accustomed to the gloom, and she perceived that he called her. He caught her in his arm as she stole forward, and placed her before him. Their breaths came quick in the same suppressed cadence. Both were far too much excited for speech, even had they dared to speak.

This was what Janet saw. A room comfortably furnished, largely curtained, dark, heavy stuff, so far as she could see in her instantaneous glance, covering the walls, a fire burning cheerfully, a small, shaded light by the side of a large sofa, on which lay a man fast asleep—so fast asleep that the very air seemed slumbering over him. She fell back upon her companion with what, had she dared to utter it, would have been a cry. The pale old face, long and tragical, the crown of white hair, the long white beard, half hid by the great red coverlet which enveloped him, were the same which she had seen at the window. It was, then, no fancy, no trick of reflection. Janet for a moment, in her agitation, was unconscious of all the circumstances round her. She gasped dumbly, paralyzed, yet thrilling with wonder, terror, and dismay.

Meredith's face touched hers as he whispered "Come away." He almost carried her through the anteroom, the dark staircase, the faintly-lighted passage, lingering at the door for a moment to see that all was quiet. They came out into the hall, anxious but safe. The crowd was still about the door of the dancing-room, but the music bore witness that the dance was just at its conclusion. Meredith hurried Janet back to the sheltered corner which they had left for this quest.

"One moment; I must speak to you for one moment more," he whispered behind a bush of evergreens, which concealed them entirely. "You don't know how important this is—Janet, have you got those papers——"

"The copy-book?"

"I don't believe it was a copy-book. Try to give them to me quietly the next time I am here, or send them—that would be the safest—United Universities Club. Dearest, I can't say half I want to say to you to-night."

"To me there is nothing to say," said Janet, drawing away from him. "I have forgotten myself in the excitement—but don't think, Mr. Meredith——"

"Yes, I will think," he said. "Don't warn me off, for you can't do it. I have thought of you since the first moment I saw you. Is it my fault if they take things into their heads, Janet?"

"I will not have you call me Janet," she said, with angry vehemence.

"But I must. I never call you anything else—to myself—darling! We'll meet again before long, and be able to say everything to each other."

He let her go suddenly, and in a moment had joined the crowd of the lookers-on, who had been awaiting the end of the Lancers, and now were scattering to permit the exit of the more dutiful couples who had been performing that now somewhat despised dance.

Janet seized the opportunity to fly upstairs to the shelter of her own room, which she reached breathless and agitated. She could scarcely realize what had passed in this strange evening so full of excitement. Meredith's presumption—was it presumption? his unpardonable freedom of speech—but was it unpardonable? the confidences into which he had hurried her; the extraordinary discovery they had made together; the way in which he had assumed her consent and acquiescence, taking possession of her as if she belonged to him. Janet tried to be angry; she said to herself that it was detestable, unpardonable; that never more would she speak to him again; that, if *that* were true, then his behavior to Gussy was villainous; and if it were false? Her breath came hard; her veins swelled as if they would burst. How dared he speak to her—look at her—hold her so? Janet saw herself in her glass, with eyes blazing, lips quivering, nostrils dilating, and wondered at herself. She could see that she had never looked like that before—never so brilliant, so much excited, or taken out of herself. Oh! how did he dare—he who was as good as engaged to Gussy Harwood? It was *that* she thought of—not of the mysterious secret tenant of the wing. That strange habitation with its tenant had died out of her mind. She found herself thinking only of Charley—of whom? Good heavens! what had she to do with his name—of Mr. Meredith and his impertinence and presumption. He had told her to tell Dolff (with a laugh) of Vicars' impertinence; but what was that of Vicars to his? He had taken possession of her against her will. He had made her a traitor to the people whose bread she was eating. He had made her the instrument of humiliation to Gussy. Oh! would he go now and whisper to Gussy, and laugh with her at Dolff and the governess?

Janet clinched her hands and bit her lip till it almost bled. Was this what he would do? Tell Gussy perhaps that the governess was a silly little thing, and believed everything that was said to her—or was it Gussy that he would slight and scorn, after so long holding her in suspense? Janet felt that she abhorred Charley. Oh! to think that his name should come to her lips without any intention, when she had nothing to do with it! and he had called her by hers—the insolent, the scoundrel, the deceiver! Janet wrought herself up into a passion, and raved at him within herself like a little fury: and then she suddenly changed her mood, and fell a-crying, soaking up the tears that would come with her handkerchief lest they should make her eyes red, and saying to herself "Poor Charley!" from the bottom of her heart.

CHAPTER XXVI.

MEANWHILE, all was going on merrily below, dance succeeding dance. The music was good, the floor was good. "Dolff's men" had fully made up the number of partners necessary, and left a few over to support the doorway lest it should fall. Dolff himself, in the midst of the gay crowd which had been collected to give him pleasure, wandered about distractedly, seeking Janet, but unable to find her, and teasing Gussy, who had certainly enough to worry her without his constant questions, by demands where Janet was.

Gussy had plenty of her own affairs on hand. The hours were passing—those hours which she had felt to be so full of fate—and nothing was happening; and her heart was sore with unfulfilled expectations. To think that while her mind was thus torn asunder, while she was almost unconsciously, but with the keenest anxiety, watching for one figure in the crowd, yet carrying on the necessary conversations, listening to what ever nonsense might be said to her, laughing at the smallest jokes, presenting generally the aspect to all around her of a disengaged and cheerful spirit, while suffering an endless torture of suspense—to think that then Dolff should assail her with his questions:

"Where is Miss Summerhayes? Have you seen Miss Summerhayes? This is our dance. Where has she disappeared to? What has become of her? Gussy, have you seen Miss Summerhayes?"

Gussy tried to push off her brother's inquiries with trifling answers, but finally found that this last straw of provocation was more than she could bear.

"I am not Janet's keeper," she said, with angry impatience. "You had better attend to your guests, Dolff, and let Miss Summerhayes look after herself."

"By Jove!" said Dolff, who was almost as exasperated as she, "I knew you were selfish, Gussy, but never so bad as that."

They glared at each other for a moment, both at the end of their patience, distracted, abandoned, left to themselves. It was a kind of relief thus to snarl at each other, to let out their offence and trouble, persuading themselves each that the intolerableness of the other was the cause. But Gussy's case was by far the harder of the two. Janet had given Dolff no right to resent her absence—but the other—the other! It did poor Gussy good for a moment to be able to be angry with Dolff.

When Meredith came to her for the third dance she had given him, the two first of which he had danced conscientiously all through without a word that could not be breathed in the course of the twistings and whirling, Gussy declared she was too tired to dance any more.

"Then let us sit it out together," he said; "there is a nice corner I know where we may be as private as if we were all alone, yet see everybody—if you wish to see everybody. I think it must have been arranged expressly for you and me there are two such comfortable chairs."

"You have put that corner to use before," said Gussy.

"Several times," he answered, promptly; "one must do something with one's partner if, for example, she doesn't dance well, or there is any other drawback. I have been conducting myself more or less like the son of the house to-night. You may think me presumptuous to say so, but I think, after Dolff, I have almost the best right to look after your guests, Gussy, and see that it goes off well. Do you allow my claim?"

In that dark corner which he had occupied a little before with Janet it was not possible to see the warm blush, like a fresh tide of life, which came over Gussy's face; but something of that warm, sweet flood of consciousness could be made out in the melting of her voice.

"Oh, yes," she said, with a happy tremor, "you have known us longer than any one here—almost all your life."

"All our lives," said Meredith, with a little emphasis on the pronoun. "I can't remember the time when we didn't know each other, can you, Gussy? There is nothing else can come so near as that. And I have been taking it upon me to entertain your guests as if they were my own."

"Thank you very much for that, Charley."

"Oh no, you need not thank me. You will do as much or more for me when the time comes—when I shall have guests of my own. But I am not well enough off to think of that yet. A little patience and then my turn will come."

"I thought," said Gussy, "you were telling mamma the other night——"

"Oh, that I have made a beginning. Yes, I have made a beginning; and you may be sure it will not be my fault if it does not go on: a year perhaps, or so, and I shall feel that I am justified—ah, Gussy, I wish that time was come."

"You must not insist on too much," said Gussy, softly; "to begin is the great matter."

"So it is; but I must have the means to get a nice house and everything suitable before—— When it comes to having guests, you know, there must be something to give them, and—better things even than that. Ah, me! waiting is slow work." Gussy echoed the sigh from the bottom of her heart. "But I hope there's a good time coming," continued Meredith, with a smile, putting his hand upon Gussy's, and giving it a warm pressure.

He looked many things which he did not say, and poor Gussy sat in a sort of trance of mortified happiness, feeling herself put back, checked, as if it were she who was over-eager and impatient, yet so assured of his tenderness, so moved by the high-mindedness of his determination to have everything worthy of her before he should ask her to share his fate, that her heart melted within her in answering tenderness and consent. No, she would never, could never doubt him more. His hand laid upon her hand was not enough for the response she was so ready to give: but he knew and trusted her, as she felt she ought always to have known and trusted him. And there was a moment's silence, to Gussy more eloquent than any words; a sort of noiseless betrothal, binding them to each other till the time for full disclosure and explanation should come. He stooped down at last and kissed her hand as if his feelings were getting too much for him, and then broke into remarks upon the dancers, who were once more streaming out into the cooler space at the end of the waltz. He called her attention to two or three, and made her laugh. She felt no longer any difficulty in being amused.

"But I am afraid I must go soon," she said; "I am engaged for the next dance."

"Sit close," said Meredith, "and the man will never find you. Dolff's men are all as blind as bats. They know nobody, and they go prowling round trying to recognize some girl they have only seen for a moment. There is one who has begun his round already, peering at everybody. I hope he is not your man?"

"Perhaps he is," said Gussy, drawing further back; "I don't know him any more than he knows me."

"Then you had far better stop with one who does know you, and—something more," said Meredith. "There! he has passed and you are safe. Ah, so here is old Vicars again! Where does he always appear from, whenever you want him, that old man?"

"He appears—from where he lives, Charley. You know mamma lets him have the coachman's room in the wing."

"That wing has always seemed a most mysterious place to me. How do you get into it? Do you strike upon a trap-door, and does he start up through it like a jack-in-the-box?"

"Nonsense," said Gussy. "There is a door at the back, as I am sure you must have seen."

Her tone was quite simple and unembarrassed, and Meredith for a moment was silent. He went on again, however, immediately.

"There must be some nice rooms up there. I can't think why you never use them. Almost enough for a young *ménage*. For Dolff and his wife, for instance, if he was to make a match with Miss Summerhayes, or even——"

"Charley, I wish you would not always make fun of those two. There is no chance whatever of Dolff making a match with Miss Summerhayes. My mother would be furious; and it is really unkind to Janet, who, I am sure, has not the least idea——"

"Well, my dear Gussy, well, I'll say nothing more; but if Dolff is the person that has the idea, so much the safer is it to come about. You know your mother never denied him anything. And the wing looks as if it could put up a pair of people famously. It is a great pity to leave it without use."

"Mamma does make some use of it," said Gussy; "but," she added, after a pause, "there is not so much room as you think."

"I know what use I should put it to if it were mine. I suppose Mrs. Harwood keeps the lumber in it. I should clear away all that ivy, and open the windows, and turn out the rubbish, and then—— Ah, well, I must put away all these dreams for the next year."

Gussy sat with one hand still in his, with her heart full of happiness, yet conscious of something wanting. She was melted beyond expression by his tone, and by all that he said or inferred but did not say. She was not even aware at the moment of what it was that was wanting. The ache was calmed. She was subdued and charmed away into an enchanted land. To have less than perfect faith in him would have been an offence against every tradition of her heart, and yet——

Meanwhile, Dolff was rushing everywhere, winding his way among all the groups, seeking Janet.

"Mother, have you seen Miss Summerhayes? Where is Miss Summerhayes? The next is our dance" (it was the second or third which he had thus described), "and I can't find her anywhere. Ju, where is Miss Summerhayes?"

"She must have run up to her room. Perhaps she tore her dress. Perhaps she is mending up somebody else's gown. Perhaps she was tired."

These were the explanations that were rained upon him, till Dolff became desperate. He seized Julia by the arm, and conducted her perforce to the foot of the stairs. Julia was enjoying herself very much, dancing every dance, and determining in her own mind that no force should get her to bed before everything was over. She was very indignant, and struggled as Dolff rushed her through the room without the least regard for her opinion.

"Go and fetch Miss Summerhayes. Tell her it's our dance, and I'm waiting. Go and fetch Miss Summerhayes, Ju."

"But it's my dance as well as yours," said Julia. "I'm going to dance with one of your men—the man with the red hair. Oh, it's a shame! If Janet went away it must have been because she was tired. I won't go! Oh! I won't go!"

But there were some points on which Julia was constrained to yield. Dolff was very good-natured, but there were moments when nothing was to be done with him. She was finally compelled to obey, and flew like an arrow from the bow upstairs and to the locked door of Janet's room, against which she threw herself in her impatience.

"Janet, you're to come directly," cried Julia. "Dolff says it's his dance. You're to come directly, or else I shall lose mine, for I daren't go back without you, and my partner will get some one else. Janet, Janet, come away!"

After a minute the door opened, and Janet came out. She was wiping away the tears from her eyelashes, but, notwithstanding these tears, she looked so resplendent that Julia was dazzled.

"What have you been doing to yourself? Crying generally makes one's nose red, but you look as if you were all made of diamonds," said the girl. "Come along, come along. I shall lose my dance, and it will be all because of you."

Dolff was standing impatient at the foot of the stairs.

"Oh, here you are at last, Miss Summerhayes," he cried. He held out his arm for her hand, and led her away hurriedly. "You have almost spoilt my night for me," he cried; "where have you been? I did not get up a dance, and rummage up men, and all that, for you to hide yourself upstairs."

"But I did not want you either to give a dance or to rummage up men," said Janet, with a laugh.

"I know you don't care," he said. "It is nothing to you that it's all as dull as ditch water to me when you are away: and now we must dance when I wanted to talk. I have a hundred thousand things to say, and I quite calculated upon to-night for that: for I can't talk to you at all most days. Let's dance and get it over, and then we can go away somewhere and talk."

But Janet did not want to be talked to by Dolff. She would not let him off a single round, but danced till the very last bar. And poor Dolff got out of breath easily, and could not talk while he was dancing. He did not dance very well. He was not very fond of it, he allowed, on ordinary occasions, and he was most anxious to break off now. When at last the waltz was over, he hurried her off to find a corner somewhere—one of those which he had himself arranged so carefully for the accommodation of stray pairs of wanderers, and in which he had imagined himself pouring out his heart to Janet. But, to his wrath and dismay, Dolff found that every one was filled. He made a hurried round, holding Janet's hand tightly within his arm, to keep her from slipping away. But wherever Dolff had placed a couple of chairs consecrated to himself and the lady of his affections there were a frivolous pair established before him—the gentleman lolling with his legs crossed, the lady sitting prim beside him—the most uninteresting, the most prosaic of couples. Dolff set his teeth when he came to the end and found no place.

"Will you come and have some tea?" he said, dolefully, "or an ice, or something? As every nook is filled, it must be quiet there. Oh, Miss Summerhayes, this is not what I hoped: I have been looking forward to it so long, and there is not a spot where you can sit down."

"Really. I don't want at all to sit down," said Janet; "let us walk about. We can talk just as well as if we were sitting down. And I am not tired."

"No, it is not all the same," said Dolff. "We can talk, I suppose; but not about what I wanted, Miss Summerhayes—about the ladies in white and the ladies in blue, perhaps, and who is flirting and who is not, and the man with the red hair, and all that. That is what ladies talk about between the dances; but that's not my style, Miss Summerhayes."

"Is it not?" said Janet, "it seems very innocent talk."

"Innocent enough—meaning nothing," said Dolff, with scorn; "like what we talk about in the evenings, when we're all together, and you scarcely say anything at all. I hoped we might have had a little real conversation to-night."

"I am very sorry," said Janet. "I fear it was my fault, but I forgot. I am very fond of dancing. Who is that lady that looked at you so significantly, Mr. Harwood?"

"Oh," said Dolff, with a groan, "I am booked to her for the next dance. And there are those infernal fellows—I beg your pardon, Miss Summerhayes—beginning to tune up!"

CHAPTER XXVII.

CHARLEY MEREDITH walked home from St. John's Wood to his chambers, which were in one of the streets about Berkeley Square, between two and three o'clock in the morning. It was in the week between Christmas and the New Year, when the fashionable parts of London were very quiet, but the other parts—the domestic quarters, so to speak, where people live all the year round—more lively than usual. Yet it is needless to say that he had on the whole a quiet walk; and it was a long one—a capital opportunity for thinking, which is an exercise that often goes on best when it is accompanied by physical movement, and the sensation of the fresh air in one's face.

Meredith had spent an exciting night. Had it been nothing but the two interviews above recorded, he would not have been without something to think of, and the consideration of the fertile crop of embarrassments and conflicting questions which no doubt would spring from them might have occupied him not unprofitably for an hour or two. He had gone further in one way than he had ever done before, having deliberately deceived Gussy and given her to understand that within a definite period he would present himself as an avowed suitor for—nay, claimant of her hand. In the passing thought he gave to this subject he said to himself that it was silly to have indicated a definite time. Yet, as nobody could prophesy what a year might bring forth, there was perhaps but little harm, and a hundred things might happen in the meantime to blow all that nonsense away. And he had also committed himself in respect to Janet, for whom he felt a real inclination as much resembling love as anything he knew of. Yes, if circumstances permitted, if it should turn out to be anything but the last folly to a man in his position, he felt that he should like to carry off that little girl, to marry her, and pet her, and be amused by her quick understanding and her piquant looks. She was not too rigid about duty and so forth, though she took upon her that little schoolmistress's manner and reproved him for his levity.

It was perhaps not quite the most appropriate thing she could have done to betray the secrets of the house, and help him to the means of satisfying a long-smouldering curiosity; but it was very clever of her to find out, and, very engaging as well as serviceable to choose him for the confidant of her discoveries. Poor little thing! He felt that henceforward his attentions to Gussy, which it would now less than ever suit him to break off, would plant thorns in the bosom of the governess, which was a pity, for she was a nice little thing, far more tempting than—— But these thoughts were all disposed of before Mr. Charles Meredith got to the end of the street; or at least before he got to the boundaries of St. John's Wood: and a much more important matter filled the foreground of his thoughts.

To enter into a history of the Harwood family at this period of our story would be too great a tax upon the reader, and it may be enough to say that this most respectable family had not been altogether so spotless as was supposed by the respectable inhabitants of St. John's Wood. There was a break in the tradition, and that a very recent and important one. The husband of Mrs. Harwood and father of her children had been one of those bold speculators who often ruin whole communities. When a number of bubbles burst which he had been instrumental in blowing about the world it had been necessary for Mr. Adolphus Harwood to disappear; and he had done so, leaving but one feeling of pity for his wife and young children, and for his father—an old man, who was said to be bowed down to the dust by his son's iniquities.

After a while, though the interval was one of several years, information was received that he had died in Spain, and imperceptibly things mended for the family. His father being dead, Dolff became without any trouble the legitimate heir of the little entailed property upon which his grandfather lived, and the money matters of the house in general were cleared up, though I cannot explain how, having small knowledge of such subjects. It was found that Mrs. Harwood was not so badly off as had been supposed. She had some money of her own, which it was said formed the greater part of her living, and there were other resources of which nobody knew any particulars except, it is to be hoped, her man of business. She had at once rejected any quixotic notion of giving up what she had for herself and her children to satisfy the creditors of her husband. It would not have been enough to give them a pittance all round, and in the meantime she and her son and the girls would be added to the army of the destitute without doing anybody good. Some people think differently on such matters, but Mrs. Harwood had never wavered in her determination, and in general her conduct was at least not disapproved by her friends, who thought her an excellent woman of business and as full of integrity and steadiness as her husband had been the reverse.

These things had happened when the children were very young, and they were now forgotten, save in the tenacious memories of a few who had suffered through the failure of Mr. Adolphus Harwood, and who did not fail to bear a certain grudge against his family. It had all taken place at a distance, in Liverpool, where his business was, and where failures and ruin are commonplace matters such as occur every day; and their home where old Mr. Harwood lived was in North Wales, far away from any communication with St. John's Wood.

Mrs. Harwood had never lived in that house, which had been let from the period of her father-in-law's death, and was not known much in the neighborhood. She had been nearly fifteen years in St. John's Wood, where she had soon become known as a liberal supporter of the parish charities and an acquisition to the neighborhood in every sense of the word; and where nobody inquired into the family history of an agreeable widow, very well off, and with nice children. Now the description of the household was changed—nice young people with an agreeable mother was how they now presented themselves to the knowledge of the world; and any little episodes that had happened in Liverpool or in the wilds of North Wales were totally unknown.

Meredith, however, was an exception to this ignorance. He was a Welshman. He had known them all his life, and he knew everything about them. It had been at first unpleasant to Mrs. Harwood to acknowledge his claims, for she preferred to ignore altogether their previous circumstances. But, seeing that it was impossible to shake him off, she had taken the part of making the best of him and speaking freely to him of relations and connections like a woman who had nothing to conceal. Meredith had friends who were well off, if he was not, for the present, very well off himself; and when it became apparent that there was a mutual inclination between him and Gussy, Mrs. Harwood was glad of it, partly because his father had been one of the sufferers by her husband's failure, and might thus be partially recouped for his losses, and partly because Meredith's mouth would thus be effectually stopped, and no revelations need be apprehended from him—though, as she sensibly remarked, "What does any scandal matter after fifteen years?"

Meredith's motives were perhaps more difficult to read. They had indeed been easy enough at first, for he had really liked Gussy, and had felt her to be as good a match as he could aspire to. Latterly, however, several circumstances had struck him as strange in the house with which he was so familiar. They had been scarcely of note enough to call for any consideration singly; but put together they had awakened a suspiciousness not unnatural in a mind trained to the complexities of the law.

Had he been ignorant of the history of the Harwoods; had he been altogether without the tradition of animosity which lingers in the mind of a man who has a hereditary injury in his thoughts, it is probable he would not have remarked these little incidents. The chief of them was Vicars, whose countenance seemed one of evil omen to the young man. He had come by degrees to the belief that there was something in the house to be found out.

Nothing, however, had prepared him for Janet's extraordinary revelations and for the discovery more extraordinary still which he had himself made.

It was this which he turned over in his mind, viewing it from every side, considering it in every possible light, as he walked briskly along the long line of silent streets. It seemed a thing almost incredible that an unsuspecting family could have a man hidden in their house with such elaborate precautions, shut up in rooms which were given out to be uninhabitable, yet surrounded with comforts, kept from all air and vision yet manifestly cared for—a mystery in the midst of the commonest matter-of-fact details of life.

The face which he had seen, though but for a moment, communicated no idea to Meredith's mind. It was not like anyone whom he had ever seen before. The long white hair, the long pallid countenance, was more like those of a hermit in the desert than of a dweller in an ordinary English house.

The eagerness with which the young man had followed up the mystery had fallen somewhat blank when he got to the climax and saw the cause of all. The thread which he had seemed to hold in his hand broke off short. He had not known or been able to imagine to what it might lead, yet had associated it somehow with the story of the family, and expected it to throw some light upon that. But the light he had been hoping for seemed suddenly to go out as he gazed through the curtains at this strange old man. Who was he? What connection could he have with the family in whose house he was hidden? Was it Vicars who was responsible—Vicars, who was the representative of mystery in the house—the old servant who was no longer a servant? Could this be some private undertaking of his own of which not even Mrs. Harwood was aware?

But when Meredith thought of the curtains, the softly-moving noiseless spring doors, all left, no doubt, that Vicars at a moment's warning might rush back to his patient, or his prisoner, or his victim—which was it? he was again stopped suddenly as by a blank wall of impossibility. Vicars could not have fitted up the rooms with all those elaborate precautions. He could not without Mrs. Harwood's knowledge have arranged everything for secrecy and at the same time for comfort in that way. Was it then some one whom Mrs. Harwood was hiding? But whom? But whom?

Gussy and Janet and all the embarrassments connected with them died away from Meredith's mind as this problem presented itself to his intelligence. Who was it? That curious curtained room—it suddenly flashed upon his mind that it might be a padded room prepared for a lunatic: and this seemed for a moment to throw an illusive light upon the problem, but only for a moment: for he could not think that Mrs. Harwood would permit Vicars to harbor a lunatic in her house, in the near neighborhood of her children; and who could it be whom she could shut up like that in lawless disregard of all rules? Nobody. There was not a madman in the family that he had ever heard of.

This last idea, however, seized upon Meredith with greater force as he considered. He remembered the cry which he himself had heard more than once, and which had been put aside with careless explanations as something which was to be heard from time to time from a neighboring house, or from the streets, or a shriek from the railway, or the effect of the wind when it blew in certain directions. He remembered even to have asked, "Is there any private asylum near?" and how it had been suggested by some one that there was somebody out of his mind next door. He had said that in that case he hoped the people next door were aware that it was unlawful to keep a maniac capable of uttering cries like that in an unauthorized house.

This forgotten conversation suddenly surged up before him as if it had been laid up in his memory for future use. Was the man mad? Was it Vicars who had him in charge, backed up by his mistress, injudiciously kind, or was it she who was the prime mover and Vicars only the instrument? He puzzled about this insolvable question, turning it a long time over and over in his brain, until at last he came back to the fact that even were this matter solved to his full satisfaction it would leave him as much in the dark as before. For who was the man? This, after all, was the only thing that it was of any importance to know.

Meredith made a long excursion as he walked along into all the connections of the Harwood family of whom he had ever heard. He was something of a genealogist, and he had the excellent memory of a country-bred individual for all the cousins, and brothers-in-law, and connections generally of people near home. No; he could think of nobody related to the family on either side who had been mad or who had disappeared or failed to be accounted for. There was nobody. It could not be a mere connection, a far-off friend, who was thus cared for. It must be some one whose life was of importance, for whom secrecy was necessary; whose madness was either to be concealed under a pretence of absence, or who was so near in love that to retain his custody the law was transgressed and defied.

But there was no such person, none. Everybody that had to do with the Harwoods was respectable, known, above suspicion, except the scoundrel of a husband who had died so many years ago. Could it be that the widow, already in middle age when her husband died, had loved some other man, and perhaps secretly married, or at least taken him into her house when attacked by the dreadful malady?

Meredith was in a very silent bit of the way when he came to this hypothesis, and its effect upon him was such that he stopped short and laughed aloud. Mrs. Harwood, the most irreproachable of women and mothers, more than middle-aged, never moving out of her wheeled chair! That she should have a postscriptal romance—a love-affair in her fifties: and that the man should go mad—of love probably—and be guarded thus as the apple of her eye! She seemed to rise before him in all her comfortable ease and motherliness—poor lady! not able to walk—to rebuke the wild imagination. He laughed, but then all at once became grave again: for that same easy-minded woman, the respectable mother, the elderly mistress of so correct a household, must be in the mystery one way or another. She it must be who had settled and arranged the whole elaborate business. It could not be Vicars, who was a man-servant in no way above the level of his class. He could not have done it; could not have the means to do it, or the knowledge. The mistress of the house must be involved. Her purse and her brain must be in it, whoever the mysterious patient or prisoner was. Who was the man? Beyond that question Meredith, with all his acuteness, could not go.

What a strange sight it was, looking in at him through the curtains! Meredith said to himself that the man must have been drugged to lie in such a deep stupor of sleep. Something must have been given to him to keep him quiet, to make it possible to fill a house in which such an inmate was, with music and the sound of the dancers' feet and the hum of a lively crowd. And the incredible rashness, temerity, of doing so—of carrying on all the gayeties of life in a house occupied by such a spectre, on the other side of the wall only from the unconscious merrymakers! It was like a woman to do that, with a regardlessness of all consequences, a want of natural logic which belonged only to women: for everybody surely must see that one time or other such a thing must be found out. Nothing in the whole matter was so certain as that—that one time or other it was bound to be found out. It was like a woman to do it: but even a woman, one would have thought, possessing such a secret would shut her house up and keep society at least at arm's length. But no; on the contrary, all sorts of pleasant things went on in the house. It was open to all the friends of the young people, who visited it, stayed in it, came there as freely as to the most commonplace of houses. And all the time that man shut up in the wing! Any one of them might have pushed open the door at some careless moment as Janet and he had done, and found his or her way upstairs. Any one of them might have seen the spectre, so notable as he was in appearance; not a face to forget. And what then?

But Mrs. Harwood, with the incredible inconsequence of a woman, had ignored all that. No doubt Vicars, to spare himself trouble, had got into a way of leaving the door unfastened, the spring uncaught, to save himself trouble. And they thought they never would be found out. They gave dinners and dances and asked all sorts of people to come and pass within sound of the maniac. They might drug him, but they could not drug the spectators, who, one time or other, as sure as Nemesis, must have found out—as Charley had done.

But who was the man?

CHAPTER XXVIII.

JANET had been so quickly summoned downstairs after her strange adventure that she had no leisure to think it over, until, about the time when Mr. Meredith set out on his walk, she escaped upstairs. Meredith had been the very last to go away, he had stayed for the little family supper which the house-party had made after the guests were gone. He was evidently regarded, in short, entirely as one of the family, and in that capacity claimed Mrs. Harwood's applause for his exertions in making everything "go off."

"I have danced with all the plainest women," he said, "and taken at least three dowagers in to supper. I ought to be very much petted now to make up."

Mrs. Harwood looked from him to Gussy uncertain what to reply. But Gussy did not meet her mother's eyes, as she most certainly would have done had there been anything to tell.

"Oh, yes, you have been of great use," she said, "I don't know what we should have done without you. But I don't believe in such magnanimity as that. And you ought to be more civil about the dowagers when you are talking to me."

"You are not a dowager—you are the head of the house," Meredith said, bending over her affectionately to say good-night.

It was not possible that Janet could be otherwise than on the watch, considering her own share of his attentions during the evening. He had cast a laughing glance at her when he spoke of the plain women, and when he turned to leave the house he shot another look of leave-taking, tender yet laughing too, over the head of Julia, who was still at supper, consuming as many forbidden dainties as was possible in the short space of time that remained. Meredith put his hand on Julia's shoulder, which she flung off with a rapid twist, and said good-night to Janet with his eyes, so that nobody could see; and then he turned round with a laugh, complaining that all his civilities to Ju were without effect. Gussy, who was pleased by this supposed attempt to conciliate her young sister, accompanied him with Dolff to the floor. And Janet could not but wonder what kind of farewell would take place there, with something between mirth and misery in her heart.

Oh, he was not true. It was certain that he was not true; but we do not somehow condemn the man who cheats another on our account, as we denounce him when he deceives us on account of another. The two things are different. He should not perhaps have pretended to be affectionate to Julia in order to be at liberty to look love at Janet; but the expedient prompted Janet to laugh. There is always something that tempts the lookers-on to laugh in a lover's wiles. And the person who is preferred is apt to pardon and take such deceits lightly. How could he otherwise have found it possible to give her that parting look? And Julia's wrench of her shoulder made Janet laugh in spite of herself. How ridiculous of the girl to suppose that it was for her he did that!

And, to tell the truth, Janet could not think of the leading incident of the night for the shadow of these other things which pushed in front as if they were more important. What he had said to her—what he had looked, which was more than what he had said, the touch of his hand, the curious union that had been formed between them by their mutual discovery, that discovery which was owing to Janet, and which her observations had alone made possible—all these things were in her mind rather than the discovery itself. When she tried to think of it she found herself thinking of him, and going over and over his words and his looks, and every particular of that so confidential and lover-like talk which had taken place under the shadow of the evergreens. What would Gussy have said if she had seen them sitting there? What would she have thought if she had heard them?

It gave Janet a keen prick of pleasure, of gratification, and trouble to think that the governess should be placed so much above the young lady of the house. Janet did not know what would come of it, or if anything would come of it, or if she were to blame or not. But, in the meantime, she could not help enjoying the triumph. It was not Gussy he cared about, who was so much better off, but her, little Janet the governess. She forgave him his falseness—was not everything to be forgiven to a sudden love springing up in a man's heart when hitherto he had been giving himself up to consideration of what was best to be done in the way of a respectable marriage? She could not get these incidents out of her mind.

When she tried to think of the other matter, the thing which Meredith was studying so intently on his way home, her mind eluded that subject and came back and back to the other, the more interesting, the subject which made her youthful heart beat. She had been much excited once by her own discoveries, by the face at the window, and indeed by the scraps of paper, until she had discovered as she thought that they were only from a copy-book; and it was inconceivable how little she cared now for this far more important discovery. But then there were things more important, events more exciting to Janet's little self, which came in the way. Her heart had suddenly been roused within her, a new life had opened before her. It was not noble, nor did it come with that elevating and purifying effect which a first love so often exercises, making all beautiful and excellent things congenial to the awakening spirit in the first fervor of that new emotion.

Janet felt guilty, she had a breathless sense of something secret, forbidden, in her excitement and happiness. The best she could feel was the mischievous clandestine pleasure of a child in balking some little rival, and triumphing over some one who had been elevated above her. She did not dare to think of Gussy, save in a ludicrous sense, as being so silly as to be taken in. Oh, how silly she was not to see that his looks, his secret inclinations, were not for her, that ever since Janet appeared upon the scene it was towards her that his thoughts had turned! She thought of Gussy only in this way, scorning her for being deceived; and there was nothing softening, ameliorating, or ennobling in Janet's *vita nuova*. It was made up of clandestine communications, secret looks, communings in dark corners. There had been only one of these, and yet she felt as if it had been going on for years. And she did not know what would come of it, or if anything could come of it. He had stepped into a lover's place without, in so many words, telling her that he loved her; without that proposal of marriage which is the inevitable formula of love to an English girl. He had said nothing about all that. Janet did not know what he intended, or if he intended anything; but this only made her heart beat all the more.

Thus two young women in that seemingly tranquil house retired to their rooms with hearts high-beating, moved to their inmost depths by Charley Meredith, who was not in the least worthy of the agitation of either, not even of Janet's half-guilty agitated excitement which she thought love, and certainly not of the emotion which made Gussy Harwood hide her face in her hands, in humiliation and misery which all the sweetness of their recent interview could not overcome. It was sweet: and his implied assurance of the cause that kept him silent, and certainty of a definite term to the suspense, had flooded her being with happiness for the moment; but by the time she had gained the privacy of her own room, and the excitement was over, Gussy's heart once more had sunk into the depths. To wait in this humiliating way till he should signify his pleasure, to be dependent upon him for something like life itself, to attend like a handmaiden on his leisure and his choice of a time and manner of signifying his will—all this filled Gussy with humiliation and shame, still more deeply felt in that her consciousness was pervaded by it, and she felt, even while she revolted, that her happiness was in his hands, and that she could not escape. He was not a man of great qualities, there was nothing in him to make him worthy of being the arbiter of a life. And yet, so he was.

Janet went to bed, but she found that, with all these fumes of excitement hanging about her, she could not sleep. If she dozed for a few minutes she was again with Meredith, walking along wonderful dark passages, peering through half-opened doors, seeing dreadful visions—sometimes of coffins and dead people, sometimes of threatening faces looking out upon her.

In the end Janet jumped out of bed again and lighted a candle. She had suddenly thought she heard some one touch the handle of her door, and a sudden vision—the face of the old man with his white beard seemed to spring out of the darkness before her. After all, there were but a few doors between them, doors which were sometimes left unsecured. What if, waking like herself in the middle of the night, the prisoner should find a practicable way as she had done, and come out and pass through her door as she had done through his? The impression of some one standing beside her bed was so strong upon her in the dark, that Janet made but one spring to the opposite side, and trembling, managed, though with difficulty, to strike a match.

The light relieved her from that sickening spasm of terror. There was nobody there—of course she knew there could be nobody there: but it was impossible to think of going to sleep again, thrice impossible to return to the darkness and once more imagine stealthy steps about the room and the pallid face bending over her. She put on a dressing-gown, and, taking out the scraps of paper, began with more leisure and real pains to put them together. Now that she knew it was not Dolff's name that was written at the bottom of the page, the sense of mystery returned to her mind. It seemed impossible that his father's copy-books should be still in being, or that it could be of any importance who saw them.

Janet shivered with cold, but it was better than lying trembling in the dark, thinking that the old man of the wing was walking about the room. And she had promised to send the bits of paper to Meredith. She put them all together, piecing them as well as she could. Sometimes she could only join a triangular or oblong scrap to a square one. Sometimes there was an absolute break which in no way could be filled out. She succeeded in making out something like this:

"I can't get—— I want to get out. I can't get out. I can't g—get out: could pay—could p——can't get——can't get—out, out, out——Money, plenty money. Could pay, could p——but can't, can't, can't get out."

It was mere gibberish Janet thought. She knew no meaning in it. After she had worked for an hour at it, she had almost thrown it away again, feeling that it was mere nonsense; whether written by the prisoner, whether, as was more likely, some childish repetitions out of a copybook, she could not tell; but at all events nonsense, throwing no light upon anything, doing no one any good. She fixed the scraps on a sheet of paper, however, as well as she could piece them together, and especially the sprawling, childish signature "Adol——Char—es Har—w——."

She was very cold, very tired, and sleepy by the time this task was done. She would put it in an envelope since *he* had asked her to do so. It would make him none the wiser, still it should be done, because he had desired it. She forgot altogether the central incident of the night as she went back to bed with little, cold feet, shivering and sleepy. The foolishness of the words she had been so carefully picking out and pasting together somehow emancipated her from her terror, they were so silly and without meaning. She did not believe, after all, they could have any connection with the mystery in the wing. But as she thought of the address, and that she must take it herself to the post lest any one should see it and think it a communication of a different kind, a thrill ran through her, and she could not help thinking of perhaps a time to come when there might be other communications that would not be so colorless. Janet's heart felt the lifting tide of a secret happiness. She fell into a delicious drowsiness, in which all his words and looks and movements came back upon her in a maze of pleasant confusion: and then, with the privilege of her age, she fell fast asleep.

Janet posted her letter next day, glad to be rid of it; for she could not, all the morning, get over the terror in her mind lest she should pull the letter out of her pocket with her pocket-handkerchief, or somehow expose it to be looked at, and so call forth the comment which she felt already ringing in her ears, as if any one she met in the street might come up and call it out to her:

"Oh, are you in correspondence with Charley Meredith?" "What have you to say to Charley Meredith?"

She thought she could see Gussy's look if that dreadful contingency should come to pass. It would not be she that would make that exclamation—wonder would be the sentiment in her face, wonder and a sort of mild haughtiness which Miss Harwood knew how to put on. She would take no notice. But she would never forget; she would go on wondering, perhaps divining at last: proudly and entirely ignoring that strange incident—but she would not forget it. Henceforward her eyes would have another aspect towards Janet, and even perhaps towards her lover.

Janet breathed more freely when it was safely out of her pocket and in the post-office box. Nobody could see it now; she was safe, at least for the time. It is needless to say that she added not a word, explanatory or otherwise, to that curious piece of paper. She wrote the address with the greatest care in her neatest hand. She was so girlish as to think that her pretty handwriting, the fresh glossy envelope which she selected so carefully, rejecting one which had a small speck upon it, and which was a little brown at one corner—would go to his heart, and that he would remark those signs of her care to please him. Poor little Janet! She was not a girl of lofty sentiments, nor a very loyal soul; but she was very young, and had a world of foolish expectation still in her inexperienced heart.

Thus her former terror about the mystery which she had discovered so close to her was quieted in her mind almost entirely by the coming in of something more powerful. Sometimes a vague thrill of terror would pass through her when she looked at the door so hermetically closed, the door which had once trembled and given way under her slight fingers. In the middle of the night she sometimes woke with a start thinking she heard some one at her door, afraid to open her eyes lest she should see the whiteness in her room of the white beard and pallid face.

She took to locking her door from that time, a practice for which she was much scoffed at by Julia, who discovered it at once and wished to know, satirically, what she was afraid of? Was it robbers, and did Janet think they would come up all the way to the second floor for her, instead of going at once to the pantry for the plate? Janet could not make an answer to this assault, but she continued to lock her door and to look carefully around her room every night to make sure that no one was there.

This, however, was the only effect that the vision in the wing had upon her. Another matter, far closer and more urgent, was introduced into her thoughts. There were now two people whose whole attention was bent on the sounds outside in the still evenings when they sat over their needlework, listening intently for a step, for the sound of the bell. To meet him and Gussy within the same four walls, to see his eyes turn to her, and know that Miss Harwood looked on, this was far more difficult than any mystery for Janet to bear.

CHAPTER XXIX.

GUSSY HARWOOD awoke next morning with a sense of exhilaration in her mind, as if, during the night, some burden had rolled off her shoulders. Had any burden been rolled off? The first sensation in the morning of pain or pleasure is not always a true one, but there is none so poignant or which leaves so much impression on the mind.

A year—she said to herself—what was a year? If it were two years, what would it matter so long as all doubts were removed and she was assured that as she thought of him so he thought of her? How much better would it have been, in that point of view, if he had opened his heart to her at once!—not waiting for business or wealth or the means of setting up a house which he could ask her to share. All these were secondary matters. The thing she desired to know was his heart and what was in it. If he really loved her, as she sometimes believed he did, yet sometimes doubted, how happy it would be to watch the growth of the practice, the coming of the time when prudence and good sense would permit them to set up a new household together!

Gussy did not desire in the least to forestall that moment, to reject the guidance of prudence. Far from that. Her own actions were always regulated by that rule. All that she wanted was the full understanding, the power to believe that she knew his heart as he knew hers. But she said to herself, with a sigh,

"Men do not understand this. They think it not honorable to engage a woman before they are able to carry their engagement out, not knowing, not guessing, how very different is the woman's view—how that what she wants is the understanding, the link between heart and heart, the privilege of sharing their thoughts and being bound to them."

She sighed, and there was impatience and weariness in her sigh. How was it that they would not understand—that he would not understand? She would wait for him for years if it were necessary, so long as there was no doubt left upon the mutual sentiment, so long as the bond was made which he thought it more honorable not to make till it could be quickly fulfilled.

And this feeling went on growing stronger every hour of the day. The first exhilaration departed, and the weariness came back. A year! And who could tell that in a year there might not be some new drawback, some further suspense necessary. If men would but understand that it is not to be married that the woman wants, but to know the lover's heart, to be assured of his love!

When Molière made his *Précieuses* contemn the vulgar haste with which their suitors would have jumped to the last accomplished fact of marriage, he had (perhaps) touched a secret of the feminine heart which few men divine.

Gussy, who was not poetical, still less *précieuse*, who was indeed a very matter-of-fact and most sensible person, would have been like the foolish Cathon and Madelon, quite pleased with the *pays du tendre*, so long as her lover had led her with a faithful hand into that enchanted country. She did not insist upon the new establishment, the immediate conclusion. She only wanted him to say frankly half-a-dozen words, and so to bind them together forever. It was half an injury to her that he should feel it necessary to wait for such a practical reason. Did he think that her love was a less thing than her word, and that so long as she had not audibly pledged that, she was free? Did he think himself free because he had not said to her, "Be my wife!"

These questions flitted through Gussy's mind, drifting across the sky like clouds, throughout the day. She shook her head at the vanity and shortsightedness of the thought. She free, when she loved him! Would a mere promise bind her more than the devotion of her whole being? And then there came a cold shiver over Gussy's heart. Did he think perhaps that *he* was free so long as he had made no promise—that all the silent fascination which bound them together and the link that had been growing for years, and which he had woven by so many tender words and looks and fond regards, was nothing, so long as no pledge had been given or received?

Gussy would not allow herself to think this. She shook her head over the defects in men, the absence of a finer feeling, the want of that intuition which everybody said women possessed in a higher degree. He could not see that there was a more delicate honor in avowal than in silence. It was strange, but she was obliged to conclude that this was how men felt, and that they did not understand.

Gussy was also a little cast down, ashamed, almost humbled, by the thought that he was in no such doubt of her sentiments as she was of his. But, then, she asked herself—for such a problem awakens metaphysical tendencies in the most simple mind—whether perhaps her doubt of him was not as much the weakness of the woman's point of view as his reticence was of the man's? Perhaps it had never entered into his mind that she could doubt him after all that had come and gone. Perhaps he felt the bond between them to be so assured and true that no declaration could make it stronger. Perhaps, just as he did not understand her, she did not understand him, and exemplified the woman's deficiency just as he exemplified the man's. This thought sufficed to clear Gussy's brow for the whole afternoon.

She told her mother, who was very eager for news, and had also expected much from the dance, that Charley had been talking about his profession, and that he was now really getting on, and felt, he believed, the ball at his feet.

"He thinks that in another year or so he will be able to think of a house of his own," said Gussy.

"Oh!" said Mrs. Harwood, with somewhat blank looks, "in a year or so!"

"Yes, mamma; did you expect him to jump to the heights of his profession in a moment? A silk gown in six months and the woolsack perhaps in——"

Gussy broke off with a laugh. She had replied to her mother with a look equally blank, incapable of understanding (as it seemed) what could be looked for more.

"I am not so silly as that," said the mother. "I know it is very slow work getting on at the Bar. Still, I thought——"

"What did you think?" asked Gussy, with a certain scorn in the corners of her mouth.

"My dear, if you take that tone I shall say nothing more. I had thought nothing that was not quite reasonable, whatever you may think; but I shall say no more about it. You young people have your own ways of managing matters. I don't think much of them, but that, I suppose, is because I am old-fashioned and can't understand anything so superfine as your modes of action. You are a great deal too superior for me."

"I notice," said Gussy, "that whenever people are arguing, and don't know what to say, they call those who think differently superfine and superior. It is as good an argument as another, I suppose."

Thus Gussy punished her mother for putting into words the troubled intuition of her own heart. It was enough, however, to put a stop to the discussion, which was what she desired most. Mrs. Harwood was so much moved that, wanting an outlet somewhere, she was driven to confiding in Janet, who came down to the drawing-room earlier than usual. Gussy had gone out somewhere to tea.

"I don't seem to understand the simplest questions nowadays," she said, fretfully; "they all think me so old-fashioned that I am not worth considering. Do you think it an honorable thing, Janet, or right, or wise for a man to flutter for years about a girl, always coming after her, never letting her alone, so that everybody has remarked it, and yet never saying a word that could compromise him, though he has quite compromised her? Do you think there is any sense in which that could be called right?"

"No," said Janet, in a very low tone, smitten by sudden compunction.

She had her back to Mrs. Harwood, pouring out the tea.

"What do you say? Oh, I suppose you are just like the rest, and don't see any harm in it. But I assure you I do. If anyone haunted you like that, my dear, under my roof, I should certainly think it my duty to interfere."

"Oh, I hope not, Mrs Harwood; isn't that surely the very worst thing that can be done—to interfere——"

"Interfere!" said Mrs. Harwood, indignantly; "I should soon interfere. I should not let anything like that go on, I promise you. The worst is," she went on, with a troubled countenance, "that with one's own——"

She stopped here, finding further revelation, perhaps, injudicious; but apparently the mere suggestion of interference in one case showed the possibility of doing so in another. She had taken the cup of tea from Janet's hand, who sat down opposite her, in a way which was very familiar and home-like, and Mrs. Harwood's mouth was opened. After a pause she began, with a little laugh,

"My son is not of that kind. I wonder, by the way, what has become of him that he is not in for tea? He is rather the other way. He goes a great deal too fast. If ever he thinks he is in love he will blurt out everything at once, and perhaps find himself bound for life to some one whom he has only known for a few days."

"That is even more dangerous than the other way," said Janet, with exceeding demureness, in the half light.

"Worse for the man, but not for the woman, who gets everything she wants. The other is a great deal better for the man, who holds off until he is quite sure——"

"One would think, then, that you rather approve of that last way, though I thought you had condemned it; but perhaps it is only for your son you would like it, and not for other people——"

"I don't approve it at all," cried Mrs. Harwood, hotly. "A girl's best years may be wasted like that—always waiting and waiting—and perhaps some other cut her out in the end. You can't think I should approve of that, my dear. I only say that Dolff, poor boy, is all the other way, and will most likely fling himself at the head of the first girl he fancies, which would be a pity for the girl too, for Dolff will not be very well off. He has got his grandfather's little property in Wales, which is entailed on him, but he has in reality nothing more: though perhaps people might think otherwise, seeing him always treated as if he were the master of the house."

Janet made no answer for a minute or two, and then, with a not unnatural instinct of combativeness, it occurred to her to carry the war into the enemy's country.

She asked: "Have you been very long in this house, Mrs. Harwood?" in her most childlike voice.

"Eh? Oh! in this house? We came about fifteen years ago when Julia was a baby," she answered, briefly.

"You must have done a great deal to it to make it so pretty. And have you really never used the wing?"

"The wing?"

Mrs. Harwood, in the first impulse of astonishment, raised her eyes and stared at Janet, but said no more.

"It looks," said Janet, "as if it must be such a nice, well-shaped room—or perhaps there is more than one room? Many people would be so glad to have that little additional space."

"You seem to know a great deal about it," said Mrs. Harwood, "though I don't quite know how, for it has been shut up for years, and none of the servants even have ever been in. It is full of old furniture from my home in Wales—and other lumber."

"To be sure," said Janet, "a nice lumber-room where you can put everything is of great use."

"Yes, it is of great use; and, as it happens it would be of no particular use in any other way; for we have as many rooms as we want, and two or three for visitors—which is as much as anybody could desire in London. Of course it is a different thing in a country house. How is it that you have formed such a very clear idea of the wing, Janet? Many people never find it out."

"I suppose," said Janet, "because I have been walking so much in the garden lately, and one goes all the round of the house, and one speculates——"

"On what, I should like to know?" cried Mrs. Harwood, sitting bolt upright in her chair.

"Oh, nothing; only on the shape of the house, and what a nice corner it seems, and so much sun. Perhaps I was so bold as to think it would make a nice school-room," said Janet, with a little laugh, "and so shut off from the rest of the house."

"Oh, if that is all!" said Mrs. Harwood. She resumed, after a moment, "I would not advise it for that use. Of course I don't myself believe in anything of the kind, but there are curious stories about it, about things that have been heard—and seen too, I believe. The last people who lived here were very queer people. I can't tell you all that was said of them. The door of communication used to be open, but the servants in a body begged that it might be shut up. You have noticed, perhaps, that it is quite done away with."

"Is it built up?" asked Janet, with great innocence.

"Built up? oh, no, that's a strong step to take. After us there might come somebody who would want to use it, and building up is a strong step. But it's almost the same—it is fastened up very effectually, so that no one can either come or go—not even," said Mrs. Harwood, with an abrupt laugh, "a ghost."

"But Vicars," said Janet, pursuing the investigation, "can go out and in, I suppose?"

"Vicars?" cried Mrs. Harwood. "What do you suppose he has to do with it? Oh, I know now. You have heard that he lives on the ground-floor. So he does; but his rooms open from outside, as you may have seen. You must keep your eyes very well about you, Janet, to have found out all that."

"No," said Janet; "I only can't help seeing things—that is, some things. And, to tell the truth, I have heard once or twice a curious noise which has frightened me very much. And I never had heard any of the stories, so it was all the more strange."

Mrs. Harwood looked at her for a few moments with a fixed look; veiling her face, however, by means of the cup of tea which she had raised to her lips. Then she relapsed again into a laugh.

"You must not take such foolish fancies into your head, my dear. *I* don't believe in anything of the kind. You may be sure there is some quite simple explanation of it—the wind in a chimney, or some other trick of acoustics, as they call it. You are far too sensible to believe in ghosts or mysterious noises. There is Dolff, I think, at the door."

"I hope the tea is strong enough for him. He likes it strong," said Janet.

"Oh, I am sure it will do very well. Janet! be careful how you mention such a thing to Dolff. He is very imaginative and impressionable. I don't want his mind to be disturbed about the house. Pay a little attention to me, my dear; I am quite in earnest in what I say."

"I shall certainly pay attention to whatever you tell me, Mrs. Harwood."

"I know you will. I know you will! Not another word about it, as he is just coming in—nor to anyone, if you please, my dear. The servants get hold of such things, and make a story out of them, however small the incident may be; and there is a continual fuss, with their frights and their imaginations. You may mention it to Gussy if you like, but to no one else. Well, Dolff, we were just wondering what kept you so late for tea. Gussy and Ju have gone out to a tea-party, but I always calculate upon you to hand me my piece of cake."

"You have got Miss Summerhayes, mother," said Dolff, as if that was all that anyone could require.

CHAPTER XXX.

JANET withdrew as quickly as she could from the drawing-room when she had given Dolff the tea which he now took so regularly, and which his family considered such a sign of mental and moral reformation. There was indeed no chance of being left alone with him, which was the thing of all others she most wished to avoid, for Mrs. Harwood could not go away, and was always present when she had once been wheeled into the room; but Janet knew that Dolff would ask her to come to the piano, and take advantage of the withdrawal there to say things to her which made it very difficult to keep him at arm's length as she wished. She turned away while he was talking to his mother, stealing out of the room, knowing that her absence would be felt by both, but longing to escape, feeling the agitation and excitement more than she could bear. And there could be no doubt that to-night that agitation would be stronger than ever, for Meredith was sure to come to talk over the dance, as was almost necessary considering his intimacy in the house; and her heart beat wildly when she thought of meeting him again in the presence of them all, Gussy and Dolff, and the mother whose secret they had discovered. All of the three were more or less wronged in that secret alliance which had been formed between Meredith and Janet; an alliance, was it, or a conspiracy? The girl shrank into herself for a moment when she thought of this, and of the unsuspecting family who knew nothing of it, and would receive Meredith with such warm kindness, and was so good to herself. She shrank—but then forgot everything else in the consciousness that she should meet him to-night— that once more they would be in the same room, and that with his eyes at least he would say to her many wonderful agitating things.

Perhaps this secrecy, and the absorbing excitement there was in meeting him under the eyes of those who were so deceived, who were so little aware of what was going on beneath, held Janet's interest more than anything else. A conspiracy has always a strange fascination in it, and to carry on secret communications in the face of every scrutiny, and balk suspicion, and baffle watchfulness, has, especially to the very young, a piquancy which legitimate intercourse often does not have. Janet could not escape the sense of guilt, but the interest, the dramatic combinations that would be gone through in the evening, her own position as the heroine of the situation, a place which Gussy thought was hers, but which was not hers, was too strong, or Janet's conscience too weak to conquer. Everything yielded to the thought of what he would say. How he would manage all the conflicting elements, whether he would be able to say a word to her to tell her if he had received her letter. It was far more engrossing, far more absorbing than any play.

And it may be imagined what a party it was that sat awaiting Meredith in the bright room where Mrs. Harwood sat, with the dimmer one beyond, where all the light centred in the white keys of the piano. Gussy was full of an expectation, not quite serene indeed, but calmer than might have been supposed; for, now that she knew all immediate change to be impossible, she had schooled herself to think that what had been said about a year was in itself a sort of decision upon which, since better could not be, her position for the future might be founded. She awaited his coming, accordingly, with more composure than usual, with a sort of secret assurance, as almost her betrothed—kept from being so only by that exaggerated sense of honor which made her impatient sometimes, yet was nevertheless, in its way, in the mistaken way of men, a high quality. To be able to think highly of the man she loves, although she may think him mistaken, or even wrong—to believe that he is wrong in what is, according to his lights, a chivalrous and high-minded way, is always delightful to a woman. She had reasoned herself into this view of the matter, and she sat accordingly in what poor Gussy thought was her most becoming dress, with a countenance full of light and a heart full of trembling comfort, awaiting her lover.

Dolff was a little sulky: he was disappointed and troubled that Janet had run away from him after tea, just when they might have had, he said to himself, a quiet hour, undisturbed by anyone, either for music or talk. Now that fellow Meredith would come and take possession of the piano, and make an exhibition of himself and his singing all night—keeping everybody else out in the cold. Dolff thought that it was not fair. He ought to be the first to be considered in the house; not a fellow who has not even the pluck to speak out, who was dangling on forever without coming to anything. That would never be Dolff's case. Difficulty in making up his mind was not a fault of his. He knew what he wanted, and, by Jove, he would have it, too, whatever his mother might say. They would want him to marry somebody with money, he knew; but there was only one woman in the world whom he would ever marry, and what did it matter to him whether they gave their consent or not?

Thus he mused, sitting as near as he could to Janet, talking to her about the music. Talking about music threw dust in the eyes of his mother and sister, and stopped any interference on their part—and *she* understood well enough what he meant. She was so quick—at the first word, almost before you were aware yourself, she knew what you meant. She was the most wonderful creature that had ever been born; there was none like her, none.

I wonder if Mrs. Harwood, sitting by the side of the fire, had any idea what was going on in the minds of the young people who surrounded her, and who were ready to start, at a word from her, to do anything she wanted. They all thought she had not. Gussy believed that her mother, save for the momentary surprise she had expressed, was entirely satisfied with Meredith, and calmly considered him as one of the family. Dolff thought that his rising passion for Janet would burst upon his mother as a great discovery, calling forth her wrath and (ineffectual) resistance when he should announce it to her. And Janet? Janet was the only one who was not so sure. She was quicker in perception than either of them; and there were looks in Mrs. Harwood's eyes sometimes which did not consist with the quiescence of her *rôle* as a mere good-natured mother of a family, living only to humor her children. Besides, Janet was aware of the secret in this genial woman's life. She knew that there must have been something deeper, something more tragical in it than anybody suspected.

Mrs. Harwood, motionless in her chair, taking every accident with such perfect good-humor, smoothing everybody down, no doubt observing everything, was the one in the party of whom Janet was afraid. But her children were so well accustomed to her, so dutifully, habitually disregardful of her, taking her for granted, as children do, that they made little account of her watchfulness and knowledge. "Mamma takes no notice," they said and thought.

"I wish you'd just try over this thing with me, Miss Summerhayes. I want to have it perfect," said Dolff.

"Oh, please do give us a little respite, Dolff—we know all your songs by heart."

"I did not ask you," said Dolff, with fraternal rudeness. "So do I know all your songs by heart—and Meredith's—and I don't think much of them. Besides, this is none of my old songs," he said, with a little shyness. "It's one Miss Summerhayes looked up for me, and I know you'll like it, mother—something old and nice—not classical, which is not in my way——"

"I should think not, indeed," said Gussy, with scorn.

"Or the other, which I used to like: but I don't care for them now. Miss Summerhayes—oh," he continued, rudely, "here's that fellow; I suppose we shall have to give it up for to-night?"

"There is no reason why you should give up, Dolff. You speak as if Charley—who has far more sense—would ever interfere with you."

"Oh, I know!" said Dolff, digging his hands into his pockets. He brought the song he had intended to sing to Janet, and standing behind her chair showed her how he had marked it in consonance with her teachings. "You said this was to be very *piano*" said Dolff, "it's not how the stupid printers have done it, but I am sure you know best."

This appeal to her, though she felt it almost intolerable, carried Janet through the moment of Meredith's entrance. Gussy rose to meet him, going forward a step involuntarily with the instinctive air of being the person most concerned. He shook hands with Janet as with the rest, pressing her hand as she hoped he did not press the others, till she had nearly cried out, and giving her a look under his eyebrows, which she felt to mean that he had received her communication. And then he sat down, and Dolff retreated, giving up to the superior influence. Meredith brought in with him a changed atmosphere altogether. The humdrum family routine, with all its little subdued oppositions and disagreements, but dull surface of unity, quickened into interest. He divided his smiling looks, his little flattering bantering speeches, among them all.

"Well," he said, "let's talk of last night. I suppose that's still uppermost in all our minds. I hope that you are all quite convinced that it was the greatest possible success."

"You know," said Gussy, "we are not very sanguine people in this family. We are always seized with secret doubts afterwards whether all our friends were not making believe to enjoy themselves."

"I cannot say that is my frame of mind," said her mother; "yes, I thought it went off very well. Everybody looked pleased; they ate a very good supper, and there was no getting them out of the house. I don't at all think they were making believe."

"Ah, mamma, but you're not quite a Harwood, as I often tell you."

"You are the best judge, Mrs. Harwood," said Meredith, "for you look on and see the game. We are all so much engaged in thinking of our own parts that we never take in the whole."

"I see, perhaps, more that I am supposed to see; but I don't pretend to be omniscient, Charley, as you give me credit for."

"With an eye for everything," he said, laughing—"for our vagaries, all and sundry, and for the supper, and for Vicars and who knows how many private matters besides."

"Vicars," said Gussy; "he is the least of mamma's cares, I should think. He is the most invaluable person for such a party as we had last night. He is the best servant I ever saw, though one might think, as he does so little household work, that he would get out of the way. But he doesn't. He never forgets anything———"

"Oh, that's a great deal to say," said Meredith, again with a laugh. "I think I've seen occasions on which he has been caught out."

Mrs. Harwood took no notice of this, though her attention quickened.

"Vicars," she said, tranquilly, "is a very old servant; but I think you may give me some credit, for I superintended everything last night."

Meredith gave Janet a look. Did anybody see it, could anyone notice it, but herself? The secret that they both knew seemed to burn between them like a link of fire.

"Everything," he said, "is a big word."

The laugh with which he accompanied this seemed to Janet full of suggestion, and as if he intended his hearers to understand that there was something beneath; but this was probably only her excited consciousness, for he began at once to plunge into details of how Miss Robinson danced all the evening with Mr. Green, and the hard ado he himself had to prevent two rival mothers from coming to blows.

"For I hope you all saw how I devoted myself to supper and the old ladies," he said.

"You did not dance very much, I perceived," said Gussy.

"No; and chiefly with the plain people, the people who had no partners." He sent a laughing glance towards Janet. "Indeed, I think I may give myself credit for having quite fulfilled my *rôle* of the next friend—the next after the son of the house."

"Dolff does not understand his duties in that way," said Mrs. Harwood. "He dances with all the prettiest people, and never goes near the dowagers; but Charley, I think, is taking too much credit to himself."

"You seem to me," said Dolff, returning from the outer room still with his hands in his pockets, "to be making a great deal of talk about nothing. I didn't see that it required such dreadful exertions to make the dance go off. It went off of itself, as dances usually do, so far as I can see."

"Dolff settles the matter like a Daniel come to judgment. Well, I can only say for myself that last night is one that I shall remember all my life. For finding out more things in heaven and earth than are dreamt of in anyone's philosophy, commend me to a dance."

"Finding out?" said Gussy, with a look of surprise.

"Oh, yes; the hearts are uncovered like the shoulders, and all the corners of the house open. Don't you agree with me, Miss Summerhayes?"

Janet fell a thrill of terror come over her. What did he mean? Was he going to disclose their discovery, to demand explanations?

"I don't think," she said, faltering, "that I—wanted to find out anything. It was a very nice dance."

"That's what I say,", said Dolff. "I don't understand metaphysics. But it was not quite such a nice dance as I hoped," he said once more, stooping over Janet's chair.

It is probable that this last little speech was not intended to be heard, but there was a pause at this moment, and as a matter of fact it was audible enough. Mrs. Harwood and Gussy both looked towards the speaker, whose boyish face was a little flushed as he looked down upon the governess. It diverted their attention from the fact that there was something strange, not quite comprehensible, in what Meredith had said. They were not susceptible about the discoveries that could be made in their house; perhaps, Gussy thought, though his language was a little strange, that all he said was directed to herself, to impress upon her the communications of last night, and to make it more and more evident to her that, little as had been said then, he considered the evening a turning-point in his life. She was very willing to adopt this view. It flattered all her feelings, and confirmed her wishes. He was wrong, oh, very wrong, in that point of honor of his; but he was very anxious. And that, notwithstanding the visionary necessity that sealed his lips, she should fully understand him she threw herself into the discussion and led him on to the gossip of which he was a master, and which amused Mrs. Harwood. They took all the ladies and their toilets to pieces, and Meredith had various stories, funny and otherwise, to tell of the men.

In society of every kind the characters of the absent are often torn to pieces with no particular motive, or one which is half good, to divert the minds of the audience from more important things. The friends of the Harwoods suffered in this way, because the situation had become, nobody knew how, somewhat strained, and the conversation, no one could understand wherefore, uncomfortably significant—and this holocaust was offered up with the usual advantageous results.

CHAPTER XXXI.

IT was certainly impossible that any communication could take place in words between Janet and Meredith on the evening above recorded. He squeezed her hand significantly indeed, and looked volumes at her from under his eyebrows—but looks, though they may express volumes of tenderness and sentiment, are not much to be relied upon as regards facts, and explanations cannot be given in them nor appointments made. Janet was accordingly more tantalized and excited than satisfied by these glances; and she found that when Meredith drew Gussy as usual to the piano, and the ordinary duet began, it was with feelings considerably changed that she regarded this pair, who the last time they performed together she had watched with a half-comic, satirical sense that the woman was much more deeply moved than the man, and a mischievous half pleasure in perceiving how he played with her.

But now Janet was conscious of other feelings; not all the confidential glances he could bestow upon her could keep her from feeling a keen pang as she watched the two together, the close approach of his head to hers, the caressing gesture with which he would bend over Gussy. She had smiled at all that before with a kittenish amusement, half guilty yet undisturbed by any pain, thinking if Gussy only knew what her lover's looks said to the looker-on! But now Janet had ceased to be a looker-on. She was one of the players in the drama, the one secretly preferred, to whom all those sweetnesses were due. She felt a silent pang rise in her instead of the amusement. She was very angry, not sorry, for Gussy, the deluded, and angry beyond words with him. How did he dare to do it? What was his motive? If it was she, Janet, whom he loved, what was the use of keeping up this pretence and flattering Gussy with the vain imagination that she was the object of his thoughts?

It was a great change to have been made in a single night, and it altered Janet's views of many things. She had no longer the feeling of superiority which her spectator position gave her, and from which she had despised Gussy for her easy subjugation and delusion, as well as pitied her. Now Gussy had become her enemy, stealing what belonged to her, since she could talk to him freely, go away with him into the background, where they were comparatively alone, and could say what they pleased to each other.

Thus the evening was full of torture to Janet. She began to pay the penalty. She could not endure Dolff, who came to her perpetually with some little remark or reference, and whom she repulsed with an impatience which took him entirely by surprise; nor Julia, whose retirement from the scene necessitated also the withdrawal of the governess. Julia was very tired after the dissipations of the previous night. She yawned "her head off," as Dolff eloquently said; her eyes would not keep open.

"You had better go to bed, Ju," said her mother; "you were up so late last night."

Julia, after the inevitable resistance which every child, even of fifteen, and however sleepy, offers to that suggestion, rose at last to obey it.

"Are you coming, Janet?" she said; "you must be tired too."

Janet rose after a struggle with herself. She had the greatest mind to rebel, to break the bondage of custom, to ask whether she might not stay. But what was the use? only to have another look perhaps, or squeeze of the hand, as he went away, more exasperating than consolatory. As she followed Julia out of the room she gave a glance, at the pair and saw that Meredith was stooping over Gussy's chair, saying something in her ear, at which she, leaning back almost upon his shoulder, smiled with her face half turned towards the door. Was he carrying it so far, false and cruel as he was, as to make a jest at Janet's expense after all that had happened? Janet felt herself stung to the heart. She ran upstairs with a burning sensation in her breast, as if a knife had gone through her, and flung herself upon her bed in a paroxysm of anger and misery. To make confidences to her on the subject of Gussy was one thing—it made her laugh, though no doubt it was bad of him (yet humorous) to do it, but to make confidences to Gussy about her—this idea fired Janet with anguish and rage beyond words.

It was the custom in the Harwood family, as in many other virtuous houses, that the letters should be placed by the side of the plates at breakfast, each member of the family finding his or her correspondence when he or she appeared—a custom which has its inconveniences if any individual of the family has anything to conceal. It had never occurred to Janet before to receive any letter which had not the Clover postmark, or at least came from some one in that old home; and it was an object of curiosity to Julia to see a litter of letters lying by the governess's plate.

"Oh, what a lot of letters Janet has to-day," she said.

Dolff, who sat on Janet's side of the table, cast an involuntary look at them as he passed. She was herself a little late that morning, not yet downstairs, and it gave the foolish boy pleasure even to read her name. But as he glanced a look of consternation came upon Dolff's face. He uttered a suppressed exclamation, and looked again, then flushed crimson, an effect which was not so pretty on his boyish bearded face as it is on a girl's.

"What is the matter, Dolff?"

"What a cad I am! I am looking at Miss Summerhayes' letters," he said.

"I daresay," said Gussy, "you won't do much harm. She has no letters but from the vicarage and her old friends where she came from."

Dolff did not say anything more, but he was very watchful till Janet appeared, which she did immediately after, with many apologies. He saw her, too, look at the address on the envelope that was uppermost with a start, and then she put her letters hastily away in her pocket.

"You know we all read our letters, Janet," said Gussy, "and stand on no ceremony."

"I know, thanks; but it does not matter. My Clover news will keep: it is much diluted generally, and I am so late this morning. I cannot think what has made me so late."

Dolff was very silent at that morning meal. He scarcely spoke to anyone. He had none of the remarks to make which he was generally so anxious to expend upon Miss Summerhayes. If anybody had been specially interested in Dolff it would have been seen that he watched every movement Janet made—not as he usually did, but with a suspicious, anxious inspection. But his sisters were indifferent, and Janet herself too much excited to pay any attention to him. She did not know that he had seen her letter. When she saw it, she cast a quick glance at the other side of the table to see if by any chance Julia or Gussy had noted a handwriting which must have been familiar. But they were both entirely unconscious, at their ease; and she never thought of Dolff. It was unlikely that a man should have looked at her letters, but one of the girls might have done it with that more lively curiosity which girls have about little things. Julia might have done it "for fun;" but Janet did not think of Dolff. She was, therefore, quite at ease so far as they were concerned, though the letter burned her pocket, demanding to be read. As soon as she had an excuse to rise from the table she did so, still unaware of the spectator, full of heavy thoughts, who said to himself, "Now she is going to read it. She will not trust herself to read it before any of us." He did not know that there was any special reason why Meredith should write to Janet. Had it been Julia who had seen it she would have said so, and Janet would doubtless have found an explanation. But Dolff said nothing. A letter in Meredith's hand—Meredith, who was, or should be, his sister's pledged and affianced lover—who could have nothing to do with Janet that was not clandestine and guilty. Dolff's colorless countenance—with its light hair and light mustache, a face which was more foolish than comic, a half-innocent, half-jovial countenance—was stern as that of a judge. What had she to do with Meredith? What did she know of him, save as Gussy's lover? Was she so far ignorant of honor and virtue that she should allow another woman's lover to write to her? and what to Janet could Meredith have to say?

It was at once less, and more guilty than Dolff imagined—for it was touching the papers she had sent him that Meredith wrote—but the manner of the writing was not exactly that of a business communication. Meredith wrote as follows:—

"MY DEAREST—

"Do you know you have set me on the right track, as I believe, by your mad scraps of paper? They are mad, but there's method in them. I am coming to your house to-night, but I shan't dare, you know, to speak to you. Come to the library, where we have met before, at about four o'clock. You can make an excuse to change books or match worsted or something—any pretext you like, but come. It will be dark, and I can walk with you part of the way home. There is no telling what may come out of those papers of yours— freedom, I think, in the first place, and the power to decide upon my own life. Come, my little Janet, my sweet little girl, at four, to your devoted—C."

While Janet read this her heart beat and thumped upon her bosom, and took away her breath. He had no right to write to her like that. It was abominable of him, a great liberty—"My dearest!" She was not his dearest, she was only an acquaintance whom he had known about two months. And to bid her come "where they had met before," as if she had been in the habit of meeting him before—as if it had not been merely an accidental or chance meeting. Janet was very angry, and shed hot and bitter tears. But yet to be called his dearest, though it was false, was somehow sweet. "His little Janet!" She was not his little Janet; he had nothing to do with her. How dared he?—how dared he?

Janet went with scarlet cheeks to the school-room, when she heard Julia moving about there; and with her soul as much disturbed as her face. How difficult it is to attend to verbs and spelling when your heart is rent between two things—the good which you can barely see, and are doubtful of, and which as so painful; and the evil, which has everything to recommend it except that it is evil. Janet tried to put that conflict aside while she attended to Julia's lessons, thinking all the time how trifling was the one in consideration of the other, what loss of time to worry concerning the way in which she spelt disappointed. It was just as miserable a word if you spelt it one way or the other; diss-apointed does not look so well, but Julia knew no difference. Poor little girl! it is perhaps as vain writing down the tale of Janet's little troubles, while the narrator perhaps has a heart filled with things that hurt and wound a great deal more. But Julia could not fail to remark those scarlet cheeks.

"Why are you so red?" she said; "you look as if you had been scorching your cheeks, as mamma says I do, reading over the fire."

"It is nothing," said Janet; "have you got out all the books?"

"And your eyes look as if you had been crying," said Julia.

How the lessons were got through it would have been difficult for Janet to tell. As it happened, in the afternoon things arranged themselves for her in the most wonderful way so as to leave her free. Julia went out with Gussy to another tea-party, which was a thing she detested, and an old friend of Mrs. Harwood's came to call. The old lady liked to be left alone with her visitor when it was an old friend, so that Janet had perfect command of her time. It seemed done on purpose, she thought, by some spirit opposed to good resolutions, for she had thought that she could not, must not go. She would not, it was treachery to her present home, it was undignified on her own part, obeying a call which was really a careless command, which was given as if it would be beyond her power to resist it. She would not go!

But then came the other side of the question. It might, he had said, be very important to him to get the clue, and he had found it. He would wait for her, and be terribly disappointed when she did not come. He might have some other important question to ask her, something in which she could give him real help. The woman who deliberates is lost. After a great deal of self-discussion, Janet put on her hat hastily, as if by stealth, and went out. It was half dark already, though it was not four o'clock. It occurred to her vaguely that it was a happiness she could scarcely have anticipated not to have Dolff on her hands, who was almost always waiting for the opportunity of falling upon her. But she had scarcely seen Dolff all day.

If ever man spent a miserable day it was Dolff upon this occasion, when all his faculties were roused to watch the girl whom he had thought so perfect. Poor boy, his mind was full of the most dolorous conflict. He was angry, jealous, wretched, longing to go down on his knees to ask her what the letter meant, to implore her to tell him that it was all right and there was no harm in it, yet not daring to betray that he knew anything at all, or that he had any suspicions, and all the time declaring to himself that he was a brute to suspect her that could do no wrong. If she was wronging anyone it was not him, to whom she had never given any hearing, but Gussy. And Dolff's mind waxed fierce at the thought of the other, the man who was Gussy's lover, yet had dared to write to Janet. Sometimes it gleamed upon him that there might be nothing wrong in Meredith's letter to Janet, that it might be some question, something of no importance: but it was very hard for him to believe that there was nothing in it, and the desire in Dolff's heart was to take the fellow by the throat, to knock him down, to kick him, to annihilate him. It was his fault. If Janet was in the wrong, it was he that had beguiled her and led her away.

"Let me but get my hands on the fellow!" Dolff said.

He kept up a very rigorous watch all day, and when in the afternoon he saw Janet steal forth alone, Dolff followed in the growing darkness, determined to see where she went. He kept her in sight along the line of garden walls to the little shop, such an innocent, feminine shop, and his heart was relieved at the sight of it. Surely there could be no harm there!

Dolff thought at first of following her in, his heart swelling with sudden relief. He would go in and ask leave to walk home with her, and forget all his evil thoughts. But as he passed the pretty shop-window, with all its Christmas cards laid out, and paused to look in for the pleasure of seeing her trim little figure with the big boa, looking, as he thought, like no one else he had ever seen before, distinguishable anywhere at any distance, something else struck his eye—a black coat, an uncovered head, a greeting, even the sound of the voices coming to him, recognizable, though he did not hear what they said. It was to arrange a meeting that the letter had come. Dolff's heart swelled as if it would burst from his breast; the veins in his temple began to beat. The traitor! The false wretch—false to Gussy, false to everybody, disgracing and betraying the house in which he had been received!

Dolff's passion ran in his veins like wine. He was drunk with the impulse of vengeance that came upon him. If he could but seize the fellow by the throat, dash out his brains against the stones, he thought he would be happy. He could not have spoken; he could scarcely breathe. Poor Gussy betrayed! And this—this little deceiver—— He stopped himself with a gasp in his throat. It could not be her fault—it was the villain's fault—the intolerable wretch who deserved no mercy. *She* was his victim, too. Dolff stood with eyes of fire gazing at them through the trumpery little veil of painted papers, the Christmas cards and pictures that were stuck all over the window, taking hold of himself, so to speak, with both hands to keep his fury down. After all, it occurred to him, almost with a sense of disappointment, this might, it was possible, be a chance meeting. He must do nothing rashly. He must not strike till he knew. He stood and watched the conversation; how he smiled and advanced, and Janet looked up shyly with at first reluctant looks, withdrawing a little. No, she was unwilling, she drew back. God bless her! She did not, indeed, look up at all at first, only after a time, when he had flattered and cajoled her, the villain. No, she had not meant it, poor darling, he had been lying in wait for her. It was not she, not she, that was to blame!

Dolff followed every movement with blazing eyes; he pulled up the collar of his coat, and held his hat down over his brows, that they might not by any chance see and recognize him. Now they were coming out together. He turned half away with his shoulder to the pair, but his ears drinking in every sound, and Meredith did not seem afraid of being heard.

"You were a little angel to come," he said, as he came down the steps. "I half fancied you would take fright."

It was a settled thing; an arranged meeting. Dolff was almost glad, though with a sense of anguish in his heart. He had his arm thrown out to strike, when with the impulse of rage and jealousy which prefers to feed its flame, to hear a little more of the depravity it means to punish, he restrained himself once more and followed. How it was they did not hear him following almost in their footsteps close behind them he could never tell. They were entirely absorbed in each other. Meredith took that hand which Dolff scarcely dared to touch, and drew it familiarly within his arm.

"It is dark, nobody will see us," said the well-known voice. "Just for this once."

What did he mean by his "just for this once," the shameless villain? If it was for once, should it not be forever? Dolff strode on behind close as their shadow; it was quite dark, and the few lamps in St. John's Wood gave a very moderate light. They did not see him, they were too much absorbed in each other. But he could no longer make out what they said. Meredith was discoursing upon something which Janet did not seem to understand any more than Dolff did; but when he stooped down over her, holding the hand which was upon his arm in his, and said, "My little Janet," both Janet and Dolff, with his supernatural hearing, understood very well. Thus they came in their temerity, trusting to the darkness and to the loneliness of the deserted, silent streets, close to Mrs. Harwood's door.

CHAPTER XXXII.

DOLFF blotted himself out against the wall, under the tree which bent over the wall of his own garden, and threw a rugged shadow on the pavement. He was invisible in the gloom of the wintry night. They went up in their boldness almost to the very door, and stood there whispering, yet starting at every noise. Dolff could scarcely hear Janet's hesitating little voice, but he drank in every sound of Meredith's.

"No, no; there will be nobody out at this hour. Don't be afraid. Ah! there might be Dolff. No; Dolff's waiting for you to come in to teach him his new song, Janet. Little daring! to train a lout like that. Well, you'll keep your eyes open, and if you hear or see anything further, report to me at once. It's very important. What do you say? Don't be in such a fright, dearest; nobody will see us."

Then there came a murmur from Janet, too low to be heard.

"Yes, there you're right. There might be Vicars, the everlasting Vicars whose occupation will be gone, and who will have to return to be a butler, like the others. Oh, no, I've no pity for Vicars. I daresay it was he who put his mistress up to it. Mind you keep a good look-out. You don't know how important it may be for me. Yes, I know I must go. It will be droll after this, won't it, to meet solemnly, as if we had not seen each other for ages, and didn't care if we never met again? Eh? To be sure, I'm going to dinner, and you are never seen on those occasions. Poor little Janet, eating her morsel up in the nursery, like a naughty child, and knowing there's some one downstairs. Never mind, I shall only think of you the more."

"And make fun of me with her?" said Janet, in a sharper, more audible tone.

"With Gussy, bless her! No, she never lets me make fun. She don't understand it. You needn't be jealous, little one, though I avow it's droll enough, the position altogether: to keep her in good humor—and then you, you little spitfire."

Janet was not audible but in the movement of her figure, the twist of her shoulders, the poise of her head, there was a question and remonstrance as clear as words.

"Why do I do it? Oh, it's all very complicated, very difficult to understand. I couldn't explain unless I had time. Unfair! no; there's nothing unfair, don't you know, in love or in war. Don't be afraid; she's of the careless kind, it will do her no harm. I ought not? Well, perhaps not, strictly

- 195 -

speaking. But when does one do everything one ought? This is not right—perhaps not; but it's all the more sweet, eh, little one? And as for Gussy!" he laughed, that triumphant laugh which, even to Janet's bewildered ears, was not without offence, "for Gussy——" with a gurgle of mirth in the words.

Janet could never understand how that horrible moment went, nor how it all happened. Something seemed suddenly to hurtle through the air, a dark, swift, rapid thing, like a thunderbolt. She had scarcely felt the sensation of being pushed away when she was conscious of Meredith lying at her feet, his white face upturned to the faint light, and of that dark thing over him seizing him, dashing his head against the pavement. Janet uttered a cry, but it was not her cry that brought flying feet along the road in both directions, and evoked a little tumult round the insensible figure. She mingled with it instinctively; she could not tell why, keeping silent, partly that she was struck dumb with terror, partly with an instinct of self-preservation, which seized her in this strange, sudden, awful emergency. When the door was opened—and her senses were so acute that she saw it was Vicars who had rushed to see what the commotion was—she managed to steal in unseen, to fly upstairs, and shelter herself in her room. What did it matter where she went? He had been killed before her eyes, with the laugh on his lips. Killed—struck dead at a blow! And she had seen it done, and knew who had done it, and was all mixed up and involved in the horrible, horrible catastrophe. It may seem cruel that this was Janet's first thought, but she was so young. She had done her share of all this wrong so carelessly, with no particular meaning, thinking not much harm.

"Not much harm," she said to herself, piteously.

No harm, no harm—only to amuse herself; and lo! it had come to murder, to sudden, swift fate. She was all one throb from head to foot, of horror and panic and wild excitement. Had any one seen her? Would she be mixed up in it? Would she have to stand forward and avow it all before the world in the light of day! Oh, what could Janet do? Where could she fly? How escape the dreadful revelation, the story which would be spread over all the world, the horrible fact of being mixed up in a murder? For the second time, when he seized Meredith by the shoulders, and dashed his head against the stones, she had recognized Dolff's face, distorted, almost beyond recognition, by passion. What could be more dreadful than to be the witness of it all, the only one who could tell—mixed up in it as no one else in the world could be?

By and by she heard sounds of men tramping, and a great commotion below. They were bringing him in here—him—it—the body. Janet's head went round, she was on the verge of fainting, but called back her senses by a supreme effort, saying to herself that if she were found fainting she would be betrayed, and that nothing but her own self-possession and courage could now save her. She dipped her head into a basin of water, put off her outdoor things, even her shoes, on which there were signs of her walk, and stole out to the gallery to look over the banisters. She was pale, and there was horror in her face, but that was no more than the circumstances called forth.

He was lying on a couch which had been wheeled into the hall, and round him there was a little crowd, a doctor, who seemed to have sprung out of the earth, as everybody did, and who stood over the prostrate figure examining it. What was the use? Janet could scarcely keep herself from crying out, when she had seen him killed. Killed! Oh, what was the use? Gussy, very pale, but with all her wits about her, stood at the foot of the sofa. There was a policeman in the hall, and an eager crowd filling up the doorway with a ring of staring heads. And there he lay killed, killed! And Janet, horror-stricken, speechless, mixed up in it! the only witness of what had been done. That dreadful instinct of self-preservation presently impelled her to further steps; that and the anxiety she felt to know everything, to know especially how far it was known that she was mixed up in it.

"What is it? what is it?" she whispered to Gussy, feeling herself by Miss Harwood's side; "is it an accident?"

"We can't tell what it is: it is Mr. Meredith," said Gussy, in a low, stern tone.

Janet uttered a cry—what more natural?—and, stealing one glance at the white upturned face, hid her own in her hands. It was only what an inexperienced girl would naturally do brought suddenly into such a presence. Nobody noticed her or thought of her. In the dark she had escaped entirely unseen.

Then there stole a little balm into her despairing soul. The doctor, after a hurried examination, turned round to say that the man was still alive, and begged that a well-known surgeon in the neighborhood should be immediately sent for. Gussy, who was very pale but perfectly calm, and complete mistress of the situation, herself superintended the removal of the couch into the dining-room, which was spacious and well aired, and had everything removed which was out of place.

The table was already spread for the dinner at which Meredith was to have been one of the chief guests and Dolff to have occupied the place of master of the house. Fortunately Gussy did not as yet know the double misery involved. It was dreadful enough to have this calamity fall so suddenly without warning upon the domestic happiness and calm. The dinner-table, with all its pretty arrangements of flowers and shining crystal and plate, was such a mockery of the sudden, unexplained, incomprehensible catastrophe, that this touch of the familiar and commonplace almost broke down Gussy's composure. She dismantled it noiselessly with her own hands, assisted eagerly, as she remembered afterwards with compunction and gratitude, by Janet, who clung closely to her like her shadow, following where she went with an anxious endeavor to be of use, which went to Gussy's heart. They removed the incongruous ornaments in less time than half-a-dozen housemaids would have done, and pushed the table aside.

When the surgeon arrived, Janet was ready to be sent on any errand, and did everything with noiseless rapidity, looking not at the figure on the sofa, which she seemed incapable of regarding, but at Gussy for her orders. She was like an obedient, docile slave. When the ladies were sent out of the room she still clung to Miss Harwood like her shadow, moving only when she moved. In the hall the policeman still held his place, with several of the people who had surged in after him and who were giving their several accounts of the transaction.

"I see it all," said one. "I was on the other side of the road, and I see it all. There was a woman with the poor gentleman. I can't tell you what kind of a woman; not much good, I shouldn't think—or perhaps she was a-begging. There wasn't light enough to see. And all in a moment some one made a spring upon him. I don't know where he came from, officer. I see him dash on the gentleman as if he had fallen out of the sky. And down he went like a nine-pin, and afore I could get across the road the other lifts him up again and down with his head upon the ground."

Gussy was standing by, listening intently, and Janet behind, half-hidden in her shadow, listening too, with such wild yet paralyzing sensation, wondering would he know her if he saw her—this man who had seen it all—shrinking behind her protectress faint and sick with the unreality, the fact and falsehood mingled in which her feet were caught.

Gussy's voice so close to her even made her start, "Have they got the man? Is he known?"

The witness turned to her with an instinctive transfer of his attention.

"He just disappeared, mum, as he came. Afore I could come up to them he was gone."

"I saw a man running round the corner," said another, "but I took no notice, for I didn't know then what was up."

"I'll tell you what, miss," said another, "the fellow's in your garden if he's anywhere. I see some one dart in when your man-servant came out. I'll take my oath he did."

"In our garden! Has there been any search? Have you done anything to secure the man? Can anyone identify him? What are you standing there for," cried Gussy, "doing nothing, if that wretch is within reach? Policeman——"

"I'm a-looking after the murdered man, miss," said the policeman. "I did sound my rattle, and there's two of my mates about. I shouldn't say but it might be a good chance to search the garden, unless they've got him outside."

"Go then, go, for heaven's sake, and do it," cried Gussy. "He may have escaped by this time. Mr. Meredith's friends will give a reward. I myself—" she suddenly faltered and grew pale, leaning back upon Janet for support. "Go, go," she cried, faintly, "go and find the murderer."

Janet had to put her arms round her to support her. Oh, what things were beating in the breast that afforded that support. The murderer! was not she too the murderer? she, whom no one would recognize, who would never be punished, save by the consciousness which would be her inheritance forever. Horror and trouble, and the dreadful fear of betraying herself, of being mixed up in it, kept Janet upright as if in a frame of iron. The murderer! Oh, heaven! if they should find him, and if he should point her out and let all the world know how deeply she was mixed up in it! She supported Gussy, yet clung to her, looking with eyes of anguish at the policeman who got out his lantern and prepared to go.

"I think Mr. Harwood is in the garden," she said, "he was—walking there—a little while ago."

"Dolff!" said Gussy, recovering herself; then she added, "I hear my brother is in the garden; he will help you. Oh, do not lose any more time; go! go!"

Was it to save Dolff that Janet said this, or to betray him? Oh, not to betray him certainly, for that would be to betray herself. It seemed to her that the sight of him would kill her; yet could she but warn him by a word—only a word! If he had the presence of mind to be calm, to make that rabble understand that he was the son of the house.

Her heart sank within her as they trooped out into the dark garden; the policeman with his lantern, a few of the boldest of the men following him, the rest hanging about in the front of the house talking over this wonderful adventure, which was so terrible, an unthinking, unoffending man struck down in a moment; but a godsend to all the idle loiterers who spring out of the earth whenever such an excitement is to be had.

The hall was cleared of all the intruders that pushed into it; the servants who had been hanging about retired; Gussy went into the drawing-room to carry the dreadful news to her mother: and Janet, who could not rest, to whom some outlet for her overwhelming excitement was necessary, went out into the porch, and, raising her voice, told the spectators to go away.

"Don't you see that the noise you make will do harm?" she cried. "It may hurt the—the poor gentleman who is—so ill. It will warn the—the man who did it if he should be here. Oh, go away, go away, for God's sake. What do you want here? Go away! oh, go away!"

She went out in her excitement, moving them towards the garden door, which still stood open, haunted by some mere lookers-on to whom the news had been carried by the extraordinary rapidity of rumor, which would call forth a crowd in the midst of a desert. Though she was so slight and young, so little able to influence them, yet they yielded before her, moving out, indistinguishable in the darkness, obeying the natural right of a member of the household to clear its precincts, though with a little grumbling and remonstrance.

"We want to get hold on the murderer." "We want to see as he doesn't escape." "He's far enough off by this," cried a sceptic. "The police get hold on a fellow like that! not as I ever heard tell on."

"Oh, go away, go away," cried Janet, following them to the door.

She pushed it close after them, shutting it with a sharp snap, comforted a little to have got rid of so many at least; but not, it seemed of all. As she turned back some one caught her by the arm. All Janet's composure, her courage, her over-mastering resolution not to betray herself, could not withstand this new shock. She gave a cry. It seemed to her in her dreadful agitation as if the next thing would be that some one would thunder, "You are the woman who was with him" in her ear.

It seemed almost tame to her that the tragic whisper she heard, hoarse and miserable, emphasized by another crushing pressure of her arm, was "Is he dead? Is he dead?" and no more.

CHAPTER XXXIII.

THERE is nothing in the world that so suddenly sobers wild excitement and passion as to carry out its practical suggestions. A blow brings down the pulses of wrath as nothing else can do. It is a dangerous remedy, but it is a sure one.

Dolff was like a devil incarnate as he swooped down upon his victim and beat his head against the stones. The moment he had done it—the moment he had done it, he became a horrified, miserable, remorseful boy, miserable beyond any words to describe. As soon as he heard that dull thud on the pavement, and saw the white face turn unconscious in a blank which he never doubted to be that of death, his own being came back to him. His passion ended like the blowing out of a candle. What had he done? What had he done? Instinctively he sprang back under the shadow of the tree and the wall; but he had no thought of escape, or of anything but the dreadful thing he had done. After a minute, when other people crowded round the prostrate figure, he stole among the crowd and entered with them, pushing like the rest through the narrow doorway, as if he, too, were a spectator, to know all that happened. After the first awful sobering and coming to himself, there came over him a passion of eagerness and curiosity—a desire to know which for the moment made him feel himself a spectator, too. He even asked the other lads who crowded in along with him what it was, what had happened, and heard half-a-dozen versions of his own deed as he shouldered his way on to get a place near the door, with a strange feeling of being cut off from the house and all in it, of being but a wretched spectator and inquirer, though with that misery in his veins like molten fire. What was to hinder him pushing his way among them, going in boldly, he whom nobody could suspect, the son of the house, to see what was the matter? But Dolff could not do it. Janet had been stronger of mind than he. She had managed to disengage herself at once from the tumult, to steal in while attention was diverted from her, to escape in the darkness and confusion. And so might he have done: but he was incapable of thinking of himself or his own safety, though instinct made him herd among the intruders, concealing himself in the crowd. What he wanted to see was what had happened, whether it was real, and the man killed, or if it were only, as he almost hoped, a dreadful dream. He heard it said that the gentleman was not dead, but it conveyed no impression to his mind, and he pushed forward, peering over the shoulders of the others who crowded and gazed at the unknown interior, with a horrible sense of familiarity yet distance. There was the couch wheeled out of the library, the couch on which he had himself lounged so often; there was Gussy, clasping her hands together as if to keep herself up, standing as pale as death by the foot of the couch; there was—heaven! was it Janet standing behind, half concealing herself in the other's shadow? It was not Janet then, he said in his dull brain—not Janet that was the cause of it all, only some horrible delusion to tempt him to his fate. There had been nothing wrong except in him. He it was alone who had been to blame. She could not have been there at all, since, she was here, horrified, full of pity, helping, when he had killed. Oh, God! what had he done? He had killed a man in some horrible mistake. Perhaps it was not Meredith at all; if it was, it was his friend, Gussy's betrothed, the friend of the family. He had killed him—for what, for what? For nothing. His rage had died off like fever. He was quite calm now, like one fallen from some horrible height, shaking with the shock, and as miserable as if all the miseries of earth had gathered on his head. It did not seem to him unnatural that he should stand there among the crowd, struggling to get a glimpse of what was going on in his own home, within his mother's open door.

He did not, however, follow the others when Janet drove them away. Though it had filled him with consternation to see her there, and the dull, dreadful thought that there had been no provocation, nothing but delusion and mistake—it was yet with a kind of stupid fury and repugnance that he saw her taking upon her to send away the crowd, to act as if the house was hers. He hung behind in the dark, and seized her arm with a wild feeling that he would like to crush her too to make her feel, though apparently she had done no wrong. But these gave way to the other anxiety, the deeper interest. After all there was but one thing that it was, or would be, now or ever, of the slightest importance to know—was he dead?

Janet gave no direct answer to his question. She said quickly,

"Come in now, take your place, and nobody will ever suspect. It is all in your own hands."

He did not understand what she meant. Suspect? What did it matter? There was only one thing of consequence—was he dead?

"No," said Janet. "No, no, no; do you understand! Go in, and say you were in the garden. Oh, do you hear me? The men are coming round again. Come in, and look as if—as if you were yourself."

As if he were himself! He did not understand. He was not himself. He did not know who he was. He had nothing to do in that house. He stood and stared blankly at her, not knowing what she meant. But Janet was as keen as he was dull. A passion of energy, of life, and purpose was in her. His hand had dropped from her arm, but she seized him with both hers, and dragged him into the house. She flew at him as if she meant to assault him, putting down the collar of his coat, pulling off his cap, thrusting a hat into his hand—a few hours since how those touches, this familiarity, would have moved them both. She did it all now like a nurse dressing a child, while he stood stupid, not resisting.

"Say you have just come in, and ask what has happened. For God's sake don't mix them all up in it, and kill your mother. Nobody will ever suspect—ah!" Janet saw through the open door the advancing gleam of the policeman's lantern. She left him with a little shake to rouse him to energy, and ran forward to meet the constable. "Have you found the man? Have you found anyone? Oh, here is Mr. Harwood, just come in; you can speak to him. He doesn't know what's happened. I was trying to tell him. Come in," she said, "policeman; but don't let all those people come in. Come in and talk to Mr. Harwood; but shut the door."

The policeman came in heavily, putting down his lantern on the floor.

"We've found nothing, miss, and I didn't expect as we should. It was my mate's business to see as no one escaped while I saw after the gentleman; but he's got clear off, as they always do, along of men not minding their own business. Evening, sir. It's a dreadful business, this is, to happen just at a gentleman's door, and a friend of the family, as they tell me."

"I have just come in," said Dolff, saying his lesson stupidly. And then he added the only question that had any interest for him: "He's not dead?"

"Not at present," said the policeman; "but the doctors say as they can't tell what an hour or two may bring forth." He spoke hopefully, as of a favorable turn the case might take. "It's a deal of trouble for you, sir, and the ladies, to have such a thing as this happen, as I was a-saying, at your very door."

"It's very well, though," said Janet, "for the poor gentleman to be so near a friend's house."

Janet felt that the safety of this house, which she had perhaps betrayed otherwise, but in which her own safety now lay, demanded all her exertions. Despair had given her force. She was beginning to recover her color in the stimulation of this dreadful emergency.

"That's one way of looking at it, miss," said the policeman. "My mates they are busy a-hearing all the nonsense that them fellows can tell them. I don't believe they knows anything about it, for my part. I'll just wait here, sir, if I may, with leave, till I hears the doctor's last report."

"Mr. Harwood is just going in, and he'll bring it to you," said Janet.

She dared not say any more, but she pointed towards the dining-room door with an imperative movement. It was fortunate for Dolff that, at this moment, his sister appeared. She came quickly into the hall, with an exclamation of satisfaction.

"Oh, Dolff, you are here! I am thankful you are here. Have they got the man? I have told them there will be a reward——"

Dolff could say nothing to his sister. His tongue clave to the roof of his mouth. He repeated as he had done before, with a dull reiteration.

"Is he dead? He is not dead?"

"Oh, no, no, no, God be praised! That's the chief thing, isn't it?"

Gussy went up to her brother and twined her arm within his and, leaning upon his shoulder, cried a little, with faint sobs. She was not a demonstrative person, and the movement took him entirely by surprise. He stood with his hands in his pockets, dully supporting her, saying nothing, his mouth open and jaw dropped. There was no power of tragic expression in Dolff's commonplace countenance; but there was a dumb sort of quiescent misery in it. He was capable of nothing, not even of a word to shield himself. But then there was no one there who suspected him—only Janet, who knew, and whose interest it was to protect him—to silence all possibility of suspicion. She stood looking on, conscious of the respectful sympathy of the policeman with the brother and sister, and feeling a new and fierce impulse of hatred rising in her heart towards the young man whom she was exerting herself so strenuously to save.

In the midst of these efforts there came into her mind so strong an impulse to denounce him that Janet was afraid of herself. Even while she was scheming how best to divert all suspicion the voice seemed to struggle up in her almost audibly—"Take him! take him. That is the man!" How could she be sure that she would not yield to it at some moment when the sight of him had driven her frantic with indignation and impatience? That Gussy should seek his sympathy; that everybody should look to Dolff to direct the search; that the very constable—and all the time he was the man—he was the man!

A spasmodic shiver ran through Janet; she could hardly keep silent, and yet her mind was busy inventing devices to protect him. She stood there longing to fly from them all—to be alone, and able to relax her self-bondage. But Janet felt that she dared not go away. He might betray himself—or worse, and more likely still—he might betray her. He might tell Gussy what share she had in the matter. It was what men did—to punish a woman, regardless what trouble might fall upon themselves. She stood with her hands firmly clasped, like a sentinel on guard.

This dreadful evening, however, came to an end, as all evenings do. The crowd was made to pass on, to leave the house in quiet, though there were still an unusual number of passengers and people loitering about till far on in the night, notwithstanding the policeman who was on duty near to keep them unmolested. And within all became quiet, except in so far as dangerous illness in a house disturbs its habitual repose. A nurse had been installed in the room in which Meredith lay, and Gussy came and went throughout the night, holding occasional whispered conferences in the hall with the doctor, who remained too.

The patient still lay insensible, entirely unconscious of what had happened to him, with that utterly mournful and pathetic look which a face that is unconscious takes. He had concussion of the brain, as well as external injuries of a serious description, but it was as yet impossible to pronounce whether he would die, or if he might yet recover. Two of the servants were up in case anything might be wanted during the night, a quite unnecessary precaution—one of the results of the great and unusual excitement which had convulsed the house—but except these women, who appeared now and then at the end of the passage which led to the kitchen, very sleepy and with an air of conscious self-sacrifice on their faces, no one else was suffered to be about. Janet had asked to stay to be of use, but had been dismissed by Miss Harwood—not unkindly.

"It's not that I am not grateful, Janet. You stood by me this evening in a way which I shall not forget; but you're too young," said Gussy, with a sigh, "to sit up, unless it was a case in which your heart was concerned."

This speech of his sister's for the first time roused Dolff a little. He had been sitting all the evening with a stupefied air, saying nothing, calling forth much sympathy and admiration from his mother, who whispered to Janet how tender-hearted he was, how much he felt it. But Gussy's words roused him. He glanced at Janet, as Janet had glanced at him with the same impulse, to say, "She's the cause of it all," as she had felt to say, "That is the man."

Their eyes met, and they both read what was in the other's looks; a certain fear, yet defiance, awoke between them. They were in each other's power. Janet had Dolff's life in her hands, and he had her reputation in his. They were both liable to all the risks of a sudden impulse, to let the truth slip in a moment of provocation.

Janet watched the hardening and darkening of the face which had once expressed only devotion and admiration, with a sinking of her heart. He was more dangerous to her than she was to him. It was evident that to see his sister's trust in her was more than he could bear. After this, however, they withdrew into their rooms with their different burdens. Dolff sat smoking and dozing in his, not knowing what he was to do, or how to meet the morrow. He was still stupid with misery, unable to use his faculties, or to think for himself, as, poor fellow, he was but little used to do at any time. He could not think, but only sit miserable, feeling the night to be a century long, yet without any desire for the morning. As for sleep, it was impossible, and yet, though it was so impossible, he slept the greater part of the night.

As for Janet, there was no rest at all for her; the shock of the terrible events which she had witnessed, which she knew she was the cause of, had affected her nerves, and more than she was aware of: but she had been obliged to thrust it aside from her, to control herself with a hand of iron, to act with an independence and energy which she did not know she possessed, which she had never had occasion to employ before. How could she have had occasion to display them? could such a horrible emergency ever occur twice? could it be possible that ever again she should be placed in such a situation? Even now, when alone and free from all immediate alarm, it was a continual struggle to keep from giving vent to hysterical sounds, crying, or screaming aloud; or convulsive sobbing, which runs into horrible pretence of laughter.

She was not a girl who had ever been humiliated by any such mastery of her nerves over her will and mind. But a hundred frantic impulses seized her during this terrible night. Sometimes she felt as if she must precipitate herself from the window and escape for ever and ever into the darkness; sometimes she felt disposed to tear everything about her, even herself, in wild rage and excitement. Sometimes she walked about—walked, run, flew, from one end of her room to another—unable to calm herself down. And in calmer intervals she stole out of her room and stood looking over the banisters, seeing Gussy come out of the room where she was keeping watch, holding whispered conferences with the doctor at the door, passing in for a moment to the other room where the patient lay, from which the white-capped nurse, with her large apron creating a high light in the partial darkness we aid out to get something that was wanted.

All these noiseless movements of the watchers Janet looked upon from above as if they were the incidents of a dream. It was all going on before her in dumb show—an awful little dream, significant in its silence. And the strange thing was that she felt no interest in the patient round whose unseen bed these watchers were coming and going. All the facts stood out before her. The horrors of the attempt, the touch as she thought of sudden death, the panic of all that might follow, the dreadful fear of being mixed up in it and exposed in her *rôle* of traitor to all the world, to the people at Clover who were fond of her—but any other sentiment was wholly wanting.

She had brought all this upon herself and Meredith and Dolff, through something which she had supposed to be love. It was all love, jealousy, double dealing, the stratagems and deceits which are supposed to be legitimate in love as in war. And yet it did not occur to Janet to care whether Meredith lived or died. The others thought that the chief thing, but she did not. What she would have liked most would have been that he should disappear out of her consciousness altogether, and never be more seen or heard of. She was almost impatient of the watchers and of all the anxiety there was about him, as if it mattered what became of him! She had felt as if she could almost strike at Dolff in her impatience when, instead of attending to the precautions she prescribed to him to save his owe life, he asked, "Is he dead?" For herself, if an earthquake could have taken him away, buried him in the earth, so that his very name should be extinguished, that was what Janet would have liked: but——

CHAPTER XXXIV.

A WEEK flew over the house in St. John's Wood like a dream. Yet nothing could be more erroneous than to say that it flew the days went on feet of lead, not on wings—every hour was as long as a day. The room which had been devoted to Meredith became the centre of the house. The nurse, with her white cap and white apron, was now a recognized member of the family. She came and went when the doctor was with the patient, or when Gussy took her place, cheerful, though she had not very much that was encouraging to say. She told everybody who asked that the poor gentleman was very much the same, but her own opinion was that he was going on well. How he could be going on well while he remained unconscious she could not indeed say.

Gussy spent a great deal of her time by that melancholy sick-bed. There is no such melancholy sick-bed. The breathing form from which the soul seems to have departed is a terrible sight to have before one's eyes day by day.

Gussy had not the use and wont of nursing, and Meredith lying thus helpless before her, rapt from the world and all its ways, with pathetic eyes that saw nothing, acquired the new power of utter and saddest helplessness over the woman who loved him. She would have taken the nurse's place permanently had she been permitted. She was never weary, or would never, at least, acknowledge it, but she grew thinner and paler, disinclined to say anything, sitting silent at the meals over which she still dutifully presided, and doing everything she had been in the habit of doing with a sort of solemnity, as if that sick-bed, death-bed—which was it?—had made the rest of the world unreal to her.

Dolff had become silent, too. He came to no resolution, did nothing; fell back into a sort of sullen use and wont. But all the gayety which he had brought to the house in the days of the music-hall songs, all the attempts to please which had gratified his family during the time when Janet was the light of his eyes, had departed. He no longer spoke to Janet or cared for her society, though he would sit and gaze at her sometimes with the strange, stern expression which was altogether unlike Dolff.

That this change should have been caused by Mr. Meredith's accident was very bewildering to Mrs. Harwood, who, to tell the truth, soon became very weary of Meredith's accident, and longed for his recovery chiefly as a means of getting him away. She did not for a moment believe that it was the effect of this which had changed Dolff. She believed that there must have been some quarrel with Janet—a premature proposal, perhaps, which the governess had rejected. A pretty thing indeed, Mrs. Harwood could not but reflect angrily, that a little governess should reject *her* son! but yet no doubt the best thing that could have happened. This she felt was what it must have been, and she was glad of it, on the whole, though angry with Janet for having treated Dolff as she wished him to be treated. She would have been much more angry had Janet accepted his boyish proposal. As it was, all would no doubt turn out for the best; but she resented her boy's changed looks, and could not but feel a grudge against Janet for causing them.

To tell the truth, in the blank of that anxious week, when everybody was absorbed in Meredith's condition, and the house was exceedingly dull and the days very long, Janet would not have objected to resume her friendly relations with Dolff. Her mind had got over the horror of the position, and somebody to talk to would have been pleasant to her. But Dolff was not disposed to listen to the voice of the charmer. He gazed at her for long times together without saying a word, but it was the stare of anger he directed upon her, and not that of love.

In the meantime the police were coming and going about the house, bringing reports which Dolff had been deputed to hear and examine. Gussy herself for a day or two had insisted upon doing this herself, but presently, as she became more and more engrossed in the sick-room, it became impracticable. She had offered a reward for the ruffian who had so desperately assaulted her lover, and the list of men who had been taken up in succession, examined, and dismissed as having no evidence against them, seemed endless; though no one would seem to have been more likely than another. Dolff was made after a great struggle to take this duty upon him, and stolidly heard the stories which were brought to him, making no remark. Scarcely a day passed in which a detective did not appear with the account of a failure; all of which Dolff listened to in a grave, dazed manner, as if he but partially understood.

As it happened, however, there were some who admired this manner as judicial; and even Gussy in her trouble approved with a smile her brother's action for her, and said in her grave, but gentle voice that it was a good thing he was showing himself so well adapted for his future profession.

The sight of these officials arriving almost daily gave Janet always a pang. She was never sure that things might not some day become intolerable to Dolff—that he might not cast off this dreadful bondage that was eating into his soul, and startle everybody by saying that the man was found, that he was here ready to give himself up, and that it was Janet that was the cause. Thus she was never at rest—she had no certainty of him, no confidence. It seemed to her that the question stood always open, that there was no telling when it might burst forth as fresh as at first, and become a story which would be edifying to all the world.

Dolff, however, had no intention of this kind, nor had he any fear. He knew she would not betray him, and he did not care whether she did so or not. He went on dully, as it was his nature to do, taking no initiative. He was not one who would ever have taken the grave step of giving himself up: but had anyone said to him, "Thou art the man"—had anyone asked him, "Did you do it?" he would not have denied it. And perhaps to be found out was the least miserable thing which could have happened to this unfortunate boy.

They were all sitting in the drawing-room dully enough, after the first week was over. Julia, perhaps, was happiest, who was left quite to herself, and who lay on the rug all the evening with a succession of novels, with her selection of which nobody attempted to interfere. She got them from the library herself, neither her mother nor anyone else attempting to control her. Mrs. Harwood, too, with a piece of white fleecy knitting on her knees, perhaps, was not more dull than usual. She regretted much not to hear Dolff's cheerful voice; but then, of course, singing was impossible, and he had never been a great talker; and if there had been an unfortunate explanation between him and Janet it was all very comprehensible, poor boy. No doubt he would get over it. Young men always did get over these things; but the good mother began to turn over in her mind the desirability of getting rid of Janet—not in any hasty way, of course, but quietly, during the next term, so that Dolff might not be made uncomfortable again by the too close vicinity of the girl who had been so silly as to refuse him. She thought this over while Janet wound her wool for her, and while she called the girl "My dear," and was quite affectionate to her; but these are things which occur continually in domestic life. Dolff was seated at a little distance, with a book open before him; but he did not make any pretence at reading. His eyes were often intent upon Janet from behind the page, and she was conscious of the look, but asked herself why? for there was no love now in Dolff's sullen eyes.

This silent party, enlivened chiefly by Mrs. Harwood's occasional advices or directions to Janet about the winding of the wool, had been passing the evening together, as they often did, with scarcely a change of attitude; and when the door opened suddenly they all looked up with expectation, hoping at least for a break in the monotony somehow. It was Gussy who stood in the doorway, her eyes shining with moisture and joy, and a little flush of color on her face.

"Oh," she said, "he has spoken, he has come to himself!" She came round quickly to Mrs. Harwood, and, throwing her arms round her mother, sank down upon her knees by the side of the chair. "Oh, mamma," she said, "he has come to himself: all in a moment, when we were looking for nothing but another miserable night." She knelt there, facing them all with that sudden revelation of happiness in her face. "He knew me," she said. "I went and kissed him, I was so happy. I thought it might help him to wake up and throw the stupor off—but chiefly because I could not help it, because I was so happy."

"My darling!" said Mrs. Harwood, taking her into her arms.

Dolff and Janet, who were the spectators of this scene, unconsciously and involuntarily looked at each other, as poor Gussy made her confession. Their eyes had never willingly met before, but something, neither could tell what, compelled them to this involuntary, more than involuntary, unwilling confidence. They looked at each other, the sharers of a secret which neither dared reveal. Janet's pale face was suddenly suffused with burning color— and Dolff looked at her with a dull flame in his eyes. The thought flashed through both their minds with one impulse.

Poor Gussy, betraying herself in the rapture of her gladness over her false lover's recovery, had not the faintest conception of this dark secret: but to hear of that sacred kiss of joy aroused something of the old fury in Dolff's mind. He could not bear that Gussy should disclose her weakness, and in presence of the other, the woman for whom this man had nearly died. To sit composedly in the same room, as if they knew no better, to hear these innocent words, to see the full faith of the deceived but happy woman, who had thus her betrothed given back to her from the gates of death, was to Dolff unbearable. He sprang up from his seat, casting a look at Janet of rage and reproach unspeakable, and hurried to the door.

"Oh, Dolff!" said Gussy, springing up and hurrying after him, "you must not, you must not! The nurse says we cannot be too careful; to look at him even might be too much—even I must not go back to-night."

"I was not going near—the fellow," said Dolff, sullenly.

"Oh, I know what your impulse was! Dear Dolff, you have been so kind, so sympathetic, never saying anything. And perhaps you thought I didn't see it: but I have been very greatful to you—very grateful, all the time. Now I can speak," Gussy cried. "Oh, what a time it has been! I was beginning to despair. It looks like a year since that dreadful night. Oh, thank you all, you have been so good to me—Janet, too. And now at last I dare to hope. But you must not go near him, nobody must go." Gussy loosed her hands from her brother's arm, and sat down on the chair he had left. "I can have the pleasure of a cry now," she said, smiling pathetically upon them all.

"We're not crying people in the family, are we, mamma? but it is a great relief when you have been down to the very gates of the grave and come back."

"I hope now you will let them bring you something to eat," said Mrs. Harwood; "you have not had a proper meal for a week. Tell Priscilla to bring a tray, Ju, and some champagne. She must have a little support before the reaction sets in. I know what it is," said the mother, shaking her head; "now that her mind is solaced she will find out that she is as weak as water. And, my dear, you'll not be able to nurse him when nursing will be a real pleasure, when you will see him come round every day—if you don't take care."

"Oh, whatever you please, mamma," said Gussy, in the docility of her happiness. She added, "Tell Dolff not to go. He must not—not for any reason—be disturbed to-night."

"I going—to disturb him? I wouldn't—not for a fortune; but I can't stand this any longer. Gussy crying, and all the rest—I am going away."

"Not out?" said his mother, anxiously. To think there should never be a good thing without the ugly shadow of a trouble after it! He had quarrelled with Janet, and now there was nothing to keep him indoors, to make home agreeable to him. "It is quite late, my dear," she said. "I was just going to bed. Don't, oh! don't go out to-night."

"Don't, Dolff: somebody might be wanted to run for the doctor."

"Did I say that I was going out? I am going to my room. I am going to do some work. Everything here is swallowed up in Meredith, I know; no one thinks of my comfort. But, after all, I'm something more than a man kept on the premises to run for a doctor. I am going to my room to do some work. Good-night."

"Good-night, dear boy," said his mother, holding out her hand to him. "Yes, go and do a little work—that's always good for you. Don't take him at his word, Gussy. He is as glad as any of us; but that's a boy's way."

"I know, mamma," said Gussy, with a serene smile. She beamed upon her sullen brother as if his very ill-humor were something to thank him for. "They will never let one see what they feel," she said.

Had she but known! Dolff went to his room with a surging of blood to his head and trouble in his heart. It was partly relief—for no doubt to be free of the horror of blood-guiltiness was much: and his heart was unspeakably lightened by the thought that Meredith had recovered, that his own hasty fury, the boiling rage into which he had been driven, was not to have fatal consequences. There was to be no stigma on his soul. He need not now spend all his life with blood upon his head, never knowing when he might be found out and hunted down.

But this very relief opened the doors of his mind to the sentiments which had been repressed under the influence of that horror and fear. That Gussy should believe in the man whom he had heard and seen so false—so false! who had jeered and laughed at her devotion and talked of her to another woman, another traitor! that she should hang over his bed and kiss him when he came back to himself! Dolff ground his teeth and muttered an oath of fury. The last thing in the fellow's consciousness must be that lingering talk with Janet, holding her hands, making love to her—and the next would be Gussy's kiss! Dolff felt that he could not bear it—the villain, the rascal, the cad!

And now he would be courted and petted back to life, he would be surrounded continually by the tenderest care and attention, he would be caressed, and flattered, and consoled, while he, Dolff was desired to be in the house solely that he might, if necessary, run for the doctor! It was too much. Dolff set his teeth, and the thought flashed through his mind that if he had such a deceiver in his hands, nobody near! But if it had not been for the relief of knowing that he had failed that time he would not have dared to think such a thought now.

CHAPTER XXXV.

JANET was not moved either by Gussy's rapture or Dolff's rage. To say that she was not relieved would be untrue, for it was, no doubt, a great relief to know that she was not in any way responsible for a man's death. But beyond this her strongest feeling was annoyance, a painful sense that she was not quit of the consequences, that he was still there to be reckoned with, more near than ever, under the same roof. Would he be changed as she was by the catastrophe which had nearly cut off his life? or would he, returning to life from his unconsciousness, and probably knowing much less about it than any of those round him, take up everything from the moment the thread had dropped from his hands and expect her to do the same?

Janet had got a tremendous lesson, such a lesson as not one foolish girl in a million is ever exposed to: and all her lighter feelings—the mischievous pleasure of taking another woman's lover from her, which is so often merely a piece of fun to an unthinking girl; the excitement of being made love to; the fascination of contact with the first man who had ventured to seize upon her attention, to take her interest for granted, to draw her, as it were, into the current of his own being—all these sensations had died in the horror with which that sudden murderous assault had filled her, and the double horror of being mixed up in it, held up before the world as the cause, with a stigma upon her forever. Janet had liked to amuse herself all her life, and it was irresistible to triumph over the composed and self-confident Gussy, to take her lover from her, and watch sarcastically behind backs the self-exposure of the victim, and laugh internally, though never without a half shame, at the "silliness," which wounded Julia's sharp perception, in her sister. Julia saw it as well as Janet, though she did not know the cause. And she had liked the bold love-making, the wicked looks aside which had at once placed her on a platform above Gussy; those confidences which Meredith had begun to make to her from the first, and which had at once established a secret link between them. He had been the interest and amusement of the dull life which Janet had never had time to get tired of, so interesting was the drama he had played for her and made her play; and she had liked to be made love to in that bold, presumptuous way. There was something piquant in it, especially in contrast with the clumsy devotion of Dolff. It had carried her at last a little out of her own control, in the hurrying sensations of the night of the ball: and the touch of jealousy after, and the complication of the events of that night—of the discovery of the papers which she was compelled to send him, and the meeting she was compelled to grant him for the sake of clearing up that mystery—had all added an impetus to the downward stream upon which Janet was going.

Had it not been interrupted so abruptly, it is probable that she might have been floated on beyond her own control, carried to depths beyond her anticipation, and become Meredith's slave and victim, if not his wife. But it had scarcely got beyond the stage of amusement to Janet when it was thus cut in a moment, the link which was twisting round her severed at a blow. And now how glad she would have been to be done with it, to hear of him no more, to wipe it entirely out of her life! It had occurred to her, indeed, that she might do that by leaving the Harwoods; but she was too young, although so independent and self-sustaining, to make up her mind easily to such a trenchant proceeding. She would have to explain to her friends at Clover why, after all her praises of the Harwoods, she left them so soon. She would have to take a great deal of trouble, probably to sacrifice much of her comfort—for Janet was not so entirely inexperienced as not to know that few governesses were treated so well as she was. Therefore, she rejected the idea of going away, or rather, it but flew through her mind as a suggestion which was much too decided and important to be adopted on her own responsibility.

But to hear of Meredith's progress towards recovery troubled Janet extremely. It was like thrusting him upon her again, recommencing a business which she had been glad to believe concluded. She was annoyed and impatient—scornful of Gussy's rapture, indisposed to hear anything further of the matter. When she left the room with her pupil, leaving the mother and daughter going over and over the minutest details—of how the patient had opened his eyes; how he had looked around with a bewildered glance; how his face had lighted up at the sight of Gussy, etc., Janet was almost angry at the fuss they were making, and provoked beyond description by their delight and endless anticipations.

"After this he'll make progress every day," Mrs. Harwood said.

"And oh, mamma, to think he is himself again—to think that he recognized me!" cried Gussy.

Oh, cried Janet to herself, if they but knew! She thought, like Dolff, of the last scene that had been present to his consciousness before that awakening, and Gussy's kiss; of how he had stood laughing, holding her hands, not letting her go, making fun of Gussy; and the next thing he was aware of—a dim sick-room, a nurse in a white cap, and Gussy, who kissed him in her joy! It was all Janet could do not to burst out with something contradictory, something that would express all the contrariety of her feelings. It was a good thing to get out of the room, to be out of temptation. She did not remark Julia's keen inspection of her in the vehemence of the perturbation in her own mind.

"Well," said Julia as they went upstairs; "it's a good thing he is better, though I wish Gussy would not be always so silly about him. Aren't you glad he is better, Janet?"

"Did you think," said Janet, "that I wished him to be worse?"

"Oh! I don't know. I used to think you liked Charley Meredith; but I'm almost sure you don't now."

"One may not care for a man, and yet one may be glad he is better. I am sick," cried Janet, unable to control herself, "of hearing his name."

"Oh, so am I!" cried Julia. "Isn't it enough to make one ill? And now there will be more of it than ever. We shall all be wanted to rejoice over him. I wish he had gone to his own chambers to be killed, and not here."

By this time they had reached the school-room, which was their common property, and where no one could interfere with their talk. Julia threw herself into a chair before the fire and pursued her inquiries.

"Did you ever think to yourself," she said, "Janet, how it was that Charley should have been assaulted like that?"

"Think!" said Janet, faltering. "I don't know what good thinking would do."

"That may be," said Julia, "but one can't help thinking, though it may do no good. I hate him so much myself that I understand it better than you can, who used to like him. It must have been some one who hated him—even more than me."

"Don't talk so about a—a crime, Julia: and don't say me instead of I," Janet cried, hoping to stop this embarrassing discussion.

"Oh, what does stupid grammar matter! My opinion is that it must have been something about a girl."

"Julia!" cried the governess, taking refuge in the shock of conventional horror at such a suggestion from such a quarter.

"Oh, you know as well as I do what Charley was. I have heard even mamma say that he couldn't resist making himself agreeable, whoever it was. That's mamma's way of putting it. Why, he has made eyes even at me—Gussy's sister, and only fifteen, and hating him as I do! It stands to reason that he did it to everybody else. And suppose there was some silly girl who thought it meant something, and somebody belonging to her who wouldn't put up with it? Oh, I've wished often I was a man and could knock him down!"

"When a man is lying so ill as he is, it is dreadful to talk of hating him."

"Oh, but you can't help it, however dreadful it may be! and, besides, he's getting better. You don't like him yourself."

"I never said so," said Janet.

"But I know. And you did like him once. What has made you change your mind? Do you know—but I won't say it; you will be angry."

"You had better say it—whatever you want to say."

"Well, then, I think—you needn't blaze out upon me, for of course I may be quite silly—Janet, I think you know something about it. There! Oh, you may kill me if you like with your eyes, but that won't make any difference! I think you've known something about it all the time."

Janet's eyes gave forth a flash. If it had been Gussy who had made this charge instead of Julia, her mind was so excited and troubled that, in all likelihood, she would have burst forth with the secret which she had been so anxious hitherto to conceal. She stood looking at the girl, happy to feel that her blood did not rush to her cheeks as it had done already this evening. She said:

"I think you are mad, Julia, to ask me such a question."

"Oh, I didn't ask any question. I said I thought—and so I do, and nothing you can say will change me. Shall I tell you what I think? I think you were out at the door or at the staircase window—where Gussy always goes to watch for people—and that you saw it, and saw who did it, and won't tell. I suppose it's from a good motive," said Julia, "to save somebody. I should do it myself, but that would be chiefly because I hate *him*, not to give him the satisfaction. However, only wait till Charley Meredith gets well. Oh! trust him to find it all out. He'll not let anybody off. He'll have no mercy. Now, that's my opinion, Janet, if you like to know."

"They are very bold opinions," said Janet; "scarcely what a girl should venture to express; but I was neither at the staircase-window nor at the door, and if all that you imagine besides is as true as what you say of me——"

Janet did not like to commit herself to an absolutely false statement, though she had no objection to deceive. She liked, when she could, to answer inconvenient questions *au pied de la lettre* in a way which might be true. Thus she was not at the door in Julia's sense of the word, but standing outside the door, perilously near it. She concluded with herself that, in saying she was not at the door, she was saying the exact and formal truth.

"Oh, I don't know!" said Julia; "you may convince me as much as you like, but I'll be of the same opinion still. The only thing is, I just warn you how it will be when Charley Meredith gets well. He won't forgive the man that did that. He won't forgive you if you're mixed up in it. Don't be mixed up in Charley Meredith's affairs, Janet. He'll get to the bottom of it as soon as he is well."

"You are a Daniel come to judgment," said Janet, with a laugh.

How strange a thing a laugh was from her at such a moment! For, though Julia was only a child, what she said was true enough. Meredith, when he got well, was not a man who would blunder about as the policeman did, hearing every story, not knowing how to separate the grain from the chaff. Even, he was a lawyer too, she reflected, with a gleam of terror. He would know how to put things together. Perhaps—this was possible, too—Dolff's face, white and distorted by passion, might have been revealed to him as he fell, as it was to Janet. He might remember as his faculties came back, and he would be able to follow it out.

Going back upon that evening, Janet began to trace with horror the evidence that might be got together. There were the people at the library who saw them meet and speak to each other, and who might have seen them walk off together, thus identifying her at least. And Meredith himself would know that she must have witnessed the attack upon him. Her anxieties had been quieted by this long want of cessation from all progress. But now that he was getting well! Oh, Julia was right. He would let no one off; he would take full vengeance for his injuries. All the world would know how she was mixed up in it! She would have to appear, to be cross-examined, to tell all she knew, and explain how she was there, and it would be in all the newspapers.

This was what chiefly struck Janet with anguish and terror unspeakable. Everybody would know it! Her friends would look upon her darkly; the vicarage—even that kind house would close its doors. To be traitor to the people who had been so kind to her—to meet another woman's lover, the betrothed of the daughter of the house! Who would have anything to say to a governess who had done that? And though she might tell the episode of the papers, and thus account for her communications with Meredith, who would believe her? Janet had an hour or two of extreme anguish turning this all over in her mind.

After this, however, she grew a little more composed. Perhaps Meredith would be kept back by the fact that he himself would be affected as much as she by any such revelation. Probably he would not, for his own sake, like it to be known that he had clandestine meetings with the governess. This was of all others the thing that would damn him, not only in St. John's

Wood, but wherever there were families to which he might wish to recommend himself. If it all came out, Gussy would no doubt be lost to him (if he had ever cared for Gussy), and not only Gussy but every young lady in his own position, and the mother of every young lady. To have clandestine meetings with the governess—to make love behind backs to the governess! Janet's heart calmed down in its tumultuous beating when this blessed thought came into her mind. No, he would not betray himself in that way. He might not care for betraying her, but he would not betray himself. He would not allow himself to be held up to the contempt of the world, put into all the papers, perhaps into *Punch*, with a shabby girl clinging to him in the dock.

Janet, who thought of everything in the sharply acute state of her perceptions, remembered too that, while the ladies would think it the blackest treachery to carry on a correspondence with the governess, the newspapers would take the other side, and would be chiefly indignant concerning the wrongs of the poor girl, blighted by her dependent position, whom this monster was endeavoring to beguile and lead astray. Ah, no! Meredith would not lay himself open to these critics. He would keep her out of it, since otherwise he himself would suffer. It calmed her entirely after a time to follow out this point of view.

But, oh! if he could but be spirited away to the other end of the world. Oh, if she could but be quit of him—but forget that she had ever seen him! Janet looked towards the room of the convalescent with a tremor. What would his feelings be? Would he expect to take up the thread where it had dropped? Would he go on telling her with his eyes what a fool Gussy was? how ridiculous was her confidence in herself! how much more he cared for herself, Janet, than for anybody else in the world! This, she thought, would be the most intolerable of all.

CHAPTER XXXVI.

AFTER this fright, however, which was—so much is that poison to one which is another's antidote—so joyful for Gussy, everything relapsed into a still and apprehensive silence which to two in the house seemed full of fate. Better and better was the news that came from the sick-room. Morning after morning Gussy came to the breakfast-table pale but radiant with the bulletin. Better, and better, and better. He not only knew her, but had smiled and said a few words. He had a long and refreshing sleep. He was promoted to a little solid food. The doctor was satisfied, nay, astonished, at the progress made. But all this took a long time.

There was a long interval of that dark and melancholy weather which gives winter its special horror in London—one day more dull and gray and dismal than the other, depressing in any circumstances, miserable when there is anxiety and suspense within. The new year had begun with the chills and snows and dreariness which so often accompany it. The only relief in the prospect was that Dolff ere many days had passed would have to return to Oxford. If it only might be that he could go without seeing the convalescent? He wished this himself in a half-and-half way sometimes, hoping that he might not be compelled to congratulate Meredith on his recovery, or indeed face him at all, though he was glad that he was getting well: yet sometimes also with a lurking desire to see him, to judge for himself how much he was changed, and if he had any consciousness of "what had happened." Dolff did not indicate to himself the tremendous moment of his passion by any more clear description than this. Perhaps on the whole he wished more than he feared to see Meredith again. Then perhaps he would get out of his eyes the white face upon the pavement, with the faint lamplight upon it, which he had never been able to forget.

The day on which Meredith was first allowed to see the family was a Monday in the middle of January. His couch was wheeled into the drawing-room in the afternoon, Gussy proudly attending and announcing her patient. The daylight was beginning to wane, and to two at least of the party it was more easy to see him than it was for him to see them. Janet had withdrawn into the further part of the room, as was becoming in her position, and Dolff stood uneasily near the door, removing himself, without intention, in the mere excitement and uneasiness of this first meeting, from the light. Meredith was still very pale, and the change in his face, which had been florid red and white, was striking. His black hair, and the beard which had grown during his illness, made his pallor still more apparent, but it was scarcely the paleness which gives refinement and spirituality to a face worn with suffering. He shook hands with them all, and turned his head, asking, "Is that Miss Summerhayes?" in a way which compelled Janet to come forward, though so much against her will. He glanced up at her with something of his old look, a sort of smile in his eyes, the telegraph of old, which implied some secret understanding between them, and which once had so fluttered Janet's heart. But it only brought a sickening thrill now of alarm and repugnance. This was the only thing she noted specially in the first interview, a look which showed her that all was not over, that he was not ready yet to relinquish the amusement which she had given him (if that was how to describe it), and that, though he had been at death's door, and was so much altered in appearance, in himself he was not changed. Janet was too young to know that to be at death's door is no sufficient reason for any change in that strange and perverse thing which is called the heart. She had been a little moved by the sight of him, so colorless and feeble, notwithstanding the change in her own feelings towards him. There is something piteous in the sight of a strong man, young, and in the flower of life, lying helpless upon a couch, ministered to like a child. It touched her heart, and something of the reverence for weakness, which is inherent in humanity, moved her as she came unwillingly, yet obediently to his side. But that side glance, the old confidential look, the smile which might have been called a leer by a more severe spectator, caught Janet in the midst of her momentary awe, and drove her back upon herself. She was not, as the reader knows, so lofty in her views, so generous in her motives, as would become a heroine; but she was startled and shocked by this, and thrown back into her original dismay and fear.

After this he saw the family every day. It became the habit of the house as he slowly recovered (and it was very slow progress) to have the couch rolled into the drawing-room every day, visitors shut out, and the whole efforts of the household, which were not very effectual in that department, devoted to the amusement of the patient. They were not very clever in the way of amusement. Mrs. Harwood talked to him, occasionally lighting upon an old story which had some interest for the invalid, and Gussy talked with no such reservoir of interest to fall back upon, generally dropping after a time into household details, which did not amuse him at all.

Janet, when she was not able to escape, sat demurely silent as far off as possible, her head bent over her work; and Dolff, who seemed to have been seized by a feverish desire to be present during these séances, as if something to his detriment might happen if he were absent, stood about, sometimes standing at one window, sometimes at another, adjured by his mother and sister not to get into the light, uncomfortable and unnecessary everywhere. Meredith, as he got able to talk a little, took up again his old habit of somewhat contemptuous banter to Dolff. He begged to know if he had not been singing lately—if Miss Summerhayes had been cruel and ceased to play the accompaniments, which she was so clever at. It was evident that his mind was far from any painful associations in respect to Dolff. He declared that it would amuse him to hear one of the old songs.

"Not the new ones," he said, with that exasperating smile, "the refined ones, which Miss Summerhayes prefers. Sing me one of those, Dolff, that you brought from the Vic."

"One of those! They're not fit for a drawing-room, Meredith; you know they're not."

"We heard them in the drawing-room often enough, didn't we, Gussy! Come, humor me—everybody humors me—sing me—that one, you know, with the chorus—" and the sick man hummed a bar or two of the most uproarious of those songs which had so startled the decorous family.

He laughed and flashed at Janet—who by some extraordinary trick of nature was aware now, when her back was turned to him, of those looks—a wicked glance. Nothing he could have asked would have been more painful, nothing could have shone more distinctly the mockery and malice of his intention. A man who had nearly died calling upon his almost murderer for a rollicking music-hall song! It was a ghastly request to the two performers, who looked at each other, or, rather, who looked each in the direction of where the other was, with a sort of helpless, mutual appeal.

"Why don't you do it, Dolff, when Charley asks you? What does it matter, if it's not very suitable, so long as it amuses him?"

Dolff muttered something about being out of practice, not having sung anything for weeks.

"No," said Meredith, "I know how everybody has denied themselves for me. Never mind; I shall like it just as much."

"Can't you go and do it, Dolff?" cried Gussy, impatiently, "when he tells you it will amuse him? It is not for you, to show off how well you can do it. I daresay it will amuse him more if you do it very badly. What does it matter if you are in practice or not?"

Once more Dolff murmured something to the effect that he did not like to be laughed at, with his head down between his shoulders and his chin on his breast.

"Good heavens!" cried Gussy, "as if it mattered! I should have thought you would be glad to be laughed at, so long as it amused him."

Dolff turned his head towards Janet in an appeal for help. She was as unwilling as he was, and felt the tragic ridicule of the proposal even more keenly, as well as the malice and cruel amusement in Meredith's eyes. She knew that he was trying to catch her attention to make her the confidante of his meaning as usual; but Janet kept her eyes fixed upon her work, and would not see. At length, however, she rose up, and putting away the needlework she was busy with, went to the piano. If it had to be done, it was better to do it without further remark. She had played the first bars of the accompaniment several times over before Dolff reluctantly followed her. It was almost the first time he had voluntarily addressed Janet in all those weeks. He said, sullenly, "Does he want to drive me mad? Is that his revenge?" over her head.

Janet replied, playing softly,

"He knows nothing yet. He wants to make us both ridiculous, for no reason. Sing; I'll help you all I can."

Dolff breathed a sigh that fluttered the music upon the piano.

"What pluck you have," he said, with unwilling admiration.

He had sworn never to trust her again, never to have anything to do with her; but how hard it was when he stood by her thus, and felt the charm of her presence, the readiness and courage and support of her little alert soul.

"Sing," she said, firmly, holding down the beginning notes to make a *bruyant*, noisy dash of sound and give him courage.

And Dolff sang—like a martyr—giving forth the uproarious, would-be fun of the words as if they were a psalm, stumbling over every second line, losing his place, forgetting what came next. The audience laughed behind them audibly, noisily, as indeed was right enough, and the effect intended by the song. But it was not at the song they laughed, but at the singer and his ludicrous gravity, and the embarrassment which was freely attributed to temper, both by his mother and sister.

Mrs. Harwood was a little offended at last by the laughter of the others though it was an absurd performance. A woman soon becomes weary of ridicule when called forth by a child of her own.

"You are very merry," she said. "I never heard you laugh so much before, Gussy, at your brother's performance."

"It is very absurd, mamma."

"It is very absurd, I know," said Mrs. Harwood, with a little rising color, "and I think it was very self-denying of Dolff to consent to make himself ridiculous for Charley's amusement. You ought to be a little grateful to him instead of making fun of him. Many would not have done it," said the mother, with a toss upward of her head.

"Mamma! why, he used to sing like that every evening when he came home first."

"Don't you interfere, Ju. If he did, he has seen since that, as he said, it was not appropriate to a drawing-room: and I think it is very good of him, exceedingly self-denying and kind, to do it—when he is more or less making a fool of himself—to amuse Charley."

"Dear Mrs. Harwood," said Meredith, from his sofa, "I am getting selfish; you are all so good to me. And I am very much obliged to Dolff. I have not laughed so much since—I hope he doesn't mind. Thanks, Dolff; that's capital. You've sung it like—like the great—what do you call the man?— Barry himself. Let us have another, please."

But Dolff hurried off as soon as he had uttered the last note, with a sense of humiliation which nothing else could have given him—humiliation, contempt of himself, misery which could not be gauged by any moral estimate. He felt as if all that he had ever done to Meredith was fully paid and atoned for by the exhibition he had thus been compelled to make: and that, if this were to go on, he would fly at the fellow's throat some day and this time make sure work of it.

His look, his laugh—which had never stopped—which began before the performance began, which was not at his song but at him, roused every grim possibility in Dolff's nature. Was that to be his revenge, the coward? a revenge like a woman's, and yet more cruel. To make him ridiculous—to hold him up to derision. And Gussy, with her smile, backing up that fellow, who had bewitched her! Dolff suddenly bethought himself of all he knew, and of what the effect would be upon Gussy if he reported to her what he had seen and heard. This thought sobered him and calmed down the tumult in his veins. If Gussy knew—if she could be made aware that, as Meredith laughed at himself, Dolff, so had he laughed at her, and that to another woman—a woman the deceiver loved, or pretended to love.

Dolff was but a rough fellow, hot-tempered, wanting in delicacy of feeling—but when he thought of the effect of that enlightenment upon his sister he shrank within himself. No; it would be too much to let her know. It was true, also, that he could not let her know without betraying his own dreadful secret, and ruining Janet. Why should he mind ruining Janet, who had cared so little either for the honor or truth of her friends! But he began to reflect, with a softening heart, that Janet had certainly stood by him. She had prevented him from giving himself up at first. She had held him up all along. She had not abandoned him even now, but supported him in that hideous song, though she hated it.

Poor Dolff! it was a sad thing for him to have stood so close to her at the piano, to have felt the spell again, though she had not so much as looked at him. No doubt it was her fault at the first, led astray by that fellow and his blandishments—but since, there was not a word to be said against her; she had stood by him, sustained him, kept him from committing himself—even in the horror of this song she had made it bearable by sharing the scorn, by covering him when he failed. Perhaps he had been hard upon Janet! Oh, if that little fact, that short, all-important scrap of time could be but blown away, made to vanish and to be heard of no more! Oh, if he could but forget, and return to what he was before! Many a man has had the same thought before Dolff: a little scrap of time, a single day, an hour or two—and to think that should influence, darken, perhaps ruin, a whole life; and that no power on earth could do away with it—not that of all the kings and potentates that ever were! At all events, Dolff added to himself fiercely, in conclusion, if only that fellow were out of the house—if only it were not the first idea of everybody to nurse and tend and amuse him. Amuse him! and that he himself, of all others, should be made to exhibit and do tricks like a monkey for Charley Meredith's sake!

"Our songster has forsaken us," said Meredith; "but it was very good while it lasted. Dolff has a great deal of expression, Mrs. Harwood. You may not like that sort of thing, which is not exactly, as he said, adapted for drawing-rooms, but he does it very well; not quite so well as before Miss Summerhayes converted him, but still well enough. It seems to me, Gussy, as if the conversion was not going on——"

"Indeed, I don't at all know what you refer to," said Mrs. Harwood; "nor how my son wanted conversion, Charley—and by Miss Summerhayes."

"I only meant musically," said the patient, with a little air of languor. He added, "I have laughed too much. It is a pleasant way of exhaustion, but it is exhaustion all the same."

"I was afraid it would be too much for you," cried the ever-anxious Gussy; "you over-estimate your strength. Lay back your head, dear Charley, and perhaps you will get a little sleep."

"I take great liberties with you all," he said, "but not so much as to go to sleep in your mother's drawing-room, Gussy."

"Oh, my dear boy, don't think of that," said Mrs. Harwood, at once forgetting his offence before this exhibition of weakness.

"You are spoiling me," he said, half closing his eyes. "How am I ever to go out into the world again after all this coddling?"

"Ask Miss Summerhayes to play one of those nocturnes she plays so well: that will do as well as sleep," said Gussy.

He put out his hand for hers, drawing it beneath the rug that covered him. Gussy's countenance beamed with a mild rapture as she sat close by the couch with her hand in his. It was pleasant to this luxurious person to hold in his—whoever the owner of it might be—a woman's hand.

And Janet sat and played—softly, entering into the dramatic situation notwithstanding the repugnance and revolt in her heart. She could not help entering into her *rôle*—soothing the invalid with soft music, rolling forth gently from the piano, in subdued notes, the spirit of a nocturne which was full of balmy night air and the soft influences of the stars—yet in herself feeling all that was unlike to this, an impatience which she could scarcely restrain, a fierce dislike and resentment. He had made her share in Dolff's ridiculousness, and now he made her play him to sleep like a slave, like something that belonged to him and had no right to contravene his will. Her heart rebelled, though her fingers obeyed. Oh, if he could but be pushed away—banished somewhere out of her sphere, never to be seen again. His laugh was intolerable; his look more intolerable still. Some time or other, she felt, she would say to him, before them all, "Don't look at me, don't take me into your confidence. I will not have your confidence." She knew what he would do if she were driven to such a folly. He would open his eyes wide and appeal to Gussy to know what was the matter. "Have I said anything to Miss Summerhayes that could convey that idea?" he would ask with the most guileless innocence. And Janet knew that there would be nothing to reply.

All this was while he had not remembered, while the events of that night had not returned to his mind. But they would return, she felt sure, as he got stronger. He would remember everything—the share she had in it, and Dolff's face in his passion. Oh, dreadful thought! for then what would he do?

CHAPTER XXXVII.

IT was not till a few days after this that Meredith's growing strength permitted a reference to the circumstances of his "illness," as they all called it, which, of course, was not at all concerted, but occurred quite unintentionally in the course of the conversation. One or two things had been said before he took any part in the talk himself. At length, rousing himself from a sort of reverie, he said.

"How was it, I wonder, that I was so lucky as to be knocked down at your door? Whoever the man was, he did me a good turn there; but how was it that I was found at your door? It was not in the evening, you say—which would have explained itself."

"It was about five o'clock," said Julia, suddenly interposing. She had treasured up all the details in her mind.

"About five o'clock!" said Meredith, looking round him with elevated eyebrows. "Now, tell me, some one, what could I be doing at five o'clock at this door?"

"And you were expected to dinner at half-past seven," said Julia again.

"Evidently," said Meredith, "she has entered into the mystery of the situation. What was I doing at five o'clock, being expected at half-past seven, at this door?"

"I have often thought of it," said Gussy, "and wondered if you were coming to say you could not come to dinner. You had clients who stopped you several times before."

He gave her a glance and laughed, but Gussy was quite unsuspicious, and instanced the clients in perfect good faith.

"Poor clients!" he said; "they have been left to themselves for a long time, but they don't seem to have been clamoring for me. I don't think it could be that."

"Perhaps you were going to call somewhere in the neighborhood," suggested Mrs. Harwood.

"I don't think it could be that either—I don't make many calls, and none about here. Try again. I must find it out."

Janet on this occasion was seated full in view. She had not been able to change her position, as she generally did when he was brought in. She did not look up or take any notice. But Janet was aware that her head was bent stiffly, not naturally, over her work, and that in her whole appearance there must be the rigor of an artificial pose. Her head was bent lower than it need to have been; her needle stumbled in her work, pricking her fingers; and her downcast face, in spite of her, was covered with a hot and angry flush. And he could see her, plainly, distinctly, near him as she had not allowed herself to be since before "the accident" had occurred. He did not take any notice for a little time, being apparently much engaged with his own thoughts; but presently he looked up, and caught the expression of both form and face as she sat in the full light of the window. Oh, that it should have so happened to-day, instead of on any of the preceding days in which it would have been of no consequence! Janet, through her drooping eyelashes, saw—as she could have seen, somehow, had he been behind her—a slight start and awakening in his face: and then he put up his hand to support his head, and fixed his eyes upon her under that shield.

"You are tired, Charley!" she heard Miss Harwood saying.

"No, no; not tired a bit, only thinking."

His thinking was done with his eyes fixed on Janet, reading (she was sure) the dreadful consciousness which she felt to be in her. She waited, trembling, for his next words.

"I think," he said, "a light begins to dawn upon me. I had been at Mimpriss's, the library; I suppose on my usual quest for music."

Janet did not know what might come next.

She had seen various glances directed towards her which made her think he would not spare her. She had made it a principle to forestall everything that could be said about herself.

"Oh, yes," she said, hastily, "now I remember! I saw Mr. Meredith there."

"You never said so before, Janet."

"I think I must have said so, the first evening. Since then nobody has thought of such details."

He looked at her doubtfully, with some vagueness.

"Now I begin to recollect," he said; "I was at Mimpriss's, and walked along, because it was his way home, with—a man I met: and then—yes, I'm beginning to remember. In a little time I shall have it all clear."

He fixed his eyes upon her again under the shelter of his hand. How they seemed to burn into her! She sat quite still, unnaturally still, with her eyes fixed upon her work. Oh, how they burned, those eyes! they seemed to make holes in her, to reach her heart. But this was as far as he had gone as yet. He was beginning to see her in the shops, on the pavement by his side—talking to him. Under the cover of his hand he kept asking her,

"What more? What more?"

"You don't remember with whom it was you were walking?" said Gussy breathlessly.

"Hush, I'm thinking—it is coming, very vaguely, like a thing in the dark."

"Janet, perhaps you saw what sort of man it was with whom Mr. Meredith was walking?"

"No," said Janet. She was unable to form more than this one word: and she never looked at him, but stumbled on at her work, steadying her hands with a tremendous effort.

He saw well enough the perturbation in which she was, though none of the others might remark it; and she saw how he looked at her. Now the smile broke out again, more malicious than ever.

"No," said Meredith, "I don't suppose Miss Summerhayes would see him. I must have met him some time after she saw me at the shop. But I begin to get hold of it all. It was a dark night, and the lamps were lighted. My friend must surely have left me——"

"I was about to say," cried Gussy, "he could not have been with you there, or he must have come in with you, and told us how it was."

"There was nobody with me, then?"

"Nobody, except the man who picked you up and the policeman, who is always coming back to say he's on the track of the murderer."

"The murderer! That gives one an uncomfortable conviction, as if one had really been killed. I have a kind of vision of a face. When does this policeman generally come? I should like to have a talk with him. He might throw some light upon my very dim recollection."

"Dolff is the one who sees him when he comes," said Mrs. Harwood. "I did not, myself, feel equal to it; and Dolff seemed the right person."

"Ah, yes; and so kind of him," said Meredith. "I have been surrounded with true kindness. Dolff, please come and tell me—what does the policeman say?"

"Not much," said Dolff, from the dark corner in which he had established himself.

Meredith turned half round towards him.

"Is the fellow any good?"

"No good at all," cried Dolff. "He has always a new cock-and-bull story. He is no good."

"And none of you in the house saw anything?" Meredith said.

"Well, Charley, it was night. There was nobody at the window; and, had there been, they could have seen nothing. We did not even hear much. It must all have been done very quickly. My dears," cried Mrs. Harwood, with a shiver, "how can we be thankful enough! You might have been killed, Charley. A minute more, and they say there would have been no hope."

Even Meredith was respectful enough to be silent for a moment. But he resumed immediately,

"It is strange that no one should have seen anything. I should have thought—And who opened the door? Did anyone ring to get in? How was it? Perhaps that would help me to pull my thoughts together. Some one must have rung the bell; some good Samaritan."

"No. It was Vicars who heard something, and ran to see what it was," said Gussy. "Vicars is very quick-eared. He runs whenever there is any commotion."

"Ah!" said Meredith again.

He put up his hand once more to cover his eyes, and under his regard Janet for the first time broke down. She got up hastily and threw her work from her.

"Shall I make the tea, Mrs. Harwood?" she said, in a trembling voice.

"Poor Janet," said Mrs. Harwood. "She has never quite got over it. It made such an impression upon her nerves."

"I think," said Gussy, "it might have made more impression upon my nerves than upon Janet's."

"Oh, please don't think of my nerves," said Janet. "If you will let me, I will pour out the tea."

Meredith said nothing. He was following out, with his brain still a little confused, the clue he had got hold of. It was Janet, certainly it was Janet. He read it in every line of her stiffened figure and conscious countenance, and in the overwhelming agitation which had at last triumphed over her self-control. Yes, he had met her in the library, and it was with her he had walked towards the ambush laid for him. What more? Was there anything more? He had in his mind a vague reminiscence of something else which he had seen, which a little more thinking would perhaps enable him to master.

She must have seen what happened if it was she who was with him, as he believed. She must be aware, if not who it was that had assaulted him, at least how it was. He kept on thinking while they talked round him, trying to quicken his own feeble brain into action, and saying to himself that she must know. If she knew, why was she silent? Then it occurred to Meredith what the reason was.

He glanced at Gussy, sitting by him, and even upon his face there came a certain uneasy color. Betray to Gussy his *rendezvous* with Janet! Ah, he understood now why Janet did not speak. She dared not. She must have stolen indoors somehow, and concealed the fact that she had ever been out. It would be her ruin to make her confess. Perhaps Meredith would not have cared so very much for this, if it had not appeared to him that he himself would cut but an indifferent figure—paying his addresses to the daughter of the house, and intriguing with the governess? He went over the same ground which Janet had already traversed, and he confessed to himself that it would not do. But what was this consciousness in his mind that he knew, or had known something more?

"Bring Charley his tea, Dolff," said Mrs. Harwood. "I am sure he wants his tea. It is a nice habit for a man, which I hope you will keep up, Charley, when you are well. I always like to see a young man find pleasure in his tea."

Her soft voice ran on while Dolff very unwillingly, and with averted face, carried the tea to Meredith. What was it that this dark, stormy, half-averted face suggested to the sick man? Dolff leaned over him for a moment, very unwillingly holding out the tea to him, offering him cake and bread-and-butter, which simple dainties were now part of the invalid's regimen. Meredith caught that view of Dolff's face with a certain shock, with a quickened interest, almost anxiety. What did it mean? There was something which he recollected, which he could not recollect—some fact that might throw light upon everything. He was startled beyond measure by the sight of Dolff's face Dolff! there could be nothing in him to excite anyone. Why was it that his heart began to beat at the sight of Dolff? He could not make it out—it had something to do with his accident. What was it. But presently Meredith felt his head begin to ache and his brain to swim. He leaned back upon his pillows with a sigh of impatience. Gussy was standing by his side in a moment asking,

"Was he tired—did he feel giddy?"

Meredith answered with a disappointment and petulance, which in his weak state nearly moved him to tears,

"I can't think, that is the worst of it. I begin to remember a trifle here and there. I have got the length of remembering who was with me, and I know there is something more."

"Don't try to think any more—leave it till to-morrow. You know," said Gussy, "dear Charley, the doctors say it will come all right; but you must do it justice, and not force it. There is no hurry, is there? You are not obliged to begin working directly again."

"No, I'm not obliged to begin working," Meredith said.

It was not necessary to enter into explanations, and to tell her how his mind was occupied. And, as a matter of fact, he remained very quiet all next day *en attendant* the great event and privilege of being allowed to walk across the hall to the drawing-room, and disport himself from chair to chair at his pleasure. From time to time during the day he did, indeed, take up the broken thread where it had dropped from him and try to tack it on to something. But he could not do it. He traced himself along the road from Mimpriss's with Janet on his arm, in the faint lamplight; but at the door he found himself stopped short. One word more would complete the task— one link and he would know all about it, as Janet did, who would never say what it was: but upon that link he could not get hold.

The event of the afternoon was accomplished with great success. He walked unassisted, though feeling as if his legs did not quite belong to him, into the drawing-room, the ladies rising to receive and admire him, as if he had been a child taking its first walk.

"Why, he's a perfect Hercules!" cried Mrs. Harwood. "He walks as well as any of you. Thank God, my dear boy, that you have got on so well. I think we may feel that you are out of the wood now."

"Oh, don't encourage him too much, mamma! He won't be kept down. He is too venturesome. Fancy, nurse tells me that he has been thinking— actually thinking all day."

"How very unguarded of him!" said Mrs. Harwood, with a laugh. And then the usual circle was made round him, and the tea poured out to refresh him after his exertion.

It was while the bread-and-butter was going round that Priscilla, the parlor-maid, came into the room which was so pleasant with firelight and smiling faces, and announced that the detective wanted to speak to the gentleman—Dolff's name was very well known since this inquiry had begun, but it was still to "the gentleman" that this official asked to speak.

"He thinks he has found out something now," said Priscilla with a faint sniff of scepticism.

Priscilla sensibly thought that a man who had been on this job for so long and had discovered nothing was a poor creature indeed.

"Who is the gentleman that is wanted?" said Meredith. "It is Dolff, I suppose, as the man of the house. But why should Dolff be bored with this?—it is my business if ever any business was. Mrs. Harwood, may we have him in here?"

"Certainly, Charley—if you are quite sure that you can stand it."

"Why shouldn't I stand it? I am quite well. I don't even feel weak. Let us have him in here."

Mrs. Harwood looked at Gussy and Gussy looked at the patient.

"I am very much afraid it will try him, mamma. Still, as he would hear the voices in the hall, which might excite him more——"

"Of course it would excite me more. Thanks, my kindest Gussy, though you scold me, you are always on my side."

Here Dolff spoke from the corner in which during these *séances* he always took shelter.

"This is a new man," he said. "He's always got a different thing to suggest, and it's very distracting—hadn't I better see him this time?"

"I think Dolff is right," said Mrs. Harwood.

"No," said Meredith, "I want distraction. Let's have him here."

He did not omit to note the fact that Dolff retired further still into his corner as the policeman came in.

The detective, who was in plain clothes, but not a lofty member of his profession, made a sweeping bow all round, and looked a little embarrassed as he found himself among a company of ladies. He looked round for Dolff, whom he knew, and then at the stranger in the centre of the group, whom he had never seen before, but who distinctly assumed the principal place.

"I beg your pardon," he said, "I don't see the gentleman I've seen before. Oh!—yes—I beg your pardon."

He turned again to the corner, from which Dolff had emerged a little.

"You needn't mind me," said Dolff, "there is the gentleman who is most interested, Mr. Meredith."

Meredith had his eyes fixed on Dolff. The young man was like a thunderstorm, dark, heavy, and lowering, his eyelids half covering his eyes, his shoulders shrugged up, his head down between them. A vague light was breaking upon the question. At this moment Dolff stooped down to recover something he had dropped. Meredith uttered a quick, low cry.

"What is it? What is it? This is too much for you Charley," said Gussy.

His eyes were fixed on Dolff in the corner. They were widening and brightening, the iris dilating, the eyes almost projecting, or seeming to project, with the intensity of his gaze.

"Ah!" he said, with a long-drawn breath.

He had found it at last—the thing which he had remembered yet could not remember. Janet's eyes, drawn to him with a sort of fascination, divined what it meant, and her heart sank. Gussy, who had no such prescience, thought only of excitement and fatigue to her patient.

"Oh, what is it? you are overdone?" she said. "You must do nothing more to-day."

When he turned to her he had a smile on his lips.

"I am not overdone," he said, "on the contrary, I have made great progress. I have got new light. I have got back my memory, and now I remember everything. Pray, Dolff," he said, quietly, "don't go away. You must help us with your experience." And he laughed—a laugh full of mockery, which somehow, to two at least of the persons present, seemed like a death-knell.

Dolff, who had made a step or two towards the door, stopped with an obedience too ready and complete. He saw the change in Meredith's face, and felt that the hour of vengeance which he had, he thought, eluded, was now about to come. He cast a dull glance at Janet, half of appeal, half of despair—and saw that she thought as he did, and was holding her breath in intense attention. She understood, but did not sympathize. She would not stand by him now, he felt instinctively, though she had stood by him before.

"Well," said Meredith, "excuse me, I have kept you too long waiting. You are after the fellow who knocked me down, officer—have you got any trace?"

"Well, sir," said the policeman, "you might say nearly murdered you. I'm glad to see you so well again."

"Thanks," said Meredith, "as I'm so well, we'll say only knocked me down: and if he hadn't taken me at a disadvantage in coming up behind me, I suppose I ought to have been able to give a good account of him."

"Ah!" said the policeman, "one of those fellows he wouldn't face a gentleman like you. I'm sorry to say we've no trace of him—nothing as I could act upon: but I've got the man as saw it from the other side of the street, and he says he could pick out the man from any dozen. He says he would know his face again wherever he saw him; he's got a notion, besides, of where the fellow's to be found. I was thinking as you might like to question him yourself; I have got him just round the corner, waiting with one of my mates, if you'd like to see him yourself."

"Ah!" said Meredith, "it wouldn't be a bad thing. What do you say, Dolff? Don't you think we might have this man—who could recognize the cad who hit me behind my back, here?"

Dolff's tongue clove to the roof of his mouth. He stood in his corner, and glanced at the speaker, but did not answer a word.

"I could have him here in a moment," the policeman said.

"It would be interesting," said Mrs. Harwood, "but a little exciting; and, if he saw him so well, why didn't he secure him there and then?"

"His attention, ma'am, was called off by the gentleman as he thought was dying; but I don't think as it is too late."

Did the detective glance into the corner too, at Dolff standing in dark shadow against the wall?

"I am only afraid it will be too much for you in your weak state," said Gussy, looking anxiously at her patient.

"We'll let Dolff decide," said Meredith, with once more that dreadful laugh. "Come, give us your advice, as you have had all the previous information. Shall we have this man in who can identify—the murderer, Dolff?"

There was a pause, which even to the unsuspecting ladies had something dreadful in it. Dolff cleared his throat and moistened his parched lips.

"You can have him—if you wish it, I suppose?" he said.

The crisis, however, passed off for the moment in an unexpected way—for Meredith's strength suddenly forsook him, and he had to be taken back to his room in something very like a faint.

CHAPTER XXXVIII.

REMEMBERING is a very slow progress when your mind is confused by serious illness, weakness, and the breaking off for a time of all threads of meaning in the mind. Meredith took it up again in the morning, though not with the momentary gleam of conviction which had flashed upon him; and he worked very hard at it, as he might have worked at a case in his practice for the Bar or a mathematical problem. But it was harder than either of those. He made out easily enough his meeting with Janet at Mimpriss's, and guessed rather than remembered that he had walked home with her, and thus exposed himself to being knocked down at Mrs. Harwood's door; but he did not make out until he had returned to the question—his faculties freshened by a night's sleep, and the new energy of the morning—why it was that he had met Janet, or that there was any special reason for their meeting. It flashed upon him all at once that he had made the appointment; that he had written to her to ask her to meet him; and then he remembered all at once the papers and the mystery which the papers had thrown so little light upon. He half started from his couch with excitement when it burst upon him that he was under the same roof as the mysterious recluse in the wing: and thus laid himself open to a grave reproof from his attendant, who called upon him to recollect that he had been very ill, that his escape was half-miraculous, and that to put his health in jeopardy by suffering himself to get excited would be "more than criminal." He believed that she meant scarcely less than criminal, but he was humble, and expressed the deepest penitence.

"I was only thinking," he said, "and something suddenly flashed upon me."

"Thinking is the very worst thing you could do," said the nurse, severely, "and to have things flashing upon you is what I cannot allow. If it occurs again I must appeal to the doctor."

The nurse was a lady, so that he could not quench her as he would have done had she been Mrs. Gamp, and had to apologize again. But the compulsory pause did him good, for when he returned to the subject without any more starts and flashes, it all became clear to him again from the night of the ball upwards. The various events of that night came back like a picture to his mind. It had occupied him entirely in the short intervals that occurred between that discovery and the assault upon him at Mrs. Harwood's door. Since then he had remembered nothing about it till now.

And now: he was under the same roof—he would have, as he got better and better, unbounded opportunities of finding out what that mystery was.

The couch was now to be altogether discarded. He was to be allowed to walk and to sit in a chair like other people. Vicars the mysterious would be under his eye, and Mrs. Harwood—and Gussy in her present condition, softened with anxiety for him, and joy in his recovery, would disclose anything he might ask from her. He knew that she could not keep any secret from him now—if it were a secret she knew.

He felt greatly elated by the idea of the discovery which was so near, which lay under his hand, which he must be able to complete with his present advantages, and the thought of it led him very far on. True, he had almost forgotten Janet and the immediate yet lesser problem which he had to solve, *i.e.*, how he came to be knocked down and almost killed at Mrs. Harwood's, and who had done it. He left the other subject with a sigh and came back to this again for the moment. Yes, he had received from Janet the papers which she had put together for him—received them, he remembered, without a word, which had piqued and made him resolve to compromise Janet, and show her what a farce it was to be demure with him—at least, to compromise Janet as much as he could without compromising himself. It was for that reason, he remembered, that he insisted upon going all the way with and talking to her as only a lover had any right to do—for that reason, and also because she had a great attraction for him, far more than Gussy had ever had. He began to recollect even the things she had said—her little struggles against his appropriation of her, her gradually yielding—all that is most delightful for a suitor of his kind to recollect.

He liked to feel himself the cause of emotion in others—he smiled as he thought of it. Poor little Janet; she was angry and she was horrified. She felt probably that it was she who had brought him into the great danger under which he had fallen, and she was desperate to see that his illness had separated them more than ever, and made Gussy mistress of the situation. He forgave her, therefore, for her averted looks and unyielding face. She must know how it had all come about. He was certain from her looks that she knew, but she would not betray herself by telling, and he would not betray her by forcing her to tell, for in that case he would betray himself too.

Who could it be, he again asked himself, who had fallen upon him, and assaulted him in that terrible way? Meredith was not conscious of having enemies of that old-fashioned kind. There might be plenty of men who did not like him, as there were plenty of men whom he did not like; but between that and trying to murder him there was a great difference. He was not a man of the highest morals, perhaps, but he did not inflict injuries which would give any man a right to fling himself upon him in this way. It was a new idea to think that it might be a lover of Janet's: but what lover could Janet have—some young fellow from the country, perhaps, driven frantic by seeing his beloved in such close colloquy with another man.

Meredith's reason, however, rejected this hypothesis. The young man from the country would not be such a tragical fool as to rush upon an unknown stranger and try to murder him solely because that stranger was walking home with his sweetheart. No! and besides, he remembered something— something which had been presented to his intelligence at the very last moment before that intelligence was temporarily quenched—something— what was it that he remembered? It was all perfectly clear up to this point. He saw every step as distinctly as if it were in a case he had studied from a brief, but here the evidence broke down. And yet it was lying somewhere in a corner of his mind if he could only get at it. He knew that it was there.

"How is our patient to-day?" said Gussy, coming in, with the privilege of her long nursing, after Meredith had made his toilette, and was lying on the sofa to rest after that operation.

The nurse shook her head.

"Our patient," she said, "has been thinking. He has been using his mind a great deal too much—he has been smiling to himself and knitting his brows as if he were trying to remember something. You will please to tell him, Miss Harwood, that this sort of thing will not do. I have done so, but he does not mind me."

"How cruel of you to say so!" said Meredith, "when you know that I mind you in everything! I never take an invigorating glass of soda-water without asking you if I may."

She shook her head again.

"It is not glasses of soda-water that are in question, but using your head, Mr. Meredith, when it's not in a fit state."

"With two or three holes in it," said Meredith, ruefully.

"No; you must not," said Gussy, soothing him. "I am glad you think you have found a clue, but that is enough for to-day."

Yes, it was enough for to-day; he was compelled in his weakness to acknowledge that he could do no more.

"And you must not think. You must not even attempt to think," said Gussy; "thinking is not a thing for you to do. Promise me you will not try."

He took her hand to reassure her, but he did not promise, and even in the act of holding Gussy's hand and looking up tenderly into her face in requital of her care, he glanced round to make sure that Janet saw this little affectionate episode. He wished her to see, with a sense of pique at the indifference she had shown, and a desire that she should be made aware how little her indifference was shared by others. In his weak state it was doubly necessary to him to be surrounded by care and attention, to have love to wait upon and consider him in all things. He was pleased for himself to caress and be caressed, but he loved to have a spectator to whom he could make those little traitorous asides which increased his enjoyment, or whom he could at least mortify with the sight of his entire mastery over some one else if he had ceased to move her.

But, though this little play with the feelings of others pleased him, he did not give up on that account the quest upon which his mind had entered. Meredith had no inclination to let off or pardon the offender who had so nearly taken his life. Whoever it might be, he was determined to hunt him out and punish him. And he only relinquished this, the process in his mind of putting together such evidence as he had got possession of and working it out, as he might have put aside any piece of manual work till his fatigue had passed away and he was able to take it up again. It would not do to throw himself back by getting a headache, by injuring his nerves or his sleep. His mind was sufficiently trained to enable him to do this; to put thoughts aside when they hurt him, to take them back again when he was in a fit state to do so—which is a capacity always very astonishing to those who have never learned to discipline and rule their thoughts.

Janet thought with relief that whatever suspicions may have gleamed across him, whatever half recollections might have formed in his mind, they had passed away like clouds, when she saw him submitting to all Gussy's half-nurse, half-lover attentions, leaning back upon his pillows, suffering himself to be silenced and soothed, smiling upon his anxious ministrant, and professing to do everything she told him.

"Was there ever so docile a slave?" he said; "I have no will but my lady's."

"You mean patient," said Gussy, with the soft flush that lit up her face, "and it is your nurse whom you obey."

"Fortunately the two things are the same in my case," he said.

To think that he could indulge in this badinage while his mind was still following out the thread upon which another man's life hung, was incredible to Janet. She thought it had all passed from his mind, and that she and her secret, and, still more, Dolff and his, must now be safe. And presently she was asked to go again and play for the soothing of the invalid, a request which she obeyed with suppressed indignation. Why should she be made to minister to him too—she whose eyes had been opened, who had just escaped, or hoped that she had escaped from him, almost at the risk of her life? Janet was impatient of him, and half disappointed after the excitement into which his tentative questions and looks had thrown her, that he had let it drop again and float off in nothingness. She was quieted in her fears, but she almost resented it, and despised the man who had so little nerve and force left.

Janet was wrong, it need scarcely be said. Meredith retired a little earlier than usual on the pretence of being tired. He lay very still in the quiet of his room, which nobody but the nurse was now permitted to enter, till his headache was quite gone, and then he returned to the search of his own mind and recollections, and to the finding out of the something which he remembered, yet for the moment had forgot.

CHAPTER XXXIX.

It all came back like lightning when the policeman came once more. The family party were almost as before, when the man was announced again, bringing back the former excitement.

No one noticed when Dolff stole out of the room. The lamps had not been brought in, though the afternoon had become dark. The fire glowed, but gave no flame. But it is wrong to say that no one noticed. Janet did not lose a movement of the unhappy young man, nor did Meredith, though he took no notice. Meredith said little: he was struggling with the force of this new discovery that had flashed upon his mind, and which not only cleared up the knotty point, but put meaning and reason into a business hitherto incomprehensible to him.

When the aspect of Dolff suddenly struck upon his dormant memory and roused it into keen life, he no longer found any difficulty in understanding the whole matter. Dolff had seen him with Janet, with whom the lout imagined himself in love. He had heard, perhaps, certain words of the conversation: he had seen the clinging of Janet to Meredith's arm, the hands held in his. Meredith thought he remembered now a figure with hat drawn down and collar up at the window of Mimpriss's shop. It was all explicable now; he understood it. Dolff! It flashed upon him without doubt or uncertainty. There was something whimsical, bizarre about it which made him laugh. Dolff, whom he had always despised, a rowdy undergraduate, a music-hall man. Dolff, a troublesome boy, wanting even in the matured strength of a man, not his own match in any way. And to think that he had been carried into the house, and nursed with the profoundest devotion under the same roof with the cub who had tried to take his life.

Nobody had the least idea why Meredith laughed. It was at the detective, he said, though the detective was not ridiculous at all. And this was what had changed the looks of Janet, and given her that tranquil air which, now he thought of it, was so ludicrous too. He had to make an effort to restrain that laugh. After the first thrill of anger, Meredith rejected as impossible the punishment of Dolff. It was not a thing that could be done. Such a scandal and disturbance of all existing ties was inexpedient, even for himself—to have it published to the world that he had been knocked down and almost killed by the son of the house in which he spent most of his evenings, was impossible. At all hazards that danger must be staved off. But Meredith saw means of torturing both those culprits which would be very effectual without any intervention of the law. He would have Dolff at his mercy; he would pierce him with arrows of ridicule from which it would be impossible for the young man to defend himself; and Janet, who had forsaken him, who held apart, and even played for him, when she was bidden to do so, unwillingly—Janet should suffer too.

Lights of malice and mockery woke up in Meredith's eyes. He anticipated a great deal of fun from the appearance of the witness, who, no doubt, would collapse and come to nothing when inquired into. Meredith saw nothing but sport in this unthought-of catastrophe. He had something of the feeling of the excited boy who has a cat or a dog to torture. He knew how to tickle Dolff up in the tenderest places, to keep him in a perpetual ferment of alarm, to hold endless threats over him; and to watch his writhings would be all the more fun that the fellow would deserve it all, and more than that if he got his due. Thus delightedly pursuing his revenge, Meredith missed the moment when Dolff withdrew. But Janet saw it, with a terror impossible to describe. She could not go after him or advise him. Since these miseries had happened, it had become her charge to make the tea, and there she sat, conspicuous even in the fading light, unable to budge. She saw the unhappy young man steal out, and she knew that all kinds of desperate resolves must be in his mind. He would not have the courage to face it out. He would go away and he would conceal himself—do something to heighten suspicion and make every guess into certainty. And she could not go after him to warn him—to implore him to stand fast! The tortures which Meredith had imagined with such pleasure had begun in Janet's breast.

Dolff got out into the hall in a condition impossible to describe—his limbs were limp with misery and fear. Great drops of perspiration hung upon his forehead. He went blindly to snatch a hat from the stand; then took his coat, for he was cold with mental agony, and struggled into it. While he was doing this, Vicars suddenly appeared by him, he could not tell how, and laid a hand on his shoulder, which made Dolff jump. He darted back with an oath, and would have that moment turned and fled had not Vicars caught his arm again.

"Mr. Dolff, what's up? For goodness' sake don't fly out like this. There's one of those d——d policemen watching on the other side of the road."

Dolff stared wildly in Vicars's face.

"Let me go," he said. "I must go; I don't care where."

"What's up?" said Vicars. "You're in some row, Mr. Dolff?"

"Don't you know?" said Dolff, wildly. "That man's coming back. If he comes back before I'm gone, it's all up with me, Vicars. Get out of my way. I'll go—by the garden door."

"And show yourself to all the women," said Vicars, "who'll tell the first word, 'Oh, he's in the garden.' Mr. Dolff, is it life or death?"

Dolff could not speak. He stared dully at his questioner, unable to reply. The sound of the outer door pushed open, and men's footsteps upon the path, came in like a sort of horrible accompaniment and explanation. The perspiration stood in great beads on Dolff's forehead. He tried to make a bolt at the passage to the garden, which led by the open door of the kitchen. Then he drew himself up against the wall, in a half stupor, as if he could conceal himself so.

"Is it life or death?" said Vicars, in his ear; but Dolff could not speak.

He had a dim vision of the man's face, of the light swimming in his eyes, of the knock upon the door of the house, ominous, awful, like a knell; and then he suddenly found himself drawn into darkness, into a warm, close atmosphere, beyond the reach of that, or apparently of any other sound.

Priscilla, always correct, but a little surprised, not knowing how to account for such an invasion of the drawing-room, ushered in the detective, accompanied by a man in a shabby coat, very inappropriate certainly to that locality. Mr. Dolff had always spoken to such men in the hall. A parlor-maid is, above all things, an aristocrat. To have to introduce two such persons to her mistress's presence offended her in her deepest sense of right and wrong.

"Is this the man?" said Meredith. "Mrs. Harwood, do you think we might have a little light?"

"Priscilla is bringing in the lamps," said Mrs. Harwood, looking with a little suspicion and annoyance at the men, who certainly were much out of place: a feeling that there was danger in them somehow, though she could not tell how, crept into her mind.

She looked anxiously at the dim figures looming against the light, and a thrill of alarm went through her. Why did Charley insist on having them here? Why did not Dolff see them in the hall, as he had done before? She had never had a policeman in her house; never, except—Trouble and tremor came over her as she sat there growing breathless in her chair. As for Gussy, she was insensible to every appeal, to every claim upon her attention but one. She was Meredith's sick-nurse, watching lest he should be over-fatigued, thinking of nothing else. There was no help or support in her for her mother's anxieties.

When the lamps were brought in matters were no better. A sort of Rembrandt-like depth of shadow fell upon the two strange figures, throwing a blackness over the tea-table at which Janet was sitting, and showing only the form of Meredith in his chair, which was full within the influence of the shaded light, and the awkward attitudes of the two men in the middle of the room.

"So this is the man who saw me—knocked down?" said Meredith. His face, which was the central light in that strange picture, was lit up with what seemed more like malicious fun than any other sentiment. "And you think you could identify the fellow who did it? Is that so?"

"You may thank your stars as you weren't killed," said the new-comer. "He meant it, sir, that fellow did."

"You think so? Well, he hasn't succeeded, you see; and you think you can identify him?"

"Among a thousand, sir," said the man. "Just you put him before me in a crowd and I'll pick him out afore you could say——"

"Then why," said Meredith, "haven't you done it before now? Here are three weeks gone, and plenty of time for him to have got away."

"He's not got away; I've kept my eye upon him, and I have said to the police, times and times, as I could lay my hands upon him as soon as ever he was wanted."

"I thought," said Meredith, "a criminal was wanted from the moment he put himself in the power of the law. You should have secured him at once; to keep your eye upon a man is not a process known to the law."

"I don't know about the law, sir," said the man. "I know that I have been ready any day. I told 'em so the very first night, but they've never paid no attention to me—not till this gentleman was put on as knows me, and knows as he can trust in my word."

"Yes?" said Meredith, solemnly, "I'm glad to hear you can have such good recommendations. Is it necessary you should have a thousand to choose from before you tell us who my assailant is?—because, you see, it would be a little difficult to have them in here."

"Oh," cried the man, angrily, "a deal fewer than a thousand will do—if you'll just collect all there is in the house——"

"In the house!" cried Mrs. Harwood, "but what is the use of that? We know beforehand that there is nobody in this house who would lay a finger——" she stopped with an indefinite choking sensation in her throat, suddenly perceiving that Dolff had gone away. It was not distinct enough to mean suspicion of Dolff—suspicion of Dolff! what folly and insanity! but why should he have gone away?

"I thought as you said the young gentleman was here," said the witness, turning to his guide. "I told you as you'd never find him when you came back."

"It don't matter much," said the other, in a low tone, "he can't go far, there's two of my mates outside."

The ladies did not catch the meaning of this colloquy, though it raised the most bewildering alarm in Mrs. Harwood's breast. Gussy still thought of it alone as it affected the health of her beloved. She stood by him, her attention concentrated on him, watching whether he grew pale, whether he flushed, if he seemed tired. Her mother's anxious look awakened no sympathy in Gussy's mind. If she observed it at all she set it down to the same cause as made herself anxious, the fear that Meredith might be over-excited or fatigued.

"Do you want the maids and all?" said Meredith, in his familiar tone of banter. "You don't think much of me, my good man, if you think I could be battered like that by—Priscilla, for instance," he said, turning to Mrs. Harwood with a laugh.

"I wasn't thinking of no Priscilla," said the man, angrily. "If it suits you to laugh at it, gentleman, it don't suit me. There's a reward out. And when I see as clear as I sees you—I should think it *was* a man, and a strong one too. Lord, how savage he took you up again and dashed your 'ead against the pavement! I should know him anywhere, among a thousand."

"Charley," said Mrs. Harwood, faintly, "there is something dreadful in all this. Do you think it could be put off to another time? or couldn't they just go and do their duty, whatever it is, without freezing the blood in our veins, and," she added, catching Gussy's look, "exhausting you?"

"I'm sorry to trouble the lady, sir," said the detective. "I shouldn't have said anything if I could have helped it; but, to tell you the truth, suspicion does attach to a person in the house. If the young gentleman had stayed and faced it, things might have been done quiet. But as he's gone away—I'm sorry, very sorry, to disturb the ladies—but I've got a search-warrant, and I must find my man. You'll explain it to 'em, sir, as I can't help it, and it was no wish of mine to upset the house."

"A search-warrant! Oh, my God! what does he mean?" cried Mrs. Harwood. She added, in her bewilderment, "That could have nothing to do with Charley," under her breath.

"I have no more idea than you have," said Meredith; "some one in this house? It must be old Vicars they mean. Come, my man, don't be too absurd. If you think that old fellow could play at pitch-and-toss with me in the way you describe, you must have a precious poor opinion of me. But I suppose Vicars can be sent for—if he's in the house."

"I don't know nothing about Vicars, nor who he is. Where's that young gentleman? What did he go away for when he knew as he was wanted? You produce that young gentleman, and then you'll see what we means," said the witness, in great wrath.

"Hold your noise," said the policeman. "I daresay it's all nonsense when we come to the bottom of it; and I'm sure I'm very sorry to disturb the ladies; but I must just 'ave a few words with the young gentleman. Most likely he can clear it all up."

"Dolff!" said Mrs. Harwood, with an amazed cry.

"Dolff!" cried Meredith, with a burst of laughter.

His apparent appreciation of this as an excellent joke confused the two men. They looked at each other again for mutual support.

"You'd not have laughed if you'd seen him, as I did," growled the stranger.

"I felt—him, whoever he was, as you didn't, my man; and it is evident you think me a poor creature, to be battered about by a boy—or a woman. Come, there's enough of this nonsense," he said. "Why didn't you seize the fellow when you saw him? What do you mean, coming with this cock-and-bull story three weeks after—and to me?"

"Produce the young gentleman, sir, and let me just ask him a few questions."

"I haven't got him in my pocket," said Meredith. "Probably he has gone out. If he were here, I should not allow him to answer your questions. I'm his legal adviser. Come, come, don't let us have any more of this."

"If he has gone out," said the policeman, "by this time he's in the hands of my mate—and if he haven't I've a right to search the house. You'd better produce him, mister—or you, lady, before it's too late."

Janet, unable to bear the scene which was thus rising to a climax, had got up out of the shadow and left the room a moment before. The hall was perfectly vacant, not a trace of any one in it—not even Priscilla going about her business, or the nurse in the dining-room, which was still sacred to the invalid. The lamp burned steadily, the silence was dreadful to the excited girl. It seemed like the pause of fate—not a sound within or without—even the voices, subdued by distance, but generally audible in a cheerful hum from the kitchen, were hushed to-night. All perfectly silent—calm as if tumult or tragedy had never entered there.

CHAPTER XL.

"I MUST go after them; I must—I must follow them! Oh, Dolff, where are you—where are you?" cried Mrs. Harwood.

She was wild with excitement and alarm, her face alternately flushed and paled, her form trembling with endeavor to move, to push herself forward, to follow those dreadful emissaries of the law whose heavy steps were very audible, now on the stairs, now overhead.

The other members of the party were in strange contrast to her anxiety. Meredith lay back in his chair rubbing his hands moved apparently by the supremest sense of the ludicrous, unable to see it in any but a ridiculous light. Gussy leaned on the back of his chair, smiling in sympathy with him, yet a little pale and wondering, beginning to realize that something disagreeable, painful, might be going on, though it did not mean fatigue or excitement to her patient. Julia, finally roused from her book, had got up bewildered, and stood asking what was the matter, getting no reply from anyone.

The door of the drawing-room had been left open, and across the hall, at the opposite door of what was now Meredith's room, stood the nurse in her white cap and apron, with a wondering face, looking out.

"I thought I knew a great deal about the folly of the authorities," said Meredith, "and of Scotland Yard in particular, but this is the climax. By-the-bye, I see an opportunity for a great sensation, which, if I were at the Old Bailey, would make my fortune. 'The prisoner, accused of a murderous assault upon Mr. Meredith, was defended by that gentleman in person.' What a situation for the press—one might add, 'who is a family connection,' eh, Gussy?" he said, putting up his hand to take hers, which was upon the back of his chair.

"Oh, Charley! but speak to mamma. Mamma is miserable. Everything about Dolff makes her so anxious."

"Even such an excellent joke?" said Meredith: but he did not say anything to comfort Mrs. Harwood.

In the midst of his laugh a sudden gravity came over him. He looked at her again with a quick, scrutinizing glance. Dolff was not all. She had been bewildered—taken by surprise, but was not really anxious about her son. Now, however, as she sat listening, waiting, her suspense became unbearable. A woman imprisoned in her chair never moving, unable to walk a step, she looked as if at any moment she might dart out of it and fling herself after the invaders. Her hands moved uneasily upon the arms of her chair, plucking at them as if to raise herself. The light in her eyes was a wild glare of desperation. The color fluttered on her face, now ebbing away and leaving her ghastly, now coming back with a sudden flush. He remembered suddenly all that might be involved in a search of that house, and that for anything he knew a secret which it was of the utmost importance he should fathom now lay, as it were, within reach of his hand. He became serious all at once, the laugh passing suddenly from his face. He got up but not to stop the examination, as Gussy hoped. He did not even stop to soothe Mrs. Harwood, but strolled out into the hall on his unsteady limbs, forgetting them all.

"I must go after them," Mrs. Harwood cried again, half raising herself in her chair. "I must go after them. Gussy, they may go—how can we tell where they may go?"

"No, mamma, there is nothing to be alarmed about. Vicars will see to that."

"How can we tell where Vicars is? I have been afraid of something of the kind all my life. Gussy, I must go myself. I must go myself!"

"Oh, hush, mamma," said Gussy; she was not alarmed about a risk which had never frightened her at all. Mrs. Harwood was always nervous; but Gussy, who had been used to it for years, had never believed that anything would happen. So long as Charley did not throw himself back—was not over-excited. This was what Gussy most feared.

"I'll take you wherever you like, mamma," said Julia, coming with a rush to the back of the chair, and projecting her mother into the hall with a force which nearly shook her out of it. Mrs. Harwood's precipitate progress was arrested by Meredith, who called out to Julia to go softly, and caught at the arm of the chair as it swung past.

"Are you coming too, to keep an eye on them?" he said.

"I don't like," said Mrs. Harwood, trying to subdue the trembling of her lips, "to have such people all over my house."

"Oh, they are honest enough; there will be no picking or stealing. As for the thing itself, it's a farce. I daresay Dolff has gone out. And, if not, what does it matter? If there is any such ridiculous idea about, you had better meet it and be done with it. It's a wonder they don't arrest me for knocking down myself."

"Oh," said Mrs. Harwood faintly, "I am not afraid for Dolff."

"You can have nothing else to be afraid of," said Meredith, in his careless tones. "A search by the police is nothing unless there happens to be something for them to find out. Nothing is of any importance unless it is true. They may search till they are tired, but, so long as there is nobody in hiding, what can it matter? Don't trouble yourself about nothing. Let me take you back to your comfortable fireside."

"No, no," said Mrs. Harwood, more and more troubled; "I will stay here."

He had not, it was evident, found the way to save her, with all his philosophy.

"No?" said Meredith, interrogatively. "It's rather cold here, however, after the cosiness of the drawing-room. I hope you'll not catch cold. If it is any satisfaction to you, of course, there's nothing to be said: but I should think you might let me look out for these fellows and send them off. Julia and me," he added, with a wave of his hand to Julia, and the smile which was so exasperating.

He kept wondering all the time where Janet was—Janet, who had disappeared without attracting any notice, and who probably, he thought, had helped to smuggle Dolff away somewhere, uselessly—because when such an accusation was once made, it was much better to brave it out. It was like the folly of a woman to try to smuggle him away, when the only thing was to brave it out.

"This is the only place where there is no draught," he said, pushing Mrs. Harwood's chair directly in front of the door which led to the wing—the door, which, on the night of the ball, he and Janet had miraculously found unfastened.

The door, he remarked once more, had every appearance of being a door built up and impracticable. To say, in a carefully-kept house like this, that it was covered with dust would not have been true, but there was an air about it as if it had been covered with dust. Meredith smiled at himself while he made this reflection. His heart was singularly buoyant and free, full of excitement, yet of pleasurable excitement. He was on the eve of finding out something he wanted to find out, and he was most particularly concerned that the circumstances which favored him should overwhelm Mrs. Harwood. He placed her almost exactly in front of the door as if she had intended to veil it, and drew over one of the hall chairs beside her and threw himself down upon it.

"This is the most sheltered spot," he said, "out of reach of the door and several other draughts. If you will stay out in the hall and catch cold, Mrs. Harwood, you are safest here."

She glanced at the door as he drew her up to it with a repressed shudder. She had become deadly pale, and in the faint light looked as if she had suddenly become a hundred years old, withered and shrunken up with age. Julia, very much startled, and with eyes wide open and astonished, stood by her mother.

"I shouldn't have put her by that nasty shut-up door; there is always a wind from under it," she said.

"Hush—oh, hush!" said Mrs. Harwood, with a shiver.

The detective and his companion were coming downstairs, led by the sniffing and contemptuous Priscilla. They came down cautiously with their heavy boots, as if they might have slipped on the soft carpets.

"Well," said Meredith, as they came in sight, "found anything? We are waiting here to hear your news."

"No, sir; the young gentleman have got clean away, so far as I can see," said the policeman; "but you know, sir, as well as me, for a man that's known to struggle with the p'leece is no good. He'll be got at, sooner or later, and it's far better to give himself up at once."

"That is exactly my opinion," said Meredith, "and I should have given him that advice if either of us had known what you meant; but, you see, a young gentleman who has nothing on his conscience does not think what is the wisest thing to do about the police—for he does not expect to have anything to do with them."

"I hope he have as easy a conscience as that," said the detective.

"I hope he has, and I don't doubt it, either. Well—what are you going to do now? You've looked through all this part of the house, I suppose?"

"We began with the upper rooms first."

"That was scarcely wise of you," said Meredith, "he might have popped out of one of those rooms and run for it, while you were busy upstairs."

"Scarcely that, sir," said the policeman, with a grin—and he opened the door, revealing suddenly a colleague erect and burly in his blue uniform upon the step outside.

This sight made even Meredith silent for a moment. It made the peril and the watch real, and brought before him all the difficulties to be encountered if Dolff (which seemed incredible) should actually be taken, committed to prison, and tried for a murderous attack upon his own life. It was so appalling, and he knew so little how to meet it if it really became an actual situation to be reckoned with, that for a moment he was stunned; then he thought it best to burst into a laugh. The effect on Mrs. Harwood was naturally still more serious. The poor lady began to cry:

"Is it my boy, my Dolff, that they are hunting down like that? Oh! Charley, you are the only one that can tell them how—how ridiculous it is—tell them it's not true."

"I'm very sorry, ma'am, to disturb you," said the policeman, "but will you just move your chair from that door? I beg your pardon, I didn't know the lady couldn't move—let me do it—thank you, miss—away from that door."

"That's not a door," said Julia, promptly, "it's been shut up since ever I remember; that other is the dining-room where Charley Meredith lives, and that is the library that is standing open. And this is the passage that leads to the kitchen and the pantry. And there's the drawing-room on the other side, And this is a cupboard, and this——"

"Beg your pardon, miss, we'll find them all out as we comes to them," the man said. "It's hard work, and it's harder still when we haves to do it in the face of a lot of ladies as is innocent of everything, and don't even know what we means when we speak. Won't you say to the lady, sir, as she'll be far better in her own room, and to let us do what is our painful dooty?"

"It is unnecessary for you to say anything, Charley," said Mrs. Harwood; "if my house is to be treated like a thieves' den, at least I shall stay here."

"If it upsets you, lady, don't blame us," said the policeman, respectfully enough.

They went through all the rooms while she sat watching, Meredith lounging beside her in a chair, occasionally getting up to take a turn about the hall. If the policeman had been a man of any penetration, he would have seen that his investigations in these rooms were of no interest to the watchers, but that their excitement grew fierce every time he emerged into the hall.

Meredith felt the fire in his veins burn stronger as they came back and forward. It was with difficulty he could restrain his agitation. Mrs. Harwood's chair had been pushed aside, leaving the access open to that mysterious door. She sat with her head turned away a little, her hands clasped together, an image of suspense and painful anxiety, listening for the men's steps as they drew nearer. Gussy had followed the rest of the party, though it was against all her principles to yield to this excitement and make a show, as she said, of her feelings. She was vexed especially to see her mother "give way."

"Let me put you back into the drawing-room, mamma. What is the use of staying here? Dolff has gone out, evidently. It is very silly of him, but still he has done so. It will do him no good for you to catch cold here. Charley, do tell her to come in. As for you, you will throw yourself back a week at least. Oh, for goodness' sake, do not make everything worse by staying here!"

Mrs. Harwood made no reply. She shook her head with speechless impatience, and turned her face away. She was beyond all considerations but one, and she could not bear any interruptions, a voice, a sound, which kept her strained ears from the knowledge of the men's movements, and where they were. Gussy's whisper continued to Meredith was torture to her. She raised her hand with an imperative gesture to have silence, silence! her heart beating in her ears like a sledgehammer rising and falling was surely enough, without having any whispering and foolish, vain, ineffectual words.

"There's nothing now but this door," said the policeman, coming out somewhat crestfallen. "He's nowhere else, that's clear. If he ain't here he's given us the slip—for the moment. Hallo! it's locked, this one is! I'll thank you, sir, to get me the key."

"I have always understood," said Meredith, blandly, "that the door was built up, or fastened up. It has never been used since I have known the house."

"I told you so," said Julia, "if you had listened to me. It isn't a door at all, and leads to nowhere. It was once the door of the wing," she continued, with the liking of a child for giving information, "but it has never once been opened since ever I was born."

"The wing! that's them empty rooms as we see from the garden—the very place for a man to hide. Tell you what, sir, I can't bear to upset the lady—but we must break in if we can't get in quietly. You might try if you couldn't get us the key, and take the ladies away—anyhow, get the old lady to go away—whatever happens, she'd better not be here."

Mrs. Harwood spoke quickly, in a hoarse and broken voice.

"There is no key," she said.

"I give you five minutes to think of it, lady," said the man; "otherwise we must break in the door."

There was a dreadful silence—a silence which no one dared to break.

"I am telling you the truth; you cannot open it, it has always been shut up. There is no key."

CHAPTER XLI.

THE policeman's epigrammatic assertion that it was difficult for a known man to struggle with the police, is still more true when it is only a door which stands before a couple of men excited and exasperated by failure and a probable discovery. The door was a strong door, it was partially plated with iron, and its lock was cunningly devised, but after a while it began to give way.

Meredith, altogether absorbed in this new turn of affairs, and carried away by the prospect which it opened to him as well as to its assailants, seemed to the bystanders to have altogether gone over to the enemy. He stood by them, encouraging them in a low tone, suggesting how to strike, examining into the weak points with the keenest critical eye; in fact, in the excitement of the moment, forgetting all his precautions and pretence of indifference, and throwing himself on the side of the assailants. He had, it is true, the safe ground to fall back upon that, as he had always been assured there was nothing there, he could do no possible harm in helping to prove that fact to the men who would not be convinced in any other way.

Mrs. Harwood sat with her face to the door, her arms crossed upon her breast, her whole frame swaying and moving with the strokes that rained upon it. When a crash came she shivered and shrank into herself as if the blow had struck her—a low moan came involuntarily to her lips. Gussy, who had abandoned Meredith after trying in vain to restrain him, came and stood by her mother's chair, with a hand upon her shoulder.

"Oh, mamma, for God's sake," said Gussy, in her ear, "don't! Don't let them see you mind it so."

The mother half turned to her a face which was livid in its terror. Her eyes, so clear usually, had lost their color even, and seemed to float in a sort of liquefication, the iris disappearing into the watery black globe—her mouth was open. She uttered a murmur of inarticulate passion, and made as though she would have struck the soothing hand. But the men at this exciting work took no notice of Mrs. Harwood. The officer of the law was more fit to break down a resisting door than to draw subtle deductions from the looks of the besieged family. The practical matter was within his sphere. He only looked round with an exclamation of triumph when the door at last burst from its holdings, and the dark passage gaped open before them with its curtains drawn back.

"There!" he shouted, turning round for a moment, "there's your door that never was used," and would have dashed in had not his attendant held him back.

"I say," said the man who had hitherto followed him like a shadow, "how do ye know that he hasn't got a revolver up there?"

The detective fell back for a moment.

"We've got to risk it," he said, with the professional stoicism of a man bound to meet danger at any time. He was not of much use in scenting out a mystery, but he could face a possible revolver with the stolid courage of his class. He made a pause, however, and added, with a rare effort of reflection, "And this one's new to it; he's not up to their dodges——" *They* were the criminal class with which a straightforward policeman is accustomed to deal.

Meredith followed with an excitement which made him forget everything, even the group of women bewildered in the hall. He knew his way, though he dared not show that he did. He followed the burly figure, and the smaller ill-trained one of the attendant informer and witness, as they wound themselves up in the curtains and came to a pause opposite every obstacle. The passage was perfectly dark, but the inner doors were not closed, notwithstanding the sounds of assault which those within must have heard. It turned out that the only individual within who had his wits about him had been too closely occupied to be able to look to those means of defence.

For a moment the group of the ladies below hung together in bewildered horror. Then Julia launched herself after the men into the dark passage, drawn by inextinguishable curiosity and the excitement of a child in sight of the unknown. Mrs. Harwood had covered her face with her hands, and lay back in her chair, fallen upon herself like a fallen house, lying, so to speak, in ruins. Gussy, with her arm round her mother's shoulders, whispered, with tears and a little gasping, frightened crying, some words that were intended to be consolatory in her inattentive ears.

"It is nothing wrong," Gussy said; "it is nothing wrong. It was to save him. It is nothing wrong."

But by-and-bye the strong attraction of that open way along which the unseen party were stumbling seized upon her also. And her patient, who had to be taken care of—who was throwing himself back! Gussy cast a piteous glance upon her mother, lying there with her face upon her hands, paying no attention, whatever comfort might be poured into her ear, and presently impatience got the better of her sympathy, and she too followed in the train. She knew the secret of the wing. She was the only other in the house, except Mrs. Harwood, to whom that secret was known. But in how innocent and simple a way! She was troubled, but she had no sense of guilt; and Gussy said to herself that it was her duty to go and explain, to make it known to the others how simple it all was, when the fascination became too much for her to resist, and, with one glance at her mother, she too stole away. As for Dolff, he had disappeared from their minds, and the incredible suspicion attached to him, as if he had never been born. From the moment that the search began it had been to Mrs. Harwood a search for her secret, and nothing more.

Janet had been all this time hanging about unseen. She could not rest, she who knew so much more than any one else in the house—both the mystery of the wing and the miserable story of Dolff and his guilt, both of them—as nobody else did: neither Mrs. Harwood, whose thoughts were concentrated upon one, nor Meredith, who had discovered or divined the other, but did not know as Janet did, who knew everything, what had been the cause of Dolff's terrible folly, and what its results, and even when and how he had disappeared. She had been hanging about now in one room, now in another, terrified to show herself, incapable of concealing herself, her very terror of being mixed up in it yielding to the fellow-felling of a general misery in which she had but her share, and that not so great a share as the others.

When she saw that the mother of the house, who was the most to be pitied of all in this dreadful emergency, was left there forlorn and alone, lying helpless, unable to go after the others, to confront the catastrophe, at least, as her children could, Janet's heart was touched. She stole down the stairs where she had been watching, looking down upon them all, and came to Mrs. Harwood's side. It was not for her to console or comfort. Janet was aware that she had been more or less the cause of all the trouble. She had found out the family secret, without in the least understanding it, and this was no blame of hers; but she had betrayed it to one who did understand it, and who might, for all she knew, use his knowledge unmercifully, being, as she knew him to be, a man with very little truth or inclination to spare another. And she had been, without any doubt, the cause of Dolff's misfortune in every way. She had taken him into her toils innocently enough, with no more guiltiness than that of any other girl who had let a foolish young man fall in love with her, and then had driven him mad by her falsehood, and led him into crime—almost to the crime of murder. All this was in Janet's mind as she stole down the stairs to his mother's side. She had plenty of excuse for herself had any one accused her, but in her heart she was impartial, and knew very well how much she was to blame. Her heart beat loudly in consonance with the sounds of that exploring party in the dark passage, going to find out—how much more than they sought! She understood it all better than anyone. Meredith's keen satisfaction in unveiling the mystery, and the stupid astonishment of the strangers, who had no suspicion, and Gussy——but what Gussy would feel was the one thing that Janet did not divine, for she was unaware how much or how little Gussy knew.

She stood by the chair in which Mrs. Harwood lay, all sunken upon herself like a fallen tower, her face hidden, her shoulders drawn together, sinking to her knees. Janet dared not say anything. She put her hand upon the arm of the chair, not even upon the unhappy lady's arm, which she felt that she dared not touch—and stood by her. It was all that any one could do. The two were left there like wrecks on the shore, from, which everything had ebbed away, even the tumult and the storm which had been raging round. The sounds went on getting fainter, the voices dropped, the footsteps seemed to mount and then grow still, stumbling at first a little, gradually dying out. Mrs. Harwood did not move, nor did Janet, standing by her, scarcely breathing. Were they both following, in imagination, the darkling way which both knew, or had the mother, at last, fallen into a blind insensibility, hearing and knowing no more?

This imagination was, however, suddenly put an end to by a moaning from the chair.

"I can't bear this any longer; I can't bear this!" said Mrs, Harwood. "Oh, my God! my God! Have they got *there?*" Then she cried, loudly, "I can't bear it! I can't bear it!" and with a sudden wrench, as if she were tearing herself like a limb from its socket, the disabled woman rose.

Janet, terrified, gave a cry of dismay as, stumbling and tottering, she flung herself out of the chair. Whether Mrs. Harwood had been aware of her presence before this she could not tell; but, at all events, now she was beyond all sentiment of displeasure or reproof. She put out her shaking hand and grasped at Janet's arm as if it had been a post. The girl's slight figure swayed and almost gave way at the sudden weight flung upon it; but the burden steadied her after the first moment's uncertainty. Mrs. Harwood's face had collapsed with the extreme anguish of the crisis past; her features seemed blurred, like the half-liquid, vaguely floating eyes, which did not seem to see anything. She made a heavy, uncertain step forward, carrying her prop with her by mere momentum of weight and weakness.

"Come," she said, hoarsely, "come!"

Janet never knew how these dark passages were got through. She was herself enfolded, carried away in the burden of the helpless woman who leaned upon her guidance for every step. Their progress was wildly devious and uneven, every step being a sort of falling forward, which nevertheless carried them on with spasmodic rapidity, though terrible effort. The voices and steps in front of them grew audible again, but before they reached the last door, which stood open with curtains drawn aside, disclosing a warm blaze of light, there arose a sudden tumult, a roar as of some wild creature, with answering cries of panic and dismay. The opened doorway suddenly darkened with a crowd of retreating figures, and Julia darted out from the midst and came blindly flying upon the tottering group that was struggling forward.

"Go back, go back!" cried Julia, "whoever you are. There's a madman there!" and then she gave a shriek as wild as the sounds that came from the room, "Oh," cried the girl, her shrill voice dominating even that riot, "it's mamma! My mother's here!"

CHAPTER XLII.

NEXT moment they had surged as on the top of a wave to the room within. Nothing could be more strange than the scene presented there. The room was curtained all round with red, hung above a man's height with ruddy thick folds, upon which the firelight threw a still warmer flicker. A shaded lamp filled it with softened light, and from above, from what seemed a large skylight, a white stream of moonlight fell in, making a curious disturbing effect in the warm artificial light. These accessories, however, though they told afterwards, were as nothing to the sight that burst upon the eyes of the new-comers. In the centre of the room stood a tall old man, with a long pallid face, straggling white hair, and a white beard. His face was distorted with excitement, his voice bellowing forth a succession of cries, or rather roars, like the roars of a wild animal. His loose lips gave forth these utterances with flying foam and a sort of mechanical rapidity:

"I know what you've come for? I can pay up! I can pay up! I've plenty of money, and I can pay up! But I won't be taken, not if it costs me my life!"

These were the words that finally emancipated themselves from the stammering utterance and became clear.

Vicars stood behind this wild figure holding both his arms, but it was only by glimpses that the smaller man was visible holding the other as in a vise.

"Come, sir, come, sir, no more of this; they'll take you for a fool," he said.

And then this King Lear resumed. The foam flew from his lips; his great voice came out in its wild bellowing, the very voice which Janet had heard so often. It had seemed to her to utter but an inarticulate cry, but this, it would seem, was what it had been saying all the time—words in which there was some meaning—though what that meaning was, or whether the speaker himself understood it, who would say?

The policeman and his attendant had edged towards the doorway, and stood there huddled upon one another. The leader of the search had been willing to face a revolver, but the madman was a thing for which he was not prepared. He stood against the doorway ready to retreat still further in case there should be any further advance. Meredith and Gussy had passed into the room, and stood together, she very anxious, he very eager, at the side, where those wild eyes had not caught them. Behind was Dolff very pale, standing half concealed by the group formed by the madman and his attendant, raising his head to look over them to the two in the doorway who had come to look for him, and had received so unexpected a check.

Mrs. Harwood stumbled into the midst of this strange scene with her tottering uncertain stride, driving Janet with her. She put up her hand to hold back the dreadful insane figure. She was at one of the moments in life when one is afraid of nothing, shrinks from nothing.

"Take him back to his seat, Vicars," she said, "take him back. Adolphus!" The tottering, helpless woman stood up straight, and put her hand upon the madman's breast. The eyes that had been blind with misery changed and dissolved as if to dew in their orbits, consolidated again, opened blue and strong like a relighted flame. She fixed them upon the staring red eyes of the maniac. "Adolphus, go back, be silent, calm yourself. There is no need for you to say anything. I am here to take care of you. Let Vicars put you back in your chair."

"I will not be taken," he said, "I will not be taken! I can pay up. I have got money, plenty of money. I will pay up!"

"Vicars," cried Mrs. Harwood, imperiously, "put him back in his chair."

She held her hand on his breast, and fixed her eyes upon his, pushing him softly back. The roarings grew fainter, fell into a kind of whimpering cry.

"I'll pay it all—I have plenty of money. Don't let them take me away—I'll pay everything up!"

"Go back and rest in your chair, Adolphus. Put him in his chair."

The astonished spectators all stood looking on while the old servant and this woman, whom force of necessity had moved from her own helplessness, subdued the maniac. Vicars had partially lost his head, he had lost control of his patient, but this unlooked-for help restored him to himself. Between them they drew and guided the patient back to the chair, which was fitted with some mechanical appliances, and held him fast. Mrs. Harwood seemed to forget her weakness entirely; she tottered no longer, but moved with a free step. She turned round upon the frightened policeman at the door.

"Now go," she said, "you have done your worst; whatever you want, go; you can get no further satisfaction here."

The intruder breathed more freely when he saw the madman sink into quietude. He said, with a voice that quivered slightly.

"I am very willing to go: but that young gentleman has to go along with me!"

"Come on," cried the other man, whose teeth were chattering in his head. "Come on; we've got nothing to do here."

"I'm going: when that young gentleman makes up his mind to come with me."

"What young gentleman? Why, bless you, *that* ain't the young gentleman!" said the man, who had struggled out into the passage, and was now only kept from running by the other's strong retaining grasp.

It was not wonderful that the policeman was indignant. He let his friend go with an oath, and with a sudden push which precipitated him into the outer room.

"You d——d fool! to have led me such a dance; and as much as our lives are worth, and come to nothing at the end."

The man fell backward, but got up again in a moment and took to his heels, with the noise as of a runaway horse in the dark passage. The policeman, reassured to see that the madman was secured, had the courage to linger a moment. He turned to Meredith with a defiant look.

"It has come to nothing, sir, and I ask your pardon that I've been led into giving you this trouble by an ass. But I make bold to ask is this house licensed? and what right has anyone got to keep a dangerous madman in it without inspection, or any eye over 'im? I'll have to report it to my superior."

"Report it to the—devil, and be off with you," Meredith said.

The party stood round, staring into each other's faces, when the strangers thus withdrew. The madman struggled against the fastenings that secured him.

"Julia," he said, "don't let them take me!" He tried to get hold of her with his hands, feeling for her as if he did not see, and began to cry feebly, in a childish, broken voice, "Don't let them take me! I have got enough to pay everybody. I kept it for you and the children. It was for you and the children; but I'll pay up, I'll pay everybody; only don't let them take me, don't let them take me!" he whimpered, tears—piteous, childish tears— suffusing the venerable face.

"Oh," cried Gussy, "don't let him cry; for God's sake don't let him cry! I cannot bear it—I cannot bear it—it is too much."

"I'll never complain any more," said the patient; "I'm very comfortable, I don't want for anything. You shall pay them all up yourself if you don't believe me. I'll give you the money—only don't let them send me away! I've got it all safe here," he said. "Stop a moment, I'll give it you: and all these ladies and gentlemen can prove it, that I gave it you to pay up." He struggled to get his arms free, trying to reach his breast-pocket with one hand. "Vicars, get it out, and give it to your mistress. The money—the money, you know, to pay everybody up. Only," he cried, putting the piteous hands together which were held fast and could do so little, "don't, Julia—don't let them take me away!"

"Oh, mamma," cried Gussy, "I can't bear it—I can't bear it."

She fell on her knees and covered her face.

"Who is he?" said Dolff. They had all of them, and even Dolff himself, forgotten what was the cause of this revelation. The young man came forward, very pale. "I know nothing about this," he said, looking round; "nothing. I hope everybody will believe me. I want to know who he is!"

No one said a word, they all stood round, struck silent, not knowing what to think. Mrs. Harwood stood with her hand upon the table, supporting herself, asking no other support. She was perfectly pale, but her countenance had recovered its features and expression. She did not even look at her children—one on her knees, one standing up confronting her, demanding to know the truth. To neither of them did she give a word or look. Her eyes were fixed upon the man who was thus utterly in her hands. Vicars extracted an old, large pocket-book from the pocket of the patient, and handed it to her, not without a sort of smile—half-mocking—on his face. She took it, glancing at it with a certain disdain, as if the trick, often employed but no longer necessary, had disgusted her, and flung it on the table.

"There are in this book," she said, "old scraps of paper of no value. This is what I am to pay his debts with. He has given it to me twenty times before. I get tired in the end of playing the old game over and over."

"Mother who is he?" cried Dolff. "You have had him in your house, in secret, never seeing the light of day, and I, your son, never knew. Who is he?"

Mrs. Harwood made no reply.

It was a question to which no one there could give any answer, except perhaps Gussy—on her knees, with her hands covering her face—who did not look up or give any attention to what was going on. Meredith alone seemed to have some clear idea in his mind: his face shone with aroused interest and eagerness, like a man on the very trace of knowledge of the utmost importance to him. A rapid process of thought was going on in his mind, his intelligence was leaping from point to point.

"You will perhaps be surprised," he said, "to hear that I have known this for some time."

"You!" Mrs. Harwood half turned to him, a gleam as of fire passing over her face. "You!"

"Yes, I, who have several interests involved. I had just received information on the subject when that young fool, thinking heaven knows what other folly, knocked me down, taking me unawares, and nearly killed me. Oh, yes, it is perfectly true it was Dolff who did it. You start as if I were likely to make any fuss on that subject. Is it true that he had the money to pay everybody?—that is what I want to know."

"Charley, Charley, do you mean to say that Dolff——"

"Oh, I mean nothing about Dolff," he said, impatiently: "answer me, Mrs. Harwood."

"I can't answer for nothing, Mrs. Harwood," cried Vicars, "if you keep a lot of folks round him. He is working himself up into a fury again."

The madman was twisting in his chair, fighting against the mechanical bonds that secured him. He was looking towards the pocket-book which lay on the table.

"She has got my money, and she throws it down for anybody to pick up," he cried. "My money! there's money there to pay everything! Why don't you pay those people and let 'em go—pay them, pay them and let them go! or else give me back my money!" he cried, wildly straining forward, with his white hair falling back, his reddened eyes blazing, struggling against his bonds. Mrs. Harwood took up the pocket-book, weighing it, with a sort of forced laugh, in her hand.

"You think there may be a fortune here—enough to pay? And he thinks so. Give it to him, Vicars. We've tried to keep it all quiet, but it seems we have failed. You may leave the door open now—you may do as you please. It can't matter any longer. I have thought of the credit of the family, and of many things that nobody else thinks of. And of his comfort—nobody will say I have not thought of his comfort. Look round you: there is everything, everything we could think of. But it is all of no use now."

The old man had caught the pocket-book from Vicars' hands with a pitiful demonstration of joy. He made a pretence of examining its contents, eagerly turning them over as if to make sure that nothing was lost, kissing the covers in enthusiasm of delight. He made an attempt with his confined arms to return it to his pocket, but, failing in that, kept it embraced in both his hands, from time to time kissing it with extravagant satisfaction.

"As long as I have got this they can do nothing to me," he said.

While this pantomime was going on, and while still Mrs. Harwood was speaking, a little movement and rustle in the group caught everybody's attention as if it had been a new fact: but it was only Janet stealing away behind the others who had a right there which she did not possess. She had been watching her moment. She herself, who had nothing to do with it, had received her share of discomfiture too. Her heart was sinking with humiliation and shame. What had she to do with the mysteries of the Harwoods, the things they might have to conceal? What was she to them but a stranger of no account, never thought of, dragged into the midst of their troubles when it pleased them, thrown off again when they chose? Nobody would have said that Janet had any share in this crisis, and yet it was she who had received the sharpest arrow of all; or so, at least, she thought. She slipped behind Julia, who was bigger and more prominent than she, and stole through the bewildering stairs and passages. How well she seemed to know the way, as if it had been familiar to her for years! And it was she who had given the information—she who had been the cause of everything, drawn here and drawn there into affairs alike alien to her, with which she had nothing to do. They were all moved by her departure; not morally, indeed, but by the mere stir it caused.

Gussy rose from her knees, showing a countenance as pale as death and still glistening with tears. She said,

"Mamma, shall we go away? Whatever there may be to be said or explained, it ought not to be done here." She went up to the old man in the chair, who was still embracing his pocket-book, and kissed him on the forehead. "If any wrong has been done to you, I don't know of it," she said; "I thought it was nothing but good."

"No wrong has been done to him—none—none," cried Mrs. Harwood, suddenly dropping from her self-command and strength. "Children, you may not believe me, since I've kept it secret from you. There has been no wrong to him—none—none. If there has been wrong, it has not been to him. Oh, you may believe me, at least, for I have never told you a lie. Everything has been done for him. Look round you—look round you and you will see."

"Who is he?" said Dolff, obstinate and pale, standing behind the chair.

"You have no thought for me," said the mother. "You see me standing here, come here to defend you all, in desperation for you, and you never ask how I am to get back, whether it will kill me—— No, no, Janet has gone, who supported me, who was a stranger, and asked no questions, but only helped a poor woman half mad with trouble and distress. Ah!" she said, "he could go mad and get free—he who was the cause of it all: but I have had to keep my sanity and my courage and bear it all, and look as if nothing was the matter, for fifteen years. For whom? Was it for me? It would have been better for me to have died and been done with it all. For you, children, to give you a happy life, to do away with all disgrace, to give you every advantage. Yes, I'll take your arm, Ju: you have not been a good child, but you know no better. Get me to my chair before I drop down; get me to my chair——" She paused a moment, and looked round with a hard laugh. "For I am very heavy," she said, "and I would have to be carried, and who would do it I don't know. Ju, make haste, before my strength is all gone. Get me to my chair."

CHAPTER XLIII.

GUSSY was the last to leave of that strange procession, of whom no one spoke to the other. She closed the door after her, and the curtains, and followed the erect figure of Dolff, drawn up as it never had been in his life before, and walking stiffly, as if carrying a new weight and occupying a position unknown. They all came into the hall, defiling solemnly one after the other, to find Mrs. Harwood deposited in her chair and awaiting them, almost as if the whole events of the evening had been a dream and she had never left that spot. It was with a strange embarrassment, however, that they looked at each other in the pale, clear light as they emerged from the doorway, almost like making new acquaintance, as if they had never seen each other before. Nobody certainly had seen Dolff in that new manifestation; nor was Gussy, she whose very existence had been wrapped up in that of Meredith, who had only lived to watch him for weeks past, recognizable. It was she who came out the last, but who made herself the first of the group.

"There may be a great many things to say," said Gussy; "but not to-night. We have all had a great many agitations to-night. My brother has been hunted for his life. My mother has done a thing which, so far as we know, she hasn't been able to do for years. Mr. Meredith has had a bad illness, for which it appears this unfortunate family is responsible too. I only and my little sister"—she paused here with an effort—"no; I will not pretend; I have had my share of the shock, too. We'd better all separate for the night."

"Gussy!" cried Mrs. Harwood, with a sharp tone of appeal.

"Gussy!" cried Meredith, astonished, trying to take her hand to draw her towards him.

"Gussy!" said Dolff, with a certain indignation.

"It is of no use," she said, quickly, "to appeal to me. I think I am the one who has been deceived all round. I thought I knew everything, and I've known nothing. Whatever may be the meaning of it, I for one am not able for any more to-night, and none of the rest ought to be able for it. I don't know whether I may have been deceived there, too, about how much invalids could bear. Good-night, mamma. I advise you to get to bed."

Gussy waved her hand to the others without a word, and walked upstairs without turning her head. The sudden failure of a perfect faith in all the world, such as she had entertained without entering into complications for which her mind was not adapted, is no small matter. It is alarming even for others to see. They all stood for a moment huddled together as if a rock or a tower had fallen before their eyes. They could scarcely see each other for the dust and darkness it made. All the other events of this startling night seemed to fall into the background. Gussy! who had been the central prop of the house, who had kept everybody together, done everything! When she thus threw up her arms they were all left in dismay, and fell into an assemblage of atoms, of units—no longer a united party ready to meet all comers.

Meredith, perhaps, he who had been the most eager, was the most discomfited of all. He had claimed Gussy's interest as his right for years. When she thus withdrew, not even asking if he were fatigued, speaking almost as if she thought that fatigue a pretence, he was so bewildered that he could do nothing. An anxious believer like this is accepted perhaps with too much faith and considered too inalienable a possession; and when she fails the shock is proportionately great. Without Gussy to stand by him, to make him believe himself a universal conqueror, always interesting, always important, Meredith for the moment was like an idol thrown from his pedestal. He was more astonished than words could say. He exclaimed, hurriedly,

"I think Gussy is right, as she always is. Mrs. Harwood, I will say good-night."

Mrs. Harwood was altogether in a different mind. The period of reaction had not come with her as yet. She had got herself deposited in her chair in time enough to save her from any breaking down. And her spirit was full of excitement.

"I am ready," she said, with a panting hot breath of mental commotion, "to explain—whatever it is necessary to explain. Take me back to my room, Dolff. It is cold here."

"Good-night," said Meredith. "I will not encroach upon you longer to-night."

"As you like," she said. "I warn you, however, that to-morrow—— Dolff, take me back to my fire."

Dolff was unsubdued, like his mother. The reaction from a long period of suspense, and the sense of safety after a great alarm, no doubt acted upon his mind: though, so far as he was aware, he was moved by nothing save the overwhelming discovery he had made, and his indignant sense of wrong in finding such a secret retreat unsuspected, in his mother's—in his own—house.

"We'll be better alone," he said, in the stern tone which was so new to him, putting his hand upon her chair; "but perhaps you could walk if you tried," he added, with rude sarcasm.

He drove rather than wheeled her before him into the deserted room, where all was so brilliant and warm, the light blinking in the bright brass and steel, the lamps serenely burning, everything telling of the tranquil life, unbroken by any but cheerful incidents, which had gone on there for so many years.

"Now, mother," said Dolff, "we have got to have it out. Who is that man upstairs?"

Julia had followed them unremarked, and remained behind her mother's chair. Dolff stood before them, in the full firelight, very erect, inspired with indignation and that sense of superiority which injury gives. It had elevated him altogether in the scale of being. His own shortcomings had fallen from his consciousness. He was aware of nothing but that he, Dolff, in reality the head of the family, had been deceived and compromised.

Mrs. Harwood took but little notice of her son. She took up her work which had been thrown upon the table and turned it over in her fingers.

"Gussy was right," she said, "though she was a little brusque in her way of saying it. I am certainly unable to bear anything more to-night."

"I suppose, however, you can answer my question," said Dolff.

"Go to bed, boy," said his mother, "and don't worry me. We have two or three things to talk over, you and I, which are too much for to-night."

"I am not a boy any longer," cried Dolff; "you have made me a man. Who is it you have been hiding for years upstairs?"

She gave vent to a little fierce laugh.

"For my pleasure," she said; "for my amusement, as anybody may see."

"Whether it is for your amusement or not," said Dolff, "I am of age, and I have a right to know who is living in my house."

"In *your* house!" Her exasperation was growing. "Don't force me, Dolff, to go into other questions to-night."

"Whose house is it?" he said. "There's been no question, because you have kept everything in your hands; but if I am to be driven to it, and claim my rights——"

"Your rights!" she cried, again repeating his words. "Was it one of your rights to knock down a man like a coward from behind? It appears this is what you think you may be permitted to do with impunity—to have your home searched in every corner and to destroy all that I have been doing for years, and to bring shame and disgrace to a house that I have kept free of shame, almost at the risk of my life!"

"I did not," cried Dolff, interrupting her eagerly. "I did not knock him down from behind. I had not time to think. I let fly at him as I passed. It's a lie to say I knocked him down from behind."

"You did the same thing; you took him unawares. And you dare to question me! You killed a man at my door—or meant to do it—and never breathed a word to warn us, to keep us from the disgrace——"

Dolff was not clever enough to know what to say. His snort of rage was not attended by any force of bitter words. He only could repeat, with rage and incompetence,

"At *your* door?"

"Perhaps," said Mrs. Harwood, half carried away by passion, half influenced by the dismay which she knew she had it in her power to call forth, "it would be better, since you are exact, to say at your father's door."

Dolff responded with a strange cry. He did not understand it, but he felt all the same that a blow which stunned him had been directed at him, and that the ground was cut from beneath his feet.

"He has neither been tried, nor sentenced, nor anything proved against him," cried Mrs. Harwood, carried away now by the heat of her own excitement. "All that has to be gone through before he can be put aside. And at this moment everything's his—the roof that covers you, the money you have been spending. It is no more your house—*your* house!—than it is Julia's. It is your father's house."

"My father is dead," said Dolff, who had again grown very pale, the flush of passion dying out of his face.

"Yes," said Mrs. Harwood, "and might have remained so, had it not been for your cowardly folly and Vicars's infatuation for you. How was it the man had not the sense to see that a fool like you would spoil all?"

"You are dreaming, you are mad," said Dolff; "you are telling me another lie."

But, though he said this with almost undiminished passion, the young fellow's superiority, his erect pose, his sense of being able to cow and overwhelm her, had come to an end. He fell into his usual attitude, his shoulders dropped and curved, his head hung down. He could fling a last insult at his mother, but no more. And his own mind began to be filled with unfathomable dismay.

Julia had been very uncertain what side to take. Her mind went naturally with her brother, who was most near herself. But a mother is a mother after all. You may feel her to be in some way your natural enemy when the matter is between yourself and her; but when another hand plucks at her it is different. A girl is not going to let her mother be insulted, who after all means her own side, without interposing. Julia suddenly flew forth from behind her mother's chair and flung herself upon Dolff's arm, seizing it and shaking him violently.

"How dare you speak to her like that?" cried Ju, "you that can't do anything you try—not even kill Charley Meredith when you have the chance! I should be ashamed to look any one in the face. Go away, go away, and leave us quiet, you that have done it all: that brought the police into the house, and yet did not hurt him to speak of, you great, useless, disappointing boy!"

Dolff did not know how to sustain this sudden assault. He looked round stupidly at the active assailant at his shoulder with a little pang, even in his agitated and helpless state, to find that Julia was no longer on his side. His head was going round and round: already in his soul he had entirely collapsed, although he still kept his feet in outward appearance. And it would have been difficult to end this scene without an entire breakdown on one side or the other, had not the pensive little voice of the parlor-maid become audible at this moment over their heads, making them all start and draw back into themselves.

"If you please, ma'am," said Priscilla, "for I can't find Miss Gussy—shall I take Mr. Meredith's tray to his room, or shall I bring it in here?"

"I think Mr. Meredith is going to bed," said Mrs. Harwood; "he is a little tired. Take it into his room, Priscilla. And Miss Gussy has gone to bed; you may come now and help me to get into my room, and then shut up everything. It is later than I thought."

"Yes, ma'am," said Priscilla, in those quiet tones of commonplace which calm down every excitement.

Priscilla indeed was herself bursting with curiosity and eagerness to find out what had happened. The long-shut-up door stood ajar, and every maid in the house had already come to peep into the dark passage and wonder what it led to: and the keenest excitement filled the house. But a parlor-maid has as high a standard of duty as any one, were it an archbishop. It was against the unwritten household law to show any such commotion. She took hold of the handle of her mistress's chair as she did on the mildest of domestic evenings, and drew her very steadily and gently away. The only revelation she made of knowing anything was in the suggestion that a little gruel with a glass of wine in it would be a proper thing for Mrs. Harwood to take.

"You may bring me the glass of wine without the gruel," Mrs. Harwood was heard saying as the sound of her wheels moved slowly across the hall, an hour ago the scene of such passionate agitation. "I don't think I have caught cold. A glass of wine—and a few biscuits," she said as by an afterthought.

Was this part of the elaborate make-believe intended to deceive the servants and persuade them that nothing particular had happened? or was she indeed capable of munching those biscuits after such a night of fate?

"Ju, don't you turn against me," said Dolff, feebly, throwing himself into a chair when they were thus left alone.

"Oh!" cried Julia, still panting with her outburst, "to think you had hold of him and didn't really hurt him, not to matter! I can never, never forgive you, Dolff."

"Oh, hold your tongue, you little fool; the only thing I'm glad of is that I didn't hurt him—to matter! You don't know what it is to live for a long week, all the time he was insensible, thinking you have killed a man!"

"When it was only Charley Meredith!" Julia said.

CHAPTER XLIV.

IT was strange that it should be Gussy, who was not ideal or visionary, but very matter-of-fact in all her ways, who was the most cruelly offended and wounded by the events of this night. It seemed to Gussy that she had been deceived and played upon by everybody. By her mother, who had never confided to her the gravity of the position, though she had known the fact for years; by Meredith, who had seemed to know more of it than Gussy did, and whose eyes had been keen with understanding, following every word of what was to Gussy merely the ravings without consequence of a madman; he knew more of it than she did, who had helped to take care of the secret inmate. And then Dolff, her brother. What was the meaning of this cloud of tempest which had come into Dolff's trivial, schoolboyish life? Why had he tried to kill, if that was what he wanted, or, at least, to injure, to assault Meredith?

It was all a mystery to Gussy. She understood nothing except that many things had been going on in the house which she either did not know at all or knew imperfectly—that she had been possibly made a dupe of, brought down from the position which she had seemed to hold of right as the chief influence in the family. She had thought this was how it was: her mother's confidant, the nurse and guardian-angel of her lover, the controller, more or less, of all the house. And it turned out that she knew nothing, that there were all kinds of passions and mysteries in her own home with which she was unacquainted, that what she knew she knew imperfectly, and that even in the confidences given to her she had been kept in the dark.

Gussy was not imaginative, and consequently had little power of entering into the feelings or divining the movements of the minds of others. She was wounded, mortified to the depths of her heart, and angry, with a deep, silent anger not easily to be overcome. She did not linger nor ask for explanations, but went straight up to her room without a moment's pause, careless that both her mother, whom she generally attended through the troublesome process of undressing, and Julia, whom she usually held under such strict authority, were left behind, the latter in contempt of all ordinary hours. Janet, whose charge that was, was not visible; she had stolen away, as it had lately been her habit to do. Janet, Gussy felt sure, was mixed up in it too; but how was she mixed up in it?

Think as she would, Miss Harwood could not make out to her satisfaction how it could be that Janet could have influenced Dolff to assault Meredith. Janet had no quarrel with Meredith, could not have. He had been very civil to her—too civil, Gussy had sometimes thought. She remembered that there was a time when she had felt it very tiresome to have to discuss Miss Summerhayes so often; and on the night of the ball, certainly, they had danced and talked together almost more than was becoming. How, then, could Janet have moved Dolff to attack Meredith? It seemed impossible to discern any plausible reason: and yet Gussy had a moral certainty that Janet was somehow mixed up in it. Could it be that the joke about Dolff and his accompaniments had been the cause? Gussy felt involuntarily that it must be something more serious than that.

She went to bed resolutely, for, indeed, there are times when it requires a severe effort to do this—to shut out the commotions which are around, and turn one's back upon all the questions that require solving. Gussy felt bitterly that she had no certainty as to what might be going on in the house, which she had lately been as sure of as if she had created it. Her mother, for anything she knew, might be going from room to room, her chair set aside, and all her pretences with it. To think that she, Gussy, should have been taken in by it so long, and have believed whatever was told her! Her brother Dolff, so good-natured, of so little account as he was! might have caught Meredith again at a disadvantage, and have accomplished now what he tried before.

The house, her calm and secure domain, seemed now full of incomprehensible noises and mysterious sounds to Gussy. But she would not even look over the banisters to see what was going on. She would not open her door, much less steal downstairs, as another woman might have done, to find out everything. She went to bed. She asked no explanation. She shut her door and drew her curtains, and closed her eyes. Whatever might be going on within or without, the gateways of her mind were closely fastened up, so that she might hear or see no more.

It was Priscilla who put her mistress to bed: and Mrs. Harwood was very angry with her children, feeling that Gussy had deserted her and that Dolff had insulted her. But it takes more than that to make a woman betray her sons and daughters. With the flush of anger still on her cheek and the tremble on her lips she told Priscilla how tired Miss Harwood was, how she had been overdoing herself, how she had made her go to bed.

"I told her you could see to all I want quite nicely, Priscilla."

"Yes, ma'am," said Priscilla; but it was doubtful how far she was taken in, for, of course, the servants knew a great deal more than they were supposed to know, and where they did not know they guessed freely, and with wonderful success.

It was curious to see them all assemble in the morning at the breakfast-table as if nothing had happened. Nay, that was not a thing that was possible.

There were traces of last night's excitement on every face; but yet they came in and sat down opposite to each other, and Gussy helped Dolff to his coffee and again wondered how in all the world Janet could be the cause of his attack on Meredith: for it was evident that now, at least, Dolff was not in a state of mind to do anything for Janet. He never spoke to her during breakfast. He avoided her eye. When she spoke, he turned away as if he would not let her voice reach his ears if he could help it. How then could Janet be mixed up in it? Gussy was sorely perplexed by this problem. As for Janet, though she was pale, she put on an elaborate appearance of composure and of knowing nothing which (in her readiness to be exasperated with everything) provoked Gussy most of all. She said to herself that it was a worse offence to pretend not to know when everybody was aware that she must know, than to show her knowledge in the most irritating way. No doubt, however, that if Janet had betrayed any knowledge, Gussy would have found that the most ill-timed exhibition that could be.

There was very little conversation, except between Janet and Julia, during this embarrassing meal. And Mrs. Harwood came out of her room as she had gone into it, unattended by her daughters. There were less signs about her than about any of them of the perturbation of last night. Sometimes an old woman will bear agitation better than the young. She has probably had so much of it, and been compelled to gulp it down so often! Her eyes were not less bright than usual—nay, they had a glance of fire in them which was not usual in their calmer state, and the color in her cheeks was fresher than that of any one else in the house. The girls were all pale—even Julia, and Dolff of a sort of dusky pallor, which made his light hair and mustache stand out from his face. But Mrs. Harwood's pretty complexion was unchanged—perhaps because though they had all made so many discoveries she had made none, but had been aware of everything and of far more than any one else knew, for years.

Early in the day the policeman of last night appeared with a summons to Mrs. Harwood, directing her to appear before some board to show cause why she should have kept, unregistered and unsuspected, a lunatic shut up in her house. Mrs. Harwood saw the man herself, and begged to be allowed to make him a little present, "for your great civility last night." The policeman almost blushed, as he was a man who bore a conscience, for he was not conscious of being very civil; but he accepted the gratuity, let us hope, with the intention of being civil next time he was employed on any such piece of business.

While he spoke to Mrs. Harwood in the hall, whither she had been wheeled out to see him, Meredith came from his room and joined her. He had not escaped so well as she the excitement of the previous night, and it was with unfeigned astonishment that he contemplated this old lady, fresh and smiling, her pretty color unimpaired, her eyes as bright as usual. She was over sixty; she had just been baffled in an object which had been the chief inspiration of her life for years, disappointed, exposed to universal censure, perhaps to punishment, but her wonderful force of nature was not abated; the extraordinary crisis which had passed over her, breaking the bonds of her ailment, delivering her from her weakness, had left no signs of exhaustion upon her. She looked like a woman who had never known what trouble or anxiety was as she sat there smiling, assuring the policeman that she could fully explain everything, and would not fail to do so in the proper quarter. She turned to Meredith as he appeared, and held out her hand to him.

"Good-morning, my dear Charley; I hope you are not the worse for last night's agitation. You see our friend here has come to summon me to make explanations about my poor dear upstairs. You will appear for me and settle everything, won't you? You see this gentleman is a barrister," she explained, smiling to the man who stood looking on.

"Of course I will," Meredith said.

Upon this the policeman took courage, and with a scrape made his *amende honorable.*

"I ought to beg your pardon, sir, and yours too, lady, for all the trouble last night. I had every confidence in Jim Harrison, the man that said he could identify the culprit—that is the fellow as nearly killed you, sir—and rumors have been getting up all over the place as it was the young gentleman here as had been a bit wild, and hated you like poison."

"Dolff never hated me like poison, did he?" said Meredith, elevating his eyebrows and appealing to Mrs. Harwood.

"Never! you have always been one of his best friends."

"Well," said the officer, who was not too confident either in this assurance or in the conclusion he had been obliged to come to, "there was a parcel of tales about. You can never tell how them tales gets up. However, it's all been a mistake: for when Jim sees your young gentleman he says in a moment, 'Nothing of the sort—that's not 'm.' So it all falls to the ground, as you'll see, sir, being used to these questions, as the lady says—for want of evidence."

"Exactly," said Meredith, "and you'll do me the justice to say, officer, that I told you it would from the first. It's worth while occasionally taking a man's advice that knows something about it, you perceive, instead of your Mr. Jim, who evidently knows nothing but what he thinks he saw or didn't see."

"That's it, sir, I suppose," said the policeman, "and if he did see it, or if he didn't I couldn't tell, not if it was as much as my place was worth."

"He would have looked rather foolish though, don't you think, in the witness-box? You see," added Meredith, with a laugh, "you might have spared this lady the trouble of last night."

"No, I don't see that, sir," said the policeman, promptly, "for if it didn't answer one purpose, it did another. I'm very sorry to upset a lady, but she didn't ought to bottle up a madman in a private house without no register, nor information to the commissioners, nor proper precautions. You know that, sir, just as well as me."

"How do you know that the lady has no license?" said Meredith, "or that her relation's illness is not perfectly known? I think you will find a little difficulty in proving that: and then your superiors will be less pleased with the discovery. However, that's my business, as Mrs. Harwood has confided it to me," he added, with a laugh, which he could not restrain, at the man's sudden look of alarm.

"Don't find fault with our friend; he was as civil as it was possible to be. Good-morning, and thank you," said Mrs. Harwood, sitting, with her placid smile, watching her visitor, stiff and uneasy in his plain clothes, as he went away.

When the door was shut upon him by Priscilla, who sniffed and tossed her head at the necessity of being thus civil to a man who had made so much commotion in the house—much as she and her fellow-servants had enjoyed the excitement—Mrs. Harwood's countenance underwent a certain change. The smile faded; a look of age crept round the still beaming eyes.

"If you will wheel me back to my room, Charley, we can talk," she said. She could not but be conscious that he was thinking, asking himself why she could not walk, she who had found power to do so when she wanted it; but she betrayed no consciousness of this inevitable thought. She was very grave when he came round from the back of her chair and stood facing her in the firelight, which, on a dull London morning in the end of January, was the chief light in the room. Perhaps the dreary atmosphere threw a cloud upon her face. Her soft, half-caressing tone was gone. She had become hard and businesslike in a moment. "You want me to explain," she said.

"If you please. You know how much my father was involved: that craze about the money to be paid back means something. Even a mad repetition like that seems likely to have a foundation in fact. Is it true?"

She bent her head a little, and for the moment cast down her eyes.

"It was true."

"It *was* true; then you have alienated——"

"Wait a little. There were no such creditors as his own children, who would have been ruined had not I saved them. They know nothing of any question of money. They knew nothing of——"

"Of his existence at all—till last night?"

"I am bound to furnish you with every information I can. The young ones knew nothing of his existence. Gussy did; but only that I kept him there to save him from an asylum where he might have been treated cruelly— nothing more. You will not take a high moral tone against me, as she is ready to do, and Dolff——"

"No; I will take up no high moral tone," said Meredith; "but the position is very difficult. You have not, I suppose, done away with the money?"

"It is well invested; it is intact. We could not have lived as we have done on my own money. Now, of course, I must give it up—— And no injustice need be done," she added, with a sigh; "it can be paid—at last."

"With interest for all these years?" said Meredith, with a smile.

"Oh, what are you talking of?" She said, "People will be so glad to get anything so unexpectedly, that they will say nothing about interest. I even think——"

"What do you even think?" he said, as she paused.

"How can I tell how you may take it, whether it will commend itself to you or not? There might still be an arrangement by which things might be— tided over."

"After it gets into the papers and it is known that you have been concealing——"

"Oh," she cried again, "you are more dull than I gave you credit for being, Charley Meredith! Who will notice up in Liverpool a romantic story (which is all the papers will make of it) occurring in St. John's Wood? Who will link one thing to another and understand exactly what has happened, or believe that—— I might have taken him in, a miserable wreck, out of sheer love and kindness. I did! I did!" she cried, suddenly, her face melting out of its hardness, her eyes filling with tears. "You may not believe me, but I did. I thought he had not a penny. I went to all the expense of fitting up the wing for him—working with my own hands at it, that nobody should suspect— believing that Vicars had brought him back with his own money—that *he* had none—— I did, though you may not believe me," she said.

"I have not said I did not believe you. We are all very queer creatures—mixed up. And then when you found he had that old pocketbook—for it was full of something better than old papers then—you were tempted, and you——"

She nodded her head; then said, after a while,

"I do not accept that formula. I was tempted—and I did what I had a right to do. *I* had wronged nobody—I knew nothing about the debts. If I had divided *that* among them, what would it have been?—a trifle to each, but enough to dry up all the sympathy they were meeting with. He had made ducks and drakes of more than that belonging to me. And the children were the most deeply wronged. I took it for their sakes, to make up what they had been robbed of. It can go to the others now, and you will see how much it will be."

"You said something," said Meredith, "about an arrangement that might still be made?"

"Yes—if you could lend yourself to it, Charley. It could not be done without you."

"I cannot tell whether I could lend myself to it or not, until I hear what it is."

She looked at him, and two or three times made as if she would speak, but shut her lips again. Her eyes searched his face with an anxious expression.

"I don't know how you will take it," she said, hesitating; "I don't know how you will take it." Then, after a pause, she added, "I will begin by asking you a question. Do you want to marry my daughter Gussy? Yes or no!"

Meredith made a step backwards, and put his hand to his breast as if he had received a blow. In that moment various dreams swept through his mind. Janet's image was not the only one, though it had the freshness of being the last. One of those dreams, indeed, was no other than the freedom of his own bachelor estate, and the advantage of life which was not bound by any social ties. He avowed, however, at length, soberly,

"I think I may say yes, Mrs. Harwood—that is it what has been for a long time in my mind."

CHAPTER XLV.

THE conduct of affairs in the house of the Harwoods was very dreary during the whole of this day. It was, to begin with, a very dreary day, not fog, which can be borne, but one of those dark days which are the scourge of London, when everything is dull and without color without and within, the skies gray, the earth gray, the leafless branches rising like a black tracery upon the colorless background, the light scarcely enough to swear by, to make it seem unnatural to shut the shutters and light the lamp, which is what every well-constituted mind desires to do in the circumstances.

And in the moral atmosphere the same thing reigned. Gussy had a countenance like the day. She, who had at no time much color, had now none. She was like the landscape: hair, eyes, and cheeks seemed the same. Every glimmer of light seemed to have been suppressed in her eyes. She kept them down, or she turned their gaze inward, or she veiled them with some film which is at the command of those who are angry, whether with or without cause. She made no inquiry even after the health of Meredith, which had been hitherto her chief preoccupation, except in so far as was implied in the conventional "How d'you do?" with which they met. Even he was daunted by the determined indifference of her aspect. When he talked of the drive which the doctor had suggested to him as a preliminary to getting out on foot, Gussy never lifted her eyes or made the least inquiry. Yesterday this step of decided progress would have been the most exciting event in the world to her. She took no notice of it now. There was scarcely anything said at table when they took their midday meal, with a candle or two lit on the mantelpiece, "to add a little cheerfulness," as Mrs. Harwood said.

"For certainly we are not a very cheerful party," added the mother, who was more full of life than all the rest put together.

She it was who took the lead in the conversation till Gussy retired. She talked to Meredith and a little to Janet, whom this curious aspect of the family interested greatly, though she did not quite understand it. But Gussy and Dolff both sat bolt upright and said nothing. They ate nothing, too, which, perhaps, was a more effectual weapon against their mother's heart, and, when luncheon was over, they separated gloomily, Dolff disappearing no one knew where, Gussy to her room, where she said she had something to do while Mrs. Harwood retired with Meredith, between whom and herself a curious intimacy seemed to have struck up, to the dining-room, his room as it was called, to talk there.

In this universal gloom and strangeness Julia drew Janet out into the garden. The day grew darker as it approached its end, the atmosphere became more yellow, signs as of a fog appeared in the air. The governess and the pupil put on their ulsters, and began to walk up and down the garden walks, Julia hanging with all her might upon the arm of her companion, dragging down Janet almost to the ground.

"Did you ever know," Julia said, "such a detestable day?"

"It is turning to fog," said Janet, trying to keep to what was commonplace. "It was better that we did not go out."

"Oh, was I thinking of the fog?" said Julia. "I would rather see a dozen fogs than Gussy shut up like that, pursing up her lips as if she were afraid something would drop out when she spoke. And poor Dolff, so dismal, not knowing what to do with himself. Janet, do you think there could be any truth in all that story about Dolff?"

"My dear," said Janet, "how should I have any opinion? I cannot be supposed to know about your brother, what he is likely to do."

"Oh," said Julia, "I did not ask you what you know, but what you *think*; everybody must have an opinion. Besides, after all, it is not so very little that you know about Dolff. He has been at home for six weeks, and you have always seen a great deal of him; at least I am sure he has always tried to see as much as he could of you."

"I think," said Janet, "that it is very bad taste for us to discuss people, especially for you to talk with me about your own family. You forget that I am the governess, Julia."

"I think you are very nasty, and not nice at all. Whoever thinks of you as the governess! I wonder what you mean, saying such unkind things."

"They are not unkind, they are true. Your mother and Gussy have been very good to me, but——"

"Oh, Janet, when you know we were very fond of you, and we thought you were fond of us!"

Here Janet was suddenly visited by a great compunction which changed at once her countenance and her feelings.

"Julia," she said, "don't speak to me. I feel so horrible sometimes, I don't know what to do with myself. I don't think I am nice or good at all. Perhaps," she added with a faint revulsion of self-defence after this impulsive confession, "it is not quite my fault."

"I don't understand you," said Julia. "I ask you a question, quite a simple question, and you go off into reproaching yourself and saying you are not nice. What I want to know is whether you think it was Dolff that knocked Charley Meredith down? If it was, he has not had the strength of mind to stick to it, as I should have done. And what do you think that man meant who came to identify him, and then said it wasn't he? And do you think that man last night really meant anything about Dolff, or did they only pretend to find out about the wing? And, oh, Janet, did you ever know, did you ever suspect anything about the wing? Please don't run away to other subjects, but tell me what you think."

"Where am I to begin? I can't answer all those questions at once."

"Oh," said Julia, with impatience, "how tiresome you are to-day! You don't want to answer me at all. Do you remember that first night when you heard that cry, and were so frightened? I had heard it before, but mamma told me it was nothing, it was the wind in the empty rooms. One thinks it strange," said Julia, "but at first one is stupid, you know, and just believes anything. But you see you were right; and you didn't look surprised at all, not even to see mamma walking upstairs, she who never moves. Or, do you think she only pretends not to be able to move, to take us all in?" Julia added, after a pause.

"Oh, Julia, hush! How dare you say such a thing of your mother?"

"It is because she has deceived us about things," said Julia, hanging her head. "It was Dolff that said so, not me. She has deceived us in one thing, and how are we to believe her in another. Both Dolff and Gussy think so, though Gussy says nothing; to think she has kept it secret all this time, and never let even the elder ones know: and how can we tell if it is not a deceit about the chair, too?"

"If you had seen how she tore herself out of it last night! It was only her misery and anxiety that gave her power to do it. It is very hard to judge any one like that. I daresay," said Janet, indignantly, "that the other was done for your sakes, too, not to trouble you, when you were still so young, with knowing what was a great secret, I suppose?"

"Ah, but why was it a secret? and who do you think the man is, Janet?" said Julia, clinging ever and ever closer to her arm.

"Julia, what have I to do with the secrets of your family?"

"Why, you are one of the family," said Julia; "you can't help knowing; and again I tell you, Janet, it isn't what you know, it's what you think I am asking. Why don't you give me your opinion? every one must have an opinion. Dolff and I, we don't know what to think."

Dolff himself came hurriedly up behind the girls at this moment. He had not gone out after all.

"Why do you trouble Miss Summerhayes, Ju? It is very interesting for us, but not for—a stranger——"

"That is what I have just been saying, Mr. Harwood."

"—Who can't take any particular interest, except just as a wonder and a thing to talk about, in what happens to us?"

Dolff's hands were thrust to the very bottom of his pockets, his shoulders were up to his ears, his head upon his breast. Gloom and anger and misery were on Dolff's face. As for Janet, she had stiffened more and more with every word he said, and Julia, who had been clinging, with all a child's affection, to the arm of her governess, felt herself repulsed and detached, she could not tell how, and protested loudly:

"Janet, because Dolff is disagreeable that's no reason for shaking me off!"

"I have no intention of being disagreeable," said Dolff, walking slowly with them. "I only say what every one must perceive to be the fact. We have all supposed there was a miracle to be performed, and Miss Summerhayes was to think of us as if—as if—she was, as you say, Ju, one of the family; but she does not feel like that; our affairs are nothing to her—only something that is odd and makes a story to talk about, as they would be to any other stranger."

"Oh, if you are going to quarrel!" said Julia, "you had better get it over between yourselves. I don't like people who are quarrelling. You had better have it out with him, Janet, and then perhaps he will not be so dreadful as he has been all these days."

"There is nothing for us to quarrel about. I am, as Mr. Harwood says, only a stranger," said Janet, endeavoring to hold the girl's hand upon her arm.

But Julia slipped it out and ran indoors, not without a thought that she had managed matters well. Julia had long ago made up her mind that a romantic attachment between Dolff and Janet would add great interest to her own life, and that the probable struggles of a love that would not run too smooth would be very desirable for a young lady to witness. And Dolff, under Janet's influence, had been so much "nicer" than Dolff without that. He had stayed at home; he had been ready for anything (though there was always too much of that horrid music), he had not objected even to a round game. It was true that all these domestic pleasures had come to an end since Charley Meredith's accident. But Julia, in her inexperience, could not see why they might not come to an explanation and "get over it," and everything go on as before.

Janet did not follow her pupil as she would have liked to do. She consented to the explanation as it seemed necessary, but she neither hoped nor intended that everything should go on as before.

"Yes," said Dolff, "you are only a stranger, Miss Summerhayes. My mother, I think, took to you as if you had been her own, and everybody was at your feet, but you did not respond—that is to say, you were very kind, and the things you could not help but see, being in the house with us, though we never saw them who belonged to it, you told—as amusing incidents, I suppose, to——"

"What did I tell, Mr. Harwood?"

"Oh, I have not been taken into anyone's confidence. You gave information—you heard him say it—which made a secret meeting necessary, and—all that followed. One might say," said Dolff, with a cheerless laugh, "that everything had followed. I went mad, I suppose, for a little while; and you know as well as I do what I did. Oh, I am very well aware that you know. You saved me in your way after you had ruined me. Fellows say that women are like that—driving you mad first, and then—— But I never was one that talked about women—till I knew you."

"I am very sorry," said Janet, "to have given you a bad opinion of women; but I don't know why Mr. Meredith——" Here her voice faltered a little in spite of herself.

"Ah!" cried Dolff, fiercely, "you have found out that fellow is not worth his salt, yet you could cry when you say his name."

"It is nothing of the sort," exclaimed Janet. "*I* cry—for any man in the world! You don't know me, Mr. Harwood. Mr. Meredith, I remember, walked home a part of the road with me, as it was a dark night. There are some men who think that is a right thing when they meet a lady alone; and, though I am the governess, I am not very old. I think it very old-fashioned, and unnecessary, and I am not afraid to go anywhere alone."

"You know very well if you had wished for an escort, Miss Summerhayes———"

"Yes, Mrs. Harwood would have liked her son to be at the command of the governess! Mr. Meredith walked home with me out of a civility which is old-fashioned, and he stood talking, which it seems is his way—with ladies. A man like that," said Janet, almost fiercely, "will never learn that all girls are not alike, and that some detest these old-fashioned ways of being polite. But there was not in all that any reason for knocking the man down. I supposed when I saw it that you were, perhaps, working out some old quarrel."

"You thought," said Dolff, grinding his teeth, "that I had watched him, and flew at him, by premeditation, to take him at a disadvantage—not because I was driven mad to see him holding you by the hands."

"How could I know one thing or another? There was no reason for anyone being mad about me: I can take care of myself without anyone interfering. But I did not want any scandal, I do not want to be mixed up in it; when a girl's name is mentioned it is always she that gets the whole blame. You know what they say, 'Oh, there was a woman at the bottom of it.' Now, I had done nothing wrong, I was not at the bottom of it. Whatever you choose to say, it was no doing of mine."

"One of the things that fellow says," said Dolff, "is that a woman has always reasons to show she is never wrong."

"They say everything that is brutal and cruel," said Janet, with a sound of tears in her voice, "and therefore I was determined not to be mixed up in it: and I did my best to save you from what was—not a very fine action, Mr. Harwood. You did take him at a disadvantage. I don't doubt that you were very angry, though you had no reason———"

"If you think it was all for you!" cried Dolff, transported with boyish passion and anxious to give a blow in his turn. "But to think of that fellow, jeering and laughing at everybody, those who trusted in him———"

"You see," said Janet, with a smile, "that I was right when I said I was not at the bottom of it!"

Dolff gave her a look which might have killed her where she stood, had the fire which passion struck even from his dull eyes been effectual, and yet which had in it a strange mixture of love and hate. He was not clever enough, however, to note that in Janet's smile there was a mixture, too, of malicious triumph and of mortification; for, notwithstanding all that she had said, it would no doubt have been more agreeable to Janet's pride to have been told that the sudden assault was entirely on her own account from fierce jealousy and passion. She was a little girl who was full of reason, and understood the complication of things, yet there was enough of the primitive in her to have been pleased, even had she not fully believed it, by such an asseveration as that.

"In that case," she said, "I don't know what you have to find fault with me. I did my best to smooth it all away that nobody might have known anything. What use is there in telling things that are so easily misrepresented? If it would shock anyone who trusted in him to know that Mr. Meredith had walked home with the governess———"

"Oh," cried Dolff, "you will drive me out of my senses! who calls you the governess, Miss Summerhayes?"

"I do myself," said Janet, "it is my right title. I never have been one of those who despise it; but if it would vex anyone—who trusted in him—to hear that Mr. Meredith had walked home because it was dark and late with the——"

"You are very anxious to defend Meredith," said Dolff, bitterly.

"Am I?" cried Janet. There was a dart out of her eyes at that moment that was more powerful than any dull spark that could come from Dolff's. "If I am," she added, with a laugh, "it is only for the sake of those who, as you say, trust in him, Mr. Harwood. For me I find those old-fashioned ways of his intolerable. He is like a man in an old novel," cried Janet, "who kisses the maid and gives her half-a-crown, and is what is called civil to every girl. It is eighteenth-century—it is mock Lovelace—it is the most antiquated vanity and conceit. And he thinks that he takes people in by it, which shows how foolish and imbecile it is, besides being the worst taste in the world!"

Dolff stared open-eyed at this tirade. He had a faint idea that Lovelace meant a seductive villain, but what Meredith had to do with the eighteenth century, or how he was old-fashioned, this young man, devoid of literature, understood not at all. He did understand, however, that Janet was angry with Meredith, and this went to his heart. The dull yellow sky began to look a little clearer. It became a possibility that things might brighten, that a new world might arise, that these misty shadows might blow away.

"If I could think," he said, "that you ever could forget all this, Miss Summerhayes. I heard you taking my mother's part with Ju: and you are thinking of Gussy, who doesn't deserve it very much, perhaps, and you have saved me: for I never could have faced it out but for what you said to me—though I have seemed so ungrateful: and if you think it possible that we could all forget what has happened—in time——"

"No," said Janet, "I think there are several things in it which neither you nor I could ever forget."

"I am not so sure," said Dolff. "It would depend upon you. If you would promise never to see or speak to——"

"Whom?" said Janet, rising several inches out of her shoes, and looking down upon him with a glance that froze Dolff; and then she added, interrogatively, "For you?" and, turning round upon her heel, walked away into the house without a glance behind.

CHAPTER XLVI.

JANET was passing quickly through the hall, coming from the garden by the long passage which led past the kitchen and pantry, and turning round to go upstairs, when she found herself suddenly caught as she went along. Some one took hold of the end of the long boa which was round her neck and detained her. She was a little startled and frightened at first, thinking instinctively of the mad tenant of the wing, and that now the door was no longer fastened between him and the house. Her fears, however, were instantly put to flight, and feelings very different substituted in their stead, when a voice said,

"Janet! stop a moment and speak to me, I am very lonely here."

"You have no need to be here, or to be lonely unless you like," she cried, hurriedly; "and call me by my proper name, please. I can be only Miss Summerhayes to you."

"Don't say so. You were not so hard upon me the other night. Ah! I forgot; it's not the other night, it's three weeks ago. Stop a moment; don't pass without saying a word. You ought to pay me a little attention, considering all that I have suffered since—for you."

"For me!" she cried. "I am sorry that you have suffered, but it was not for me."

"Do you think for a moment that that lout would have sprung on me as he did if it hadn't been for you? You know better, Janet. I owe it to you, my dear, that I was beaten flat like a pancake, and had my head dashed against the stones, as they did, you know, in the psalm. No, Janet; be quiet and listen to me. I've paid dear for one bit of an interview, and you ought to give me some recompense. I've lain upon my back all these many days for you, and it's for you that I grin at that fellow, instead of taking him by the throat!"

"That does me no good," said Janet, panting with excitement and alarm. "Let me go, please. I would rather die than be found talking to you here. Take him by the throat if you please. What is that to me?"

"To save you from trouble," said the other. "Don't you think I have felt how unpleasant it would be to have your name coming out? That is why I have let him off, for that reason and no other. Come, talk to me a moment, I deserve it. Nobody will hear us; Gussy is out, and the mother shut up in her room. I'm very forlorn in this house, which I had better leave, I think, at once; I'm well enough, I suppose, to do so now——"

"Don't you want to leave it? Shall you not be glad to get away?" cried Janet, under her breath.

"Glad to get away! when you are here, you little witch. Do you think it has been pleasant to go on all the time purred over by the others, and never getting a word with you."

"You will not," said Janet, with perhaps a certain revengeful pleasure, "be purred over by the others any more."

"You think so?" he said. "Don't you be too sure. If you disdain me, and refuse to hear me, there is no telling, they may purr again."

"One way or other," said Janet, "it has nothing to do with me."

"Why do you say so? Are you going to be sent away?"

"Sent away!" Janet breathed forth the words as in a gale of indignation. "Nobody," she cried, "except myself, shall send me away."

"Well," he said, "and yourself will not, I hope? It would be a changed house if you were gone. All the spirit and the understanding and the mischief—don't be angry, Janet; there is nothing so enchanting as mischief, and you know you are full of it—would be gone. I doubt if I should ever come back to the place again."

"Mr. Meredith," said Janet, "you have no right to speak to me so. It is unpardonable in a man. Who is to believe you? Miss Harwood, whom I believe you are engaged to all this time—or me, whom you venture to take hold of and—talk to, when you think nobody sees? Oh, it is quite unpardonable, Mr. Meredith! Is it her or is it me whom you want to please? You ought to know."

"That sounds very like asking me my intentions," he said, with a laugh, "as the father does in novels, or sometimes the mother. But never, so far as I recollect, the young lady herself."

Janet was angry, and she was sore. She had been made of no account among them; she who was very well aware of her own value, and had never been ignored by those around her before, had been lately treated as if she were nobody in this house. It had been necessary for her to conceal her own movements, to be prudent, to take the most urgent measures that her name should not suffer. But it had galled her to the very heart that Meredith should have spoken of her as a mere means of receiving information, and even that Dolff should have ignored her part in the matter, though it was what she wished him most to do. She was full of inconsistency in this respect, as most human natures are, and as women in particular are expected to be. Not to be mixed up in it was her most urgent desire, but to be ignored, though it was what she desired most, was bitter to her heart. It had given her a certain amount of satisfaction to assert her superiority to Dolff, and she would have been still more pleased now could she have done the same with Meredith, and issued from the double complication triumphant, setting both men in "their proper place," and proving that she was not deceived by either, but above both. But it was not so easy with Meredith as with Dolff. She had played with the youth who was not so clever as she, nor her equal in anything, but alas! it was she who had been played with in the other case, and her attempt to change the *rôle* was not likely to be very effectual.

She did not love Meredith—she was angry with him, and more or less despised him: but he had a charm for her which some men have for women, and some women for men, not only without merit on the part of the enchanter, but even with a distinct feeling of disapproval and almost contempt on that of the enchanted. This was her feeling towards Gussy's lover. He *was* Gussy's lover, probably for all she knew Gussy's betrothed; yet he had dared to play with her, to set up a secret understanding, to persuade her that he loved her best.

He did not love her at all, she declared to herself indignantly; he loved nobody except himself, he cared for nothing except to be amused, to have the best of everything, to gather sweetness on every side. She had thrown him aside indignantly in the moment of trial when he had been found wanting, and when she, too, had found herself wanting, and instinctively defended herself by dropping him. And yet now when Janet was suddenly brought face to face with him again, and there was a moment given her in which to express her final sentiments, one of those curious returns upon herself which come in every such history came over her. It was always possible that in the human mind there should be a complete change of sentiment, that the balance should turn at a touch, and truth and love vanquish all evil. The most conventional and the most lively and imaginative of minds acknowledge this possibility. It is called conversion in religion, in other matters it bears a less important title: yet it is always a possibility. A man who has been an egotist may become suddenly generous and tender; a man who has resisted every inducement to do well, and broken every heart that loved him, may by some more subtle touch be changed, and turned from his evil ways. Such a thing is always possible: and Janet, when she addressed Meredith in her indignation, had some such feeling in her mind. He had a charm for her notwithstanding her anger against him, her sense of wrong, and the no-faith she had in him; but yet he had a charm: and it was possible that something she might say, some argument struck out in the heat of the moment, might still convert him to honor and to truth.

That was, to Janet's version of honor and truth, which was, perhaps, a one-sided one. It was according to all her canons that the man finding himself not to love his *fiancée* but to love another, should sacrifice everything to that other, and leave the *fiancée* to bear it as she might. This would have been the triumph of love over worldliness and conventionality in Janet's eyes. She would not have felt it wrong for him to prefer herself, to give up Gussy: and it was quite in his power to hold by Gussy and give up herself; but one thing she felt must be done, and that at once. She would not allow him to go on, detaining her, making love to her, telling her in words and otherwise that he loved her best, if he meant after all to marry Gussy. It had to be now decided once for all.

"Since you say so," she said, with her heart beating, "I will not object to the word. I am not frightened by words: and I have neither father nor mother. Oh, don't think I forget what you said about that last time you asked me to meet you in the shop, that it was to receive information. And now you stop me and want to begin again, in a way very different from getting information. Yes, I want to know what you mean. It is quite true: which of us is it you want to please? Answer me!" cried Janet, stamping upon the floor with her foot. "Is it her, or is it me?"

"Alas, that it can't be both! My dear child, I should like to please you both, if that is how you put it," said Meredith.

It was so dark that she could scarcely see his face, but he had twisted the long boa round his arm, so as to bring her nearer to him.

She stamped her foot again upon the ground, and began to loosen her boa.

"Answer me!" she said.

"Don't put a poor fellow in a corner, Janet. I have to temporize like other people. You have almost made me lose my head; but I can't afford it, don't you know. I can't throw things up like that: and there's no hurry—we're all young enough; let us wait and see what may turn up."

"Is that all you have got to say?" said Janet, uncoiling the boa from her throat.

"What can any one say more? You women have the most confounded way of putting a fellow in a corner. There's no need for any such desperate decision. Let us wait a bit and enjoy ourselves as much as we can in the meantime," said Meredith, manipulating the boa on his side.

She left it suddenly in his hand, and quickly and noiselessly turned away, flying upstairs almost before he could call her back: and Meredith did not venture to call "Janet, Janet!" in more than a subdued tone. He dared not follow her, he did not want anybody to know of that colloquy in the hall, though he had risked it, and would have prolonged it, perhaps, to the very edge of discovery. When he felt the boa dropped upon his hands he laughed to himself, with amusement mingled with a certain discomfiture, to think how much in earnest these girls were—and he was not at all in earnest. He liked to take the goods the gods had provided, and get all the pleasure he could out of them; but to compromise his own future and bind himself forever was what he would not do for anyone: and perhaps he was half pleased to have got through the dangerous amusement of that interview, though it was he who had sought it and prolonged it, so easily upon the whole. He had not been made to commit himself to anything, and yet he flattered himself he had made no breach. Things were just as they had been before. He was not like a married man, or one who had come under solemn engagements; there was no reason that he should give up what was agreeable to him, yet, at least; but it amused him to see Janet's high spirit, her impatience, and even those questions which it was ludicrous, yet a little confusing, to be asked by her—about "his intentions," as he said. Even the sudden conclusion of the interview by which she betrayed her impatience, her displeasure was amusing to him. He felt all the more fond of her, amused and flattered by her anxiety to know what he meant, and pleased that she had not made much of her bold attempt.

"The little vixen!" he said to himself. He gathered up the boa, which was of a kind which slips through unused fingers, and laid it carefully upon the table. It escaped him once, as its mistress had done, and had to be caught again, and laid in soft, dark coils on the table, which was a thing that pleased him, and made him laugh again. Janet was in a great fright lest her conversation with him should be discovered, and she would by no means have liked it to be discovered, yet it gave him a pungent pleasure to linger and keep her there, and feel that she had fled on the very eve of detection, and get away himself to the shelter of his room, just as Gussy outside put her latch-key in the door.

He laughed as he heard her come in and call to Priscilla to light the lamps, and that the hall was so dark she could scarcely see her way upstairs. Janet had found her way upstairs like a bird a minute before. He chuckled at the thought that in another moment it might have been too late: and yet he had no desire at all that Gussy should find out that meeting in the dark.

As for Janet, she hurried to her room with hot indignation in her heart and the water in her eyes. Oh, it was not that she expected it to have ended in any other way! She had known exactly how it would be. He was not a man to behave like a man, to love one and no more. What he wanted was his own pleasure and advantage, not Gussy and not Janet. She despised him for it all, for the subdued tone in which he had attempted to call her back, for his way of putting off everything that was serious: and she half despised herself for having asked, as he said, "his intentions," and allowed him to see that she cared.

She did care, she said to herself, dashing the tears from her eyes. She had a contempt for him, and penetrated his character with the keenest perception, and to say that she loved him would have been a great exaggeration: and yet he had a charm for Janet—his mockery, his laugh, the tone of his voice, almost his want of respect and bold appropriation of her, whether she wished it or not, had a charm. Her heart would have danced with pleasure had he given her an assurance of love (which he might very well have done, she knew, without in the least meaning it), and yet she had penetrated him through and through, and had no illusion as to his character. All motives are mingled, but Janet's were so mingled that she did not understand them. She was humiliated by the result of her endeavor, yet highly excited, her heart leaping in her breast: she sat down as she was, in her hat and coat, to think it all over. Dolff and Meredith had both revealed their affection more or less—they had both allowed her to see into their hearts. And Janet, though she had provoked it in both cases, was angry, mortified, full of fury and pain. That was what men were incapable of, she thought—any real feeling, but for themselves and themselves only. Even Dolff, who had been her slave, would have consented now to forget everything, if she would give him her promise. She to him! as if he would give any promise or act otherwise than as pleased himself!

Janet sat for a long time pondering over the half-extinguished fire, her heart full of anger, disappointment, and contempt. It was themselves they had both thought of, never of her! At one time they had made her believe that she was everything, queen of their hearts, and for a moment she had been so silly as to be half-intoxicated, believing in it, accepting the high compliment, but now——. She suddenly sprang up under the impulse of the shock at the dictation of a new idea. They might be unworthy, but there were some who were worthy. Oh, what did it matter that they should have youth and a fair appearance, or any of those adventitious gifts. It was better to be true and real. It occurred to her suddenly that instead of going away to another family to exercise the mystery of a governess, instead of being liable to be dismissed, as Meredith so coarsely had suggested, instead of the state which was offensive to Janet's own good taste and feeling, of covert hostility to her employers, which she had fallen into so readily, and which in another house it was horribly possible she might fall into again—how much better it would be to go out proudly in the eye of day, as good as any of them, as independent, with a life of her own to fall back upon!

Janet flew to her writing-table at this new thought, and wrote, as quick as the pen would form the letters, a hasty letter. It was all done at flying speed, without taking time to think, a hurried, blurred, as she felt unladylike production. She thrust it into an envelope, directed it, and rushed downstairs with it to take it herself to the post, not to lose a moment. The hall was now lighted but abandoned—nobody there to call to her, to bid her pause, to stop her on the way. Her boa lay on the table carefully coiled round and round. Janet snatched it up, as if that had been an additional reason for speed, and rushed out to decide her fate.

CHAPTER XLVII.

IN the evening they were all assembled in the drawing-room once more.

The same party with so many differences. There were only Mrs. Harwood and Meredith who were unchanged. She sat in the usual warm corner, with the usual white fleecy knitting, which never changed, in her lace cap and white shawl, with her pretty complexion and her smiling looks, the woman of whom people said that she must have lain in the lilies and fed on the roses of life to preserve that wonderful complexion and eyes so clear and so bright. And he, looking so much better—really assured in his health, the tints of weakness going off, the high color which was at once his characteristic and the drawback to his good looks coming back, and his high spirits as if they had never had any check. It was only last night that he had been following up that discovery with the eagerness of a bloodhound, forgetting everything but the scent on which he was following on to the end. All that had now flown away. He was the Charley Meredith of old, playful and ready to "chaff" everybody round, talking of the new songs and what would suit "our" voices, and lamenting the interrupted "practisings." Charley was as if nothing had happened, full of fun, eager for amusement, calling upon the mother for sympathy and encouragement.

"They have all become so grave," he said. "It is you and I, Mrs. Harwood, that will have to perform our duet."

"Well," said Mrs. Harwood, "if I had been twenty years younger, there is no telling what might have happened. I should not have kept you waiting, Charley. I wish, Gussy, you would not look as if you had been to a funeral this afternoon."

"Not this afternoon—but something a little like it, mamma."

"You are talking great nonsense, my dear. If there is anybody that ought to be cast down, it is surely me. All my troubles have been forced back upon me; but I have the comfort of knowing," said Mrs. Harwood, with a slightly raised voice, "that I never meant any harm—and that I have done none—and that the last people in the world to criticise me are my children: so I desire that there shall be an end of this. I have been summoned, as I expected, to explain everything: and Charley has kindly promised to appear for me and clear it all up—and secure permission for me to look after my poor dear upstairs, as I have done ever since he was afflicted. When I have made it all clear with the Lunacy commissioners I may perhaps be supposed to have done enough, though one can never know."

"Mamma," said Gussy, "there was no need for anything but to be frank and open. You have not been open—not to me, who was taken more or less into your confidence. I suppose you were compelled to tell me something, but not all, or nearly all. A child could see there is more in it than meets the eye. And now I presume you have taken Mr. Meredith into your confidence, but none of your children."

"Why *Mr.* Meredith?" said he, with a smile, putting out his hand for hers.

Gussy made no reply. She gave him a look of indignant reproach. In point of fact, when he asked her thus, she could not have told why—after all. The truth began to steal into her mind, like the influence of a thaw, that after all he had done nothing. He had been curious to fathom the secret in the house. So would any one have been. And there was something about information that he had received—where or from whence could he have received information? But even that, she suddenly reflected, could not be his fault. If he had been told anything it would be difficult not to listen. Thus, though she gave him a look of reproach and drew away her hand, it suddenly occurred to Gussy that after all there was no particular reason why she should call him Mr. Meredith, or consider him as deeply to blame. The thaw had begun.

Dolff had kept behind backs all the evening. He took no seat, he attached himself to none of the party. For some time he had been seated in a large easy-chair which almost swallowed him up, in the other part of the room, reading, or pretending to read. Then when the conversation began he had risen from that place, and walked about in the half-light like an uneasy ghost. Now he came into the talk with a voice that sounded far off, partly because of the length of the room, and partly because of the boyish gruffness which, as a token of high contrariety and offence, he had brought into his voice.

"I don't see," he said, "what Lunacy commissioners have to do with it in comparison with the people in the house."

Mrs. Harwood turned her chair round as much as she was capable of doing, and cast a look into the dim depths of the other room.

"It is a pity," she said, "that the commissioners could not be of your opinion, Dolff; it would have saved me a great deal of trouble."

"I can't see," he said, irritably, "why you should have taken such trouble upon you at all. What is the man to you? Who is he that you should have taken such trouble for him? You have no brother that I ever heard of. Mother," said Dolff, coming forward out of the gloom, "I have cudgelled my brains to think who it could be. Is it possible that for a mere stranger— a man who is no relation to us—you should have risked all our comfort and separated us from you? I have heard of such things," said the young man, working himself up, "but to find them out in one's mother whom one has always respected——"

She gave a wondering look round upon them all and then burst into a strange confused laugh.

"In the name of wonder," she cried, "can anybody tell me what the boy has got in his head? what does he mean?"

What did he mean? They all looked at each other with perplexity; even Janet, rousing from the rigid unmeaningness to which she had condemned herself, to take share in the glance of amazement which ran round. Only Meredith did not share that amazement. He laughed, which was a sound that made Dolff frantic, and brought him a step forward with his hand clenched.

"Dolff, my good fellow," he said, with an air of superior experience which still further irritated the furious lad, "don't fly upon me again: for that sort of argument doesn't do much good in a discussion. And don't bring your ideas out of French novels here. Such things are a great deal worse when they are translated than when they are at home."

"I don't know what you mean," cried Dolff, "with your French novels! nor what right you have to be here, in the midst of us all, discussing a subject— a subject which—a subject that—makes me," cried the young man, "that I cannot endure myself, nor the house, nor so much as my mother's name."

"What does he mean?" said the ladies to each other, looking all round with perturbed looks. They were all united, from Julia to her mother, in the wonder to which they had no clue. Englishwomen, brought up in the very lap of respectability, not knowing even the alphabet of shame, full of faults, no doubt of their own kind, but utterly incapable even of imagining the secret horror and suspicion that lurked in Dolff's words, they could do nothing but send round that troubled look of consultation. Was Dolff going out of his senses, *too*? Was it perhaps in the family, this dreadful thing, and had it assailed the boy? Mrs. Harwood grew pale with sheer fright and horror as she looked back upon her son, and then pitifully consulted his sisters with her eyes.

"Dolff," cried Meredith, in a warning tone, "mind what you are about, my boy. I tell you to bring none of your French novels here. They don't explain the situation. Strike me if you like then; but don't be such an everlasting fool. Pierre et Jean, eh, *here!*" cried the elder man, with a half shriek of derisive laughter. He sat with a sort of careless courage, not putting himself even into an attitude of defence, but on his guard, looking towards the enraged youth—an air which transported both the young feminine hearts beside him into an ecstasy of admiration, though Gussy was so deeply offended (she began to think more and more without reason), and Janet more deeply still, hating and despising him as she thought.

Gussy darted forward between her brother, who had the air of springing upon his senior, and Meredith, warning Dolff in her turn with a loud cry.

"Mind," she exclaimed, "what you are about! As Charley says, enough has happened already. We will tolerate no more in this house."

Janet rose too, scarcely knowing why she did it, she who had so solemnly made up her mind that on no provocation would she take any part.

"I don't know," she said, "what Mr. Dolff means; but I hope no one will be angry if I say I found some papers torn in little pieces under the windows of the wing. I thought they were from an old copy-book and that they were Mr. Dolff's. I am sure now they belonged to the poor gentleman upstairs. They were signed 'Adolphus Charles Harwood.' I have no right to be here at all, and I am going away."

Dolff stood breathless, feeling the light fail in his eyes. He saw Meredith spring up and open the door for her, and with a pang watched while the little dark figure disappeared. For the moment he was only aware of her disappearance, of the final going out as he thought in eternal darkness of the little light which had made his life so different. He came back to himself with a gasp when the door closed, but scarcely knew what had been said to him for the beating of the pulses in his head.

"'Adolphus Charles Harwood'?" said Julia, thoughtfully; "then that, I suppose, is the poor gentleman's name; so, Dolff, you see I was right, and it was a relation after all."

"What is Pierre et Jean, Charley?" said Mrs. Harwood, sitting up a little more erect than usual, with a kindling in her eyes.

"It is a very clever French novel—far more clever and better than most—a very fine piece of work."

"But with something in it," said Mrs. Harwood, "like our circumstances? You must bring it to me to read it, Dolff. If I did not burden your minds with a secret, which would have done you no good, and been hard, hard to keep——"

"Then," he said, interrupting her abruptly, "it is a relation? but even that I never heard of before. How is it that there should be a man of that name in the family, and I should never have heard of him before?"

He still stood on the defensive, his face flushed with anger, and a sense of being wrong and inferior to all the rest somehow, though he could not tell how.

It is strange how difficult it sometimes is in such a discussion, when there is one whose invincible ignorance holds out in face of all argument and proof, to say the single word which will cut the knot. It was on Gussy's lips to say it; but she did not, perhaps because Dolff's want of comprehension was so curious to them all. And at this moment, almost before he could be replied to, there arose a little commotion in the hall. Janet's voice was heard in a faint cry, and there was a shuffling of feet, and another unknown male voice rising in the quiet. Julia, who was awake like a dog to all new sounds, rushed to the door and flung it open, and then there became visible the strangest sight.

There stood upon the threshold an old man in a strange dress, something between a long coat and a gown, with a white beard on his breast, long white hair streaming on his shoulders, and a long pallid face. His appearance was so sudden, so unlooked-for, like a stage entrance without warning, that the effect was more startling and wild than could be imagined. It was as if the conversation, in which so many complications, so many misunderstandings, were involved, had been suddenly embodied in this bizarre and extraordinary figure which was its cause. And, as if to make it more extraordinary still, this strange apparition held by the hand, with her arm drawn through his, Janet, pale, terrified, and faintly struggling, who had left the room but a moment before.

Janet was evidently wild with terror, yet did not dare even to try to escape except by the strain of reluctance in her whole figure, drawing back while he drew her forward. The most benignant aspect that is compatible with a disordered brain was in the madman's face. He smiled as he held her, dividing the fingers of the hand he held with his own, as if he were caressing and playing with a child. He stood for a moment contemplating them all, taking in the details of the picture which on their side they made, with that pleased, half-bewildered, half-imbecile look, and nodding his head from one to another, like one of those nodding figures that go on indefinitely. The weakness of the smile, the glow of foolish satisfaction in his face, the endless nodding, took much from the majesty of the venerable patriarchal figure, and made him look more like a silly old man than a picturesque and tragical lunatic. While they all stood thunderstruck, he advanced into the room with a buoyant, almost dancing step.

"Well," he said, "here I am, Julia. I suppose that you expected me? This is a merry meeting: here's to our merry meeting. Vicars says I am so much better—and so I am, quite well—don't you see I have a color in my cheeks—that I may come downstairs. He is a very good fellow, Vicars; but I want society. Julia, see what I've got here."

He drew Janet forward, nodding at her with the most complacent looks, while the poor little girl, deadly pale, trembling with terror, hung upon his arm as if suspended by a hook, holding back, yet not daring to struggle, shutting her eyes for very terror. He waved his hand, releasing hers for a moment, but holding it tight within his arm.

"Another of them?" he said. "Where does she come? I don't seem to remember what we called her, or where she comes in the family; but a nice little thing, Julia—with some feeling for her old—for her old—eh? I forget what I was going to say. What is her name?"

"Adolphus! let the child go. Here is a chair by me: come and sit down."

They all stood about helpless, gazing, Mrs. Harwood alone keeping her place in her chair, while he strayed across the floor in his half-dancing step, dragging Janet with him.

"I'll sit by you with pleasure, Julia. It is long since you have come to sit with me till last night. And these are all of them? I've said their names over in my mind, but I forget some—I forget some. They were so little once—curious to think so little once, and then when a man comes back—tse! in a moment all grown up—the same as men and women. But this," he said, with a laugh, "is still a little thing. Where shall I put her, Julia? Too big, you know, to sit on papa's knee."

He laughed again, looking round upon them all, and suddenly let Janet go, so that she fell in the shock of the release, which made the stranger laugh more and more.

"Poor little sing! but too big to tumble about. Det up again and don't ky. Julia," he put out his hand again and laid it on the elbow of Mrs. Harwood's chair, "these are all then?—between you and me——" He rubbed his long soft pallid hands.

"Who would have thought," he said, "that I should have got so well, and come downstairs again and sat by you in another chair, and seen them all men and women. It's more than we could have expected—more than we could have expected. And now there's a great deal to be done to show that we're thankful. Where is my pocket-book? I want my pocketbook. God in heaven! that villain Vicars has taken my pocket-book, and now I shall not be able to pay!"

He started up again in rising excitement, his eyes beginning to stare and his face to redden, while he dragged and pulled at the pockets of his coat. Mrs.

Harwood put her hand upon him to pull him down into his chair, and called to them all to find Vicars.

"Sit down, sit down, Adolphus," she said, holding him with both her hands. "It is in your other coat. You changed your other coat to come down, you know you did. Run—run, Dolff! for the love of heaven, and get the pocket-book out of your father's other coat!"

CHAPTER XLVIII.

DOLFF hurried out of the room so bewildered and dazed that he neither understood what this new revelation was, nor what he was sent out to do. He felt himself hustled out of the room by his anxious sisters, while Meredith was left to be the defender of the party against the madman. The madman! What was it his mother had said. To fetch Vicars—but that was not all—to get something out of his father's coat. His father! Dolff stopped a few steps from the door, out of which he had been thrust to run in haste and bring what was wanted out of his father's coat.

"My father," Dolff said to himself, "has been dead since ever I can remember. Who is my father?" He was completely bewildered. He remembered his mother very well in her widow's cap. And she was known everywhere to be a widow. "Your father!"—he could not think what it meant. He believed there must be some mistake, some strange illusion which had fallen upon them, or which, perhaps, they had thought of, invented, to prevent remark. "Your father!" could it have been said only to shut his mouth?

It was due to Providence, not to Dolff, that Vicars came in his way, drifting across the hall in pursuit of his patient. Vicars had the famous pocket-book in his hand, and Dolff wondered vaguely what was the meaning of it, and how it was that this pocket-book, like a property on the stage, should be so mixed up with the poor man's thoughts, if these distracted fancies could be called thoughts. All that he could do was to point towards the drawing-room, whither Vicars hastened. He had no command of his voice to say anything, or of himself to be able to exercise his own wits. He dropped in his dismay upon one of the hard wooden chairs in the hall, and sat there staring vaguely before him, trying to think.

There was a faint jar of the door, and a little figure came out abruptly, as if escaping. It was Janet, whose smooth hair was a little out of order, and her black dress crushed by the half embrace in which the madman had held her. Janet was deeply humiliated by that embrace, by having thus appeared before Meredith and all of them, the object of the old man's fondling. Her face was obscured by anger and annoyance, and when Dolff sprang up and put himself in her way, the little governess looked for a moment like a little fury, contemplating him with a desire in her eyes to strike him to dust if she had been able—a fiery little Gorgon, with the will without the power.

"What is it—what is it *now*?" she cried, clenching her hand as if she would have struck him, yet at the same moment holding herself in with difficulty from a fit of angry tears.

"Janet, don't forsake me," cried Dolff; "I am half mad, I don't know what to think. Who is he? Tell me who he is!"

"Mr. Harwood," cried Janet, fiercely, "you—you are not a wise child."

He looked at her with a naive wonder.

"I have never set up for being wise. You are far, far more quick than I am. I suppose you understand it, Janet. I know you don't care for me, as I do for you; but you might feel for me a little. Oh, don't turn away like that—I know you've thrown me off; but help me—only help me. Who is he? Tell me who he is."

"Mr. Harwood," said Janet, "how should I know your family history? He is your father; any one can see that."

"It is impossible," said Dolff; "my father is dead."

"Of course, I cannot know anything," said Janet, with a cruel intention which she did not disguise from herself, with her lip a little raised over her white teeth like a fierce little animal at bay, "but I will tell you what I think. Your father has done something which made it better that he should be thought dead, and your mother has hidden him away and kept him a close prisoner all these years: but now it is all found out."

"Done something—that made it better he should be thought dead!" Dolff turned so deadly pale that the girl's heart smote her. The place seemed to turn round and round with him. He fell back against the wall as if he would have fallen. "You don't mean that!—you don't mean that!" he cried, piteously, stretching out his hands to her as if she could help it.

"Oh! forgive me, Mr. Dolff. I did not mean to hurt you so."

"Never mind about hurting me," he said, hoarsely. "Is it true?"

She made no reply; what did she know about it? Perhaps it was not true—but what else could any one think who was not a fool? If Dolff had not been a fool he would have known that it must be so. She stood confronting him for a minute while he stood there supporting himself against the wall, hiding his face in his hands. And then Janet left him, running upstairs to escape altogether from these family mysteries, with which she had nothing to do. It had been very interesting at first, full of excitement, like a story. But now Janet felt that it was a great consolation to have nothing really to do with it, to retire and leave these people to manage their own affairs. And she had in her veins an entirely new excitement, something of her own enough to occupy all her thoughts.

She ran upstairs, leaving Dolff in his dismay with his head hidden in his hands—what had she to do with that?—and fled to her comfortable room, where she sat down beside the blazing fire, and turned to her own affairs—they were important enough now to demand her full attention. Since she had written that letter, Janet herself had become subject to all the suspenses, the doubts and alarms of independent life. What would be thought of it? Would he still be in the same mind? Would he come to take her away? And oh, biggest and most serious of all her questions, if he did come, if he were still of the same mind, could she endure him—could she accept the fate which she had thus invited for herself? Janet had serious enough questions of her own to discuss with herself as she sat over the glowing fire.

Poor Dolff did not know how long he stood there, with his head against the wall. He was roused at last by the sound of a movement in the drawing-room, and presently the door opened, and a sort of procession came out. First of all, the strange new inmate of the house leaning upon Vicars, looking back and kissing his hand to the others behind him, who came crowding out in a group close to each other.

"I'll come often now and sit an hour with you in the evening," he said. "Now that everybody's paid, I'll live a new life. My children, don't be frightened; I'll take care of you all. For," he said, stopping short, turning Vicars round by the arm, "I'm to have a wheeled chair and go out for an airing to-morrow. Hey, what do you think—an airing! That means it's all paid and everything right."

"I wouldn't, if I were you, say the same thing over not more than twenty times," said Vicars, sulkily; "and you won't have no airing, I can tell you, if you don't come off to bed."

"That's Vicars all over," said the smiling patient. "Vicars all over! You would think he's my master—and he's only my servant! Yes—yes, it's all paid, and everything right—or how could I go out for an airing to-morrow? There is plenty in the pocket-book for everybody. You know—in the pocket-book. Eh! My! Where's my pocket-book?" he cried, suddenly changing his tone and searching in his breast-pocket. "Vicars, do you hear? My pocket-book! Where's my pocket-book? It's not where I always have it—I keep it here, you know, to keep it safe. My pocket-book!" cried the poor maniac, tossing Vicars from him and waving his arms wildly.

His distracted eyes caught at this moment the figure of Dolff standing against the wall. Dolff had uncovered his pale and miserable countenance:

he was standing in the shade, mysterious, half seen, with that very pale face looking out from the semi-dark. The madman rushed towards him with a cry.

"There's the thief! There's the thief! Get hold of him before he gets away! He's got my pocket-book—lay hold of him! I'm not strong enough," he added, turning round with an explanatory look, "to do it myself. Never getting any air you know, as I couldn't till things were settled. I've got very little strength."

"I thought," said Vicars, "as taking that pocket-book from him was a mistake! He's always a-looking back upon that pocket-book! You'll have to give it him back."

"Don't you remember, sir," said Meredith, holding up a sealed packet, "that you gave it to me to put it up—look at the seals, you stamped them yourself. You gave it to me to pay off everything. Try to remember. Here it is, safe and sound. You gave it to me yourself."

"And who the devil are you," said the invalid, "that I should give you all my money? You're not one of them: some fellow, Vicars, that Julia has picked up. She's always picking people up. Give it back, make him give it back, Vicars—my money that's meant to pay off everybody! Give it back—back! I tell you I'll pay them all myself! I'll go out to-morrow in the wheel-chair—you know, Vicars, the wheel-chair for the airing—and pay them all myself!"

"Who is it," said Dolff, coming forward out of the gloom, "who has to be paid back? and who is this man? For you all seem to know."

"Come, come, sir," said Vicars; "it's your time for bed. You'll not go nowhere, neither for an airing nor to pay them debts of yours, if you don't come straight off to bed."

"Who is he?" cried Dolff, pushing upon the group. "Who are you? For I will know."

To the surprise of all, the madman, who had been so self-confident, suddenly shrank behind Vicars, and, catching his arm, pulled him towards the door that led to the wing.

"I'm afraid of that man," he said, in a whispering, hissing tone. "Vicars, get me home; get me out of sight. He's an officer. Vicars, I'm not safe with that man!"

"Hold your tongue, can't you, Mr. Dolff, till I get him away," cried Vicars, pushing past. And in a moment the pair had disappeared within the mysterious door, which swung after them, noiseless, closing without a sound.

Dolff was left, pale and threatening, with Meredith and his two sisters facing him. That they should know what he did not filled Dolff with a sort of frenzy; and yet how could he continue to say that he did not know?

"I wish," cried Julia, stamping her foot, "that you two who know such a lot would go away, and not speak to Dolff and me. You don't belong to us—at least Charley Meredith doesn't belong to us, and Gussy thinks more of him than of all of us together. Oh, Dolff, it only matters to you and me! I believe," cried Julia, catching her brother's arm, "that old madman's our father, Dolff. I believe he is our father. It's terrible, it's odious, and I will never forgive mamma. Why isn't he dead? as she said he was. Dolff—oh, don't mind it so dreadfully! I don't mind it so dreadfully: he's only mad—and that's not wicked after all."

Dolff pushed past them all to where his mother sat in that temple of brightness and comfort, in her chair. Everything that could be done for her convenience and consolation in her incapacity was about her. She sat there as in a sanctuary, the centre of the most peaceful house. And there she had sat for years with the air of knowing nothing different, fearing nothing, meeting every day that rose and every night that fell with the same serene composure—a woman with nothing to conceal, nothing to alarm her, occupied only with little cares of the family and sympathies with others, and the knitting with which she was always busy. To look at her, and to think of the burden that had been for so long upon her shoulders, unknown, undreamed of, was a problem beyond the reach of imagination. Never a line upon her brow, and all that mystery and misery behind.

The room, usually so orderly, was a little disarranged to-night, the chairs pushed about anyhow, and one lying where it fell, which had been pushed over as Vicars led his patient out. And she had sat there patiently and listened to the voices in the hall, knowing that another encounter was taking place—knowing that her son was desperate, that he had it in him to be violent, that it was enough to touch that secret spring of madness which, for aught she could tell, the son of a mad father might have inherited. Perhaps, had she been scanned at that moment by any one more able to judge than Dolff, the signs of a conflict might have been seen in her eyes, but to Dolff she appeared precisely as she always was in her incredible calm. He placed himself in front of her with the air of an angry man demanding an explanation from his inferior.

"Is that man my father?" he said.

"Dolff, this is not a way either to address me or to inquire about your father. Yes, it is your father whom you have just seen, afflicted almost all your lifetime, an object for pity and reverence, not for this angry tone."

"What had he done that you kept him shut up for fifteen years?"

"Done!" Even Mrs. Harwood's steady tones faltered a little. "Why should he have done anything, Dolff? He was mad. If it had been known that I had kept him here he would have been taken from me, and how could I tell that he would have been kindly treated, or humored, or waited on as he would be at home? He was never violent, and I knew Vicars could manage him. If you saw how carefully everything was arranged for him, you would not think it was from want of affection—too much perhaps," she added, putting her handkerchief to her eyes.

"And what is the meaning, then, of this about paying, and the pocket-book?" asked Dolff, half convinced.

Mrs. Harwood put her hands together with a little gesture of appeal.

"How can I explain the fancies of a mind that is astray?" she said. "He has got something into his head, some distorted recollection of things that happened before. He was not quite fortunate in his business," she added, with a slight trembling in her voice; "the worry about that was supposed to have something to do with his breakdown."

"Then there were, I suppose, people to pay—whom he thinks he has provided for in that pocket book?"

He thought she gave an alarmed glance at some one behind him, and, turning round, caught what seemed to him an answering glance in the eyes of Meredith.

"*He* knows," cried Dolff; "you take him into your confidence, but give only what you can't help to me!"

"Charley is to appear for me before the commissioners," said Mrs. Harwood, with dignity; "I have given him all the information which was ready for you had you not treated your mother as if she were an enemy trying to injure you. If you do not know, it is your own fault."

Dolff did not know what to think: his courage failed before his mother. Perhaps it was true that Meredith (though he hated him) had stood by the mother more than he, Dolff, had done, and was of more use in this great family emergency. This thought stung him, but he could not escape from it. And to think that if she had but been frank and honest—if he had known of it, as he ought to have done, as soon as he was old enough to understand——

"Oh, mother," he cried, "why did you keep it from us? Why did I not know long ago?"

A slight quiver came over Mrs. Harwood's face.

"What I did I did for the best. One may be mistaken, but I thought it best for you all," she said.

"And I think Mrs. Harwood has had enough agitation for one night," said Meredith.

"You have nothing to do with it!" said Dolff, wildly, "you—what have you to do with our family? What right have you with our secrets?—since we have secrets," the young man added, in a tone of despair.

And Meredith fixed his laughing eyes upon Dolff. He could laugh, however serious the circumstances might be.

"There are some secrets," he said, "which are supposed to be quite safe with me—which it might be awkward for other people were I to let escape."

He looked Dolff full in the eyes, and his laugh drove the young man almost to frenzy. But at the same time it recalled him to himself. He dared not meet Meredith's laughing eyes. As long as they should both live this fellow would have him at a disadvantage. Dolff drew back with a mortification and humiliation which were unspeakable. He had no longer the courage to question his mother, to assert his own rights. He had the right to know everything, to be the first to be consulted in his own house. But that look was enough to silence him, to drive him back. Oh, that he should have put such power into another's hand! And for what? For whom?

"If it will be any satisfaction to you, Dolff," said Gussy, "I knew all the time—at least, I have known for a year or two. Mamma told me, just as she has told you, that he was—afflicted soon after Ju was born, and that she knew they would not let her keep him if it was known. So it was said he had died abroad, where he was for a little while. Is that so, mamma?"

"You are quite right, my dear," said Mrs. Harwood, who had quite recovered her composure. "But with this in addition: that the news came of his death, and that I had got my widow's mourning and everything was settled, when I found out that we had been mistaken. Vicars had gone with him, and Vicars brought him back. He sent me a letter to say that your father was not dead, but afflicted, and that he was bringing him back. I could not tell what to do. I did not want to let anybody know."

"Why?" said Dolff, who had plucked up a little courage. This time Gussy and Julia both stood by him. They looked at their mother, the three faces together, all so much alike, lit up with the same sentiment. "Why did you make a mystery of it?" said Dolff. "Would it not have been easier if everything had been frank and above-board?"

For a moment there was silence in the room. Mrs. Harwood made no reply. For the first time in all these fifteen years she wavered, her confidence forsook her, she had all but broken down. Another moment and the silence itself would have betrayed that there was something else—another secret still unrevealed. As she looked at them all together, her three children all asking the same question with faces overshadowed by a cloud of doubt, her strong heart almost gave way.

"Mrs. Harwood has already told you the reason," said Meredith behind them. "She knew that she would not be allowed to keep him, that he would be carried off from her to an asylum———"

"Oh, children," cried Mrs. Harwood, with a burst of sobbing which was half relief, "it is hard, hard upon me to drive me back again to that time! I had to take my resolution all at once. I had nobody to advise me. I came up here, and took this house, and prepared it all myself. You may see for yourselves how carefully it is done. I made the curtains and things with my own hands. Oh, I did not spare any trouble to make him comfortable! And we managed everything, Vicars and I. At first, even, when he was not so weak, we managed to get him out sometimes to take the air. We did everything for him. I was not laid up then. Why should I defend myself before you as if you were my judges?" she cried, drying her eyes hastily. "It was all for you."

"Mamma," said Julia, "you said just now it was because you would not be allowed to keep him—because he would be taken from you and put into an asylum: and now you say it was for us———"

Mrs. Harwood again raised her head and gave them a look; her countenance changed, a flash of anger came over her face. She had borne everything else, but these exasperating questions were more than she could bear. She was about to answer with unusual passion when Meredith's voice came in again.

"You do not remember," he said, "that to have a father in a lunatic asylum is not the best thing in the world for a family. Mrs. Harwood desired to save you that, to save you the anxiety of knowing he was here, to bear everything herself and leave your minds free."

"Charley," cried Gussy, quickly, "thank you, you understand her better than we have done. Oh, mamma, that was why you told me so little—even me."

"I did it for your sakes," said the mother, yielding at last to an exasperation beyond her power of resistance, and bursting into uncontrolled tears.

CHAPTER XLIX.

THE explanation was over, but the family atmosphere was not cleared. Gussy indeed had been moved out of her resentment and doubt, partly for the sake of her lover, partly for the sake of her mother. To stand out against both was more than she had been capable of. And Meredith had been perhaps alarmed by her sudden withdrawal from him, or in some other way (she could not tell how) moved back towards his former devotion. He was more anxious to draw her back, to recover her attention, than he had ever been before in any of the little brief estrangements which Gussy was generally the person to bring to an end. But on this occasion it was entirely he who did it, who sought her pardon, her return of tenderness, all the old attentions that had once been lavished upon him. Gussy could not resist that silent moving back of her heart; and it pleased her that he should defend her mother, whether or not her mother was worthy of it.

But the younger ones were not moved by this influence. They were the more dissatisfied with their mother's defence, because Meredith had chimed in, to put arguments into her mouth when she was about, as they believed, to break down. Had she been permitted to break down, a more full explanation might have been had, and the children might then have forgiven their mother; but, as it was, there had been too much and not enough. An insufficient explanation is the most painful of family misfortunes. It gives a sense of falsehood and insincerity to the mind. When you do not explain at all, it is possible you may be innocent: but when you explain profusely, dwelling upon some sides of the matter while ignoring others, you must be guilty: and the impression left is all the more unhappy and unsatisfactory that it is in its way definitive and final, and all are precluded from opening up the subject again. Unless some new incident took place, or some accident which disturbed the family laws, Dolff could not ask any more questions. He was too young to know what to do, too proud and shame-faced to hazard the credit of the family by making inquiries in other quarters. An uneasy sense that everything was different, that his own position and that of everybody else was changed, that he was no longer sure of the ground on which he stood, or the relations of those around him, was in Dolff's mind. It must make a difference that his father was alive, even though that father was a madman: and vague notions came into his painfully exercised brain—ideas half seen, uncomprehended, of some sense in which his mother might have done what she had done for their sakes, although she had professed in the same breath that it was for her husband's sake she had done it, that he might not be shut up away from her. Julia, on the other hand who was much more sharp-witted than Dolff, had seized like lightning upon this inconsistency, and could not forget it.

"She said it was for him and then she said it was for us," cried the girl. "How could it be for us when it was for him? It could not be supposed good for us that there should have been some one shut up there in the wing, and when we might have found it out any day."

"I never found it out nor thought of it," said Dolff. "If I had been told of it I should not have believed it. I should have said my mother was the last person in the world for mysteries—the very last person in the world—and that everything in this house was honest and above-board."

"I never thought like that," said Julia, shaking her head. "There was always something queer. Vicars, that was our servant, and yet not our servant, and that cry that one heard——"

"What cry?"

"Oh, an awful cry that we heard sometimes. Janet heard it when she had only been here a week, and she was dreadfully frightened. So was I at first," said Julia, with dignity. "It has only been for a few years: mamma explained it to me: she said it was the wind in the vacant chimneys that were not used. Oh, Dolff, though she knew very well it was not the wind, and the chimneys were not vacant! Dolff, mamma has said a great many things that are——"

"Don't talk of the mother, Ju—I'm very fond of the mother; and to think she should ever—— Don't—I think perhaps there might be reasons for our sakes, as she said. The property, you know, came from my grandfather to us. If he were known to have been alive, perhaps—I don't know so much about business as I ought—perhaps—— It makes my head a little queer to think of all that. She might have reasons."

"If it was simply for *him*, as she said first, to keep him from being sent to an asylum, it could not be for us as well."

"I'm not so sure of that," said Dolff stroking fondly, but with a very serious face, his youthful very light moustache, light both in color and texture.

"I have noticed in ladies," said quick-witted Julia, "that they like to have a motive, don't you know—something nice, as if they were always thinking of others, never of themselves; when they do anything, it's always for their children. Mamma is not like that, to do her justice; when things are going on she says she likes it, not for us only. Oh, Dolff! to think of the parties and romps we have had this Christmas, and people coming to dinner, and *him* there all the while!"

They were both overawed by the thought, and silenced, not venturing even to look at one another, when Julia suddenly cried out,

"There's a party to-morrow, Dolff."

"It mustn't be," said the young man; "they must write and say it can't be."

"What can they say? Nobody is ill; you can't shut the people out who come to call, and they would see mamma was quite well, and know it was not true. Oh, no; mamma will say we must keep up appearances; and she will be there, looking as nice as possible at the end of the table, and Vicars behind her chair."

"Ju, what did they do with *him* when Vicars was at all the parties behind her chair?"

"He was fastened in, I suppose, the doors all locked. I don't know. Dolff, suppose he had come downstairs one of these times, as he did last night!"

They looked at each other with a shudder.

"Perhaps on the whole," said the young man, "it *was* better for us that we did not know."

This was how they came to a partial approval of their mother. It rankled in their hearts that she had said to them what was not true, that she had made explanations which they could not refuse yet could not receive; that this tremendous crisis had come and gone in their lives and everything been changed, and yet that they were little wiser than before. And it was still more bitter for Dolff to perceive, what he could not help seeing whenever the family assembled together, that the knowledge that was kept from him was given to Meredith: but yet it had gleamed upon him that after all there might be something reasonable in his mother's plea.

There came, however, in this way to be two parties in the house—one which knew and discussed everything, the other which knew nothing and imagined a great deal, and chafed at the ignorance in which it was kept, yet found no means of knowing more or understanding better. Mrs. Harwood talked apart with Gussy and Meredith, who were always about her chair. When the others came into the room there was a momentary silence, and then one of the three would start an indifferent subject. It was enough for Dolff or Julia to come near to stop all conversation of any importance. They were shut out from all that was serious in the house as if they had nothing to do with it, as if their lives were not bound up with it as much— nay, far more than the others! What had Meredith to do with it, at all? Only through Gussy, who, if she married him at last, would go away with him and be a Harwood no longer; whereas Dolff, whatever happened, would always be the representative of the family, though shut out from its councils and kept in ignorance of its affairs.

Mrs. Harwood had decided, as Julia foresaw, that the party was to take place, that the world was not to be permitted to see any difference. Such whispers as had crept out could be silenced in no other way.

"Of course they have heard something," she said, "and if they were put off, if we made any excuse, they would believe the most of what they heard, whatever it was; but if they are received the same as ever and have as good a dinner, and see us all just as usual, even the worst-thinking people will be confused. They will not believe we could be such hypocrites as that. They will say whatever it is that has happened must be much exaggerated. The Harwoods look just as usual. Oh, I know the world a little," she said, with a half laugh.

Even Gussy, who knew her so well, was bewildered by her mother's fortitude, and by the clearness of her vision.

"I know the world a little," Mrs. Harwood said. "I have lived in it a great many years. Nothing makes quite such an impression as we expect. The people who can piece things together and understand exactly what has happened, are the ones that don't hear of it, and those who do hear haven't got the clue. I have told Charley already what I think. If we stand together and are bold, we'll get out of it all, and no great harm will come."

"Yes, you have told me, and I begin to believe," said Meredith.

"What do you mean by harm coming?" said Gussy, surprised. "Gossip about one's family is not pleasant; but that is all, and what other harm could come?"

Her mother and her lover looked at each other, and a faint sign passed between them; they did not venture to smile, much less to laugh, at the simplicity which understood nothing. Dolff, too, overheard this talk with an ache of wonder. What did they mean? Something more than gossip, he felt sure; for what did it matter about gossip? The madman in the house would scare and startle the neighbors, but it was not that his mother meant. What did she mean? He was the one that was likely to betray himself at the dinner-party, where he was compelled to take the foot of the table as usual, much against his will.

"Why can't you put Meredith there?" he said; "you trust him a great deal more than you trust me."

"And if I do so," said Mrs. Harwood, "have I not good reason? He is not always flinging my mistake—if it is a mistake—in my face. He is willing to do what he can for me. To help me without setting up for a judge."

"I have not set up for a judge," said Dolff.

"You have," his mother said; "you are judging me and finding me wanting whatever I do."

"Why should you have this party?" cried the young man; "why fill the house with strangers when we are all so miserable?"

Dolff could have cried with trouble and discontent and a sense of wrong had not his manhood forbidden such an indulgence. He was all wrong, out of place, wherever he turned.

"I see no cause you have to be miserable. I am not miserable," said Mrs. Harwood, "and I hope you will have the sense not to look so, making everybody talk."

This effort, however, on the part of Dolff was impossible. He sat at the foot of the table like a ghost. He scarcely opened his mouth, either to the lady on his right hand or the lady on his left. He ate nothing, making it very evident that he had something on his mind; and it became quite clear to all the guests that Dolff was in great trouble. Rumors about him had flown through the neighborhood, as well as rumors on the other subject, perplexed stories of which it was difficult to make anything. But when his mother's guests saw Dolff's looks, they were instantly convinced that the true part of the story was that which concerned him.

"Didn't you remark what a hang-dog look he had? Depend upon it, it is Dolff that is at the bottom of everything. The other thing is probably great nonsense, but Dolff is evidently in a bad way."

This was the conclusion arrived at by Mrs. Harwood's guests, which that inscrutable woman had foreseen, and for which, perhaps, she was scarcely sorry. It is so common for a young man to get into a scrape—and when the said young man is only two-and-twenty it is not so difficult to get him out of it. Even the hardest of judges are tolerant of misdemeanors—when they are not dishonorable—at that age. Therefore, perhaps, the mother calculated—being forced to very deep calculations at this trying period— that it would do no harm to the house to have the trouble in it saddled upon Dolff. "Is that all?" people would say. Whereas to have a family secret divulged—to have curious minds in St. John's Wood inquiring what was the meaning of that story about a secret inmate in the Harwoods' house, and who the Harwoods were before they came to that house, and what there was in the antecedents of the family to account for it—that would be a very different matter. When a sympathetic friend, anxious to find out what she could, condoled with her after dinner in the drawing-room about her son's looks, Mrs. Harwood accepted the kind expressions gratefully.

"No," she said, "I am afraid Dolff is not looking very well, poor boy; he has had a good deal to trouble him: but I hope everything is now in a right way, and he will have no more bother."

"Was it some trouble with his college?" asked the sympathetic friend.

"Oh, no! nothing with the college," said Mrs. Harwood. "He has stayed down for an extra week to look after some business, and he is going back to Oxford in a day or two—it is nothing of that kind."

The friend concluded from this that it was debt which was troubling Dolff, "like all the young men." And his mother, no doubt, had been obliged to draw her purse. It must have been some writ or something of that sort— which is a thing that still always seems to involve dungeons and horrors to women—which had taken the "police" to the Harwoods: for that the "police" had been at the house of the Harwoods everybody knew. Poor Dolff! but he had evidently got a lesson, and probably it would do good for him in the end, these good people thought.

Thus Mrs. Harwood's plan was successful more than she could have hoped, and it seemed as if all would settle down again, and go well. Meredith had arranged everything for his appearance before the commissioners on her behalf. He had a very touching story to tell. The poor wife distracted by the arrival of her husband, whom she had supposed to be dead, but who was brought back to her when she was in her widow's weeds, not dead, indeed, but mad, and as much severed from life and all its ways as if he had been dead indeed; and how she had no one to advise her, no one to consult with, and had come to a rash but heroic resolution to devote herself to him, to provide for his comfort secretly in her own house; and how he had been carefully tended by an experienced servant, and by herself until rheumatism crippled her and confined her to her chair—which still did not prevent her now and then from paying him visits, at the cost of great agony to herself, to see that all was well.

"Such things rarely get into the papers unless there is some special interest in them," said Meredith. "I think with a little care we may keep it quiet, and then——"

"Then all will be safe," said Mrs. Harwood, "and no secrecy whatever. Oh! my dear Charley, what I shall owe you!—the relief to my mind, above all."

"You will owe me no more than you will pay me," he said, with a laugh; "which will satisfy *him* also, as clearing off those debts which are so much on his mind. It is a transaction by which we shall all gain."

This was not a point of view which was agreeable to Mrs. Harwood.

"I wish," she said, "that you would not treat it in that way. It will be Gussy's fortune. I have a right to give Gussy what I please. She has not said anything to me, but I hope you have spoken to Gussy——"

"As soon as the business is over," he said, "when I shall have won—not only Gussy, but my share——"

"Oh! for heaven's sake," cried Mrs. Harwood, "do not speak of it like that."

CHAPTER L.

MEANTIME Janet, who had nothing to do with dinner-parties or anything of the kind, and who in the agitated state of the house appeared but little, and did not linger a moment longer than could be helped downstairs, had been passing through a period of suspense which was intolerable to her— far more terrible to bear than all the burdens, involving so much, which were on the accustomed shoulders of Mrs. Harwood. It was on Tuesday that she had written that momentous letter—that appeal of her impatient young soul to fate. She had written begging that she might be delivered at once from the position which she could not bear.

"All that I was threatened with before I left Clover has come true," she said, "though not in the way they thought: and I can't bear it any longer; and, if you meant what you said, come—come and take me away at once. If you don't come I will know that you didn't mean it, or that you have changed your mind: and I will do what I can for myself."

On Tuesday! Thursday at the latest should have brought a letter—though what she had expected was, that on Wednesday, the very day he received hers, he would come at once, answering it in person. This was the natural thing to expect. He would come—full of that ardor which had made Janet laugh when in October he had pleaded with her not to go away, to let him take care of her, provide for her. It had seemed to Janet the most ridiculous of suggestions that she should give her hand to the old doctor, and settle down for life in the familiar place where she knew everybody and everything, and where novelty was not, nor change of any kind.

And it was only January, the end of January, not much more than three months! was it possible that life had so disgusted this little neophyte, who had faced it so valiantly, that she gave up the battle already? She had asked herself that question as soon as her letter was in the post-office and beyond her control. What was there to hinder her from going on to another chapter, from spurning from her this prelude in which she had not come off a conqueror—three months only, and to throw down her arms!

The moment that Janet had dropped her letter into the box at Mimpriss's that place which had played so large a part in her life, her heart made a great leap, a sort of sickening rebound against what she had done. Oh no; her first beginning had not been a success. She had betrayed people who had been so good to her; her quick wit had seen too much, known too much, in the house where she ought to have been a grateful spectator only, making no discoveries. She had not been unwilling, by way of mere fun and distraction, to take Gussy's lover from her. She had not been unwilling "to make a fool of" the son of the house. She had been there like a little free lance to get what amusement and advantage she could out of them, without giving anything in return.

But Janet, though she had succeeded in the most remarkable way in both cases, had come to such a failure in the end as made her loathe herself. She had been met by her match, she had been deluded by a stronger practitioner of those arts, intent upon fun and distraction too, and with as little intention of promoting Janet as of anything else that would involve trouble to himself. How could she ever have thought it? A man who betrayed the woman who loved him to her, a stranger, how could she have supposed that he would be true to her and give up his own interest to proclaim his devotion to the governess! And Dolff, the dolt whom she had said to herself that she could turn round her little finger—Dolff, who had nearly killed the other man who had played with her; but not even that for Janet's sake. For his sister's sake, whom Janet had never taken into consideration—Dolff, too, had thrown her off as easily as an old glove when he got into trouble, and more serious matters occupied his mind.

These extraordinary failures had altogether overset Janet's moral equilibrium. Had she been driven out of the house by the jealousy of the women, with the secret sympathy and support of the men, a victim to the spitefulness of her own sex, but assured in her power of attracting and subjugating the other, Janet would have felt this to be quite natural—a thing that is in all the stories, the natural fate of the too attractive dependent. But this was not at all her case. The ladies had been very kind to her; they had never discovered her misdoings. Even Gussy, if she suspected anything, had taken no notice, which was to Janet very humiliating, an immense mortification, though the thing most to be desired by anyone who had retained a morsel of sense.

Janet had a great deal of sense, but in this emergency it forsook her—the kindness of the ladies had added a sting to the humiliating insincerity of Meredith and the indignant self-emancipation of Dolff. She had failed every way. It was she who was jealous—the one to be thrown aside; the legitimate sentiment had triumphed all along the line, and the little interloper had failed in everything. She had thought that to prove to them at last that she had no need of them, that she had but to hold up a finger to bring her deliverer flying to the rescue, to be carried off triumphant to her own house, to her own people, would be a triumph which would make up for all, while still Meredith was in the house, while Dolff was at home, while everyone could see how little necessity she had to care what they thought! Janet knew, she was certain, that the moment she held up a finger—— And she had held it up—she had summoned her deliverer—without pausing to think.

But when she dropped the letter in the letter-box at the window of Mimpriss's there suddenly came over Janet a vision of Dr. Harding as she had seen him last, rusty, splashed with mud, his hat pushed back on a forehead that was a little bald, his coat-collar rubbed with hair that was iron-gray. He was nearly as old as Meredith and Dolff added up together; a country doctor, called out day and night by whoever pleased to send for him, not even rich. Oh, the agitated night Janet had after that rash step of hers! She had called him to her, and he would come flying on wings of love—*i. e.*, by the quickest express train that never stopped between Clover and London, which flew even past the junction—that terrible train which frightened all the Clover ladies; as quick as the telegraph almost would he be here.

Janet held her breath and asked herself how she could have done it? And what if, when he came, holding out his arms to her as he would be sure to do, her heart should fail and she should turn away—turn her back on him after she had summoned him? Oh, that was what she must not, dare not do. She had settled her fate; she had committed herself beyond remedy. If Meredith and Dolff should repent, and fling themselves one after another at her feet, it would do no good now. He might be ready to sacrifice Gussy to her, but she could not sacrifice Dr. Harding to him. Oh, not now—she had settled her fate now!

All Wednesday morning Janet was in a state of suspense which defies description. She expected every moment to be called downstairs, to be told that a gentleman had come asking for her. The train arrived at half-past ten, just half-an-hour after the hour at which she sat down with Julia to lessons. Lessons, good heavens! They had never, perhaps, been very excellent of their kind, these lessons, though they had been gone through with steadily enough; but Julia had been quite well aware from the first that Janet's heart was not in them, just as Janet had discovered from the first that Julia would learn no more than she could possibly help learning. And it may be supposed that, with this indifferent mutual foundation, the agitated state of the house, and of the minds of both instructress and instructed, had not improved the seriousness of the studies. Janet calculated that half-an-hour would be wanted to get from the station to St. John's Wood; half-an-hour would be enough, for of course he would take a hansom, the quickest to be had, instead of the slow four-wheeler which had conveyed her and her luggage on the occasion of her arrival. Then at eleven o'clock! Oh, what should she do, what could she do? There were but two things she could do—run downstairs at the first summons, and rush into Dr. Harding's arms—or fly away, somewhere, she knew not where, before he came.

Sitting dazed by this suspense, her heart beating in her ears, taking no notice of Julia's proceedings, which were very erratic, listening for the sound of Priscilla's steps on the stair with the summons feared yet desired, Janet came to herself with a shock at the sound of twelve, struck upon the little French clock on the mantelpiece, and by the larger church clock in St. John's Wood, at a minute's interval. Twelve o'clock! It must be eleven, it could not be twelve! It was impossible, impossible! But, like so many other impossible things, it was true. Her heart seemed to sink down into her slippers, and a horrible stillness took the place of all that beating. He had not come! Could such a thing be? He had not come! Then he had not meant it, or he meant it no longer. Dr. Harding, who had been her slave since she was a child, who had pleaded, oh! how he had looked at her, what tones his voice had taken, how he had implored her as if his life depended upon it! while she—had laughed. Her voice had trembled, too, but it was with laughter. She had not given a moment's consideration to that proposal. She, before whom the world lay open, full of triumphs, she marry the old doctor! It was ludicrous, too absurd to be thought of; she had not been unkind, but she had let him know this very completely; there had been no hesitation, no relenting in her reply.

And now he had done the same to her.

But Janet could not believe it—she went on expecting him all day. Something might have happened to detain him in the morning. He might have gone out upon his rounds before the letter came—sometimes the postman was very late, at Clover. She knew the life there so well that she could calculate exactly when the letters would reach the doctor's house. The bag was always heavy in the beginning of the year. Clover was one of those places where all the people hear from their friends in the early part of the year. Perhaps there were still some belated Christmas cards or premature valentines to give the postman more to do. And some one might have been ill, and the doctor called out before his usual time. All these things were possible—but not that he should have received her letter and not come. But when Thursday passed without even a letter in reply, and Friday— Friday, the third day!—Janet fell into a state of depression that was miserable to see. She could think of nothing else. Her doubts about the doctor's age, about his appearance, about his gray hair, and all his disadvantages, disappeared altogether from her mind.

Astonishment, humiliation, the sense of having fallen altogether from her high estate, of being a miserable little failure abandoned by everybody, filled Janet's mind. He had not come, though she had sent for him; he had turned a deaf ear to her appeal. Where could she now go? Never to Clover to give him the chance of exulting over her, though Clover was the only place in which she could find a home. Oh, how foolish, how foolish she had been!

She might have gone back to the vicarage with no more ado than saying that she was not happy in her situation. The vicar and his wife had expected as much—they would not have been surprised. But now she had closed in her own face that friendly refuge. She had longed for a triumph, though it would be a homely one, and again she had failed—again she had failed! Anything more subdued, more troubled than Janet could not be. The doctor was no longer in her eyes a makeshift, an expedient—something to restore her *amour propre*, but whom she shrank from even in appealing to him. She forgot his rusty gray hair, his bald forehead, the mud on his boots. Oh, if he would but still come, if he would come! To let them see that she had someone who cared for her, a man who thought her the first of women while to them she was only the little governess. But when Friday came, Janet gave up the hope. He too had decided against her. She was not the first of women to anybody, but a poor little foolish girl who would not when she might and now had to be said nay.

The lessons went on all the time, not, I fear, very profitable lessons, and the two girls went out to have their walks as usual, with what comfort they might, and everything continued like a feverish dream. Janet sat upstairs and heard the sounds and commotion of the dinner-party and did not care. What did it matter that they were feasting below, while she was left all alone, neglected by everybody? By everybody, yes! even by people who had loved her: nobody loved her now. She was forgotten, both by those at home and those here. And what did it matter? The school-room, that was the place for a governess. They ought never to have brought her out of it. It was true she ought not to have been deceived by any other thoughts—and it was true that she must calculate on spending all the rest of her life, nobody to give her any triumph, nobody to carry her away like a conqueror, nobody to vindicate her importance so that the Harwoods would see their mistake, and Mr. Meredith bite his lips with envy and dismay. No, that had all been a dream; there was nobody to deliver Janet, and nothing for her but to take a new situation, and perhaps go through the whole again, as poor governesses so often do.

On Friday afternoon she had come in from her walk depressed beyond description, feeling that everything had failed her. Julia had gone into the drawing-room to her mother, while Janet, dragging a little behind, as she had begun to do in the prostration of her being, lingered in the hall, loitering by the umbrellas in the stand, untwining her boa from her throat, the boa which Meredith had held, by which he had detained her until she had thrown it upon his hands and escaped from him on their last interview. She was very low; expectation was dead in her—she no longer looked for an answer to her letter, nor for anything that could happen. So dull, indeed, was she in her despondency that she did not heed the ring at the bell, nor the hasty step upon the path when Priscilla opened the door. It would be some visitor, some one for the others—nobody any more for Janet. It was a noisy step which came in at the door, firm, a little heavy, and very hurried and rapid.

It was almost twilight; the hall was dark, and Janet in the darkest corner, with her back to the door, slowly untwisting the boa from her neck, when—oh, what was this that burst upon her ear?

"No," very hastily, with an impatient tone, "not Mrs. Harwood. I said 'Miss Summerhayes.' I want to see Miss Summerhayes."

"Oh!" Janet turned round and came forward, feeling as if she had wings, as if her feet touched the ground no longer. She called out of the darkness, "Is it you, is it you?" as if she did not know who it was at the first thrill of his voice!

"Janet," he cried, and came forward and caught her—not exactly in his arms, but with his hands upon her shoulders, clutching her with a sort of hungry grasp ("as if he were going to eat me up," she said afterwards). She felt him trembling, thrilling all over, and perhaps it was as well that it was dark, that she could see nothing of the gray hair, etc., but only that the middle-aged doctor had a vibration of haste, of anxiety, of emotion in his arms and hands, and the very lappels of his coat which touched her breast, which was more real than any words, convincing her in a moment, as no explanation from Meredith, for instance, could have done, that the delay was none of his doing, that he was here as quickly as if he had come by that express train.

"Janet! You mean that?" he asked, with eyes that glowed even through the darkness, and a voice that thrilled and trembled too.

"Yes, Dr. Harding, if you do."

"If *I* do?" he said, with a sort of suppressed shout, "did you ever have any doubt of me? My little darling! I'm like your father, ain't I? I'll be father and mother and husband all together now you'll have me, child! If I do! How dare you say that, you little torment; you little delight! as if I shouldn't have rushed head over heels from the ends of the earth!"

"You have taken your time about it, Dr. Harding," Janet said, "you might have been here on Wednesday, and now it is Friday afternoon."

"You little love! Have you counted the days?" cried the poor man, who was such a fool; and then he burst into his explanation, how he had indeed come from the ends of the earth, from one of the great towns of the North where he had found "a noble practice" awaiting him. "They'd heard of me, dear, fancy that! How surprised the Clover people will be! And there will be fine company and grand parties, and everything she likes, for my little Janet," he cried, with a sort of sobbing of joy and triumph in his voice.

To tell the truth, Janet was as much bewildered by the thought that Doctor Harding had been heard of, as anybody in Clover could have been. But she concealed this with a throb of delight in her heart to hear of the great town in the North, and the fine company and grand parties. No Clover then and seclusion, but the world and all its delights. Janet's heart beat high with satisfaction in her own wise impulse, and the sense of the triumph to come.

As they stood talking, the door of the drawing-room was thrown open, and, looking up at the sound, they both had a view of the interior of the room illuminated with its bright firelight and with the lamp, always the first brought in, which stood on Mrs. Harwood's table. She in her white shawl, with her white hair and cap and the mass of white knitting on her knees, stood out like a mass of whiteness made rosy by the light from the fire, a most brilliant figure seen from the twilight of the hall. The doctor started a little, and took his hands from Janet's shoulders.

"Mrs. Adolphus" he said.

"It is Mrs. Harwood; do you know her? But, indeed, her husband's name is Adolphus."

"You mean was: don't let us speak of him. She is an old friend of mine. But if it had not been for Adolphus Harwood I should never have been doctor at Clover, and perhaps never have seen my little Janet, so for every trouble there is compensation, my dear."

"What trouble?" she said, eagerly.

"Never mind. Come in and introduce me, Janet—though we know each other very well."

Janet took the arm he offered her and walked in, with all her spirit and courage restored, to Mrs. Harwood's room. She wished they had been all there, every one to see that she was not the lonely creature they had thought her. But there was nobody but the mistress of the house, with Julia behind, telling her mother what they had seen during their walk. Mrs. Harwood was smiling; she had the air of a contented and cheerful mother with no trouble in her way. She looked up to receive the new-comers, saying, "Why, Janet!" with a little surprise, quickly divining from the girl's attitude and the air of the pair that something unusual had come in the governess's way.

"I have brought an old friend to see you," said Janet, faltering a little.

"John Harding, at your service, Mrs. Harwood, now as long ago," the doctor said.

Mrs. Harwood uttered a low cry, the color went out of her face, and the light out of her eyes. She sat and looked at him, with her under lip falling and dismay in her heart.

CHAPTER LI.

NOTHING, as Mrs. Harwood herself said, is so bad as you expect; and the great shock which the sight of this stranger evidently gave her soon subsided in the extraordinary composure and self-command which she was able to bring to bear against every accident. By the time that it had been explained to her who the visitor was, and what was his errand, which he insisted at once upon telling, the conversation became what an uninitiated person would have thought quite cosy and pleasant. Mrs. Harwood drew her breath more quickly than usual. She looked at the door with some anxiety, and she even sent Julia with a message whispered in her ear.

"Don't let Dolff come in here."

"Why not?" said Julia, aloud.

It is inconvenient to have a daughter who has not the sense to obey. Mrs. Harwood made no answer, but pushed the girl away, and after a moment's pause Julia went, though whether to fulfil the message in the manner intended, her mother could not say.

"Things have changed very much for us all," she said, in her cheerful voice; "I have a daughter on the eve of marriage, like you, Dr. Harding—a man who does not marry keeps so much longer young. You may remember my Gussy as a child——"

"I remember my little wife that is to be as a child," he said, heartily, "and she might well have despised an old fellow. Yes, things have changed. It was very good for me, as it turns out, that I could not go on in my old way. I've been a hard-working man, and kept very close to it for a long time, and now things are mending with me. I shall be able to give this little thing what they all like—a carriage and finery and all that. I am going back—to the old place, Mrs. Harwood——"

"To Liverpool?" she said with something like a repressed scream.

"Yes, to Liverpool; they had heard of me, it appears, and then some of the old folks remembered I was a townsman. You have not kept up much connection with the old place, Mrs. Harwood."

"None at all; you may suppose it would not be very pleasant for me."

"Perhaps not," he answered, drumming a little with his finger on his knee; "and yet I don't know why, for there was always a great deal of sympathy with you."

"Dr. Harding," said Mrs. Harwood, with some eagerness and a nervous thrill in her voice, "may I ask you a favor? It is, please, not to speak of me to any of my old friends. You may think it strange—there is nobody else in the room, is there, Janet?—but I would rather the children did not know more than is necessary about the past."

"I understand: and I honor you, madam," said Dr. Harding, in an old-fashioned, emphatic way.

A faint tint of color came over Mrs. Harwood's face, which varied from red to white, no doubt with the agitation caused by the sight of her old acquaintance.

"I ask for no honor," she said, hurriedly, "so long as it is thought that I have done my duty by the children."

"I should think there could not be much doubt of that," said Dr. Harding, who, in his own high content and satisfaction with himself saw every one round him in a rose-colored light. He would have sworn she was an example to the country, had anyone asked him. So she was, no doubt, for had she not given shelter and protection to Janet, and somehow led her by example or otherwise to see that there was nothing so good in this world as to trust yourself to the man that loved you, whatever his age or his appearance might be?

Janet listened to this conversation with a great deal of her old curiosity and desire to find everything out. She did not see why her doctor should be bound by a promise to Mrs. Harwood not to speak to her of Liverpool. Janet felt happy that it was not upon herself this injunction was laid, and that she was free to talk about the strange occurrences which had happened in St. John's Wood, and perhaps get to understand them better. Janet, however, gave only a part of her mind to this. The rest was filled with her own affairs: her heart was beating still with the startling sensation of his arrival and the realization of all that must now follow. She had been a little afraid, when she brought him into the bright light, of the revelations it would make. But the Dr. Harding who was about to enter upon a 'noble practise' in Liverpool was not at all like the Dr. Harding of Clover. His clothes were new and well-made, his hair carefully brushed, his linen dazzling—oh, he was not at all like the man who rode over on a shaggy cob to see Miss Philipson, and was at everybody's beck and call around the Green.

Looking at him again in this favorable new light, Janet decided that he was not so very old—older than herself, no doubt, older than Meredith or Dolff, but not _so_ old—at the utmost no more than middle-aged—a man still in his prime. She did not do any talking herself, but let him talk, and she thought he talked well. All her thoughts had undergone such a revolution within the last half-hour. She had felt herself abandoned, a creature all alone, cast off from everything, scorned on all sides. And now all at once she had a defender in whose presence no one dared utter a jibe or make a scoff of Janet. She had wealth within her reach—a carriage (he said), all the prettinesses that life could bestow. No such prospect was before Gussy, though she thought herself so happy;—and the more Janet looked at him in these spruce clothes, the more her breast expanded with satisfaction. He was not merely Dr. Harding—he was something that belonged to herself. And so manly—not a person to be despised. Meredith himself—why did she keep thinking of Meredith?—Meredith was a weakly person, a man who had let himself be almost killed, not one who would stand against the world like John Harding. Pride and satisfaction swelled her breast. She too looked at the door as Mrs. Harwood did, but with a different meaning. She desired that they should all come in to see how much changed her position was, and that she had now someone belonging to her—someone who was better than them all.

Both these ladies accordingly sat and listened to Dr. Harding without taking much notice of what he said. He filled them with emotions of different kinds, neither of them entirely on his own account. They both listened for sounds without while he talked, intently, anxiously praying and hoping on one side and the other that some one would or would not come. Mrs. Harwood had perhaps never been so deeply moved before. To have made sure that no one would come—that this dangerous man might be got out of the house, without meeting Dolff at least, she would have given a year or two out of her life. There were sounds, several times repeated, of people coming and going, doors opening and shutting, the usual sounds of a house full of people, which brought the blood coursing to the mother's heart. She put up her handkerchief to her face as if the fire scorched her. But it was her trouble that scorched her, the great anxiety in which she was consuming her very soul.

At last, in a moment, it was stilled, as our fears of an evil are stilled, either because it has become impossible, or because it has happened. The latter was the case in this instance.

Dolff came into the room, and behind him Julia, very curious, and after her Priscilla carrying the tea-tray. Priscilla and the tea-tray were things in which there was hope—but what Mrs. Harwood dreaded had happened. She had no resource, but to say:

"My son, Dr. Harding. Dolff, Dr. Harding is a friend of Janet's and—and an old acquaintance of mine."

"How do you do?" said Dr. Harding, rising up, formally giving the young man his hand. "I did not know your son was grown up. I thought he was the youngest."

"No, it is Julia who is the youngest," said the mother, breathlessly, indicating the girl, who came forward and shook hands with Dr. Harding too. Though she had been in the room at his first appearance, there had been no thought of introduction then.

"It is quite curious," said the doctor, with his hearty voice, "to find myself among old friends. I expected to find only my little Janet, and here I am surrounded by people whom I knew in the old days in Liverpool before she was born."

"But we have nothing to do with Liverpool," said Dolff.

"Welsh," said Mrs. Harwood, with breathless brevity.

"Ah, yes, by origin; the little property's there, isn't it? But Harwood has been a well-known name in Liverpool for longer than any of us can recollect. I remember when it was talked of like the Bank of England," said the doctor, shaking his head a little and with a suppressed sigh.

"Oh," cried Mrs. Harwood, "I am not fond of those old recollections; they always lead to something sad."

She had made another tremendous effort of self-control, recovered her voice, recovered her composure. She sat bolt upright in her chair, her eyes shining out like watch-lights, and all her color concentrated in two red spots in her cheeks.

"This is very interesting to me, for I never heard of it before," said Dolff. "My mother has told us very little, Dr. Harding; I should be very grateful for a little information."

"My dear young fellow," said Dr. Harding, "I daresay your mother's very wise. Least said is soonest mended. That's all over and done with. It all went to pieces, you know, when your father"—he paused a moment, visibly embarrassed, not knowing what word to use; then added softly, "when your father—died."

Mrs. Harwood drew a long breath. She sank back a little in her chair. The dreadful tension was loosed.

"If you think that this is satisfactory to me," said Dolff, "you are making an immense mistake. Why should least said be soonest mended? Is there any disgrace belonging to our name? Besides," he said, himself a little breathless, with an instinctive sense that his words were words of fate, "my father—is not dead."

"What?" said Dr. Harding. He jumped up from his chair as if he had been stung. "What? Adolphus Harwood not dead? My God! Adolphus Harwood? What does this mean?"

Mrs. Harwood was making convulsive efforts to speak, to rise from her chair, but nobody heeded her. Dolff stood confronting the stranger, in his ignorance, poor boy, fearing he knew not what, angry, beginning to awake to the fact that there might be need for defence, and that the danger was his own. He said:

"I don't know why you speak in such a tone. There is no harm, I suppose, in my father—being alive. We never knew till the other day. Perhaps *she* can tell you why. Is there any harm in my father—not having died?"

His voice had grown hoarse with an alarm which he did not himself understand.

"Harm!" cried Dr. Harding. "Adolphus Harwood alive!—harm! Only this harm—that I can't let old friendship stand in the way. I dare not do injustice; he must be given up to answer for his ill-doings. Harm! The fool! He never did but what was the worst for him! to live till now—with all the misery and ruin that he brought——"

Dolff frantically seized the doctor by the breast.

"Stop," he said, "tell me what has he done? I knew—I knew there was more in it; what has he done?"

"Done!" cried the doctor, flinging the young man off from him, "done! ruined everybody that ever trusted in him! Don't stop me, young man! Keep yourself clear of him! I cannot help it; I am sorry for your sake—but he must be given up."

"To what?" cried Dolff, "to what?" He put himself in front of the doctor, who was buttoning his coat hastily and had seized his hat from the floor. "Look here! to what? You don't stir a foot from here till you tell me."

He had his arm up in mad excitement as if ready to strike, while Dr. Harding, a man of twice his strength, stood slightly drawn back prepared to defend himself. Then there suddenly came between them, with a cry, a moving, stumbling figure, white shawl and white cap showing doubly white between the dark-clothed men. She put one hand on Dr. Harding's breast, and with the other pushed her son away.

"John Harding!" she cried, "John Harding! listen to me. He is mad—mad, do you hear? Mad! What is that but dead?"

"Mother, let this man answer to me!"

"Oh, go away, go away with your folly! He is mad, John Harding! He came back to me mad—could I turn my husband to the door? give him up to the police? Listen to me," she cried, holding the doctor's coat as if it had been a prop to support her; "you can see him yourself, if you doubt me—he is mad." The poor woman burst into a shrill hysterical laugh. "Mad as a March hare—silly! Oh, John Harding, John Harding, hear what I have got to say!"

A sudden transformation came over Dr. Harding, such as may be seen in his profession in the most exciting moments. He became a doctor and not an ordinary man. He threw down his hat and took her by the elbows, while she still held fast by his coat.

"Wheel her chair forward," he said. "Young Harwood, gently, send for her maid. Heavens, boy! be gentle; do you want to kill your mother? Janet, come round here and put the cushions straight, to support her head. There! quiet all of you. Let her rest; and you, Janet, give her air."

"She has done it before," said Dolff, with passion. "Oh, I am not taken in, mother! Let her alone, man, and answer me!"

"Go to the devil," cried the doctor, pushing the young man away. "You confounded cub, be quiet, and let the poor woman come to herself?"

Had he forgotten all about the other, altogether, as if it had never been? He looked like it, bending over Mrs. Harwood in her chair, giving quick directions, taking the fan out of Janet's hand to give her air, moistening her lips with the wine he asked for, absorbed in her looks as if there was nothing in his mind but the care of her. Janet, too, ran to get whatever he asked for, stood at hand to do what was wanted, inspired by the doctor's devotion. As for Dolff, he turned away as if he took no interest in it. His mother to him was a deceiver, getting sympathy by an exhibition of weakness. Julia, half moved by her mother's faint, half by her brother's rebellion and excitement, wavered between the two, uncertain. Janet and her doctor alone gave themselves up to Mrs. Harwood as if there was nothing else in the world to think about.

"Such an effort as that to a woman in her state might be fatal," said the doctor. "She must have the constitution of an elephant. Once before, did you say? Janet, my little darling, you're made for a doctor's wife! Hold this fast—and steady as a rock. Now, raise her head a little. There! Now I hope she'll come to."

"You make yourself busy about my mother," said Dolff, coming up to him, striking him upon the shoulder. "There's nothing the matter with my mother: but you've got to explain to me—What does it mean? What do you want with him? What has he done? I never knew he was there," cried the lad, "till the other day. And then I never suspected he was my father. Oh, don't you know when one never has had a father, what one thinks he must have been? And then to see—that! but I must have satisfaction," cried Dolff. "What has he done? What are you going to do?"

At this moment the door was opened hastily, and Gussy came in, followed by Meredith. There had been so much excitement in the house that they all came together for every new incident.

"Is my mother ill?" she said, with a glance at Mrs. Harwood in her chair. "Something has gone wrong. Dolff, who is this gentleman? and for heaven's sake tell me what is it now? What has gone wrong?"

Only a glance at her mother, who was still but half sensible, supported in Janet's arms, and then Gussy came and stood by her brother's side, and looked at the stranger. She had no doubt that he had something to do with the secret in the house. Everything clustered round that, and was drawing to it like flying things to the light.

Dr. Harding, on his side, looked at the little crowd round him, meeting their eager eyes with reluctance and embarrassment.

"I presume that you are Miss Harwood," he said, "but I cannot explain this matter to you. The less you know of it the better, my dear young people. I have no ill-feeling to your poor father—not the least, not the least: though I was one of the victims, I hope I've forgiven him freely. But justice is justice. If Adolphus Harwood is in this house, he must be given up."

"Dear Gussy," said Meredith behind her, "will you take my advice and go away, and get Dolff to go? Let me speak to this gentleman. I know all about the business affairs. I am to appear for your mother, you know. Let me speak to him, and hear what he has to say."

Gussy gave him a look and a faint smile, but did not move. They all stood still gathered round the doctor like a ring, more anxious than hostile, and yet hostile too, hemming him in with a sort of enclosure of pale faces. Dr. Harding was greatly moved; he put out his hands as if to put them away— to deliver himself.

"God knows," he said, "how I feel for you, you poor children! You break my heart; but if Adolphus Harwood has been living quietly here, living in comfort and luxury here, after bringing so many to ruin——"

"He has been living," said Meredith, "concealed in a couple of rooms, for fifteen years. I don't know who you are, or what right you have to be here, or to inquire into the affairs of this family."

"Oh, hush," cried Gussy, "he will be a friend, he has a kind face!"

"His name is Dr. Harding," said Julia, breaking in. "He came for Janet, but mamma said he was an old friend: and Dolff told him by chance that *he*—*he*, you know—was living, and not dead."

"This is all mere madness," said Dr. Harding. "I did not want to know anything about the affairs of the family, but I have my duty to do—I must do what is my duty."

There came a faint voice from behind—from the chair in which the mother lay, only as it seemed half-conscious, propped by pillows.

"See him," it said. "See him, see him; a doctor, he will know."

They all turned round startled, but it was Meredith alone who caught up the meaning of this half-stifled utterance. He put his hand on the doctor's arm.

"Come here," he said, "and look at the man for yourself."

He opened the door softly as he spoke. There had been sounds outside to which no one had paid any attention till now. The lamp had been lighted in the hall, and it threw a strong light upon a man in a wheeled chair with white hair and beard. He was speaking in a note of half-whispering complaint.

"Why do you bring me in, when I don't want to come in, Vicars? Dark—I like it when it's dark and nobody can see."

"It don't do you no good, sir," said Vicars, "to be out in the dark."

"Vicars, you're a fool! A man with money about him, a lot of money like me—you want me to be robbed, you villain! And then how can I pay up? When you know it's my pride to pay up, whenever I'm called upon. Whenever I'm called upon—everybody! There's plenty for everybody. Ah! there's an open door! I'm going to see them, Vicars. Their mother tells them lies, but when they know I have it all here to pay up——"

"No, sir," said Vicars, "you can't go in there to-night."

"Why not to-night? Did she say so? She wants to get my money from me, that's what it is! Swear, Vicars, you'll never tell them where I keep my money! She got it and gave it to that fellow, but it came back, eh! Vicars? It knows its own master, and it always comes back." Here the old man burst into a foolish laugh, but presently began to whisper again. "Where are you taking me? You are taking me upstairs. You want me to be murdered for my money in that dark hole upstairs."

The two men stood at the door, hidden in the curtain that hung on it, and watched this scene. They stood still, listening while the wheels of the chair rumbled along, and the door of the wing closed upon it. Then Meredith spoke.

"Is this the man you are going to give up to punishment?" he said.

The doctor turned away and covered his face for a moment with his hands. When he turned round again to the audience, who watched him so intently, almost without seeming to draw breath, he met the gaze of Mrs. Harwood's eyes, wide open, full of agonized meaning. She had come to herself and to a consciousness of all that depended upon the decision he would make.

"What does he mean about the money?" he asked in a low tone.

"He means," she said, answering him before any one could speak, "what he thinks he has in his pocket-book—money to pay everybody. Oh, John Harding, that's no dishonest meaning. He gives it to me, to pay up—and then he is restless till he has it back again. There's nothing but old papers, old bills, worth nothing. He thinks," she said, carried on by her eagerness, "that it is the money he took to Spain."

"And where is the money he took to Spain?"

She had not meant to say that; but there was only one in the company who was aware that she had betrayed herself, or understood the look of bewilderment that for a moment came over her face. She paused, and that one who was in her confidence trembled. She raised herself up by the arms of her chair, and looked round upon them. Then she burst into a strange hysterical fit of laughter.

"He thinks that I know everything," she said. "How can I tell? Where are the snows of last year?"

CHAPTER LII.

THERE are times when Nemesis appears unwitting at the door of a doomed house, and, however unlikely that might be, before she crosses the threshold, with the mere wind of her coming, the cunning webs of deceit are shattered, the blow of vengeance falls. But there are other cases in which Nemesis comes and stands in the doorway and departs again innoxious, either because some veil has been thrown over her clear-sighted eyes, or because the heart of that inexorable goddess has failed.

Nemesis turned and departed from the house of the Harwoods when Dr. Harding went upstairs to the school-room with his little Janet. The middle-aged gentleman there spent an ecstatic hour, the happiest of his life, and he forgot that there were such people as the Harwoods in existence, or anybody worth thinking of except the little girl who had called him to come and take her to himself— Janet, who had flung him over that dark October evening on the edge of the windy common at Clover, but who had now whistled him back and put her little hand in his.

Which was more true to her real meaning—her refusal then, or her delighted acceptance now? The doctor never asked himself any such questions. He was too happy to be allowed to think that when Janet compared the others, all the rest of the world, with him, who had loved her since she was a baby, she had found that none were so much to her taste as her old lover. That she had "them all" at her feet, Dr. Harding had no doubt—how could it be otherwise? seeing there was no one like her, no one! It seemed clear enough to him that both that cool fellow downstairs who had taken the management of the business, and the dolt—Dolff— what did they call him? had been at Janet's feet, and had been rejected. The young fellows had done him a good turn. They had shown this little captivating creature, this darling little capricious woman who did not know her own mind, that there was nobody like her old doctor after all.

When he took his departure that night for the hotel where he meant to stay until he could take Janet down to Clover to the vicarage from which he was to marry her, there was no thought in his disturbed and rapturous mind of the awful part which for a moment he had seemed about to play. Not Nemesis—but Dr. Harding, an old fellow in love, and more silly than any boy.

As for Janet, when her old lover left her, her little head was partly turned by his raptures, and by the opinion he had of her as if she had been a queen, and all the gratitude and honor he seemed to think he owed her. A little thing who had not a penny, and who, indeed, had thrown herself into his arms in a kind of despair because of her first disappointment and disgust with the world. But he did not know that at all, and she scarcely remembered it, when he took his leave with a privileged kiss which made her cheeks burn, and a promise to come for her as early as possible in the morning, to take her out shopping, to buy what she would want against the great event, which was to be delayed only as long as was necessary—not a day longer, he vowed.

"For you have cheated me out of six months," he said. "I might have had you six months ago."

"Oh, no, no, Dr. Harding," said Janet, with gravity, remembering that nothing in the world would then have made her accept the old doctor.

But she had no such feeling as that now. She did not even remember that he was a *pis aller*, and she looked forward to to-morrow, when she was to be taken out shopping, and to buy such things as she had never hoped for—dinner-dresses, morning-dresses ball-dresses; for she would require a great deal of dress, she had the sense to perceive, in that great rich town in the north, which was so very different from Clover.

Janet could scarcely think for the moment of anything beyond this, for it was a delight she had never enjoyed before. To buy, is a pleasure to every woman—to get a number of new dresses, is a delight to any girl. If these things are accompanied by a heartbreak, as when she is going to be forced to marry a man whom she does not love, the pleasure evaporates. But this was not Janet's case. She had made up her mind to have her old doctor, it is true, in a moment of pique and disappointment, and perhaps if he had come instantly as she had expected, if he had not kept her waiting, if he had been still only the doctor of Clover—but none of these things had been. Her heart had been racked with the thought that he, too, had forsaken her; and then he had arrived a new man, in those new, well-cut clothes, with all the confidence of a great success about him.

And he had no sooner appeared than he had taken a commanding position. The father of the family had been in his hand. Dolff was nothing but a foolish boy beside him, and even Meredith—Dr. Harding had held the upper hand easily of them all. He had been able to put aside Janet while that crisis which she but half understood was going on, and then he had come back to her, and poured out gratitude and admiration; and she was to have a handsome house in Liverpool, where there was a great deal of gayety, a great deal of wealth—and a carriage—and a day of shopping to-morrow with nothing to do but to say, "I like this," or "I like that!"

Thus Janet's mind was satisfied, and her fancy delighted. Those little vagaries which had troubled her rest had all dropped into oblivion. Meredith? Yes, he was going to marry Miss Harwood, to struggle into a practice at the Bar, though he was not at all hardworking, and probably would never be known except as an amateur tenor among his friends. Janet wondered maliciously whether they would sing as much together after they were married, or, if not, what they would do to amuse themselves? and could not help the reflection that Gussy's accompaniments would probably tire her husband, and that he would not conceal the fact from her in these after days. She wished them no harm whatever, none at all, they had done her no harm: but still in her own room, as she was going to bed, Janet could not but laugh at this thought.

Mrs. Harwood had recovered in the most wonderful way. It was she who kept up the conversation at dinner, talking to Dr. Harding of old friends, and, with her head high and another cap on, looking as if agitation or trouble had never come her way. She kept it up all the evening with a courage that never faltered. It happened before they all separated for the night that there was a moment in which Meredith and she were left alone. He went up to her, and took her hand in his.

"You are wonderful!" he said. "I could not have thought it possible. You are able for any emergency."

She began to cry a little, with a laugh running through the sobs.

"Oh, Charley," she said, "I hope it will all be forgiven me. What could I do? I had to hold by it. And what would that have been among so many? I shall be able to do justice to Gussy."

"No," he said, ignoring these last words, "it would have been nothing among so many."

"You see that, too?" said Mrs. Harwood. And then she added, raising her hands in an appeal to the roof or the skies, "Heaven knows that it was *them* I thought of—my children—always, always! all the time."

Nobody was aware of this momentary confidence, for Gussy came into the room a little afterwards, and Meredith led her up to her mother.

"Of course," he said, "you have known it, dear Mrs. Harwood, for long, and, though there has been nothing absolutely said between us, I think that Gussy and I have understood each other for a long time. You will give her to me, won't you? I will try to be worthy of her."

Mrs. Harwood's eyes were filled with tears. There was no hypocrisy in this, nothing but nature.

"That I will, with all my heart, Charley!" she cried, and held out her arms to her daughter, who in the moment of emotion forgot everything, and forgave her mother who had done so much—had she done so much?—for her children. Gussy did not know all that the mother had done, nor at what cost she herself was to be "done justice to." She only knew that there had been clouds upon the domestic firmament, and that they were now all blown away by delicious breezes of happiness and sweet content.

Everything was arranged afterwards with the authorities, and Adolphus Harwood, proved to be a harmless though hopeless lunatic, was left in the custody of his wife. When the story stole out, it was as the story of a wife's devotion, which indeed it was, in some sort. It was said that he had wandered back to England, scarcely recognizable in his madness after he was supposed to be dead, and that she had then and there taken the tremendous task upon her of concealing him, caring for him, watching and providing for his safety and comfort. It was a tremendous task: nobody could exaggerate the weight of the burden that had been upon her shoulders. And those of the victims who heard of it in faint rumors after a time, were more disposed to shed tears over Mrs. Harwood's martyr life and her wonderful devotion then to take any steps—if any had been possible—to interfere with her custody of the madman.

The vengeance of Heaven had overtaken that criminal who had been the ruin of so many. And, as for his poor wife, what was she but the first of the victims, the one who had suffered most? The story of the pocket-book with which he was going to pay up every claim touched still more the hearts of those who heard it. They thought it proved that, underneath all the misdoings which had overwhelmed his brain, there had still been an honest instinct, and that perhaps he had never intended but to give the money back. If Dr. Harding felt sometimes, when he looked back upon that strange scene, that there was something beneath, he was the only one to whom that idea came. And nobody suspected even, what there had been in the pocket-book the first time Adolphus Harwood's wife got it into her hands!

Dolff threw up the university, which did him but little good, and the music-halls, which did him less, and went down to the little property in Wales which had come to him from his grandfather. Notwithstanding that scene with Dr. Harding, he never understood clearly what his father had done. He married there, and was in a small way a gentleman farmer, and got perhaps as much good out of his life as if he had pursued the course his mother intended. Perhaps on the whole, even she admitted, it was as well that the name of Adolphus Harwood, which is a conspicuous name, should not flourish at the Bar, which was a thankless profession; and where even Charley Meredith, who had been always thought so clever, did not flourish as people had hoped, though fortunately he and his wife were sufficiently well off not to care.

As for Janet, the little governess, the wife of the great Liverpool doctor, who acquired such fame in that northern capital, and was knighted, and as great a man as any in the place, her career is too brilliant for these simple pages. And yet when I say that she was beyond question the best-dressed woman in the north of Lancashire, which is saying a great deal, where could there be found a sign more eloquent of the apotheosis and grand culmination of a favorable fate?

THE END.

9 789362 928399